MEDAL WINNERS

MEDAL WINNERS

HOW THE VIETNAM WAR
LAUNCHED NOBEL CAREERS

RAYMOND S. GREENBERG

The University of Texas Health Press

Requests for permission to reproduce material from this work should be sent to:
Permissions
University of Texas Press
P.O. Box 7819
Austin, TX 78713-7819
utpress.utexas.edu/rp-form

∞ The paper used in this book meets the minimum requirements of ANSI/
    NISO Z39.48-1992 (R1997) (Permanence of Paper).

Library of Congress Cataloging-in-Publication Data

Names: Greenberg, Raymond S., author.
Title: Medal winners : how the Vietnam War launched Nobel careers /
    Raymond S. Greenberg.
Description: First edition. | Austin : The University of Texas Press, 2020. |
    Includes bibliographical references and index.
Identifiers: LCCN 2019015011
  ISBN 978-1-4773-1942-0 (cloth : alk. paper)
  ISBN 978-1-4773-1943-7 (library e-book)
  ISBN 978-1-4773-1944-4 (non-library e-book)
Subjects: LCSH: Goldstein, Joseph L. (Joseph Leonard) | Brown, Michael S.,
    1941– | Lefkowitz, Robert J., 1943– | Varmus, Harold. | Physicians—United
    States—Biography. | Scientists—United States—Biography. | Nobel Prize
    winners—United States—Biography. | Vietnam War, 1961–1975—United
    States—Influence.
Classification: LCC R153 .G75 2020 | DDC 610.92/2—dc23
LC record available at https://lccn.loc.gov/2019015011

DOI:10.7560/319420

CONTENTS

ACKNOWLEDGMENTS

Researchers who have achieved success at the highest possible level, such as Nobel Prize winners, might be expected to bask in the brilliance of professional accomplishment. It was an unexpected experience, therefore, to encounter true humility and modesty among the Nobel laureates featured in this book. Drs. Joseph Goldstein, Michael Brown, Robert Lefkowitz, and Harold Varmus tended to attribute their many successes to good fortune, in addition to the positive influences of their mentors, rather than to their own evident and considerable abilities. They were candid in relating personal stories to help illuminate the "Golden Era" when they served together as trainees at the National Institutes of Health (NIH). Asking them to recall events that occurred a half-century ago was an unfair test of their memories. Nevertheless, the clarity with which they all remembered their stints at NIH only served to underscore how vital those few years were to each of them.

Parenthetically, it should be noted that the experience of having four Nobel laureates read and critique one's work can be more than a little intimidating. To my great relief, these distinguished scientists could not have been kinder or more generous with their thoughtful suggestions. When the writing lagged at times, the unsolicited chorus of enthusiasm and encouragement from these masters was a powerful motivator to complete the project. I benefited from an up-close and personal view of the coaching skills this quartet of effective mentors provided to literally hundreds of aspiring investigators.

The two surviving NIH mentors, Drs. Ira Pastan and Jesse Roth, were equally helpful in sharing their personal recollections about their Nobel Prize–winning trainees, Harold Varmus and Bob Lefkowitz. Well into their eighties, both Pastan and Roth remain active researchers and continue to mentor young scientists who follow in the footsteps of Varmus and Lefkowitz. Others who were NIH Associates at the same time, including Drs. Thomas Caskey, Maximilian Buja, Mahlon De-Long, and Thomas Boat, all of whom went on to very distinguished academic careers, kindly shared their NIH memories as well. Dr. William Lovejoy, who was a few years ahead of Bob Lefkowitz and Harold Varmus at Columbia-Presbyterian Hospital, also generously offered his recollections of their days together.

An invaluable resource to this project was the Office of NIH History, which provided access to previously conducted oral histories, the Clinical Associate program application cards for the four protagonists, and photographs of the mentors and facilities. Helpful advice and guidance were provided by the founding director of the Office of NIH History, Dr. Victoria Harden, as well as Christopher Wanjek, director of communications of the Office of Intramural Research. Barbara Harkins, the office's librarian/archivist, spent many hours searching for relevant material, and Michele Lyons, the curator of the Office of NIH History and the Stetten Museum, provided additional support. The prior interviews of NIH Clinical Associates conducted by Melissa Klein and Drs. Buhm Soon Park and Sandeep Khot provided a rich detail of background information. Dr. Alan Schechter, NIH senior historical consultant and chief of the Molecular Medicine Branch of the National Institute of

Diabetes and Digestive and Kidney Diseases, was kind enough to share his many insights into the Clinical Associate program.

The Board of Regents of the University of Texas System and two chancellors, William McRaven and J. B. Milliken, allowed me the time and support needed to research and write this book. It is a privilege to work for leaders who view scholarship as a possible route to salvation for an aging educational bureaucrat. The University of Texas Southwestern Medical Center, the academic home of Drs. Goldstein and Brown, provided generous financial support for the publication of this book. My thanks go to President Daniel Podolsky and Executive Vice President for Business Affairs Arnim Dontes for helping to identify the necessary funding. My very capable and perennially cheerful executive assistant, Trisha Meloncon, did yeoman's work in transcribing the interviews, collecting permissions for the reproduction of photographs, and incorporating multiple iterations of edits. Without her loyal support this project would not have been possible. The University of Texas Press, under the leadership of David Hamrick, embraced this project with enthusiasm and helped to bring it across the finish line. Robert Kimzey, managing editor at the University of Texas Press, served capably as the project manager, and the copy editor, Jon Howard, drew the short straw to guide me through the developmental editing process.

With great ardor I thank my wife, Leah, for her sacrifices of time and companionship that allowed this book to be written. She was the first person to read and critique the text, and in so doing she reaffirmed, once again, the wisdom of marrying an English major.

The story of the "Yellow Berets" and their contributions to the advancement of science and medicine is one of the most remarkable and underappreciated chapters in American history. The stories of these four Nobel doctors—Goldstein, Brown, Lefkowitz, and Varmus—can inspire a new generation of accidental scientists to stand on the shoulders of such giants.

Raymond S. Greenberg, MD, PhD
AUSTIN, TEXAS

MEDAL
WINNERS

PROLOGUE

One of the most memorable dinners hosted by President and Mrs. John F. Kennedy at the White House was on Sunday, April 29, 1962. The event honored living Nobel Prize winners from the Western Hemisphere, and among the 177 guests, forty-nine Nobel laureates attended along with other luminaries in the arts and sciences. Scheduled at the height of the Cold War, the evening's subtext was American dominance in science and technology. In the first six decades since the Nobel Prize was awarded beginning in 1901, seventy-six Americans had been so honored—more than any other nation and accounting for nearly a quarter of all laureates. Russia could muster only eight recipients. This celebration came about a year after the Soviet cosmonaut Yuri Gagarin became the first human in outer space. The Kennedy administration was eager to spotlight America's heroes in science. Invitees included the writers James Baldwin, John Dos Passos, Katherine Anne Porter, William

Styron, Lionel Trilling, and Robert Frost, the nuclear physicist Robert Oppenheimer, and John Glenn, who just two months earlier had followed Gagarin into space and successfully orbited the earth.

Another guest, the 1954 laureate in Chemistry, Linus Pauling, had that weekend protested along with 3,000 others outside the White House against the resumption of atmospheric testing of nuclear weapons by the United States. Earlier that Sunday, Pauling, carrying a placard with a message to Kennedy and the British prime minister Harold Macmillan ("we have no right to test"), managed to change into black-tie attire by eight o'clock. The president greeted Pauling at the door with a smile and his familiar wry sense of humor: "I understand you've been around the White House for a couple of days already." Pauling, who soon would win a second Nobel for contributions to Peace, acknowledged as much. President Kennedy was gracious in reply: "I hope you will continue to express your feelings."[1]

The evening is remembered for Kennedy's toast to laureates, departing from remarks prepared by the Harvard historian and special assistant to the president Arthur Schlesinger Jr.:

> I want to tell you how welcome you are in the White House. I think that this is the most extraordinary collection of talent, of human knowledge, that has ever been gathered together at the White House, with the possible exception of when Thomas Jefferson dined alone.

Later in the toast, Kennedy again spoke unscripted, expressing the hope that the dinner would also "encourage young Americans and young people in this hemisphere to develop the same drive and deep desire for knowledge and peace."[2]

Kennedy, a month shy of his forty-fifth birthday, was a big believer in the powers of both technology and bold visions. Three weeks after Gagarin's spaceflight, the president stood before a joint session of Congress and famously declared: "I believe that this nation should commit itself to achieving the goal, before the decade is out, of landing a man on the moon and returning him safely to Earth." Now, his broader charge to the next generation of Americans was equally audacious. Many of those who would bring Kennedy's Nobel vision to reality had no idea that they would become scientists—much less Nobel laureates. Among the unsuspecting future researchers were three college seniors and a first-year English literature graduate student. Joe Goldstein, a native of rural Kingstree, South Carolina, was nearing graduation as the valedictorian at Washington and Lee University in Lexington, Virginia. Mike Brown, raised in the Philadelphia suburbs, was preparing to graduate at the top of his class at the University of Pennsylvania, where he briefly served as editor of the student newspaper. Bob Lefkowitz, a hometown prodigy from the High School of Science in the Bronx, was about to graduate from Columbia University at nineteen. All three were chemistry majors and aspired to be practicing physicians, and none had any mentored research experience.

The graduate student among this quartet was Harold Varmus, who was struggling between pursuing a passion for English literature versus following his father's path into medicine. Varmus grew up on the South Shore of Long Island and matriculated at Amherst College, where he majored in English literature (and barely survived a premed prerequisite in organic chemistry). Even though he won a Woodrow Wilson Fellowship to attend graduate school at Harvard, Varmus soon became disenchanted with the program there and applied to medical school. As with Goldstein, Brown, and Lefkowitz, Varmus avoided any opportunity to pursue laboratory research experience, anticipating a career in patient care.

All four young men were stellar undergraduates and were admitted to excellent medical schools. Goldstein, the lone southerner in the group, made a last-minute decision to attend Southwestern Medical College of the University of Texas. Brown remained at the University of Pennsylvania, and Lefkowitz and Varmus became classmates at Columbia University's College of Physicians and Surgeons. All four finished at or among the very top of their medical school classes in 1966, securing clinical training positions at two of the premier teaching hospitals in the country. Goldstein and Brown became fellow interns at Massachusetts General Hospital in Boston, and Lefkowitz and Varmus stayed at Columbia-Presbyterian Hospital in New York City.[3] All four anticipated futures as professors at medical schools, primarily serving as clinicians and teachers. They thought that they might dabble in research but had only vague notions of what that would entail and saw it as more of a sidelight than a primary focus.

With the Vietnam War escalating in 1966, all four (as well as other newly minted physicians nationwide) faced the likelihood of being drafted involuntarily into military service. Since the Korean War, there was a mandatory draft of physicians in order to meet the medical needs of the United States Armed Services. There were few viable alternatives, but one especially attractive option was selection for a two-year commission to conduct basic research and care for patients at the National Institutes of Health (NIH) in Bethesda, Maryland. With a handful of positions available and thousands of highly motivated applicants, admission into the NIH Associate program was, at best, a long shot. Although Goldstein, Brown, Lefkowitz, and Varmus all had sterling academic credentials, their paucity of research experience did not bode well for their selection. Fortunately for them, and for the NIH, all four managed to find an interested staff scientist who saw a reason to bring them aboard.

This quartet of rising stars arrived at the NIH in July 1968, a period when the country seemed to be coming apart at the seams. The Vietnam War saw an alarming rise in casualties, and antiwar street protests roiled campuses and divided the nation. Reverend Martin Luther King Jr., the civil rights icon and movement leader, was assassinated in Memphis that April, sparking violent riots in at least ten major cities, including the nation's capital. In June, the United States senator and Democratic presidential candidate Robert Kennedy had been gunned down in Los Angeles, just five years after his older brother met a similar fate in Dallas. Come August, with November's presidential election in the balance, the Democratic National Convention in Chicago was stained by bloodshed, the result of a police crackdown on protesters. Amid the chaos and uncertainty, four young physicians were introduced into a different world—the compelling, challenging, and exciting pursuit of medical research.

Brown and Goldstein used "Golden Era" to describe the NIH at that time.[4] Five of its senior scientists would go on to win Nobels in their own right, the first going to Marshall Nirenberg only a few months after the four Clinical Associates arrived. Three more NIH investigators would win the Nobel in the following eight years: Julius Axelrod (1970),

Christian Anfinsen (1972), and Carleton Gajdusek (1976). It would be another eighteen years before another NIH scientist, Martin Rodbell, was selected in 1994. He would be the last scientist employed by NIH so honored. To the extent that Nobel awards are markers of achievement in science, there is little question that NIH was a prodigious contributor during the 1960s and 1970s.

The matching of brilliant basic scientists with a cadre of gifted physician trainees occurred in an environment at NIH that was well-resourced, collaborative, and open to people, such as religious and ethnic minorities, who often felt less welcome on traditional university campuses. The period also marked a revolution in biomedical research, as technological advances were made in the methods used to isolate, purify, and study important biological molecules such as proteins and genes. Indeed, a high percentage of the physicians who would become future leaders in American medicine trained at the NIH during those halcyon years. As Goldstein and Brown pointed out, nine future Nobel laureates were trained at the Bethesda campus between 1964 and 1972.[5] Even more remarkable, the class that entered in 1968, including Brown, Goldstein, Lefkowitz, and Varmus, accounted for nearly half of the total number of future Nobel laureates to date.

The Vietnam War left deep wounds—physical and emotional—on a generation of Americans. If there is a silver lining to the war, perhaps it is the unforeseen salutary effect it had on bringing some of the brightest minds of that generation into scientific careers. Collectively, this group of former Public Health Service[6] Commissioned Officers is referred to by the nickname "Yellow Berets," an obvious counterpoint to the celebrated Green Berets—the US Army's Special Forces troops in Vietnam. Although Goldstein, Brown, Lefkowitz, and Varmus are too modest to stake the claim, a credible argument can be made that their work made possible many of the advances in medical care over the past quarter-century.

Brown and Goldstein formed a lasting partnership, still thriving five decades later, that led to fundamental discoveries about how cholesterol levels are controlled within the body. Their work helped to pave the way for the popular statin drugs that are improving the lives of those who have or are at high risk of developing heart disease. Varmus teamed up with another former Yellow Beret, Michael Bishop, and discovered how a normal gene can be altered and give rise to cancer. Their findings opened the door to more precise cancer treatments that target specific underlying genetic defects. Lefkowitz, for his part, characterized the molecules on the surfaces of cells that recognize members of a large class of chemical messengers, triggering the appropriate biological responses. His insights helped to advance the development of medications for treating a multitude of conditions ranging from allergies, to heartburn, to diabetes, to heart disease, to cancer.

The awarding of the Nobel Prize for each of these discoveries provides objective evidence of the importance that experts in the field attach to such work. There are many accolades given for scientific accomplishment, but none has the history, global visibility, prestige, pomp, and ceremony associated with the Nobel Prize. Established by Alfred Nobel, a Swedish inventor and explosives manufacturer, in his 1895 will, the series of annual awards was intended to honor work that conveyed "the greatest benefit to mankind." Virtually all of Nobel's fortune was bequeathed to create the prizes in five specified domains: Physics, Chemistry, Physiology or Medicine, Literature, and Peace (a sixth area—Economics—was added in 1968 with financial support from the Bank of Sweden). A foundation was created to manage the operational aspects of the prizes (but not the actual selection of recipients). For the award in Physiology or Medicine, the Karolinska Institutet in Stockholm is assigned the responsibility for choosing the honoree(s), whereas the other scientific prizes are selected by the Royal Swedish Academy of Sciences.

The first Nobel Prizes were awarded in 1901 and have been granted annually since then, with the exception of interruptions during World War I and World War II. For all of the hoopla over the announcement of winners, few are household names. The best-known recipients in Physiology or Medicine include Ivan Pavlov (digestion, 1904), Robert Koch (tuberculosis, 1905), Alexander Fleming (penicillin, 1945), and James Watson and Francis Crick (structure of DNA, 1962). Although the identities of honorees and the technical details of the work may be unfamiliar outside scientific circles, the impact of the discoveries is easier to appreciate, at least in retrospect. Some of the featured areas of innovation in Physiology or Medicine include the discovery of insulin, the development of key technologies such as the electrocardiogram, computed tomographic and nuclear magnetic imaging, the identification of blood groups, the introduction of high-impact procedures such as heart catheterization and in vitro fertilization, and the determination of causes of disease such as the human immunodeficiency virus. In Physiology or Medicine, the selection process is overseen by an assembly of fifty professors at the Karolinska Institutet, with a five-member committee that screens nominations and selects candidates.

Sometimes, potential recipients are excluded because they do not meet the award guidelines. For example, Nobel rules do not permit an award to someone who has not been nominated, regardless of how deserving that individual may be. This has been suggested as one of the contributing reasons for the underrepresentation of female laureates. Another exclusion factor is a prohibition against posthumous recognition. So, when Rosalyn Yalow was selected in 1977, her deceased colleague, Solomon Berson, who partnered on the prize-winning work on radioimmunoassay, was not designated as a corecipient. Similarly, only three honorees are permitted in any prize category in a single year, which is increasingly challenging as science becomes more of a team sport. Deliberations in the selection process are maintained under strict confidentiality for fifty years, so the underlying rationale for inclusion or exclusion of any potential candidate remains shrouded in mystery for generations.

Even with all of these constraints, the Nobel Prize still remains the worldwide gold standard for scientific achievement. Part of its appeal is its longevity, now well into its second century. It also benefits from the halo effect of past winners—a virtual Who's Who of Scientific Heroes, including such revered historical figures as Ernest Rutherford, Marie Curie, Max Planck, Albert Einstein, Neils Bohr, Werner Heisenberg, Erwin Schrödinger, and Enrico Fermi. To be associated with these giants, if only in an indirect way, provides an enduring legacy for each awardee. Then there is the masterful and media-savvy manner in which the announcements of winners are made in October every year. Each discipline has its own designated day, and collectively there is a full week of global attention to the awards. Finally, there is the incomparable pageantry of the award ceremony itself, held every year on December

10—the anniversary of the death of Alfred Nobel. The white-tie ceremonies are hosted at the resplendent Stockholm Concert Hall, followed by an elaborate banquet at the Stockholm City Hall. The prizes are presented to honorees by the king of Sweden, with each winner receiving a gold medal emblazoned with the image of Nobel, as well as an ornate diploma. A handsome cash award, currently valued in excess of $1 million, is provided in each discipline and divided if there are multiple recipients.

The mystique of the Nobel Prize and the work that underpins the honored discoveries have inspired popular books on the subject. Perhaps the best known is *The Double Helix*, the autobiographical account of the discovery of the structure of DNA by James Watson.[7] Of more immediate relevance here is the excellent autobiography written by Harold Varmus, *The Art and Politics of Science*,[8] and the equally entertaining memoir *How to Win the Nobel Prize*, written by his colleague and corecipient Michael Bishop.[9] Both of these accounts are invaluable sources for this book and are recommended highly to the reader who is interested in a firsthand perspective on the experience of becoming a Nobel laureate. Goldstein, Brown, and Lefkowitz have yet to pen their own autobiographies, but they have been generous in sharing their personal stories in various articles and interviews. These publications proved helpful in constructing this synthesis and are commended to the reader.[10]

The article written by Goldstein and Brown on the NIH's Golden Era drew attention in scientific circles to the remarkable cohort of future Nobel laureates who trained at the institutes on the Bethesda campus and posed a question: "Was there something particular about these recipients, the time, and the place that account for this unprecedented record?"[11] They mention many contributing factors they deem important, namely, the involuntary draft that funneled top medical students to the NIH; the focus of the research experience on fundamental biological processes; and especially the rigor of the NIH's veteran scientists who served as mentors. Interestingly enough, three senior researchers (Marshall Nirenberg, Earl Stadtman, and Ira Pastan) oversaw two each of the nine future Nobel awardees.

Others have attempted to characterize circumstances associated with the development of Nobel laureates. Arguably, the most influential study of this topic was published by Harriet Zuckerman in 1977.[12]

Then a sociology professor at Columbia University and later a senior vice president at the Andrew W. Mellon Foundation, Zuckerman studied the lives of all American Nobel laureates selected between 1907 and 1972. Of the fifty-six honorees, Zuckerman conducted personal interviews with forty-one, creating a rich trove of information that she described as a "group biography." Not surprisingly, given her disciplinary background, Zuckerman approached her research subjects from the perspective of the social organization and operation of the world of science.

Key findings from Zuckerman's work were that Nobel laureates show early promise and tend to be educated at a small number of prestigious private and public universities. Often, they served apprenticeships with prior recipients, learning how to choose and approach important topics, how to adhere to the highest research standards, and how to develop self-assurance, especially when facing uncertainty and criticism from others. Future Nobelists tend to begin publishing early and in greater volume than peers. This entire picture of early success led Zuckerman to propose that the laureates benefit from "the accumulation of advantage: the spiraling of augmented achievements and rewards for individuals and a system of stratifications that is sharply graded."[13]

More than four decades have passed since Zuckerman's study. And though many aspects of the socialization process that she documented likely persist in the upper ranks of scientists, there have been some significant changes to the research landscape that affect how scientific leaders emerge. Some of these trends include older ages at which training is completed[14] and first grants are awarded,[15] heightened competition for grant funding,[16] declining percentages of physicians pursuing careers in research,[17] the emergence of a new breed of research universities, particularly on the West Coast,[18] the rise of "Big Science," which requires large, interdisciplinary research teams,[19] and the expansion of industry-funded research and a parallel emphasis on ownership of intellectual property.[20] The extent to which any of these factors (and others) shape the current and future scientific elite remains to be determined.

To some extent, Zuckerman's work can be updated by a close examination of the Yellow Berets, who were being trained just when the last of her Nobel laureates were being chosen. All nine of the NIH Associates who later won Nobel Prizes are worthy of consideration, but an attempt to cover the full cohort in a single book would fail to do justice to any one of them. Out of respect for both the laureates and the reader, this book is confined to the four Yellow Berets who arrived at the NIH in 1968. In recounting their odysseys and trying to weave together their storylines in a coherent narrative, this book is organized into three sections. The opening chapters in Part I ("Soldiers for Science") build our foundation by describing the circumstances that brought the four trainees to the NIH and the environment they entered. The middle chapters in Part II ("Mentors and Apprentices") represent the beating heart of the story, covering mentors and the research these four Yellow Berets conducted while at NIH. The final chapters in Part III ("Four Laureates") covers their days after NIH leading up to, but not beyond, the award of their respective Nobel Prizes. The intent throughout is to illuminate the science and its implications for medicine without becoming immersed in technical jargon and concepts.

As the reader will appreciate, there is no single uniform path to great achievement—whether scientific or otherwise. Although each story is unique, there are some commonalities and themes that emerge. To the extent that these personal histories reveal larger truths about the NIH in the 1960s and 1970s—and more generally what it takes to prepare young people to achieve the highest levels of performance—this book humbly extends President Kennedy's 1962 challenge to yet another generation of young Americans.

PART I

SOLDIERS FOR SCIENCE

CHAPTER 1

ANNUS HORRIBILIS

1968 and America's Conflict on Two Fronts

For President Lyndon Johnson, Vietnam was an unwanted distraction from his ambitious social agenda, known as the Great Society. In late May 1964, with America's commitment still limited to providing advisers, financing, and matériel, Johnson made clear his reservations about Vietnam to Special Assistant for National Security Affairs McGeorge Bundy: "It looks to me that we're getting into another Korea. It just worries the hell out of me. I don't see what we can ever hope to get out of there with once we're committed. I believe that the Chinese Communists are coming into it." Johnson added prophetically: "I don't think it is worth fighting for and I don't think we can get out. And it's just the biggest damn mess I ever saw."[1]

About two months later, a limited exchange of fire ten miles off the coast of North Vietnam turned into a critical test of Johnson's reservations. On August 2, an American destroyer, the USS *Maddox*, operating in international waters in the Gulf of Tonkin, was monitoring North Vietnamese radar and electronic transmissions. Suspecting that the US ship was engaged in naval commando raids occurring along the coast for several months, three patrol boats from the North Vietnamese Navy pursued and fired on the *Maddox*.[2]

The *Maddox* was unscathed in the attack, but two days later a second incident occurred or, more accurately, was thought to have occurred. The crews of the *Maddox* and a second destroyer, the USS *Turner Joy*, mistakenly interpreted phantom radar images as an indication that they were under another torpedo-boat attack. The suspected second attack was communicated to military leaders back in Washington, but further assessments from the Gulf of Tonkin over the next several hours raised serious doubts about the credibility of initial reports.[3] Secretary of Defense Robert McNamara, reflecting on this incident, observed: "It was just confusion, and events afterwards showed that our judgment that we'd been attacked that day was wrong."[4]

To some extent, a rush to judgment and action may have been influenced by events two weeks earlier at the 1964 Republican National Convention in Daly City, California, where Arizona's hawkish senator, Barry Goldwater, was chosen as the GOP presidential candidate. In his acceptance speech, Goldwater declared: "Yesterday it was Korea; tonight it is Vietnam. Make no bones of this. Don't try to sweep this under the rug. We are at war in Vietnam. And yet the president, who is commander in chief of our forces, refuses to say, refuses to say, mind you, whether or not the objective over there is victory, and his secretary of defense continues to mislead and misinform the American people."[5]

As midnight approached on August 4, mere hours after reports about the second confrontation, President Johnson announced via nationwide broadcast his conclusion that American forces had been attacked on multiple occasions and would respond accordingly. Johnson stated: "Repeated acts of violence against the armed forces of the United States must be met not only with alert defense, but with positive reply. The reply is being given as I speak to you tonight."[6]

A series of air strikes were launched against North Vietnamese attack boats and other targets. Of much greater consequence was the so-called Gulf of Tonkin Resolution: at the president's behest, the United

States Congress, with only two dissenting votes in the Senate and none in the House, rushed to authorize the president, without a formal declaration of war, "as Commander in Chief, to take all necessary measures to repeal any armed attack against the forces of the United States and to prevent any further aggression." It went on to authorize the president to "take all necessary steps, including the use of armed force, to assist any member or protocol state of the Southeast Asia Collective Defense Treaty requesting assistance in defense of its freedom."[7] This gave Johnson the political cover necessary for direct American military intervention in Vietnam.

Three months later, the presidential election resulted in a landslide victory for Johnson, who received more than 60 percent of the popular vote and 90 percent of the Electoral College. With this mandate and the Gulf of Tonkin Resolution in his back pocket, Johnson's military advisers urged him to expand the US role in Vietnam. The government in Saigon (South Vietnam) was unstable and ineffective. It's military, the Army of the Republic of Vietnam, was losing territory, and, not surprisingly, troop morale was very low. Yet Johnson hesitated. He was not particularly concerned about fighting North Vietnam, which he characterized in private as a "raggedy-ass fourth-rate country."[8] Johnson's recurring nightmare was that sympathetic communist governments in Beijing and Moscow would come to the aid of the North Vietnamese and that the war would escalate into a showdown between nuclear-armed superpowers.

Meanwhile, North Vietnam's communist National Liberation Front, commonly known as the Vietcong (VC), had a sizable force in South Vietnam allied with the North. The Vietcong controlled substantial areas of countryside in the South, and VC guerrilla warfare tactics were taking an increasing toll. A series of VC attacks on American military bases in February 1965 finally convinced President Johnson that he had to increase US pressure, starting with airstrikes against North Vietnamese Army (NVA) camps. The knockout punch was supposed to be a massive air operation code-named "Rolling Thunder."

Launched on March 2, 1965, the initial targets of Rolling Thunder were supply lines just north of the border that were used to transport men and matériel in support of VC insurgents in the South. In addition to the tactical objective of disrupting and degrading the opposition forces, the strategic goal was to demoralize the enemy through a massive show of force and determination.[9] Over time, the bombing expanded to military and industrial targets throughout North Vietnam, enemy-held targets in South Vietnam, and regions in neighboring Laos and Cambodia. The major cities of Hanoi and Haiphong, with their large civilian populations, and the border area near China were spared.

Rolling Thunder was undertaken on a scale unprecedented in military history. Between 1965 and 1967 alone, the United States dropped more bombs than during the entire Korean War or the Pacific campaign in World War II.[10] Rolling Thunder was estimated to have destroyed three-quarters of all ammunition depots, more than half of North Vietnam's power plants and bridges, and 10,000 military vehicles.[11] In spite of this devastation, the bombing was unsuccessful in breaking the fighting spirit and capabilities of the North Vietnamese and the Vietcong.

The initial commitment of US ground troops to the war effort began on March 8, 1965, when 3,500 Marines from the 9th Expeditionary Brigade were deployed to protect the air base at Da Nang. Three months later, for the first time, US troops engaged the Vietcong in combat. On July 28, President Johnson announced at a noon press conference at the White House that he would authorize sending forty-four combat battalions to Vietnam. His public words made it evident this decision weighed upon him: "I do not find it easy to send the flower of our youth, our finest young men, into battle." He added: "I think I know, too, how their mothers weep and how their families sorrow."[12] Even as he commenced the ground war, Johnson had doubts about the prospects for victory. Speaking privately to his press secretary, Bill Moyers, Johnson confessed: "Light at the end of the tunnel? We don't even have a tunnel; we don't even know where the tunnel is."[13]

The die was cast, however, and within five months US troop levels had reached nearly 185,000, almost sixfold more than a year earlier. By the end of 1966, there were more than 385,000, with another 100,000 added in 1967.[14] As the US troop presence grew, so did the number of casualties. In 1965, US forces suffered about 6,000 nonfatal injuries and nearly 1,400 deaths. In 1966, the number of wounded was five times higher and the number killed nearly four times higher. And in

1967—with fighting in Vietnam at its peak—60,000 Americans were wounded and more than 9,000 killed.[15] This was roughly 70 percent more than the total nonmilitary deaths of eighteen- and nineteen-year-old males back home.[16] The gruesome numbers were weighing heavily upon the nation.

As the fighting expanded and intensified more than 8,000 miles away, Americans at home had a front-row seat to the action. The Vietnam War was the first military conflict to be televised, and by that time more than 90 percent of American households had a television.[17] By 1963, television surpassed newspapers as the leading source of international news for the American public.[18] Even more telling, television was becoming the news source that Americans considered most trustworthy.[19]

Television and other media coverage of the war was not censored, and reporters were given free access to the troops and the action. Nevertheless, Johnson felt that TV coverage of the war was excessively negative: "The Communists already control the three major networks and the forty major outlets of communication," he groused to his aides.[20] Tensions about the role television played in influencing public sentiment toward the war emerged as early as one week following Johnson's commitment of large numbers of US ground forces. On August 5, 1965, the CBS correspondent Morley Safer reported on a mission conducted by US Marines in Cam Ne, a hamlet near the Da Nang air base. As film rolled, Marines used a variety of devices, including a Zippo cigarette lighter, to set fire to thatched huts while villagers, including old men and women, fled in terror.[21]

Accompanying the images of 150 homes being destroyed, Safer narrated: "Today's operation is the frustration of Vietnam in miniature. There is little doubt that American firepower can win a victory here. But to a Vietnamese peasant whose home means a lifetime of backbreaking labor, it will take more than presidential promises to convince him that we are on his side."[22] The Marines and the administration were incensed over the report, which they felt provided selective and biased information, omitting, among other key details, the hamlet's known connections to the Vietcong.[23]

Whether or not there was bias in media coverage, brutal images combined with American lives lost impacted attitudes on the home front. A

Gallup public opinion survey conducted around August 1965 revealed that only one-quarter of Americans thought that sending troops to Vietnam was a mistake. By early 1968, after nearly three years of unrelenting warfare, the number of Americans who opposed the commitment of troops to Vietnam had doubled.[24]

Internal documents from the Pentagon's Systems Analysis Office reveal concern about the eroding public support for the war: "If we are to stay, we must have the backing of the U.S. electorate. As we divert resources from other national goals, as U.S. lives are lost, and as the electorate sees nothing but endless escalation for the future, an increasing fraction will become discouraged. . . . [I]f we are not to lose everything, the trends will have to be changed."[25]

In public statements, Johnson and his advisers did their best to counter mounting opposition. On Veterans Day 1967, the president delivered an address from the deck of the USS *Enterprise*, posing a question on the minds of many: "How many nights must we suffer the nightmare of war?" His answer was upbeat but, in retrospect, overly so: "Not many more nights. . . . Not while we stand as one family, and one Nation, united in our purpose."[26] Ten days later, General William Westmoreland, commander of US forces in Vietnam, appeared before the National Press Club in Washington, DC, and predicted: "With 1968, a new phase is now starting. We have reached an important point when the end begins to come into view."[27]

However, the new phase that began in 1968 was not one Westmoreland saw coming. In Vietnam, the Lunar New Year known as Tet is the most sacred time of the year. Homes are cleaned in preparation for the holiday, symbolically removing the bad luck of the past year. Good fortune in the new year is thought to be encouraged by performing acts of kindness. Tet is a time for families to be together at home. (Even during the height of the war, it was standard practice to suspend hostilities to allow combatants on both sides to spend time with families.) In advance of the Tet holiday in 1968, both the NVA and VC insurgents in the South announced that they would honor a one-week cease-fire from January 27 through February 3.

The Tet holiday began January 30, and in the early-morning hours of January 31 the Vietcong and NVA launched a coordinated series of attacks on more than a hundred cities and towns in South Vietnam, including the capital (Saigon) and the former imperial capital (Hue). With the element of surprise, and a massive force estimated at 80,000, the attackers were able to penetrate many targets, including the United States Embassy in Saigon. During the second day of fighting, the brutality of the conflict was captured in a Pulitzer Prize–winning photograph. On a street in Saigon, the Associated Press photographer Eddie Adams captured the exact moment that, at point-blank range, the South Vietnamese chief of national police, Nguyen Ngoc Loan, fatally shot in the head a handcuffed VC death-squad captain, Nguyen Van Lem. The following day, the startling photograph appeared in newspapers worldwide, putting faces to the violence occurring in the capital.[28]

The defenders were able to repel attacks quickly in many locations, but there was fierce and protracted fighting in other locations, particularly Hue. By the end of the twenty-five-day assault, losses in Hue were heavy on both sides—and even more so for the resident population. It is estimated that nearly 6,000 civilians died there, half being executed and then buried in mass graves by communist forces. Three-quarters of the houses in the city were destroyed, and more than 100,000 persons were left homeless.[29]

From a strictly military perspective, casualties suffered by the NVA and Vietcong during the Tet Offensive were staggering. It is estimated that as many as 32,000 fighters were killed, representing 40 percent of the forces amassed.[30] On the American and South Vietnamese sides, losses were much smaller, but still they represented some of the costliest days of the war. Nearly 3,000 South Vietnamese soldiers died; the Americans lost more than 1,500.[31] It was hardly a victory for the communist forces, however. When they were repelled from Hue, the North Vietnamese and Vietcong had lost all of the territory they had seized, and their infrastructure was decimated.

For Americans back home, the Tet Offensive fed a growing sense of pessimism. In his State of the Union Address, which he delivered just prior to the beginning of the Tet Offensive, the president declared that "the enemy has been defeated in battle after battle."[32] Yet only two weeks later, this same enemy was able to mount a series of surprise attacks, deploying unprecedented numbers of troops in coordination. To see the walls of the United States Embassy, a symbol of American strength, penetrated by Vietcong fighters was jarring to even the most hawkish supporters of the war.

As questions mounted across the country, Walter Cronkite, the legendary anchor of *CBS Evening News*, traveled to Vietnam for some answers. Cronkite, whose program was the most popular among the three national networks, felt that news should be presented in an objective manner without editorial commentary. However, when his special documentary report from his tour of Vietnam aired on the night of February 27, Cronkite ended the broadcast with a brief personal assessment: "To say that we are closer to victory today is to believe, in the face of the evidence, the optimists who have been wrong in the past. To suggest we are on the edge of defeat is to yield to unreasonable pessimism. To say that we are mired in stalemate seems the only realistic, yet unsatisfactory, conclusion."[33]

Legend has it that President Johnson reacted to the CBS broadcast by observing to press aide Bill Moyers: "If I've lost Cronkite, I've lost middle America."[34] Regardless of whether this is an apocryphal story, it is undeniable that Johnson was losing the support of the electorate. Two weeks later, he would barely beat an antiwar Democratic presidential candidate, Senator Eugene McCarthy of Minnesota, in the New Hampshire primary. It was an ominous sign for a sitting president to face such strong opposition from a relatively unknown challenger within his own party.[35] Four days after the New Hampshire primary, sensing Johnson's vulnerability, Senator Robert Kennedy of Massachusetts announced that he would join the race as well.[36]

On March 31, Johnson delivered a televised address from the Oval Office. He was not yet sixty years old, but he appeared worn down by the burdens of office. He spoke for forty minutes about the war, announced a unilateral suspension of the bombing campaign, and entreated the North Vietnamese to come to the negotiation table. Johnson concluded his address with a stark acknowledgement: "There is division in the American house now. There is divisiveness among us all tonight." He then stunned the national audience by declaring: "I shall not seek, and I will not accept, the nomination of my party for another term as your President."[37]

Three days after Johnson's surprise announcement, Reverend Martin Luther King Jr., the thirty-nine-year-old civil rights champion, accompanied by several fellow leaders of the Southern Christian Leadership Conference, boarded a plane in Atlanta bound for Memphis. King went there to support a strike by the city's African American sanitation workers. The strike was launched seven weeks earlier to protest unsafe working conditions as well as poor wages and benefits. Although such grievances were long-standing in Memphis, the situation boiled over when two sanitation workers were crushed to death by a trash truck's compactor. The workers wanted to be able to negotiate with the city through union representation, but the city refused to even recognize the union.[38]

King had traveled to Memphis several times in support of the strike, hoping to hold a peaceful march. A massive, restless crowd gathered on March 28 for a scheduled protest in downtown Memphis with King in the lead, but violence and looting erupted and King was forced to call off the march. Shaken by the riot and its damage to the cause of nonviolence, King and his closest associates returned to Atlanta to plan a response. After intense debate, the Nobel Peace Prize winner convinced the others that a return to Memphis was the only way to demonstrate that a peaceful protest was possible and that ultimately it would prevail in securing workers' rights.[39]

King's arrival in Memphis on April 3 was delayed because the airline had received a bomb threat on his life, necessitating a search of all baggage onboard. In Memphis, King and some associates checked into the Lorraine Motel at midday and that afternoon received a court injunction barring the march, which was planned for the following day—April 4. While lawyers strategized into the evening about how to lift the injunction, an exhausted King, suffering from a fever and a sore throat, sent his friend Ralph Abernathy to address the sanitation workers and their supporters gathered in the Mason Temple, one of the largest churches in the African American community in Memphis. It was filled to capacity that evening despite heavy rainstorms and tornadoes in the area. When Abernathy saw the size and energy of the assembled crowd, he called back to King and pleaded with him to come and speak.[40]

Without the benefit of text or notes, King began to address the crowd at 9:30 p.m., the winds buffeting and banging the shutters outside. King rarely spoke publically about the threats that were made against his life, but that night in Memphis, with lightning cracking outside, he confronted the issue directly. Building to the crescendo of his hour-long sermon, his message was prescient: "We've got some difficult days ahead. But it really doesn't matter with me now, because I've been to the mountaintop. And I don't mind." King continued:

> Like anybody, I would like to live a long life. Longevity has its place. But I'm not concerned about that now. I just want to do God's will. And he's allowed me to go up to the mountain. And I've looked over. And I've seen the Promised Land. I may not get there with you. But I want you to know tonight, that we, as a people, will get to the Promised Land. So I'm happy, tonight. I'm not worried about anything. I'm not fearing any man. Mine eyes have seen the glory of the coming of the Lord.[41]

King's "Mountaintop Speech" that night, one of his greatest and most moving, is tragically prophetic. The following evening, King stood on the second-floor balcony outside his room at the Lorraine Motel as his party prepared to visit a local minister for dinner. Below King, in the parking lot, was a tenor saxophone player, Ben Branch, who was to perform at the dinner. King leaned over the railing to request that Branch play Thomas Andrew Dorsey's gospel song "Take My Hand, Precious Lord" at the gathering. Branch responded that he played it all the time and would be happy to perform it that night as well. Pleased, King added: "But tonight, especially for me. I want you to play it real pretty." These words were the last that King spoke. As he turned to go back inside Room 306, a forty-year-old escaped convict named James Earl Ray pointed his Remington Gamemaster pump-action rifle from 200 feet and fired a single bullet that struck King in the chin and neck, killing him.[42]

"Take My Hand, Precious Lord" includes the following haunting lyrics: "When my life is almost gone, hear my cry, hear my call, hold my hand lest I fall, take my hand, Precious Lord, lead me home."[43] Although King did not hear it played that night in Memphis, at his prior request the renowned contralto Mahalia Jackson would sing it five days later at King's funeral in Atlanta.

On the night of King's assassination, Robert Kennedy, now a Democratic candidate for president, was scheduled to make a campaign appearance in Indianapolis. Kennedy arrived to news of King's death and, against warnings for his own safety, discarded his prepared remarks in speaking to the heart of the African American community. From the back of a flatbed truck, he delivered a short, moving appeal for peace and understanding. He began by announcing to the audience—many did not yet know of the events in Memphis—of King's assassination. Screams of disbelief and anguish rose from the crowd. Kennedy expressed empathy in deeply personal terms: "For those of you who are black and are tempted to be filled with—filled with hatred and mistrust of the injustice of such an act, against all white people, I would only say that I can also feel in my own heart the same kind of feeling. I had a member of my family killed, but he was killed by a white man."[44]

Kennedy echoed King's call to nonviolence: "What we need in the United States is not division; what we need in the United States is not hatred; what we need in the United States is not violence and lawlessness, but is love, and wisdom, and compassion toward one another, and a feeling of justice toward those who still suffer within our country, whether they be white or whether they be black."[45]

Indianapolis remained quiet that evening, perhaps in part because of Kennedy's calming influence. But a hundred other cities across the country erupted in a spasm of arson, looting, and violence. In the nation's capital, unrest started on the night of the assassination, and by the middle of the following day a full-scale riot was under way. The DC police force was overwhelmed by an estimated 20,000 rioters; federal troops were called in for assistance, with Marines guarding the Capitol and the 3rd US Infantry Regiment protecting the White House. Over four days of tumult in Washington, more than 1,200 buildings were burned, a dozen people killed, a thousand-plus injured, and more than 6,000 arrested.[46]

Riots in Baltimore started a day later than in Washington but quickly matched the level of ferocity. Over the weeklong nightmare of burning and looting in Baltimore, more than a thousand businesses were damaged or destroyed, six people were killed, 700 were injured, and nearly as many were arrested as in Washington.[47] In Chicago, especially in the largely black communities on the West Side, two days of violence left eleven dead and 150 injured, and more than 2,000 people were arrested.[48] Empty lots in some neighborhoods—still impoverished and never rebuilt—attest to the enduring devastation caused by events in 1968, the annus horribilis.[49]

There had been deadly riots in American inner cities before, including the Watts section of Los Angeles in August 1965 and Newark in July 1967. The riots reflected the growing frustration of many black Americans that, despite federal programs and outlays to improve education, economic status, and housing, little progress was made. Lyndon Johnson's ambitious Great Society agenda was aimed at making America fairer and more just for all citizens. A flood of legislation had been passed, starting in 1964 with the Civil Rights Act and the Economic Opportunity Act, followed in 1965 by the Voting Rights Act, the Housing and Urban Development Act, and the establishment of Medicaid.[50]

In 1968 many blacks in urban America saw meager progress in daily life. The median number of years of educational attainment was 9.8 for African Americans, compared with 12.1 for whites.[51] The black unemployment rate was more than twice as high as for whites.[52] And the median household income of whites was 60 percent higher than that of African Americans.[53] Centuries of inequity could not be erased overnight, or even a few years, and discontent among black communities nationwide might have turned toward rioting without the catalyst of Martin Luther King's assassination. His murder instilled in African Americans a sense of hopelessness and despair atop their stagnant prospects.

Racial tensions impacted the 1968 presidential election. George Wallace, the segregationist former governor of Alabama, ran as a third-party candidate, appealing to poor white voters with law and order and by attacking liberal social policies. The Republican presidential nominee—the former vice president and unsuccessful 1960 candidate Richard Nixon—chose then-Maryland governor Spiro T. Agnew as his running mate to secure the conservative base. Little known to voters nationwide, Agnew's local record was controversial. He had quickly mobilized the National Guard during the Baltimore riots, and more generally he demonstrated contentious interactions with black leaders.

Nixon presented himself as a law-and-order candidate, and his "Southern Strategy" to capture the anti–civil rights white constituency in the Old South still echoes in politics more than a half-century later. Here is Nixon in his acceptance speech at the Republican National Convention: "As we look at America, we see cities enveloped in smoke and flame. We hear sirens in the night." His solution? "To those who say that law and order is the code word for racism, there and here is a reply: Our goal is justice for every American. If we are to have respect for law in America, we must have laws that deserve respect."[54]

The Democratic race had become a referendum on the current administration. Eugene McCarthy's potent antiwar message versus then–incumbent Lyndon Johnson in New Hampshire impelled RFK to get into the race. And with the president out of the picture, Vice President Hubert Humphrey entered the race, focusing on states without primaries. As the Kennedy campaign was gearing up, McCarthy tallied a string of victories in early voting. Kennedy then won in Indiana and Nebraska, then lost a close race to McCarthy in Oregon.

The next primary, in California, was key to each campaign.

McCarthy focused on campuses, where his peace platform was the motivator among most students; for his part, Kennedy appealed to African American and Hispanic communities. On June 4 in the late hours of the night, Kennedy—forty-two years old—won California by a close margin. Around midnight, Kennedy delivered a victory speech to nearly 2,000 supporters in the Ambassador Hotel ballroom. His remarks rallied them to the next step toward nomination: "Now on to Chicago and let's win there!"

Everything ended moments later when a gunman wounded Kennedy and five other persons in a cramped pantry leading to the Colonial Room for press interviews. The assassin Sirhan Sirhan, a Palestinian Orthodox Christian with Jordanian citizenship, immigrated to the United States twelve years earlier and opposed Senator Kennedy's support of Israel.

The nation, still recovering from the assassination of Martin Luther King and the violent reaction that it triggered two months earlier, was in shock from another killing of a national leader. On the day of Robert Kennedy's funeral, the playwright Arthur Miller wrote a commentary in the *New York Times* that exhorted his fellow Americans: "Face the fact that the violence in our streets is the violence in our hearts." Miller went on to link the injustice at home with the fighting in Vietnam, which Kennedy had sought to end: "A country where people cannot walk safely in their own streets has not earned the right to tell any other people how to govern itself, let alone to bomb and burn that people."[55]

Two weeks after Robert Kennedy was slain, Robert Angell, editor and writer at *The New Yorker*, assessed the nation's state:

> Each morning since the death of Robert Kennedy, we have awakened to the familiar knowledge that some terrible piece of news, some jolt of the intolerable, awaits us just beyond the borders of sleep. We open our eyes to a corner of the bureau, a soft glint of mirror, morning sounds, and then it comes back.... Like an invalid, we are each day less shocked to find that we are ill, each day more absorbed with our symptoms.[56]

In this dispirited state, the country limped into the national political conventions, with the Republicans gathering on August 5–8, followed by the Democratic meeting on August 26–29. The Republicans nominated Richard Nixon on the first ballot over Nelson Rockefeller and Ronald Reagan, in part because the Southern Strategy brought support from conservative delegates opposed to racial integration. The convention was held without disruption in tony Miami Beach, but only a few miles away, in the predominately black, poor, overcrowded section of Miami known as Liberty City, unrest was brewing. Reminiscent of the riots following King's assassination, Liberty City erupted in looting, arson, and violence on August 7, with local police bolstered first by state troopers and then by the National Guard. The fighting over the next two days resulted in three deaths, numerous injuries, and almost 200 arrests.[57]

Even with President Johnson off the ticket, the Democratic National Convention, held at the International Amphitheatre in Chicago, amounted to a referendum on his policies, particularly escalation in Vietnam. In Johnson's absence, Vice President Hubert Humphrey stepped into the race and was seen as the standard-bearer for the administration. The candidate who had been in the race the longest, motivated by his opposition to the war, was Senator Eugene McCarthy. After Robert Kennedy's assassination, Senator George McGovern of South Dakota, also an early opponent of the war, joined the race. The peace vote, previously divided between Kennedy and McCarthy, now was split between McGovern and McCarthy, providing Humphrey a clear path to nomination. Antiwar forces in fifteen states attempted to bolster their representation through repeated challenges of the credentials of Humphrey delegates, but it was to no avail and Humphrey was nominated.

The biggest battle of the convention, however, was fought outside on the hot and humid streets of Chicago. Beginning five months before the convention, plans were laid for large-scale antiwar protests involving more than a hundred groups. Tens of thousands of protesters came to Chicago. In a show of strength, Mayor Richard J. Daley refused permits for parades, established curfews at public parks, and amassed a force of nearly 12,000 Chicago police, 7,500 Army troops, 7,500 National Guardsmen, and 1,000 Secret Service agents. Violence erupted when law enforcement attempted to relocate protestors from areas in which they were not permitted and when protestors attempted to march to the convention site. Scenes of police in full riot gear, using tear gas, and wielding clubs to beat protestors were telecast live around the country. Reporters who happened to be caught in the crossfire were attacked as well. Nearly 600 arrests were made, and more than 100 protestors and a comparable number of law enforcement personnel were injured.[58]

Chicago only served to put an exclamation point on a year of violence and division. As soldiers fought an ocean away, the dreams of the Great Society and the nonviolence movement at home had been shattered by assassinations, looting, burning, and the heavy-handed response of elected officials and law enforcement.

CHAPTER 2

BEST IN CLASS

Goldstein, Varmus, Brown, Lefkowitz

In a contest for least likely town in America to produce a major research scientist, Kingstree, South Carolina, would have to be near the top. About 75 miles north of Charleston, Kingstree is better known for producing vinegar-spiced barbecue than for raising biomedical scientists. Kingstree's origins trace back nearly 300 years to the British governor's plan for a ring of inland townships to protect the settled coastal communities from attack by Spaniards and Native Americans. The town's name relates to a towering white pine that stood at the head of the Black River and was marked as a "King's tree" reserved as potential timber for building royal ships.[1]

In search of religious freedom, Protestant Scots-Irish immigrants settled the township, enjoying success by cultivating indigo. During the Revolutionary War many joined the legendary guerrilla commander General Francis Marion—the "Swamp Fox"—in his campaign against the British. After independence, the region began to cultivate labor-intensive crops like cotton and tobacco; large and prosperous antebellum plantations were built with the forced labor of slaves. The Civil War and Reconstruction left the community in financial and psychological ruin. Over ensuing decades, a series of economic booms and busts occurred, first with the rise and fall of turpentine production, then cotton, and finally tobacco. Much of the tree-lined downtown commercial district was constructed between 1900 and 1920. The buildings stand today as they did a century ago, undisturbed by the world beyond the fields, pine forests, and swamplands.[2]

One of the early stores on Main Street was a dry-goods business founded in 1904 by David Silverman. In 1935, the store's owner, Joseph Eron, died, and his widow, Sadie, invited her younger brother, Isadore Goldstein, to become a partner in the business and operate it. Goldstein, a recent law school graduate of Cumberland College in Tennessee, quickly adapted to the demands of running a family clothing business that was, both literally and figuratively, at the center of the community. He married Fannie Alpert of Sumter, forty miles west, in 1938. Their only child, Joseph "Joe" Leonard, was born on April 18, 1940, in Sumter, because the hospital in Kingstree had been closed due to a fire.

The Goldsteins were known as pillars of the Kingstree community, and over time Isadore served three terms on the city council, as president of the Kiwanis Club and Chamber of Commerce, chair of the local district of the Boy Scouts, and Master of the Free Masons. At their white-painted brick home on Second Avenue, built when Joe was about ten years old, Fannie was admired as a gracious hostess. In addition, she was a master gardener with a particular affection for orchids in her sun porch and pink azaleas in the yard.

Growing up in a town of fewer than 3,200, Goldstein attended segregated local public schools. The Jewish community in Kingstree had only about forty families at its peak. His parents drove Goldstein to Sumter every Sunday so that he could attend classes at Temple Sinai; he was confirmed there with three other students. His high school had only sixty students, but he had good teachers, including a chemistry instructor who sparked Joe's initial interest in science.[3]

Goldstein was voted class president for each of his last three years of high school. As a senior, among his extracurricular activities Goldstein was editor of the *Boll Weevil* student newspaper, named for the beetle that bedeviled the region's cotton farmers. Under his leadership, the *Boll Weevil* won three out of four divisions in a state press association contest and was named Best in State, beating out student newspapers from larger prominent schools.

One of Goldstein's most noteworthy assignments as a reporter was to interview the much-admired statesman Bernard Baruch. A Jewish native of Camden, South Carolina, Baruch was born five years after the end of the Civil War. His father, Simon, a physician educated at the state's medical school in Charleston, had served as a surgeon in the Confederate Army. When Bernard was eleven, Simon moved the family to New York City, where the elder Baruch became known for medical writing and public health efforts.[4] Bernard chose not to follow his father's career path into medicine, instead becoming a stock broker and making a fortune in commodities trading. Baruch served as an adviser to Presidents Woodrow Wilson and Franklin D. Roosevelt during World War I and World War II.[5]

Baruch reconnected with South Carolina when he bought a massive landholding on the coast, which he named Hobcaw Barony and maintained as a hunting preserve. A second, smaller Baruch landholding—this one a paltry 3,700 acres or so—was located eight miles east of Kingstree and was known as Little Hobcaw.[6] Among the dignitaries who came to visit Baruch at Little Hobcaw was Eleanor Roosevelt. While in high school, Goldstein observed the former first lady's arrival in Kingstree on the Atlantic Coast Line Railroad. As in many Southern towns, the railroad tracks divided the community by social and economic status. Roosevelt's arrival was greeted with cheers from the assembled African Americans on one side and jeers from whites on the other side.

In February 1958, the eighty-seven-year-old Baruch consented to be interviewed by Goldstein at Little Hobcaw. The elder statesman clearly charmed the young reporter, who variously described the elder statesman as spry, robust, warm, and friendly. Of particular note, Baruch emphasized to Goldstein, that while the three *R*'s of education—reading, writing, and arithmetic—are important, equally important are the three *C*'s—*c*haracter, *c*ourage, and *c*ompetence. This lesson would shape the young editor's life for years.[7]

More than 700 miles to the north and a cultural world away lies the village of Freeport, New York. Located on the south shore of Long Island, the town's name reflects its history as a so-called free port where ships during colonial times could unload cargo without paying customs fees. The town became an artist colony in the early twentieth century, with many vaudeville performers such as Fanny Brice, Sophie Tucker, and Will Rogers establishing residences there. Freeport grew as a tourist destination, noted for its water sports and fishing in the summer months. With a population of about 20,000, Freeport welcomed a new resident on December 18, 1939: Harold Eliot Varmus. Harold's father, Frank, was a physician who had attended Harvard College on a lacrosse scholarship. After graduation, Frank worked as a waiter to earn enough money to enroll in Tufts University Medical School. Frank would undertake a residency at Kings County Hospital in Brooklyn, where a friend introduced him to his future wife, Beatrice "Bea" Barasch. Bea grew up in Freeport and attended Wellesley College, where she majored in psychology and later trained as a psychiatric social worker. Together, they settled in her hometown, where Frank launched a family medicine practice.[8]

Harold grew up with his younger sister Ellen in a Victorian house surrounded by vegetable and flower gardens. Even as the son of a physician, Harold's school interest was literature rather than the sciences. A product of public schools, Varmus augmented his high-school studies by arranging an informal summer tutorial on James Joyce. Taught by a young English professor from Hofstra University, the once-per-week evening seminar reinforced Harold's interest in, and appreciation of, great literature.[9]

In Brooklyn, less than twenty-five miles west of Freeport, Harvey and Evelyn Brown celebrated the birth of their firstborn, Michael "Mike" Stuart Brown, on April 13, 1941. Harvey was a salesman who marketed textiles to clothing manufacturers, and Evelyn was a homemaker.

Harvey knew the frustrations of working for a boss, and he wanted something different for his son. He believed that if Mike could become a physician his son would enjoy greater independence and freedom. From an early age, Mike was encouraged to become a physician, and he internalized this desire.

When Mike was eleven, the Brown family, by then including a daughter, Susan, moved to Elkins Park, located within the sister suburban townships of Cheltenham and Abington about six miles north of Philadelphia. Together, the two townships had about 50,000 residents when the Browns arrived. Elkins Park was named after businessman William L. Elkins, who made his initial fortune in oil refining and then diversified into the streetcar and railway businesses. At the turn of the twentieth century, Elkins built an opulent Italian High Renaissance summer retreat there. At the time, it was said that "there were more millionaires in Cheltenham per square inch than anywhere else in the country."[10]

When Brown was growing up, Elkins Park was far more diverse economically, and the Browns lived in an apartment in the less affluent part of town. Not long after arriving in Elkins Park, Michael developed a keen interest in operating amateur radios and obtained a license when he was thirteen. He built radio transmitters and receivers from kits, and he learned how to troubleshoot problems in a systematic way. These skills would serve him well in later years when he was trying to solve problems of an entirely different nature.

Brown attended Cheltenham High School, one of the oldest public high schools in Pennsylvania. Cheltenham alumni have been successful in many fields, including business (dealmaker and billionaire Ronald Perelman, class of 1960), athletics (baseball Hall of Famer Reggie Jackson, class of 1964), and politics (Israeli prime minister Benjamin Netanyahu, class of 1967).[11] At Cheltenham, Michael played baseball and developed an interest in journalism, serving as the sports editor of the school newspaper. During this period, one particular book left a lasting impression, as it did for many young people who aspired to careers in medicine: *Arrowsmith* by Sinclair Lewis. This 1925 satirical novel tells the story of Martin Arrowsmith, a physician who traveled a fanciful odyssey from private practice, to hospital work, to research, to fighting a plague, and finally returning back to private practice.[12] Young Brown was fascinated with how a career in medicine might open up so many doors of opportunity.

On April 15, 1943, during World War II, Max and Rose Lefkowitz welcomed their only child, Robert "Bob" Joseph Lefkowitz, into the world. After four prior miscarriages, Rose's delivery of a healthy son was the realization of a dream, and Rose was advised against attempting any further pregnancies. She had grown up in Manhattan and worked as an elementary-school teacher. Husband Max grew up in a large family on the Lower East Side of Manhattan, studied accounting at Brooklyn College, and worked in the garment industry. The Lefkowitz family lived in the southeast Bronx in a sixth-floor, two-bedroom, one-bathroom apartment.[13] Their building was one of about fifty that housed 12,000 families as part of a planned community, Parkchester, developed a few years earlier by the Metropolitan Life Insurance Company.[14]

Rose cherished her only child and was very protective of him, but she was uncomfortable expressing deep affection. She did manage to communicate her high expectations, however. She was a perfectionist, and she took great interest in his schoolwork and making sure that he practiced the piano for an hour every day—a task that young Bob despised. Max was a doting parent; as a Yiddish expression goes, he *kvelled* with pride over his son's every accomplishment. Max took great pleasure in any assistance that he could provide to his son. In junior high school Bob was a straight-A student, but one thing that did not come easily was athletics. When Bob struggled to meet physical education standards in tumbling and rope-climbing, Max rigged up tumbling mats in their apartment and a rope at their summer vacation home. Under his father's coaching, Bob was able to demonstrate sufficient skills to earn a passing grade.

From an early age, reading was a passion for Bob, and he devoured books, including his parents' collection. When he had read all of the books at home, he turned to the public library, always checking out the maximum number of books permitted. He deemed the library to be a poor substitute for acquiring his own books, which he did surreptitiously. He would order "free" books offered as teasers for subscriptions to buy more books over the ensuing year. In this way, he received the six-volume set of Carl Sandburg's magnum opus on Abraham Lincoln and an equally weighty six-volume edition of *The Second World War* by Winston Churchill. His unsuspecting parents were left to honor his stealth commitments to purchase the remaining contracted books, adding to his reading material. Bob's passion for books was so intense that he would occasionally feign illness so that he could stay home from school in order to read.[15]

Like Mike Brown, one novel that captured Bob's imagination was *Arrowsmith*. Another favorite was *Microbe Hunters* by Paul de Kruif, published in 1926. The latter was a collection of a dozen true-life stories of medical heroes—from Louis Pasteur working on rabies, to Walter Reed working on yellow fever, to David Bruce working on sleeping sickness. A microbiologist himself, de Kruif had been an adviser to Sinclair Lewis in the technical aspects of *Arrowsmith*. De Kruif wrote with passion and verve, occasionally inventing dialogue to spice up the story.[16]

Not surprisingly for a fan of *Microbe Hunters*, the young Bob Lefkowitz had a chemistry set and a microscope. He was also an enthusiastic stickball player and a diehard New York Yankees fan. In his heart, he aspired to be a professional baseball player, like his hero Mickey Mantle, but sadly lacked enough talent with the bat. A more realistic career choice took root by the time Bob was in third grade: to become a practicing physician. In this he had a role model, the family's dedicated physician, Dr. Feibush, who made house calls as part of his practice.[17]

Clearly, Bob had the academic chops to aspire to a medical career. In the sixth grade, he performed well enough on a Special Progress exam to skip grades. The next hurdle was admission to the highly selective Bronx High School of Science, or Bronx Science. One gained admission solely on the basis of performance on a competitive exam. At the time, Jewish students faced quotas at many private schools, but at Bronx Science no such barriers existed. The school, therefore, became an academic entry point for many talented Jewish students. As Lefkowitz described: "Everybody at Bronx Science was Jewish at the time. . . . I went back and looked and I think there were about 15 Shapiros in my class."[18] Bronx Science produced a distinguished line of graduates, including eight

Nobel Prize winners, mostly in physics, and six Pulitzer Prize winners. For the first time in his life, Lefkowitz felt challenged academically, but he still graduated within the top 5 percent of his class of about 800 students. Of course, it was an accomplishment just to graduate from Bronx Science, but Bob managed to do it two years early at the age of sixteen.[19]

These four young men—from Kingstree (Goldstein), Freeport (Varmus), Elkins Park (Brown), and the Bronx (Lefkowitz)—headed in different directions for their college educations.

Goldstein, as the only one raised south of the Mason-Dixon Line, chose a school steeped in southern tradition: Washington and Lee University, a small liberal-arts school in Lexington, Virginia, toward the lower end of the Shenandoah Valley. In 1958, Lexington had a population of about 7,500, which was double the size of Kingstree yet small enough to feel comfortable for Goldstein.[20]

Goldstein was interested in premed studies, the program at Washington and Lee was solid, and he signed up. Goldstein arrived in September 1958 among a freshman class of about 300. Joe pledged and was admitted into Zeta Beta Tau, the first Jewish fraternity. Academically, he made a smooth transition from the small high school in Kingstree to the rigors of college courses, and he was one of nine freshmen admitted into the Phi Eta Sigma honorary scholastic society.[21] Goldstein's academic success continued in his second year, when he was selected as the sole recipient of the Phi Beta Kappa honorary society's Sophomore Award.[22] The following year, he was the only junior elected to membership in Phi Beta Kappa.[23] Goldstein maintained a perfect 4.0 grade-point average through his college career. Just to prove he was human, however, he did actually earn one B—in physical education—but this was not counted in the official grade calculations.[24] With an unblemished academic record, it was no surprise when he became the valedictorian of his graduating class; on Friday, June 8, 1962, he addressed 238 graduates, their families, and friends at commencement on the front lawn of the university.[25]

There was more than academics to Goldstein's career at Washington and Lee, however. He was chair of the student library committee, secretary of the Publications Board,[26] and editor in chief of *Calyx*, the student yearbook. One of his former biology professors, James H. Starling, observed: "Pre-med students had their minds on getting into medical school . . . and to hell with the rest of it. But he [Goldstein] did the rest of it."[27] Another former professor, Sidney M. B. Coulling of the English Department, noted of Goldstein's diverse interests that "it's hard to have that kind of all-around record," adding, "he was, in short, a campus leader and a valedictorian—a rare combination."[28]

Even when it came to academics, the kid from Kingstree who graduated with a BS in chemistry summa cum laude was not monochromatically interested in the sciences. Professor Coulling recalled that Goldstein "had a perception of literary values and literary qualities. He bridged the two cultures." It was in science, however, that Goldstein truly excelled. One of his former classmates and later a judge, George E. Honts III, recalled an organic chemistry class in which Goldstein earned a 99, 30 points above the next highest grade. "He royally screwed the curve for all of the other fellows," laughed Honts.[29]

Nearly 600 miles northeast of Lexington is Amherst, Massachusetts, named after Jeffery Amherst, commander in chief of the British army in North America during the French and Indian War.[30]

When Harold Varmus arrived in Amherst, in 1957, about 13,000 permanent residents were far outnumbered by the student population. Amherst is the typical college town. In addition to the private Amherst College, there is the much larger University of Massachusetts–Amherst, the flagship campus of the public University of Massachusetts System. Nearby are two of the Seven Sisters—private women's colleges—Mount Holyoke College (in South Hadley) and Smith College (Northampton). Hampshire College, a small private liberal arts school, opened in 1970.

Varmus chose Amherst over his father's alma mater, Harvard, because he was looking for a small school at which he could have close relationships with faculty while pursuing a broad liberal arts education. His class (about 250, all male) was taught according to the so-called New Curriculum, introduced a decade earlier. This approach to undergraduate education involved prescribed two-year sequences of courses in three required pathways: history, science, and the humanities. Courses were taught in small groups, with complementary laboratory or seminar sections, and electives were reduced or eliminated during the first two years. Even when a student decided on a major in the final two years, faculty continued to exert influence, if not control, over course selection.[31]

Varmus selected English literature as his major after excluding philosophy and physics as alternatives. He was exposed to great literature and great teachers. For his thesis, Varmus was matched with a young faculty member named William Pritchard. This was the first thesis Pritchard directed, so he was particularly attentive to his young charge. The thesis focused on the role that Charles Dickens's character and life experiences played in shaping his writing. The premise of Varmus's thesis—that literary analysis must take historical and biographical contexts into account—was a counterpoint to the department's senior scholars who built reputations arguing the opposite. Nevertheless, Pritchard and other faculty members found the thesis sufficiently meritorious to advise Varmus to consider a career in English literature.[32]

When he was not immersed in Dickens, Varmus was focused on the school newspaper, the *Amherst Student*. For a year, Varmus served as the editor in chief. The paper, not limiting itself to events on campus, featured reviews of virtually every type of art form, from literature, to music, to film, to painting. Editorials were equally wide-ranging, from the amount of money spent on intercollegiate athletics, to the role private philanthropy plays in influencing academic matters, to national issues such as the presidential election and the civil rights movement.[33]

With his attention directed toward Dickens and the student newspaper, Varmus clearly was not the typical premed student. He took the bare minimum of required science courses and tackled them with little enthusiasm. Traditionally, the biggest hurdle for premeds is organic chemistry (in which Joe Goldstein screwed the curve for classmates at Washington and Lee). Harold Varmus started out at the other end of the grade spectrum and struggled even to receive a passing mark. His professor, Robert Whitney, suggested that Varmus abandon the course (and, with it, his medical school ambitions). Varmus was determined to prove Whitney wrong. He escaped the distractions of his noisy fraternity house, relocated to a dormitory, and concentrated enough to

raise his grade to a respectable C.[34] Remarkably, Varmus graduated
magna cum laude in 1961 and headed to Harvard University to pursue
English literature.

Michael Brown's choice came down to two Ivy League schools: Princeton and the University of Pennsylvania. Brown had images of himself
as a Princeton man and was "ready to buy a pipe and ascot."[35] Unfortunately, Princeton did not offer him a scholarship his freshman year,
and his family could not afford to send him there without assistance.
But Penn was prepared to foot the bill for tuition, room, and board for
all four years. Brown accepted the offer from Penn and moved to the
campus in downtown Philadelphia. Brown's four-year scholarship was
sponsored by Procter & Gamble and was awarded to two students each
year. About two months into Brown's freshman year, a dinner was held
to introduce the awardees to a representative of their corporate bene-
factor. Upon arrival, Brown immediately noticed that the seven other
scholarship recipients were large, strapping fellows.

Surprised that he was the only scholarship recipient who didn't look
like he belonged on the football field, after the dinner Brown pulled the
Penn dean aside and said: "I think that you guys made a mistake." Although Brown had played third base on his high school's baseball team,
he was no hot prospect for the Penn athletic department. The dean
graciously reassured him that no mistake had been made, confessing:
"[Procter & Gamble] stipulated that we couldn't use their scholarships
to recruit athletes. But of course we have been using it for that, and the
problem is that the grade point average is so low that they are beginning
to get suspicious. So, we had to accept somebody who would pull up
the grade point average for the whole group and that's you."[36] During
Brown's sophomore year, the Penn Quakers football team had seven
wins against one tie (Navy) and one loss (Harvard), winning the conference championship. And though Brown kept up his part of the bargain
in the classroom, his fellow Procter & Gamble scholars on the football
team went 5–13 during Brown's last two years at the school.

Brown majored in chemistry as an undergrad, but he devoted more
time and energy to writing features for the university-supported school

newspaper, the *Daily Pennsylvanian*. The editorial staff had a reputation for irreverence, which grated on the buttoned-up university administration. It was more than adolescent rebellion—it marked a turning point in social and cultural norms on campus. In the early 1960s, Penn was still a conservative bastion of tradition, with students wearing jackets and ties to classes, as well as to dinner in the freshman commons. Many, if not most, of the students were perfectly comfortable with the status quo. The staff of the *Daily Pennsylvanian*, however, felt that it was time to bury the "organization man" era of the 1950s.

The editorial staff rebelled against university-imposed curfews, dress codes, and the graduation awards handed out largely on the basis of social standing. The newspaper became a forum for raising such concerns and advocating for change. The situation came to a head when the *Daily Pennsylvanian* produced a parody of the gossipy weekly newspaper published by the separate women's college at Penn. "We basically lampooned the whole women's system," Brown recalled. "That gave the university the opportunity to close down the newspaper. At the time, the newspaper was totally funded by the university. . . . So they called up the printer and said: 'Stop the presses. We are not paying any more.'"[37]

The imbroglio did not end there, however: "They made a stupid mistake," reminisced Brown. "They didn't shut down our offices. We had offices on the campus that had telephones. So, we immediately got on the telephone and started calling up all the other Ivy League newspapers saying: 'Penn is suppressing free speech. This is horrible.'" In response, "all of the college newspapers came out with editorials saying that this was terrible." Not satisfied with support in the print media, Brown and his colleagues contacted local TV stations, but they declined coverage unless there was some sort of visual image to broadcast.

Realizing that most of the student body was not enamored of the *Daily Pennsylvanian* staff, Brown and his team had to find another way to get the campus motivated for a public protest. "We sent our freshman staffers through the dormitories saying: 'There's a big demonstration today against the *DP.*' So, we organized this whole demonstration against us, and I remember, I got up on the platform and tried to defend us. The television cameras were rolling—and my parents who lived in suburban Philadelphia—that was the first time they ever saw me on television."[38]

Within ten days, the university administration concluded that the newspaper had to be reopened, but they needed a scapegoat, so they relieved the prior editor in chief, Melvin Goldstein, of his responsibilities. The university president, Gaylord Harnwell, a Princeton-educated physicist, personally selected Brown as the interim successor, believing, as Brown later characterized with a touch of irony, that he "was the most presentable guy." Unbeknownst to Harnwell, Brown had edited the parody issue that ignited the entire controversy and, in addition, was the mastermind behind the guerrilla campaign to restore the newspaper. The headline of the first postsuspension issue read: "As we were saying . . . " Under Brown's brief tenure as editor in chief, the *Daily Pennsylvanian* continued to support greater freedom, independence, and self-determination for students.

In retrospect, these early *Daily Pennsylvanian* skirmishes with the university president seem tame compared to events five years later, when Harnwell would see his office occupied by protesting students for two days. In April 1967, as the Vietnam War escalated, students held a sit-in to object to secret research conducted on campus on chemical and biological warfare. Later that year, the editors of the *Daily Pennsylvanian* would call for Harnwell's retirement, referring to him as "an old man" and "calling for an infusion of new blood at the top."[39]

Aside from learning how to organize a protest with full media coverage, Brown's tenure at the *Daily Pennsylvanian* helped him acquire skills that he credited as serving him well later. "One is it gave me a real sense of how to work with a group—how to lead a group of people. Number two, I think newspaper writing is the best training for scientific writing because newspaper people are trained to get the major ideas in the first paragraph, because nobody reads past the first paragraph. That is certainly true nowadays in scientific papers." More generally, writing "forces you to focus your ideas. What do you do as a scientist? The same thing."[40]

Brown estimated that he spent about 80 percent of his time as an undergraduate working on the *Daily Pennsylvanian*. "You have to put out an issue every single day. The pressure of that is enormous." The paper went to press at 2:00 a.m., and at this time the printer used linotype machines, so "you would sit there all night with these linotype operators because they would print a big galley sheet and you would check for errors."[41] Even with the all-nighters, Brown found enough time to study for the courses required for his major in chemistry, as well as the liberal arts classes, which he enjoyed as much or more than his science curriculum.

In the summer of 1962, following graduation from Penn, Brown got his first taste of science in a roundabout way. His mother, Evelyn, performed temporary secretarial work, and one of her assignments was at the pharmaceutical company Smith, Kline & French, which operated a factory and a laboratory facility in the heart of Philadelphia. Evelyn Brown, who had a deathly fear of rodents, was not told in advance that her work space would be surrounded by cages of research mice. No sooner had she arrived at her desk than she fainted at the sight of her new office mates. An ambulance was called, and as she was being wheeled out on a stretcher, the laboratory head approached and asked her if he could help in any way. Without missing a beat, in true Jewish mother fashion, Evelyn replied that she was fine, but she would be ever so grateful if he could find a summer job for her son who was a student at Penn. "It was impossible to get these jobs," Brown reported, and "there was absolutely no way I could have gotten this job any other way. So, they offered me a Summer job, and even though I had a scholarship to medical school as well, I was desperate for money . . . that was the money that basically allowed me to eat during the year."[42]

The project on which he worked related to testing drugs that were being developed to reduce stomach acid secretion and the associated symptoms of heartburn. One of the undesirable side effects of these drugs was that they slowed down the rate at which food moved through the intestines. In order to assess the effect on intestinal transit, the drug company needed an experimental model in which gut motility could be measured easily. For this purpose, a meal consisting of a suspension of charcoal was introduced through a tube into the rat's stomach. The charcoal was used as a marker that could be seen and measured easily. At various times after the charcoal was introduced, the animals were sacrificed to see how far the food had progressed through their intestines. In the meantime, the medications were tested for their effectiveness in preventing ulcers that were induced by stressing the rodents.

Over the two summers that preceded and followed his first year of medical school, Brown measured the effects of various drugs on ulcers and bowel motility in literally thousands of rats. Wanting to understand the biological processes at a deeper level, he spent hours in the company's library, getting special permission to remain there after closing. It is tempting to trace Brown's later interest in both medical research and gastroenterology to those quiet summer evenings spent reading in the Smith, Kline & French library and his studies of ulcers and intestinal motility in rodents.

Bob Lefkowitz chose Columbia University for college, in part because he was granted early admission and a scholarship. He was given credit for two advanced placement courses—the maximum permitted—in chemistry. So, as a freshman, he was permitted to enroll in organic chemistry, a course usually taken during junior year. Two years younger than most of his classmates, Lefkowitz would later describe himself as "a man in a hurry."[43] His goal was to get to medical school, and from his perspective the sooner that he got there the better. He was able to pick up the already breakneck pace by combining his advanced placement credits with a heavy course load and summer school classes, thereby squeezing a full year from the normal duration of college.

At Columbia, there was a two-year required core curriculum, Contemporary Civilization. The didactic approach was to assign readings from classical works in a range of fields, from philosophy to history to social and political sciences. Then, the students would be brought together in a small group seminar format to discuss the works. This curriculum introduced Lefkowitz to a dizzying array of stimulating concepts and ideas. Moreover, he took courses from some of the leading intellectual figures of the day, including the writer and literary critic Lionel Trilling and the historian Jacques Barzun. In completing his assignments, the bookish Lefkowitz felt right at home poring over the collections of the New York Public Library in its majestic public reading room on Fifth Avenue and 42nd Street.[44]

Beyond the established academic luminaries to which Lefkowitz was exposed at Columbia, one rising star, Ronald Breslow, captured his imagination. Breslow taught an advanced seminar in biochemistry and entertained his students, including Lefkowitz, with his fast-talking depictions of the "magic stuff" of chemistry. Breslow would go on to create his own chemical magic by creating new molecules that mimic the actions of naturally occurring compounds. Three decades later, President George H. W. Bush would award Breslow the National Medal of Science for his many contributions, including the development of a drug used in the treatment of lymphoma.

Although his primary focus was coursework, Lefkowitz was active in extracurricular activities as well. He worked on the yearbook, the *Columbian*, during his junior and senior years, serving first as editor of the senior section and, the following year, the fraternities and societies section. Lefkowitz also was a member of the Political Assembly and the Pre-Med Society. In addition, he served as vice president of the Seixas Society, a Jewish fraternal organization.

Lefkowitz graduated from Columbia at nineteen and immediately got engaged to his childhood girlfriend, Arna Gornstein. A year later, the couple married, and a year after that they had their first child, David. Almost like clockwork, the following year, David's younger brother Larry was born. In his personal life, as in his educational pursuits, Lefkowitz was not interested in wasting any time.

CHAPTER 3

"MY SON, THE DOCTOR"

Higher Education in the Era of Quotas

One of the popular stereotypes about Jewish parents is their abiding desire for their children to pursue careers in the professions, whether education, law, or especially medicine. Certainly, aspirations for one's children to succeed transcend religious and cultural boundaries and are common among immigrant groups who came to the United States seeking opportunities denied to them elsewhere. First- and second-generation Jewish families in the United States often had ambitions for their children that parents and grandparents in Eastern Europe could not have imagined. And even though Joe Goldstein, Harold Varmus, Mike Brown, and Bob Lefkowitz did not feel pressured by their parents into pursuing medical careers, becoming a physician would no doubt carry the parental seal of approval.

For Mike Brown, the clues were not all that subtle. As he recalled: "We were living in this apartment complex just outside of Philadelphia.

The greatest hero in this whole apartment complex was somebody who had a son who was a resident [physician in training] at Penn. He was the god. My mother made me go and talk to this god. I guess I was still in high school, but I wanted to go to medical school. So, my mother brings me to meet this man." Once the introduction was made, Mike Brown had his eyes opened to another reality. He was told by the Penn resident: "You know, if you want to go to medical school, you are going to have to be better than everyone else because you're not competing against everyone else. You're only competing against the other Jews and there is a fixed number of places for Jews."[1]

Discrimination in admissions to American medical schools on the basis of religion took hold in the early twentieth century. Its origins trace to the flood of Russian Jewish immigrants who arrived in the United States during the three decades leading up to World War I. As these newcomers and their children pursued higher education, public institutions, such as the City College of New York, as well as private institutions, such as Harvard, saw large percentage increases in Jewish enrollment. Fearing that the white, Anglo-Saxon, Protestant heritages of the private schools were under threat, leaders at those institutions quietly instituted policies that limited the numbers of Jews admitted. But they did so behind the scenes; after Harvard president Abbott Lawrence Lowell (who also was an officer of the Immigration Restriction League) had done so publicly in 1922, strong objections were expressed both on and off campus.[2]

In an internal memorandum written that same year, the chair of the undergraduate admissions committee at Yale decried the rise of "the alien and unwashed element." In 1923, Yale implemented a 10 percent Jewish quota, known as the "Limitation of Numbers" policy, which remained in place until the 1960s.[3] At the Yale School of Medicine, applications from Jewish candidates were labeled with an H for "Hebrew." When application forms did not have explicit questions about religious affiliation, Jewish identity was inferred from an applicant's name, place of residence, or parents' place of birth. In 1940, William Sargent Ladd Jr., the dean of Cornell's medical school, acknowledged in private correspondence: "We limit the number of Jews admitted to each class to roughly the proportion of Jews in the population of the state."⁴ By one analysis, the proportion of Jewish students admitted to the Columbia University College of Physicians and Surgeons (P&S) dropped from 16 percent in 1920 to 4 percent in 1940.⁵

Even the best and brightest Jewish students faced blatant discrimination. Arthur Kornberg, corecipient of the 1959 Nobel Prize in Physiology or Medicine, recounted that he had no experience with anti-Semitism until he was a senior at "the academically prestigious City College of New York, whose student body was then 90 percent or more Jewish. Then came the disappointment of being rejected by virtually all of the many medical schools to which I applied. But it came as no surprise."⁶ Kornberg was admitted to the University of Rochester School of Medicine, and his later brilliant discoveries led to the eventual award of a dozen honorary degrees.

After World War II, following the horrors of the Holocaust, religious quotas for medical school admissions began to erode. The demise of these discriminatory practices also was hastened by the growth in the number of medical schools and the passage of prohibitions in law. Still, when Goldstein, Varmus, Brown, and Lefkowitz were seeking admission to medical school in 1962, the memories of restrictive barriers and the persistent competitive pressures among Jewish students were very real. Ironically, the medical education that they would receive was framed in large part by recommendations offered a half-century earlier by a Jewish educational reformer named Abraham Flexner.

A graduate of Johns Hopkins University, Flexner was not a physician or a scientist. But he was a serious educator and a critic of the American higher education system. Under the aegis of the Carnegie Foundation, Flexner visited every medical school in the United States and Canada and published a landmark summary of his findings in the "Flexner Report" (1910). Among the recommendations: reduce the number of medical schools, raise the prerequisites for admission, incorporate scientific advancements into coursework, include researchers on the faculty, control hospital-based educational experience, and strengthen state regulation of licensure. Flexner's ideas led to the closing of lower-quality, proprietary (privately owned, for-profit) medical schools as well as to better standards in scientific and clinical instruction among the surviving schools.[7]

When it came to choosing a medical school, Joe Goldstein leaned toward Washington University in St. Louis. During spring vacation, however, he accompanied college classmate and fraternity brother Herbert Salomon to his hometown in Dallas, where Salomon had already been accepted at the University of Texas Southwestern Medical School. Goldstein's friend arranged for him to be interviewed during this visit. Looking back a quarter-century later, Goldstein recalled his initial impressions: "I liked the city, and the school seemed to be going places. I thought there would be some opportunities here."[8]

UT's Southwestern Medical School was less than two decades old. Goldstein, who had a cousin internist, asked what he knew about it. By pure coincidence he had just returned from a national meeting where two faculty members from Southwestern spoke. The cousin reported that the talks given by those two faculty members were the best that he had heard, so he thought it would be a good medical school for Joe to attend.[9] Even though it was late in the application cycle, and he already had an acceptance in hand from a first-rate medical school, Goldstein applied and was accepted.

One of the speakers at the medical meeting was Dr. Donald Seldin, chair of the Department of Internal Medicine at UT Southwestern Medical School. Seldin, a specialist in kidney disease, trained at Yale University before coming to Southwestern, sight unseen, in 1951 as an associate professor at the age of thirty-one. Seldin arrived in Dallas to find the campus an appalling assortment of dilapidated shacks. Even more distressing, within six months Seldin became the last man standing, as other faculty members—including Charles Burnett, who recruited him—all departed. Seldin had his own attractive offers to escape. Nevertheless, he persevered, and through sheer force of character he was able to resuscitate the school. A new public hospital (Parkland Memorial) was built by the county, where medical students and residents could learn while providing hands-on patient care. The state also appropriated money to build modern facilities, and Seldin began recruiting top-notch students from Texas. He was confident the state could produce the same level of talent he encountered in the Northeast: "One thing I know is that brains are not geographically distributed."[10]

Seldin, a tall, thin, and dashing man with a magnetic personality, worked closely with students, teaching them on the wards and getting to know them personally. He was demanding, and when a student struggled to answer one of his questions on attending rounds, an oft-repeated response was: "Here's a dime, go call your mother. She'll know the answer to my question. Tell her that you're coming home." Although he had high expectations of his charges, they knew that Seldin was grooming them for success, sometimes seeing potential that they themselves did not recognize.

With his keen discernment of abilities, Seldin handpicked the most outstanding students for further development. He would work with them to map out their clinical training, relying upon his national network of colleagues at leading institutions across the country, often supplemented by research training at the National Institutes of Health (NIH). In return, Seldin promised them that, if they returned to Dallas afterward, they would become the leaders of new programs that he planned to establish. By growing the local talent and supplementing it with training at the best programs, he developed a faculty of the highest rank. The list of these homegrown stars is long and includes, among other doctors, Floyd Rector (kidney disease), Jean Wilson (hormonal disorders), Daniel Foster (diabetes), and Norman Kaplan (high blood pressure).

Among the future prospects, none was more promising than Joe Goldstein. One of the first out-of-state students accepted at UT Southwestern, Goldstein immediately impressed all who interacted with him. Even his quiet and understated demeanor could not hide the sheer brilliance of his intellect. Dr. Leonard Madison, one of the first faculty members recruited by Seldin, recalled the general perception of the student from Kingstree, South Carolina: "We always thought that Joe was something super special. There's Joe Goldstein, and then there's nobody, and then there's nobody, and then there's nobody, and then there's the second one [i.e., in the class]. He was just head and shoulders above everybody else. He has a spectacular mind."[11]

Goldstein's first research experience came in summer 1963 after he had completed his first year of medical school. Dr. Burton Combes, a specialist in liver disease, and a visiting scientist, Dr. Steven Schenker, designed a project for Goldstein to perform. It involved a test that was the leading way to diagnose liver disease at the time. The test was performed by injecting a dye, named "BSP," into a vein in the patient's arm. The bloodstream then carried the dye to the liver, the body's main detoxifying organ. Within forty-five minutes, virtually all of the dye would be cleared from the blood of persons with healthy livers, but much less was eliminated from persons with impaired blood flow to the liver or decreased hepatic function.

The mechanism by which the liver detoxifies BSP is to attach it chemically to glutathione—the body's master antioxidant. A few years earlier, Combes had identified the enzyme that accelerates this attachment process. Goldstein's project was to develop a faster way to determine the enzyme level using a technique to measure light absorption (spectrophotometry). Goldstein said: "Within several months, I came up with a spectrophotometric assay that replaced the time-consuming prior method. . . . This was my first scientific discovery and I became hooked on the thrill of scientific research."[12] By the time he graduated medical school, Goldstein had published four scientific papers based on work with Burton Combes.

To nobody's surprise, Goldstein finished first in his medical school class and was the corecipient of the so-called Ho Din Award. The title of this honor derives from a Greek acronym for the expression "the spirit of medical wisdom," and it is given each year to the graduating student who best exemplifies the attributes of the ideal physician—knowledge, understanding, and compassion.

Receiving a diploma that confers the degree Doctor of Medicine is an essential step in becoming a physician, but it is only one step. It marks the completion of the four years of core education—the first two years of science instruction and the second two years of clinical experience—collectively referred to as "undergraduate medical education." The next step—the internship—is a year of deep immersion in patient care. In 1952, the National Intern Matching Program (now the National Resident Matching Program) was established as a private, nonprofit, nongovernmental, integrated system for assigning medical school graduates to teaching hospitals. Candidates rank their choices of hospitals, and simultaneously hospitals rank their choices of interns. The goal of the system is to achieve the best possible fit on both sides.

The term "resident" was introduced in 1889 at Johns Hopkins Hospital. In its original context, resident physicians had completed an internship and were continuing hospital-based training to prepare to practice in a specialized area, such as internal medicine, surgery, pediatrics, psychiatry, or obstetrics and gynecology. Those who want to subspecialize (in, say, cardiology, gastroenterology, nephrology, or endocrinology) require additional training beyond the residency in what is referred to as a "fellowship."

The plan that Donald Seldin developed for Joe Goldstein had four steps. First, Joe would get into the best internship and medical residency possible. Second, he would undertake research training as a Clinical Associate at the NIH. Third, he would pursue a fellowship in medical genetics at one of the leading programs in the country. And fourth, he would return to UT Southwestern to establish and lead a division of genetics within Seldin's Department of Medicine. It was a six-year journey that would take Goldstein to Massachusetts General Hospital (MGH) in Boston, followed by the NIH in Bethesda, Maryland, then across the country to the University of Washington in Seattle, and ultimately back to Dallas. Goldstein gratefully acknowledged the role that Seldin played in launching him on this academic odyssey: "In combination with good grades in medical school and Seldin's influence, I got an internship at the MGH."[13]

For Harold Varmus, the path to medical school was more circuitous. As a college senior, he vacillated about what to do after graduation. One option was medicine, following his father. Although this may have seemed the obvious and predetermined course, Varmus was not convinced that it suited his personal inclinations and abilities. His English professors at Amherst College encouraged him to consider graduate school. Varmus also toyed with the idea of seeking a Fulbright Fellowship to travel to Norway, where he would study the writers Henrik Ibsen and George

Bernard Shaw. He also contemplated entering journalism and even traveling to study at a Japanese university.

When Varmus won a Woodrow Wilson Fellowship, he enrolled in the graduate program in English at Harvard in fall 1961. Soon afterward, Varmus discovered that the reality of life as an English literature graduate student was not exactly what he had pictured. Rather than being surrounded by other budding literary scholars, his classes tended to be filled with undergraduates. Often, the teaching was performed by graduate assistants rather than faculty luminaries. His courses were uninspiring, and increasingly he was drawn to readings outside the assigned topics. In particular, the writings of Sigmund Freud captured his imagination. Even though Varmus was not convinced by the psychoanalytic theories that Freud advanced, he was enthralled by the manner in which Freud wrote about patients and their lives. Clearly, the ability to tell a compelling story could be as valuable in medicine as it was in literature.

Varmus witnessed medical storytelling firsthand on Saturday-morning visits to the weekly clinicopathological conference (CPC) at MGH.[14] During a CPC, an actual patient's history and findings are presented to a master clinician, who discusses the possible diagnoses and treatments. Watching the professor sort through the information, the audience observes how an expert reasons through the diagnostic process, often made more challenging by uncertain or inconsistent evidence. The diagnosis rendered is either confirmed or countered by a pathologist's findings, sometimes relying upon a postmortem examination. If well executed, a CPC can be as compelling as a good mystery novel. For Harold Varmus, sitting with some of his former Amherst classmates (now students at Harvard Medical School), these real-life adventures were more gripping than any fiction he was studying. The excitement his former classmates expressed toward medical studies offered a striking counterpoint to his own lack of inspiration. Varmus decided to give medical school a try.

Although Harvard greeted his application with little enthusiasm, Varmus had a much warmer reception at Columbia University College of Physicians and Surgeons (P&S). His interview in New York was conducted by Dr. David Seegal. This was a fortuitous pairing, as Seegal himself had taken an indirect route to medicine, initially studying physical anthropology. A year after Varmus interviewed, the graduating class dedicated the yearbook to Seegal, a reflection of their deep admiration.[15] During his interview with Varmus, Seegal focused on the Old English expression "Ic ne wat," asking Harold if he knew what it meant. For most applicants, this would have been an obscure reference, but for a graduate student in English literature it was a softball question. Varmus replied correctly that it meant "I don't know." Seegal used this opportunity to expound, as he did in his medical school lectures, on why it is important for doctors to recognize their own limitations.[16]

Varmus matriculated at P&S in fall 1962, thinking initially that he might follow in Freud's footsteps (and even winning an essay competition by writing on the father of psychoanalysis). As he was exposed to other subjects, the lure of psychiatry began to fade. One faculty member who made a strong impression on Varmus was Dr. Paul Marks. A graduate of Columbia University and P&S (and finishing first in his medical school class), Marks undertook a fellowship at NIH under the direction of Arthur Kornberg, the future Nobel laureate whose Jewish religion almost prevented him from being admitted to medical school. Returning to Columbia, Marks studied metabolic processes in red blood cells, discovering an inherited enzyme defect that leads to anemia. Marks took a leave to study genetics at the molecular level under the future Nobel laureate Jacques Monod at the Pasteur Institute in Paris. In 1962, Marks returned to the faculty at P&S as a thirty-six-year-old professor of human genetics just as Varmus was starting medical school. Varmus had a front-row seat in the newly emerging field of molecular biology.[17]

Although enthralled by the expanding base of biological information underlying health and disease, Varmus had no personal research experience and no particular inclination to pursue it. His career goal was to become an internal medicine faculty member, with primary responsibilities in teaching and patient care. He could imagine himself engaged in patient-oriented research, but the idea of doing basic research at a laboratory bench held little appeal. If anything, he went in the opposite direction, spending the last few months of medical school in an elective working at the Clara Swain mission hospital in northern India. Today, it is common for American medical students to seek clinical experiences in the developing world, but in 1966 it was considered an unusual detour.

For Varmus, the experience was eye-opening, and it left him dismayed by the poor quality of care and the demeaning attitudes that he witnessed among some caregivers. While serving in India, Varmus learned that he had been accepted into the residency program at Columbia-Presbyterian Hospital; having ranked MGH as his first choice, he was nonetheless content to continue training at Columbia.

For Michael Brown, the decision of where to attend medical school was a matter of the heart. At sixteen, he met the fourteen-year-old Alice Lapin. Their families spent summer vacations in a small beach community on the North Shore of Long Island. More than a half-century later, he confessed: "I guess it was just love at first sight . . . I just became infatuated with her. . . . She was two years behind me in school, so when I was in second year at Penn, she was applying to colleges and her family had even less money than my family. But she fortunately got a scholarship to a school that was then called Beaver College, which was right outside of Philadelphia. Actually, a mile from my house." Brown continued: "She was a student in Philadelphia, so when it came time to apply to medical school I decided I wanted to stay in Philadelphia. We were married after my second year of medical school."[18]

As a first-year medical student, Brown won the David L. Drabkin Prize in Biochemistry. And while pursuing academic honors at Penn, Brown was repeatedly in competition with classmate Amiel Segal, the son of a prominent rabbi in Washington, DC. It was a friendly competition, and the two enjoyed studying together. Brown described the duo: "Two guys who liked to learn more than what they were teaching. So, he and I were the two guys really at the top of the class."[19]

Segal spent the summers working in a lab at the Walter Reed Army Institute of Research in Washington. This work resulted in a published monograph, an unusual accomplishment for a medical student. He was not the only Penn medical student with research experience, however; many of Brown's classmates "worked in these high-powered labs in the summer and they made no money, but they did real science." Meanwhile, Brown's summer research at Smith, Kline & French on the treatment of stress-induced ulcers and gastrointestinal motility in rats was remunerative, but it was not the kind of science likely to see scholarly publication. "All I have is these rats," Brown groused. "So, I go over all my data and I realize that . . . I could actually plot out and write an equation that described the speed of this charcoal meal. . . . The meal went the fastest in the upper intestine and as it got to the lower intestine, it slowed down more and more and more." Brown continued: "When you restrained the rat, you changed that pattern and the equation changed."[20] Although it was not groundbreaking science, Brown, by working on his own and despite limited research experience, was able to see the pattern in the data and describe it mathematically.

One of the largest medical research meetings—the Federation of American Societies for Experimental Biology (FASEB)—took place each year in Atlantic City, New Jersey. As the University of Pennsylvania was only an hour's drive, there was a "tradition for students who had done research in the medical school to write up abstracts and submit them to see if they could make a presentation at this huge national meeting."[21] Although he had not worked in a fancy research lab, Brown decided to write up "this abstract about the effect of . . . stress basically on the intestinal motility of the rat. I submitted it to the FASEB meeting and sure enough, it gets selected for a subsection of gastroenterology. So, I got to present a 10-minute talk with my data and maybe there were 20 people in the audience at this Atlantic City meeting."[22] Admittedly, it was one of nearly 3,200 papers presented at the meeting, and few people heard Brown's talk. But one of the attendees would turn out to be important to Brown down the road.

Before graduating from medical school, Brown did experience some guided research, by working under the direction of the physician-scientist Albert Winegrad, who studied diabetes. Winegrad was a "brilliant man and incredibly critical," Brown recalled. "I was almost paralyzed by his skepticism of everything. It was a tremendous experience for me to see how a laboratory worked and to see how a really critical scientist not only designed his own experiments, but also evaluated the literature. He told me what was wrong with all the papers that I was reading."[23]

This rotation doing diabetes research paid another unanticipated dividend when Winegrad visited with the chair of the Department of

Internal Medicine at Penn, James Wyngaarden. Knowing that Wyngaarden had trained at MGH and maintained good contacts there, Winegrad lobbied on Brown's behalf. As Brown recalls: "Winegrad went to Jim Wyngaarden and said: 'I've got a special student who has just done this rotation. He wants to go to MGH and you need to help him get into MGH.' So Wyngaarden called me in and we had a nice interview. Wyngaarden wrote a nice letter of recommendation and that's why I was accepted at the Mass General."[24]

At the time, MGH selected about a dozen internal medicine residents per year, with half the spots reserved for Harvard medical graduates. So the competition was fierce for the remaining spots (as Harold Varmus could attest). Even for someone as accomplished as Mike Brown, who won the Fredrick L. Packard Prize as the best student in internal medicine at Penn, getting into MGH was a long shot. A positive recommendation from someone known to the MGH medical staff could be the difference. Much as a strong recommendation from Donald Seldin opened the door for Joe Goldstein, Jim Wyngaarden's patronage helped bring Mike Brown's file to the attention of decision-makers.

Even with Wyngaarden's support, however, Brown was not assured of acceptance at MGH—there was still the matter of Amiel Segal. With his published research monograph, arguably Segal offered brighter academic sparkle compared to Mike Brown. Together the two friends headed off to Boston to interview for their residencies. The first stop was at another Harvard affiliate, the Peter Bent Brigham Hospital. More than fifty years later, Brown recalled the events vividly:

> The Brigham interviews were brutal because you had this whole series of interviews. On the second day we were supposed to go to the MGH and as we were leaving the Brigham, he [Segal] turns to me and says: 'I'm not even going to interview at the MGH.' I said: 'Why?' He said that he had a girlfriend, and they were about to get married, and she didn't want him to work every other night as an intern.
> . . .
> All of the Boston programs were every other night. But Albert Einstein

[School of Medicine] had instituted this every third night program, and so his girlfriend absolutely wanted him not to work every other night. . . . I really think that he would have been accepted over me if he had gone to the interviews.[25]

Back in New York, Bob Lefkowitz decided to remain at Columbia for medical school, selecting it over five or six other schools to which he had been admitted. He matriculated with Harold Varmus into the same class at P&S. Unlike Varmus, who had vacillated about whether to pursue medicine, Lefkowitz was fulfilling a dream he had had since third grade. Medical school only amplified his interest in biochemistry as an undergraduate under the tutelage of Ronald Breslow. His first-year course was taught by some renowned biochemists. The department chair, David Rittenberg, had trained under the Nobel laureate Harold Urey and was an expert on using radioisotopes to trace metabolic pathways. Erwin Chargaff, who would go on to win the National Medal of Science, lectured on his research on nucleic acids. David Nachmansohn, who had trained under the Nobel laureate Otto Meyerhof, taught the students about his research on chemical transmitters in the nervous system. David Shemin, a recipient of the Pasteur Medal, taught the students about chemical compounds that help to carry oxygen in red blood cells.

When it came to focus, Lefkowitz had no trouble except with his microscope. At P&S, students were required to purchase their own microscopes for lab work in anatomy, microbiology, and pathology. Because these courses were completed during the first two years, new students typically acquired microscopes from students who were transitioning to clinical work. Lefkowitz managed to negotiate a good deal for his microscope, until he started using it and realized that the fine and coarse control knobs did not work well together. With practice, however, he figured out how to apply just the right amount of pressure to bring the slides into focus.[26] The arts of applying pressure and maintaining focus would be the hallmarks of his career for many years to come.

Although inspired by the world-class scientists, Lefkowitz never contemplated following in their footsteps. He could not wait to start clinical work. The Introduction to Clinical Medicine course was taught by

Paul Marks. Just as Harold Varmus had been inspired by Marks's lectures, Lefkowitz admired the way Marks presented case histories and integrated scientific information into background readings and presentations. Lefkowitz's eyes opened to the scientific underpinnings of patient care.

Another physician model was Dickinson Richards. Trained at Columbia followed by a fellowship in London with the Nobel laureate Henry Dale, Richards was the senior statesman—sixty-seven years old when Lefkowitz entered. A quarter-century earlier, Richards had codeveloped technology for heart catheterization, leading to studies of many conditions, from congenital heart disease, to traumatic shock, to heart failure and pulmonary disease. In recognition of this pioneering work, he was named the corecipient of the Nobel Prize in Physiology or Medicine in 1956. Richards was an imposing figure and demanding of fellows in the laboratory, but he was kind and compassionate on the clinical wards.

Even with such outstanding physician-scientist role models, Lefkowitz elected for clinical clerkships, avoiding working in a research lab. He was well served by his voracious reading combined with his steel-trap mind. Bob culled through medical literature to prepare for morning rounds with attending physicians. To the chagrin of classmates, Lefkowitz compiled a daunting array of trivial facts that he incorporated effortlessly into his presentations, tossing them off as if they were common knowledge.

Throughout medical school, Lefkowitz was at the top of his class. At the halfway point, he won the Roche Prize for Excellence in Medical Science. Along with Varmus, he was one of only six students elected to the Alpha Omega Alpha Honorary Society in their third year. At graduation, he won the Janeway Prize, awarded to the student with the highest achievement and abilities. As with Varmus, Lefkowitz would pursue internship and residency at Columbia-Presbyterian. Lefkowitz interviewed at MGH but wanted to stay at Columbia; he already had two children, and all the free babysitters (grandparents) were in New York.[27]

Goldstein, Varmus, Brown, and Lefkowitz began their internships on July 1, 1966—one of the most momentous days in American health care history. On that date, the Medicare program was implemented, providing government-sponsored health insurance to the elderly. President Lyndon Johnson had signed the Medicare authorizing legislation a year earlier on July 30, 1965. In a grand and symbolic gesture, Johnson traveled to the Harry S. Truman Presidential Library in Independence, Missouri, a ceremony the former commander in chief attended. Two decades earlier, Truman became the first US president to propose a national health insurance program. His plan was opposed by special interest groups such as the American Medical Association, which branded it "socialized medicine" and its advocates "followers of the Moscow party line." With the outbreak of the Korean War, Truman was forced to abandon his national health insurance plan. Twenty years later, the political fight came full circle. After Johnson signed Medicare into law, Truman became the first beneficiary, with Johnson signing the enrollment card as his witness and declaring that it "all started really with the man from Independence."[28]

Eligible seniors were given until the end of the following March to enroll. Half of the 19 million Americans sixty-five years of age or older lacked health insurance at the time. With the introduction of a government payment system, the media stoked fears that the health care system would be overwhelmed with new demand for services. *Life* magazine ran a story during the enrollment period with the sensational headline "Medicare Is Launched into Shambles." The article featured pictures of crowded waiting rooms and hospital wards with beds crammed closely together. *Life* claimed: "Because of the nurse shortage, the weary and overworked doctors must clean up the mess."[29] The Johnson administration dismissed such claims, prompting the op-ed columnists Rowland Evans and Robert Novak to suggest that the White House's explanation "may not sit well with people who suddenly become eligible for treatment they could not afford before and then find it isn't available because of lack of space, doctors, nurses or technicians."[30]

Friday, July 1, 1966 (known as "M-Day" for the launch of Medicare), was chosen because hospital admissions were expected to be low with the Independence Day holiday weekend approaching. But for those running teaching hospitals, the beginning of July has another nerve-wracking dimension: by tradition, the annual training cycle begins in July for doctors at teaching hospitals. As all trainees assume new responsibilities at the same moment, there is a sudden drop-off in experience from the seasoned prior cohort to the incoming replacements. Given the influx of inexperienced caregivers, some evidence suggests that higher rates of hospital deaths occur during the house staff transition period.[31]

So, the combination of the start of Medicare and the yearly change-over in hospital medical staff could have produced a disaster. For Joe Goldstein and Mike Brown, new interns at MGH, the start was hectic, but it was not the calamity that some predicted. Brown was the first intern that MGH had selected from the University of Pennsylvania School of Medicine in almost a decade. The last one was John Potts, who had trained there from 1957 to 1959. Potts left for the National Institutes of Health, where he completed a fellowship under the future Nobel laureate Christian Anfinsen. Potts remained on the NIH staff until 1968, when he returned to MGH as head of the Endocrine (hormone) Unit, eventually rising to the position of chair of the Department of Medicine. Mike Brown had some very large shoes to fill, and he was curious about the other interns who were selected that year.

When Brown received a list of fellow recruits and scanned the names and medical schools, one caught his attention: Joe Goldstein from UT Southwestern Medical College in Dallas. Brown had never heard of this upstart school and, with a barely repressed smile, recalled his initial impression: "I thought it was a Bible school. And, I figured, well, if they're accepting this guy, then maybe nobody applied this year." It did not take long for Brown to reassess: "I remember admiring Joe's intellect and experience very early. Within the first two or three days of residency, it was clear that he knew more than anybody else, not only in the internship group, but more than most of the senior residents and half of the faculty. It was clear that this guy was going someplace and I just decided to ride along."[32]

Brown was not the only intern to be preceded at MGH by a star trainee from his alma mater. Joe Goldstein was following a legend as well. Charles Sanders, a Dallas native, graduated from UT Southwestern Medical School in 1955 and trained first in internal medicine at

Boston City Hospital and then in cardiology at MGH in 1958. Donald Seldin tried to convince the tall Texan to return to the faculty at UT Southwestern, but Sanders remained at MGH, where in 1962 he was appointed the founding head of the cardiac catheterization lab. A decade later, Sanders was appointed director general of MGH, where he remained until 1981.

Working in the shadows of such giants, Brown and Goldstein had to prove they were worthy successors. Goldstein had received his clinical training at Parkland Hospital, the large public teaching hospital associated with UT Southwestern. At Parkland, medical students played an important role in the care of patients, so he had developed solid clinical skills. Goldstein recalled: "I didn't really feel intimidated by the other interns, about half of whom were from Harvard Medical School and they had very little clinical experience."[33]

At MGH, the medical interns and residents had to cover two different services. One, Bulfinch, was housed in the MGH's first building, named after the celebrated architect who designed it, Charles Bulfinch. Bulfinch had also designed University Hall at Harvard, his alma mater, as well as the Massachusetts State House. His plan for the hospital in 1817 was in the Greek Revival style. The first general hospital in Boston, it featured a five-story granite structure with two lateral wings and was capped by a magnificent central dome. The rotunda was later designated the "Ether Dome" because it housed the operating room in which the use of ether as an anesthetic agent was first demonstrated publicly on October 16, 1846.

In 1966, the Bulfinch medical service was similar to what Goldstein saw at Parkland. Bulfinch patients were housed in four large open wards that, a few years after the introduction of Medicare, would be replaced with semiprivate rooms in a new building. Supervision of the four teams of interns and residents in Bulfinch fell to roughly 150 senior medical staff, or attending physicians. "The attendings on the Bullfinch [service] were more like the attendings here at Parkland—[they] were people doing research and also seeing patients, but not full-time." At MGH, however, there was a separate medical service, Baker, that the medical house staff covered for private physicians. Named after the Baker Memorial

Building, an eleven-story facility that first opened in 1930, residents on the Baker service team had responsibility for both emergency-room and in-patient care. Unlike Bulfinch attending physicians, Baker private attendings "often weren't there in the middle of the night and you'd have to sometimes call them up at home. That was an interesting experience," Goldstein recalled with a chuckle.[34]

As they learned the routine of patient care at MGH, Brown and Goldstein also discovered that they shared much in common. In Brown's words: "In those days, the interns would have a midnight meal—you'd be working all night, but you'd take a break and the cafeteria would open up for the interns. I remember many conversations that I had with Joe early on, talking about patients. 'Who did you just admit? What's wrong with them? What should be done?'" Brown continued: "Then we would get into the science. We would try to figure out . . . deeper than just simply what was wrong with the patients, but really why did the patient have it [the disease]? What's the physiology going on? It struck a chord—we were both interested in getting deeper below the surface of the disease."[35]

Meanwhile, Harold Varmus and Bob Lefkowitz, who knew each other through four years of medical school, began their graduate medical education together at Columbia-Presbyterian Hospital in New York City. Located in the Washington Heights section of upper Manhattan, the hospital was almost forty years old when Varmus and Lefkowitz began interning there. The facility was built on twenty-two acres donated by the philanthropist Edward Harkness and his mother, Anna. One of the richest men in the United States, Harkness inherited his fortune from his father, Stephen, who along with John D. Rockefeller was one of the five founders of Standard Oil.

The Harkness gift facilitated the merger of Columbia P&S with Presbyterian Hospital (creating Columbia-Presbyterian Hospital). Already a half-century old at the time, that hospital was established by another philanthropist, James Lenox, after his African American servant was denied care at all New York City hospitals. Outraged by the prejudice, Lenox was determined to establish a hospital dedicated to the care of "the Poor of New York without regard to Race, Creed or Color." For the new campus, Harkness chose Uptown, at that time a rapidly growing and vibrant neighborhood, attracting Irish, then Greek, followed by Jewish immigrants. When it opened in 1928, at twenty-one stories, Columbia-Presbyterian was the first skyscraper hospital, with more than 700 beds in open wards. Its unprecedented size and imposing façade gave rise to the building's nickname: "Fortress on the Heights." It was connected to a nine-story facility dedicated to the care of private patients and named the Harkness Pavilion after its donor.

By the time Varmus and Lefkowitz started medical school in 1962, Washington Heights was in the midst of demographic transition. After World War II, African Americans began moving there, followed by successive waves of Hispanic American immigrants. Their arrival was accompanied by the flight of the middle-class white population. Washington Heights became a focal point of racial tensions on February 21, 1965. Malcolm X, the African American Muslim minister and vocal critic of white racism, was gunned down by Nation of Islam assassins at the Audubon Ballroom. The attack occurred just down the street from the entrance to Columbia-Presbyterian, and although Malcolm X was rushed to the hospital, attempts at resuscitation were unsuccessful and he was pronounced dead.

Little more than a year later, Varmus and Lefkowitz began their internship in the trenches of a very busy city hospital. The emergency department was described by Chief Resident William Lovejoy as a "nightmare," perpetually swamped with patients, most of them very sick and indigent. Many patients needed admission for further care, and more often than not the bottleneck was a lack of available beds. With some pride, Lovejoy contrasted what he described as the "busy beehive" of activity of the Columbia-Presbyterian emergency department with the quieter, more "genteel" environment at MGH.[36]

When internal medicine patients were admitted from the emergency department to the public service, they were housed in six different open wards, similar to the Bulfinch service at MGH. Patient privacy (if it can be called that) was limited to a curtain that could be pulled around a patient's bed during an examination or procedure. Typically there were two interns per ward, each one assigned to care for about a dozen patients, although this could vary. On the public service side, in-house staff were responsible for managing patients—the intern would do the basic history, physical examination, and laboratory work, with the support of a medical student, and then present the case to the junior resident. More senior residents and attending physicians were available for advice and guidance, but the residents otherwise owned the care of the public patients. Bob Lefkowitz started his internship on the busy public service side. He tried to get a head start a week before officially starting, getting to know his patients and studying up on their care, but he still found the experience to be a "Baptism by fire."[37]

There was a separate service for private patients in Harkness Pavilion, mirroring the Baker service at MGH. At Harkness Pavilion, however, admitting physicians were faculty members of P&S, not independent practitioners. These P&S doctors were actively involved in managing patients, often meeting them at the emergency room and overseeing their care at Harkness. For private patients, house staff largely did the "scut work" of assuring that tests and procedures were ordered and results were charted.[38] For the interns, playing a support role at Harkness Pavilion, the pace was manageable, and they could even count on catching a little sleep when they were on call.[39]

Chief Resident Bill Lovejoy knew that he had two star interns in Harold Varmus and Bob Lefkowitz. He found Varmus to be brilliant and somewhat quiet, with a streak of independence. Lefkowitz was smart and enthusiastic, with boundless energy and a well-developed sense of humor.[40] The pair finished their internship year with a sense of mastery that they could care for patients as well as, or better than, anybody else. In their second year, they moved into a more professorial role. Varmus, the former English literature major, delighted in using the hospital's library to read medical articles concerning his patients' conditions and to compose the summary narrative that would go into the record.[41] (This so-called house note would provide an opportunity for the junior resident to wax eloquent about the case.) Nobody was better prepared for this literary task than Harold Varmus. Wanting to leave his own unmistakable mark, Bob Lefkowitz bought a fountain pen with a very broad nib, so that his house notes would stand out prominently.[42]

By the end of June 1968, Joe Goldstein, Harold Varmus, Mike Brown, and Bob Lefkowitz had achieved the dream of becoming skilled physicians. Each had finished at the top of his medical school class and excelled in a premier residency. As they headed to Bethesda to begin their respective two-year tours of duty as Clinical Associates at the National Institutes of Health, they were about to discover what it was like to start over yet again.

CHAPTER 4

YELLOW BERETS

*The Vietnam "Doctor Draft" and NIH's
Clinical Associate Training Program*

When Mike Brown, Harold Varmus, Bob Lefkowitz, and Joe Goldstein started medical school in 1962, about 11,000 military advisers were serving in Vietnam. When the quartet graduated from medical school four years later, 385,000 Americans were serving in the war. And when they completed junior residencies and matriculated into research laboratories at the NIH in 1968, the American presence in Vietnam peaked at more than a half-million American military personnel.[1]

The Vietnam War cast a long shadow over the lives of these four doctors, as it did for every young man of their generation. Although the United States had not formally declared war, the US government had authority under legislation passed a generation earlier to conscript males for military service. Following World War II, overall troop numbers had declined, but as the Cold War with the Soviet Union heated up, the Selective Service Act of 1948 was signed into law by President Harry

Truman. This legislation was designed to ensure that the United States could meet its military manpower needs during peacetime and in war.

The Selective Service Act required all males between eighteen and twenty-six to register with the Selective Service Administration, an independent civilian agency within the executive branch of the federal government. Young men were issued a registration form, or draft card. During times of need, 4,000-plus local draft boards would fill quotas of inductees, calling up registrants. Inductees were classified according to their eligibility to serve, with category I-A representing those available for service. Service could be deferred in certain circumstances, such as pursuing a college degree. Those classified as IV-F were deemed not qualified for military service because they failed to meet physical, mental, or moral standards. In the decade between 1964 and 1973, 8.6 million men were examined for the draft. Of those, almost half were rejected; about a third of those who qualified were inducted.[2]

The draft kicked into high gear as the ground war escalated in Vietnam. In 1965, about 106,000 men were drafted. A year later, the number had more than tripled.[3] Although draftees accounted for maybe a quarter of all servicemen during the war (the others were volunteers), during peak years half of all noncommissioned personnel were draftees.[4] A persistent criticism of the draft was that the less privileged among American society, including lower-income and minority men, were more likely to be called to serve. A 1968 study revealed that a high-school dropout from a low-income family had almost twice the likelihood of serving in the military when compared with a college graduate.[5] In addition to educational deferments, other factors favored the socially and economically well connected. As eligibility to serve was determined by local draft boards, decisions could be influenced by personal connections and social position.[6]

One might assume that doctors, with long educational preparation and critical roles in meeting society's health care needs, would be exempt from the draft. During the 1960s, there was indeed a shortage of physicians in the United States, which led to a massive expansion in the number of medical schools and an increase in the average size of medical school classes.[7] The doctor shortage, however, was not confined to the civilian population.

During the Korean War, the United States Army struggled in securing adequate numbers of medical personnel. Initially, it sought voluntary service, focusing on doctors who had benefited from government educational assistance during World War II. The Army Specialized Training Program (ASTP) was created during World War II to expand the pool of highly educated personnel, including doctors, dentists, and veterinarians. The physician component of the ASTP was designed to meet the needs of civilian hospitals for interns and residents, simultaneously creating a predictable pool that the military could call on in times of emergency. In all, more than 13,000 doctors were ASTP-trained, and at the end of World War II about a third were on active duty.[8] As the postwar military downsized, there was a diminishing need for ASTP veterans. When hostilities erupted in Korea, however, there was an urgent demand. In July 1950, when the Army contacted an estimated 3,000 former ASTP doctors, only one volunteered for service in Korea. In addition, twenty-nine physician reservists were called to active duty, and a handful of others were commissioned either in the Army or in the Reserves.[9]

With such a paltry voluntary response, the Army was forced to recall to active duty medical personnel who had served during World War II. This met an immediate shortage, but it was not a long-term solution, for these doctors were older and many were the sole source of support to their family. A way was needed to induct younger physicians who had no prior service. At the request of General Lewis Hershey, head of the Selective Service System, Congress passed an amendment to the Selective Service Act; it was signed into law on September 9, 1950, by President Truman, creating the so-called Doctor Draft.

This legislation applied to all male physicians, dentists, veterinarians, pharmacists, and optometrists under the age of fifty-one. It exempted those already in reserve units in any branch of the armed forces. A prioritization scheme was created to sequence the order of call to service.[10] The Doctor Draft was opposed by the American Medical Association for several reasons, including the perceived excessive staffing-up by the military.[11]

Professional organizations such as the Association of American Medical Colleges and the American Hospital Association had their own concerns. Objections focused on two basic issues. First, the draft could interrupt a physician's training after an internship, disrupting the educational process. Second, hospitals depended on trainees to care for patients, and the military was depleting the pool. A general lack of trust—between hospitals' and doctors' interests on the one hand, and the military on the other—led to stalemate.[12]

Enter Dr. Frank Brown Berry. A native of Dorchester, Massachusetts, Berry was a graduate of Harvard College and Harvard Medical School, then completing a Harvard trifecta with a medical internship at the affiliated Peter Bent Brigham Hospital. His internship was cut short by World War I, where he served in Burgundy, France. Upon his return from the war, Berry undertook surgical training in New York and became a senior attending chest surgeon. His medical teaching and practice was shelved a second time by World War II when he was reactivated to duty in July 1942. Berry served first as chief of surgery in a forward evacuation hospital during the Tunisia campaign in North Africa, and he accompanied the Seventh Army during the liberation of southern France. When the fighting ended in Europe, Berry served in a succession of leadership roles, ultimately being promoted to the rank of brigadier general.[13]

After discharge, Berry was appointed professor of clinical surgery at Columbia University, and he directed the First Surgical Division at Bellevue Hospital. In 1951, he was engaged as a consultant to the US Surgeon General's office. As he wrote later: "As I went about I learned much about the undercurrents of dissatisfaction on the part of many who had waited for the draft and among many medical officers in the National Guard and Reserve who had suddenly been called back to duty with great disturbance to families and themselves with their practices just started."[14]

On January 1, 1954, Berry was appointed by President Dwight Eisenhower as assistant secretary of defense (Health and Medical). From his days as a consultant, Berry had seen the military medical corps filled with young physicians whose clinical training had been placed on hold; they lacked expertise that would come only with more advanced clinical training. Also, having had his own professional career interrupted twice by war, he understood the hardships that physicians and families faced. Finally, his personal experience as an attending surgeon at an academic center gave him an appreciation of the needs of hospitals to have a reliable workforce of resident physicians.

Berry worked out a compromise that benefited all. Securing the necessary approvals, his plan was implemented as the Armed Forces Reserve Medical Officer Commissioning and Residency Consideration Program. With a name that long and cumbersome, the program soon became known simply as the "Berry Plan." It had three principal goals. First, it enabled the Armed Services to recruit a sufficient number of medical specialists. Second, it allowed draft-eligible physicians to secure a reserve commission, allowing them to enter into active duty following their internship, thereby removing uncertainty about when they would serve. Third, it allowed draft-eligible physicians to express a choice in both the branch and timing of their service (to the extent that this was consistent with the medical staffing needs of the Armed Forces). For individual physicians who participated in the Berry Plan, three options for military service were available, of which the most popular was to seek a deferment of military service until completion of a residency program in a medical specialty.[15]

One wrinkle in the Berry Plan was that a physician could alternatively apply to the Commissioned Corps of the Public Health Service (PHS), the federal workforce dedicated to preserving and protecting the nation's health. It is one of the seven designated Uniformed Services, with the others being the Army, Navy, Marine Corps, Air Force, Coast Guard, and National Oceanic and Atmospheric Administration. The Commissioned Corps includes physicians and other health professionals such as dentists, nurses, pharmacists, psychologists, and veterinarians.

The PHS traces back to its predecessor, the Marine Hospital Service, signed into law in 1798 by President John Adams. Marine Hospitals were dedicated to protecting citizens against infectious diseases from abroad that could be brought into the country by sailors and immigrants. Nine decades later, the Commissioned Corps of the Public Health Service was established as the Uniformed Services of the Marine Hospital Service. It was organized along a military model, with titles and pay grades modeled on those in the Army and Navy. In the early years, Commissioned Corps Officers were responsible for quarantine and disinfection measures to contain the spread of contagious diseases.[16]

In 1930, during the Great Depression, the so-called Ransdell Act created the Washington, DC–based National Institute of Health—later becoming "Institutes" plural. Senator Joseph Ransdell of Louisiana, who sponsored the legislation, chaired the Committee on Public Health and National Quarantine. The seventy-two-year-old Ransdell, born on a cotton plantation two years before the outbreak of the Civil War, sported a neatly trimmed white goatee and resembled a Confederate general. He pursued the creation of the NIH with determination, making three appeals to a resistant Congress before the legislation finally passed.[17] The law provided an initial appropriation of $750,000 for the construction of two buildings. The Ransdell Act was the apotheosis of his political career; he was defeated by the populist governor Huey P. Long—the legendary "Kingfish"—in the 1930 Senate election that fall.

The purpose of the NIH from its inception was to research the basic mechanisms of disease, and even during the Depression public investment in medical research was a national priority. Subsequent legislation created the National Cancer Institute (NCI) in 1937, and on July 1, 1944, an act granted the PHS broad powers to conduct and support research on human diseases and disabilities. This legislation also placed the NCI administratively within the NIH. In 1946, the Atlanta-based Communicable Disease Center—the predecessor to the Centers for Disease Control and Prevention (CDC)—was created. The Communicable Disease Center was established initially to control malaria and later expanded to address other diseases such as poliomyelitis, smallpox, and measles. In contrast to the NIH, which focused on research, the CDC evolved as an action-oriented limb of the PHS to control and prevent diseases. Another branch of the PHS was added in 1954, when Congress created the Indian Health Service (IHS) to meet the health care needs of Native American populations.

When the Berry Plan came along, applicants had several options to serve in the Commissioned Corps, including Public Health Service Hospitals, the Indian Health Service, the Communicable Disease Center, and the National Institutes of Health. Only a small percentage of those who applied were accepted to serve in one of these programs.[18] The CDC offering was built around the Epidemic Intelligence Service (EIS), an elite team of young physicians who were sent around the country and worldwide to investigate outbreaks of disease. The EIS program, founded in 1951 by Alexander Langmuir, grew famous for training so-called disease detectives. They practiced shoe-leather epidemiology, tracking down persons with a particular illness and studying the modes of its transmission. The applied research environment of the CDC contrasted with the more clinically oriented responsibilities of the physicians who were recruited into the Indian Health Service. Those trainees were assigned to serve as primary care practitioners on reservations, treating some of the most medically underserved populations in the United States.

The NIH option—the one that attracted Drs. Brown, Varmus, Lefkowitz, and Goldstein—was the NIH Associate Training Program. Launched in 1953 with an initial pool of fifteen physicians who were recruited as Clinical Associates, this training program provided the NIH young doctors who could care for patients who came to the newly constructed Clinical Center to participate in research protocols. In the early years of the program, candidates were handpicked by the scientific director of the NIH, James Shannon.[19]

A native New Yorker, Shannon attended the College of the Holy Cross and graduated from New York University (NYU) with two degrees (MD and PhD) and remained on the faculty there for fifteen years, a pioneer in the field of kidney research. During World War II, the Department of Defense needed drugs to prevent and treat malaria among GIs fighting in the mosquito-infested jungles of the Pacific. Shannon and his team made major contributions to drug development and testing, for which Shannon was awarded the Presidential Medal of Merit.[20]

After a short stint in the private sector, Shannon was recruited to the NIH to head research for the new National Heart Institute (NHI). In that capacity, he quickly recruited from his former malaria research team, including, among others, Robert Berliner, MD (who went on to a distinguished research and administrative career, eventually becoming the first deputy director for science at NIH); Bernard "Steve" Brodie, PhD (who later headed the NIH Laboratory of Clinical Pharmacology and was the recipient of the Lasker Award, often described as the

"American Nobel Prize," in 1967); and Julius Axelrod, PhD (who went on to a distinguished research career at NIH and won the Nobel Prize in Physiology or Medicine in 1970).[21]

Shannon was an imposing character—handsome, tall, and thin, with a deep bass voice, signature dark-framed eyeglasses, and bow tie. Initially, it was a challenge to convince others that NIH was a good career move. There was a widespread perception that government research was decidedly second-class. Robert Bowman, MD, later recalled the hesitancy that he and others felt about coming to NIH: "Most of us had some reservations about going to a government laboratory. We didn't think that we wanted to get involved with Civil Service red tape and other things rumored to be impediments to getting anything done."[22]

Nevertheless, Shannon was able to identify a cadre of risk-takers—those who would be willing to leave the prestige of established institutions to join the start-up enterprise in Bethesda. As Shannon later recalled: "It was new. No one had been there before, and I inherited no sins."[23] Three years after his arrival at the National Heart Institute, Shannon was appointed to oversee all research programs at NIH, including the new Clinical Center. His approach, borrowed from his days at NYU, was to rely on young trainees, and the Berry Plan created a pathway for recruiting talented doctors fresh from two years of clinical training. These Clinical Associates would spend two years at NIH, typically with their time divided between patient care and research.

Initially, Shannon relied on personal contacts with leaders at major teaching hospitals to identify rising stars. Shannon was an insider within the Northeast's academic medical establishment, and his first class of Clinical Associate recruits came largely on the basis of personal recommendation and trust, including two future directors of the NIH.[24] Donald Fredrickson, MD, a former Peter Bent Brigham Hospital trainee, went on to distinguish himself in the field of heart disease research and ultimately served as director of NIH from 1975 through 1981. James B. Wyngaarden, MD, was a former resident at Massachusetts General Hospital who became a national leader in research on metabolic diseases and would follow Fredrickson as NIH director from 1982 to 1989. With this high caliber of talent, and the added incentive of being an alternative to military service, the Clinical Associate program quickly established itself as a prized career pathway.

With growing interest in NIH training opportunities, a more formal application process was instituted a few years later. Potential candidates were required to file a written application by the middle of May during their senior year of medical school—a full two years before they would start at NIH. In the interim, they would undertake clinical training as an intern and junior resident. The applications were reviewed by NIH program leaders, and in June the most promising candidates were invited for one or two days of interviews that might be characterized as an early form of speed dating.

The candidates could, and typically did, interview with multiple laboratory directors to maximize chances of finding a good mutual fit. During the first week of July, while candidates were starting internships, the preferences of the applicants and the laboratories were matched to find the best pairings. The lucky winners were notified by a telephone call during the second week of July indicating that they had been selected for training. In theory, if the candidate was unhappy with the laboratory match, the offer could be rejected, but in practice, and with the Doctor Draft looming in the background, rejections seldom, if ever, occurred.[25]

To be sure, the Doctor Draft was a strong motivator for many medical students to apply to the Clinical Associate program. One such aspiring candidate was Anthony "Tony" Fauci, who was preparing to graduate from Cornell University Medical College in 1966—the same year of graduation as Brown, Varmus, Lefkowitz, and Goldstein. Reflecting on that time, Fauci recalled one life-changing day during his senior year: "That was the exponential phase of the Vietnam War and every single physician went into military service. I can remember very clearly when we gathered in the auditorium at Cornell early in our fourth year of medical school. Unlike today, we had only two women in the class and seventy-nine men." Fauci continued: "The recruiter from the Armed Forces came there and said, 'Believe it or not, when you graduate from medical school at the end of the year, except for the two women, everyone in this room is going to be either in the Army, the Air Force, the

Navy or the Public Health Service. So you are going to have to take your choice. Sign up and give your preferences.'" As Fauci recalled: "I had heard about the NIH and the opportunity there. At the time, the NIH was just blossoming and everyone who had any role in academic medicine spent some time at NIH." On the basis of the military recruiter's less-than-subtle message and a little prior knowledge, Fauci made a fateful decision: "I put down PHS as my first choice and then the Navy. Essentially, I came down to NIH because I didn't have any choice. I was very lucky because I knew it was a phenomenal scientific opportunity."[26]

At the time, neither Fauci, nor the military recruiter, nor anyone else in the room could have anticipated how that afternoon in 1965 would impact events for decades into the future. Although Fauci specified his preferred career choice as "academic medicine with teaching and research" when he applied to the program, he remained at NIH (unlike most of his fellow trainees), rising quickly up the leadership ladder and ultimately becoming director of the National Institute for Allergy and Infectious Diseases (NIAID) in 1984, a position he still held in 2019. Fauci became a household name during the 1980s as the Acquired Immune Deficiency Syndrome (AIDS) epidemic emerged. Fauci's calming demeanor and ability to portray issues in a way the public could understand made him an effective scientific spokesperson. One national media source even went so far as to refer to him as "the Most Powerful Doctor in America."[27] A Presidential Medal of Freedom honoree, Fauci was offered the NIH directorship by President George H. W. Bush and President George W. Bush, but he declined in order to continue his work in infectious diseases.[28]

The looming Doctor Draft was felt by other trainees as well. Dr. Harry Kimball, who much later became president of the American Board of Internal Medicine, served as a Clinical Associate between 1964 and 1967. Thinking back on his medical school years, he recalled: "We all knew we were going to serve in the military one way or the other unless we were IV-F. IV-F deferments for doctors were really difficult to obtain. You had to be really disabled to do that and so it was just a matter of trying to arrange the best possible experience during your military time."[29]

The competition to gain admission into the Clinical Associate program was fierce. At one point, two-thirds of the class from Harvard

Medical School applied to the NIH.[30] Although statistics on the annual numbers of applicants and acceptances have not been preserved, a news release from the Office of Research Administration in July 1963 gives a sense of the acceptance rate at that time. In that year's cohort, among the 1,464 physicians who applied for the program, fifty-three were selected (less than one in twenty-five).[31] The class entering in 1968, including Goldstein, Brown, Lefkowitz, and Varmus, had roughly 200 members, with thirty-three alumnae of Harvard Medical School, eleven from Johns Hopkins University, and ten from Yale. Similarly, the hospital residency training programs feeding into the Clinical Associate program were among the most selective and competitive in the country. In 1968, Massachusetts General Hospital sent nineteen participants, followed by Johns Hopkins Hospital with a dozen.

Donald Fredrickson, a former NIH director and one of the members of the inaugural class of Clinical Associates, would describe the successor, more formal selection process in the following manner:

> In 1961, when I became Clinical Director of the Heart Institute, Dr. Robert Berliner asked me to help him pick the Clinical Associates. We would sit down and go through these applications and narrow them down to about 200. We kept trying to refine the applications, to get people to answer questions and to write something. It was extremely difficult because all we really had was the scholastic record of most people. Very few had done any research. The art of picking, out of a whole group of qualified people, those who might become successful scientists was extremely difficult. The scholastic record usually meant a lot, and if somebody had shown inventiveness and had really gone into a lab for a year or two.[32]

Fredrickson went on to admit that the selection process was as much an art as it was a science:

> We still had to gamble and bet on who was going to be good. The applicants to this program were the cream of the crop and I used to tell Berliner that if we were applying for the program now, we would never make it with our write-ups. It was really just like sitting in Tiffany's and

sorting out from all of the stones what would be the highest carat. We would have to pick them with a certain amount of variety because our programs needed people with diverse interests. The main objective was getting people who would use this environment to become scientists.[33]

It should be noted that the diversity mentioned by Fredrickson pertained to research interests and not to the gender or the race of the applicants. With the Doctor Draft applying only to men, the Clinical Associate candidate pool and selection process was heavily skewed toward males. Moreover, the preference for candidates from research-intensive medical schools, which had few racial and ethnic minorities at the time, meant that the successful candidates were almost exclusively white.[34]

Of course, in the broadest sense, the potential pool from which Clinical Associates might be evaluated was defined by the demographics of US medical and dental school graduates. During the 1960s and beyond, this was a decidedly male club. For example, in 1966—the year that Brown, Varmus, Lefkowitz, and Goldstein graduated from medical school—less than 7 percent of the roughly 7,500 medical school graduates were women.[35] Even so, the clear bias against women being selected as Clinical Associates was no secret. "Several senior NIH researchers at the time indicated that they would not hire a female Associate because that would mean that a male physician would likely be sent to Vietnam," recalled Dr. Harvey Klein, a former Clinical Associate and later chief of the Department of Transfusion Medicine.[36]

The fact that women were virtually absent from the program is apparent from an analysis conducted years later in which only four female participants could be identified. In retrospect, some individuals who were involved with the selection process primarily attributed the small numbers of women Associates to the paucity of female applicants rather than to active bias against selecting them. There were some exceptions to that rule. One of the female applicants was Bernadine Healy, MD. Healy had unimpeachable credentials, having completed medical school at Harvard in 1970, followed by two years of clinical training at Johns Hopkins Hospital. She entered the Clinical Associate program in 1972 as the Vietnam War was winding down, but even then she was hired as a Staff Fellow rather than as a Commissioned Officer in the PHS, thereby not occupying a position that could be reserved for a draft-eligible male. After four years at NIH, Healy would go back to Johns Hopkins, but in 1991 she would return to NIH as its first female director.[37]

Even if the selection process had its biases and imperfections, Fauci asserted: "If you looked at the people who were Clinical Associates at that time, they were all the top of their classes, the number one intern or resident in their program. They were clearly the elite. So, the critical mass of the high quality people was one of the reasons why it was so exciting to be down here. You were sort of on the all-star team when you came down here."[38] As brilliant as these young physicians were, most had little experience in research, or even a knowledge of the techniques involved in the emerging science of molecular biology.

The success of the Clinical Associate program spawned the creation of two sister training programs at NIH. The first was the Research Associate program, designed for physicians and dentists who wanted a more intensive research experience without the patient care obligations. Research Associates accounted for about one-third of physician trainees who typically had some background in research and who wanted to become full-time investigators in a university or other setting. The two-year experience at NIH for them was geared toward acquiring skills that would allow them to become independent scientists. The laboratory work component was complemented by a series of tutorials and discussion sessions.[39] The third NIH training program was by far the smallest, accounting for about one-sixth of all participants. These physicians and dentists were called "Staff Associates" and were being prepared for careers as scientists who also performed administrative roles. They could elect to perform basic laboratory research or more patient care–oriented investigations.

As the Vietnam War escalated, so did the level of interest in the Associate training positions at the NIH. In 1965, at the beginning of the ground war, there were 153 NIH Associates. The number rose each year afterward, peaking at 229 in 1973, the year the Paris Peace Accords were signed. In 1977, two years after the end of the Vietnam War, the number of NIH Associates had fallen by 50 percent.[40] In 1974, the NIH was unable to recruit its full allotment of Associates, and one-fifth of all Commissioned Corps positions went unfilled.[41]

The connection between the Vietnam War and the rise of the NIH Associate program was undeniable. Clearly, many trainees were motivated by the Doctor Draft. If they had reservations about serving in the war effort, they were hardly alone, as many others managed to find alternative forms of service. Some drew attention decades later when they were elected to high national office. These include Vice President Dan Quayle, who joined the Indiana National Guard,[42] President George W. Bush, who was in the Texas Air National Guard,[43] and President Bill Clinton, who signed up for a Reserve Officer program before receiving a high lottery draft number that assured he would not be drafted.[44]

It was understandable that a pathway to nonmilitary service through the PHS would be viewed with reservations by military physicians. A former NIH Associate and later president of the American Board of Internal Medicine, Harry Kimball, observed: "We were doing our service obligation in a way which also was maximally enhancing our own careers. Why wouldn't they [military physicians] resent us?"[45]

Whether or not such resentment ran deep, PHS trainees became known as "Yellow Berets." It is unclear where this epithet originated, but supporters of the war in Vietnam applied it generally to anyone they felt was shirking a patriotic duty. In 1966, the singer-songwriter Bob Seger composed "The Ballad of the Yellow Beret" with the following lyrics:[46]

> Fearless cowards of the USA
> Bravely here at home they stay
> They watched their friends get shipped away
> The draft dodgers of the Yellow Beret.

The "Yellow" Beret denigration contrasted with the Green Berets worn by members of the US Army Special Forces. Green Berets were celebrated in a different 1966 song, "The Ballad of the Green Berets," by Staff Sergeant Barry Sadler and Robin Moore. The song opens with the following lyrics:[47]

> Fighting soldiers from the sky
> Fearless men who jump and die

Men who mean just what they say
The Brave men of the Green Beret.

"The Ballad of the Green Berets" was number-one in the United States for five consecutive weeks, with more than 9 million copies being sold.[48] A year earlier, Moore had published a best-selling novel titled *The Green Berets*. An action movie of the same name, loosely adapted from the novel, was produced and directed by John Wayne, who cast himself in the leading role. The movie was released in the United States on Independence Day 1968; although it made a profit, the movie was panned by the *New York Times* movie critic as "so unspeakable, so stupid, so rotten and false in every detail."[49]

Although PHS Associates may have been far away from actual combat, they were not far from military physicians. Directly across from the front entrance of the NIH on the east side of Rockville Pike is the National Naval Medical Center (now known as the Walter Reed National Military Medical Center). President Franklin D. Roosevelt had selected the site and participated in laying its cornerstone in 1940. This facility has served wounded sailors and Marines since World War II, with expansions over time and more than 1,100 hospital beds during Vietnam.

Anthony Fauci, former Clinical Associate and later the long-serving director of the NIAID, acknowledged that during the Vietnam War the view from across Rockville Pike was not always positive: "There was in fact a general feeling of some slight resentment about physicians who did not go into the service but who were here at the 'cushy' job at the NIH."[50] Fauci noted that there were exceptions. His boss at the time, Dr. Sheldon Wolff, formed the first Infectious Diseases Consultation Service because the National Naval Medical Center did not have an infectious disease department at the time. Fauci felt that by volunteering their time "to help with the workload of troops who were flown in with serious infectious complications of wounds sort of put us in a soft spot in their [Navy doctors'] heart. The infectious disease crew was well thought of by the Navy as opposed to some of the others."[51]

If tensions existed, they likely were fueled by the perception that NIH faculty and staff tended to oppose the war. In Fauci's words: "In general, the spirit on campus was much more a liberal leaning than a conservative leaning because that is generally the case with scientists. Most people were against the war."[52] The former Associate Harry Kimball recalled participating in an antiwar protest outside the NIH administration building: "I suspect that if you look at it in that time '67 and '68, the bulk of investigators at the NIH would not have favored Johnson's Vietnam policies."[53] The former NIH director Fredrickson agreed about the general antiwar sentiment on the campus: "This was a group of people that had liberal politics in the main. There were very few conservatives in those days; there are very few now."[54] Many of the Clinical Associates had strong moral objections to the Vietnam War, above and beyond their political leanings.

Leaders of the antiwar efforts at the NIH included Christian Anfinsen, head of the Laboratory of Chemical Biology at what would become the National Institute of Arthritis, Diabetes, Digestive, and Kidney Disease. Anfinsen, awarded the Nobel Prize in Chemistry in 1972, was politically active for a number of causes. He participated in a 1964 vigil held on the NIH campus after the Gulf of Tonkin Resolution passed, and he demonstrated against the Vietnam War. Anfinsen believed in peaceful protests and referred to himself as a professional petitioner and letter-signer.

A small group of activists at NIH and its sister center at PHS, the National Institute for Mental Health (NIMH), organized the Vietnam Moratorium Committee (VNMC) at NIH-NIMH. VNMC included a cross-section of personnel, from senior scientists to trainees and support staff. The group met for the first time on September 23, 1969, in Building 2, a laboratory research facility on the NIH campus. The group wanted to invite Dr. Benjamin Spock, a nationally prominent pediatrician and leading critic of the Vietnam War, to speak at the NIH. The intended date for his talk was October 15, which was scheduled to occur as part of the planned National Moratorium to End the War in Vietnam.[55]

The National Moratorium grew from an original target of 300 college campuses and evolved into a much broader protest, with a focus on events in Washington, DC. The NIH-NIMH Vietnam Moratorium Committee's invitation to Dr. Spock was endorsed within two days by the Interassembly of Scientists, the NIH's elected council of staff scientists. Spock accepted the invitation the following day, and the VNMC requested to use the auditorium of the Clinical Center to host the event. On September 29, NIH Director Robert Marston denied the request, likely because he was directed to do so by his politically appointed bosses at the Department of Health, Education, and Welfare.[56]

The American Civil Liberties Union (ACLU) represented the VNMC in a legal challenge to Marston's decision. The case was heard in the United States District Court for the District of Columbia on October 10. The presiding judge, John Sirica, would later earn national fame for his 1973 order that forced the White House to release President Nixon's secret tape recordings. In the Spock speech case, Sirica ruled against the VNMC, but on October 14 a three-judge appeals panel overturned the decision. The following day, the sixty-six-year-old Dr. Spock, looking grandfatherly, with large, heavy-framed eyeglasses, thinning wisps of white hair, a slightly rumpled dark suit, and narrow tie, appeared on the NIH campus. Spock addressed a crowd of several thousand people who had assembled on the lawn in front of the NIH administration building.[57]

There was great symbolism in the site chosen for Spock. It was Building 1, the first building constructed at NIH, in 1938. He stood between two towering, white Ionic columns on the front portico of the red-brick Georgian Revival–style building in exactly the same spot where, nearly three decades earlier, President Franklin Roosevelt had appeared. The president had come to Bethesda on October 31, 1940, to dedicate the initial six buildings of the NIH. About four months earlier, France had fallen to the Germans, and the United States was still months away from coming to Britain's aid through the Lend-Lease program. With war looming, Roosevelt searched for a silver lining: "All of us are grateful that we in the United States can still turn our thoughts and our attention to those institutions of our country which symbolize peace— institutions whose purpose is to save life and not to destroy it." The president continued:

The National Institute of Health speaks the universal language of humanitarianism. . . . The total defense that we have heard so much about of late, which this Nation seeks, involves a great deal more than building airplanes, ships, guns and bombs. We cannot be a strong Nation unless we are a healthy Nation. And so we must recruit not only men and materials but also knowledge and science in the service of national strength.[58]

In contrast to the soaring oratory of President Roosevelt, Dr. Spock's noontime address on October 15, 1969, was a hard-hitting censure of American involvement in Vietnam framed largely around the proposition "that the illegality and immorality of the War justifies dissent." Spock added with a flourish: "The only way that we can save ourselves; the only way that we can get along in the world, in the long-run, is by being able to see the realities. And when we falsify the realities by calling ourselves the 'good guys' when actually we are the aggressor, we are starting a perilous course which could easily result in annihilation of ourselves and, in fact, the whole world."[59]

Although Spock's lecture was the focal point of antiwar activities at NIH, it was by no means the only protest. The VNMC communicated its message through a periodic newsletter (*Rainbow Signs*, circulation 6,000) that featured on its masthead a quote from the Code of Ethics for Government Service: "Loyalty to the highest moral principles and to country above persons, party, or government department."[60]

There were risks associated with VNMC membership. Citing the power of the government to intimidate protesters, one of the group's founding members, David Reiss, a former Clinical Associate, later recalled: "I don't think it's fair to underestimate how frightening and how daunting and maybe just how discouraging it is to mount such an effort."[61] Such fears were anchored in the belief that careers were put at risk by speaking out against the war. The ACLU lawyer who worked with the VNMC, Zona Hostetler, remembered: "There were stories of employees actually being demoted because of their antiwar activities. Even in authorized meetings of government employees on their lunch hour, security people would come in and take pictures of the people who were attending and ask for membership lists of the organization."[62] Perhaps even more ominously, the Federal Bureau of Investigation under President Nixon conducted investigations, both public and secret, of antiwar protestors. For example, one VNMC member, Irene Elkins, recalled FBI agents interviewing her current and prior supervisors when she served as co-coordinator.[63]

For most Clinical Associates at NIH during this era, political activism was not the primary or even secondary focus. They came to Bethesda for very specific reasons: to expand their knowledge of science and to learn enough about research methods to develop a career as an independent investigator. Without question, the war and the Doctor Draft played a critical role in choosing NIH over the military, but they tended to view it more as a step in professional development than as a political statement.

For most Associates, the "Yellow Beret" epithet was tinged with a bit of sarcasm. Tony Fauci recalled: "It was somewhat of a derogatory term. Yes, it was part joke, but very much derogatory."[64]

Associates did not refer to themselves as Yellow Berets. Later, as emotions faded and many former Associates went on to distinguished careers, the term became more a badge of honor. A flavor of that sensibility can be appreciated in a poem that was written by Bernard Babior, MD, PhD, who became an Associate in 1965 and went on to head the Division of Biochemistry at Scripps Research Institute. While at NIH, Babior trained under Earl Stadtman, PhD, a few years in advance of Mike Brown, and many years later Babior offered the following poem in Stadtman's honor:[65]

> Whereas my draft board said to me "1A,"
> I from ascetic Boston made my way
> Bethesdawards, to Stadtman's realm secure
> To soldier for a while in the Yellow Beret.
> There midst foul smells, with compounds split by light,
> With black shades pulled, the lab as black as night . . .
> I strove for data pleasing in Earl's sight.

After training at NIH, Yellow Berets typically returned to academic institutions, where they had a profound impact. A survey conducted in 1998 indicated that almost a quarter of Harvard Medical School's professors of medicine were alumni of the NIH Associate program.

Similarly, more than one in five professors of medicine at Johns Hopkins had a tour of duty as an NIH Associate.[66] A dozen years later, another review indicated that Associate program alumni were twice as likely to become a medical school department chair and three times as likely to become a medical school dean. In addition, sixty-four graduates had been elected to the National Academy of Sciences, representing almost one-fifth of the members in the biomedical fields, and 125 were elected to the US Institute of Medicine. Ten alumni were awarded the National Medal of Science, and nine won Nobel Prizes.[67]

It is hard to imagine that the tidal wave of talent that washed through the NIH during the Vietnam War will ever occur again. Mike Brown, Harold Varmus, Bob Lefkowitz, and Joe Goldstein rode that wave into Bethesda, totally unaware of just how far it would carry them. Catching that wave, however, started many years earlier.

CHAPTER 5

CAMPUS LIFE

Learning Science and Serving the Nation

For NIH Associates such as Mike Brown, Joe Goldstein, Harold Varmus, and Bob Lefkowitz, the hub of the 300-acre NIH campus was the Clinical Center. This fourteen-story, red-brick, massive building housed patients and most of the affiliated research laboratories. Also known as Building 10, the Clinical Center was fifteen years old by the time Brown, Goldstein, Varmus, and Lefkowitz arrived. More recently, a surgical center was added to update the types of care that could be delivered. Even after fifteen years, it was one of the most unique and visionary patient-oriented research facilities in the world.

The $64 million funding to construct the Clinical Center was appropriated by Congress. Representative Frank Keefe of Wisconsin was an ardent supporter. Keefe chaired the House Appropriations Subcommittee that approved the funding; on January 16, 1948, Keefe proudly announced that with unanimous and bipartisan support the

subcommittee "is supremely interested in this matter of providing prop-
er clinical research facilities that will bring the sufferer, the human patient, into direct contact with the researchers."[1]

The mastermind behind the design of the Clinical Center was its
inaugural director, thirty-nine-year-old Jack Masur, MD. Masur was a
tall, imposing figure whose large ears flanked a countenance accentu-
ated by a long, straight nose and prominent chin. A native of Augusta,
Georgia, Masur was educated in New York, first as an undergraduate at
New York University, then as a medical student at Cornell University,
followed by an internship at Bellevue Hospital and a residency at Montefiore Hospital. Masur had risen to the position of assistant director at
Montefiore and was a recognized expert in chronic care administration.[2]
Broad input was solicited for planning the hospital, and design elements
were borrowed from two other New York City hospitals—Goldwater
on Roosevelt Island and Memorial on the Upper East Side.[3]

Although the Clinical Center borrowed ideas from other leading patient-oriented research facilities, it was groundbreaking in other ways.
When designed, it was by far the largest clinical research building ever
contemplated. In fact, it was thought to be one of the largest brick buildings in the world, requiring an estimated 7 million bricks for its mam-
moth façade. The basic layout of the 1.3 million-square-foot building was
a long central corridor and a series of six wings. More than 500 patient
rooms were lined up along the south-facing side of a main corridor, organized on each floor into two nursing units, each of which had thirteen
semiprivate rooms. The clinical research laboratories were located on the
north-facing side of a main corridor, allowing physicians to move easily
and quickly between patient rooms and research laboratories. The six
wings projecting out from the two ends of the building housed laboratories for basic research that did not involve patients. In all, there were
1,100 scientific laboratories within the complex.

Jesse Roth, one of Bob Lefkowitz's preceptors, described the Clinical
Center's layout: "Picture a corridor and it was laboratory after laboratory
after laboratory. You go on the far other side of the double corridor and
it was patient room, patient room, patient room. And then in-between,
there was a double set of rooms that opened to either one side or the

other, and the idea was that patient access to the labs and the lab access to the patients would be optimal." Roth continued:

It turned out that that kind of closeness was actually very dangerous because people (patients) could wander into the labs. So, you would never do that again. You would really put barriers—good barriers. Also, if God forbid, you had some kind of accident in the lab, you could . . . injure patients either physically or chemically. A design that seemed logical in principle turned out to have practical limitations. So, in retrospect, as we lived it, I thought: "God, how could such a brilliant, genius idea be so stupid?" But it helped due to the fact that we were very close to the patients. In fact, my office was on a ward and my lab was right across from that. It was very intimate.[4]

The design of the Clinical Center, besides colocating research and clinical spaces, included elements rarely seen in other contemporary patient-care facilities. Because many people would be admitted for long-term studies, services were added for patient comfort and well-being while residing on campus. There was central air conditioning, a rooftop sundeck, solariums on each patient floor, and recreational facilities. Among other amenities was a theater, a beauty parlor, a barber shop, a bank, and a post office. As Jesse Roth described: "We ate in one big cafeteria, we bought our newspapers in the same place, we got our hair cut by the same barber. . . . It was just teeming with people and they were all talking to each other and they were all having a good time."[5]

Other aspects looked toward the future. In 1948, when the Clinical Center was under design, there were only 350,000 TV sets in the United States, reaching less than 1 percent of American households. By the time that the Clinical Center opened in 1953, there were more than 20 million TV sets in more than four in ten households.[6] Anticipating this growth, patient rooms in the Clinical Center were wired for bedside television.

President Harry Truman, in a light double-breasted suit and white buck shoes, helped lay the cornerstone on June 22, 1951, when the building was about halfway complete. He declared: "Modern medicine must find ways of detecting . . . diseases in their early stages and of stopping their destructive force. That will be the major work of this clinical research center."[7]

The formal dedication ceremony occurred in sweltering heat two years later on July 2, 1953. With the Eisenhower administration now in office, the keynote address was delivered by Secretary of Health, Education, and Welfare Oveta Culp Hobby, the first person to hold that newly created cabinet-level post. In office for less than three months, Hobby, a native of Killeen, Texas, had risen to national attention as director of the Women's Army Auxiliary Corps. In January 1945, Colonel Hobby was the first woman in the history of the US Army to receive the Distinguished Service Medal. At the dedication, Hobby told the assembled crowd: "I proudly dedicate this center to medical research as a symbol of our national concern for the health of our people. . . . [T]his building and the people who work here are dedicated to the endless struggle against human suffering."[8]

The director of the NIH, W. Henry Sebrell Jr., MD, noted: "This center is not a hospital. You don't get in by just being sick. You don't get in for medical care. You get in only for research." Dr. Sebrell went on: "This Center represents a massive approach to the major killing and crippling diseases."[9]

Four days later, the first patient to be treated was a sixty-seven-year-old Maryland farmer named Charles Meredith. Meredith suffered from advanced prostate cancer and was admitted for hormonal treatments under the supervision of Dr. Roy Hertz. As with all patients at the Clinical Center, Meredith's care was provided at no cost. Patient referrals initially came from physicians in the Washington, DC, area and six local medical schools. In order to keep peace with local physicians, it was agreed that NIH doctors would not engage in private practice in the community. Area specialists were invited to serve as consultants at the Clinical Center, thereby augmenting the expertise available to patients. At the time, each of the seven institutes of the NIH[10] was responsible for admitting and managing its own patients. There were about ninety NIH physicians on staff at the time, and over the course of the first year about 150 beds—less than a third of the eventual capacity—were opened. It would take four years to reach full capacity. Within a decade, the Clinical Center averaged nearly 90 percent occupancy, and the average length of a patient's stay declined from almost seven weeks to slightly more than four weeks.

In 1968, when Lefkowitz, Varmus, Goldstein, and Brown arrived at the Clinical Center, a total of 516 patient beds were available. The largest service, with 134 beds, belonged to the National Cancer Institute, followed by the National Heart Institute—where Joe Goldstein worked—with 100 beds. The National Institute of Arthritis and Metabolic Diseases (NIAMD), where Mike Brown started and Harold Varmus and Bob Lefkowitz also worked, had sixty-eight beds. The remaining beds were assigned to the National Institutes of Mental Health, Neurological Disorders and Stroke, Allergy and Infectious Diseases, and Dental Research.[11]

During 1968, a total of 4,000 patients were admitted; about fifteen persons arrived on a typical workday. The average length of stay varied, with some visits lasting only a few days; some patients became virtual residents. The number of patients paralleled bed capacities, with NCI accounting for about a third of all admissions, followed by NHI with more than a quarter. Nearly 500 patients were admitted to the NIAMD service during the year that Brown, Lefkowitz, and Varmus started duty on those wards.[12]

There were about 1,400 different research projects under way at the Clinical Center in 1968. Not all patients had rare or life-threatening diseases. In fact, some had no illness at all. As a means of characterizing normal body functions and processes, such as those associated with digestion, metabolism, and sleep, investigators needed to study healthy subjects. In 1968, more than 200 healthy volunteers were admitted.[13]

Many study volunteers during the era of the Vietnam War were conscientious objectors—persons who sought alternatives to participating in the military. The Mennonite and Brethren Churches, for instance, opposed violence yet warmly embraced public service. The studies in which healthy subjects—all over the age of eighteen and including women—participated ranged from a few weeks to a few years. Protocols were equally diverse, sometimes requiring special diets, at other times involving deprivation of sleep, and in still other studies being exposed to new experimental drugs. The knowledge gained from this research helped to establish, among other things, the relationship between diet and blood cholesterol levels and how fatigue impacts performance of various tasks. For their efforts, healthy volunteers—human guinea pigs—received free room and board and a stipend of about a dollar a day.[14] Research on healthy subjects led to the creation of a process for reviewing clinical protocols formally, the forerunner of the Institutional Review Boards that protect the rights and welfare of human research participants.

The NIH Clinical Center was, and remains, an imposing and innovative edifice, but the talented research and clinical staff established it as a national treasure. The promise of the Clinical Center—to improve diagnosis, treatment, and outcome for patients with serious illnesses— was realized again and again through breakthrough advances.

The patient care responsibilities of the Clinical Associates varied by institute and program. When Mike Brown started on the Gastro-enterology Service, he spent about 70 percent of his time doing clinical work and the remainder working in the laboratory. For Joe Gold-stein at the NHI, it was the reverse—about 20 percent patient care, 80 percent bench research. For Bob Lefkowitz and Harold Varmus, both working with patients with hormonal disorders, clinical responsibilities were limited to an outpatient facility a half-day per week, then covering the inpatient service for a couple of months during the year. While on hospital duty, Clinical Associates would be assigned a rotating schedule for night call, typically every fifth night. When on call, they were referred to as the "Officer of the Day" and were required to remain in the hospital in case of an emergency. As most of the patients were not acutely ill, Clinical Associates generally got a respectable amount of sleep while on call. As Bob Lefkowitz remembered: "Almost nothing ever happened."[15] After two years of sleep deprivation during their residencies, when call schedules often required caring for very sick patients five out of seven nights, the slower pace of the Clinical Center was a welcome relief.

Jesse Roth fondly recalled his routine when he was a Clinical Associate taking care of patients: "I used to come in the mornings and make rounds with the nurse and then I would take a power nap until noon. They knew where they could find me because the wards and the labs were very close to each other. But I'd say: 'Don't bother me until noon—I'll be back. But if you need me, you know where to find me.' Then, I would come back at noon and write orders and take care of what they wanted." Roth continued:

> Then, I'd take off in the afternoon to go back to the lab. Then, I'd come back at five or six to work up my new patients and I'd be seeing the consults at eight at night. In fact, the Clinical Director of the Institute teased me: "Jesse, I hear you're seeing consults at nine at night." I'd say: "It's true that I am." The advantage of it was that you didn't have trouble finding the patients. They were in their room watching television. You didn't have trouble getting a nurse to help because they had nothing else to do.[16]

Regardless of how they managed daily routines when in the hospital, Clinical Associates took care of patients with rare and unusual conditions. Bob Lefkowitz recalled the patients that he saw with hormonal disorders: "It was very much the equivalent of an endocrine fellowship. The cases we saw were incredible . . . the most amazing cases which stood me . . . in very good stead, because I learned so much endocrinology during that time."[17]

Fifty years after his service as a Clinical Associate, Joe Goldstein retained the bound pocket notebook in which he kept a list of the names and diagnoses of all his patients at the Clinical Center. Flipping through that book, he quickly found the name of a certain patient: a seven-year-old girl who had familial hypercholesterolemia, an inherited disorder that results in elevated levels of blood cholesterol (and discussed at length in chapter 13). This youngster and her older brother both had the same rare and severe form of the disease, and as a result they had already experienced heart attacks and could not walk across their hospital rooms without becoming short of breath. At the time, the cause of this illness was unknown, with no effective treatments. Little did Joe Goldstein know that this young patient and her brother would be the catalyst for his life's work.

By caring for the patients of several different senior scientists, the Associates also were exposed to various approaches to patient-oriented research. Saul Rosen, who arrived at the NIH as an Associate a decade

before Goldstein, Brown, Lefkowitz, and Varmus, described his experience: "When I was a Clinical Associate in the Arthritis Institute and
was on the ward, I wasn't just seeing the patients I was studying. I was
seeing the clinical investigations going on with other people's patients
and how different investigators approached clinical research." Rosen,
who later served as acting director of the Clinical Center, added: "One
was gaining a certain amount of experience by seeing broadly how a
number of people approach areas of research."[18]

Senior physicians provided advice and guidance to the Associates. As
Thomas Boat, a member of the 1968 class of Associates, described: "We
did have clinical rounds. . . . [W]e had them with the Clinical Director
of NIAMD—a guy named Bob [Robert] Gordon—at that time. He
picked out several patients and we would make rounds." Boat, who later
emerged as a leader in cystic fibrosis research, continued: "Some of it
was discussing very practical and general patient care issues and some of
it was more detailed dimensions of care for very specific and oftentimes
rare diseases."[19]

Many other learning opportunities were provided to NIH trainees. Alan Schechter, who arrived as a Research Associate in 1965 and
remained at NIH throughout his career, recalled:

> My Institute [NIAMD] . . . had a Tuesday morning conference at 9:00
> and a Friday morning conference at 9:00 in which as many people from
> the Institute as possible were encouraged to go. Tuesday morning was
> our basic science topic and Friday morning was the clinical topic. And
> the Institute was small enough that a room that held 50 to 60 people
> could hold, sometimes via standing room, most of the staff. Most of
> the senior scientists and the postdoctoral fellows [Associates] took both
> conferences.[20]

When the Clinical Associates were not involved in patient care, they
spent much time as apprentices in research laboratories. Each had a preceptor who was responsible for overseeing the work. In some instances,
the preceptor was a physician-scientist. Physician researchers accounted
for more than half of the scientific staff in 1968. In other instances, the
adviser was a (nonphysician) basic scientist. Regardless of educational

background, most mentors focused on exploring fundamental biological questions. Sometimes research topics had a clear relationship to the disease(s) of the sponsoring institute, such as heart conditions or cancer. In other instances, the work was not linked to a specific disease. The latitude to pursue topics judged to be of the highest scientific interest and importance—without having to justify practical applications—was one of the most valued features at NIH.

In many labs, the relationship between apprentice and master scientist could be close and personal. For example, Henry Metzger, who arrived as a Research Associate between 1959 and 1961, described his work setting: "There was a technician, what one would now call a staff scientist—the principal investigator—and me. It was a three-person laboratory. . . . The principal investigator under whom I worked had no office. His desk was in the laboratory and my desk was right next to his desk. So, I literally saw him all day and every day."[21]

Physical proximity to mentors was not the only virtue of the work environment. There was a prevailing informality that transcended rank and created a sense of collegiality. An early exchange between Alan Schechter and his supervisor, the biochemist Christian Anfinsen, illustrates this point: "I remember being surprised when I said something on the second or third day to Dr. Anfinsen. I asked a question and I addressed him as Dr. Anfinsen. He said: 'Why not call me Chris?' And this was surprising because in four years of medical school and two years as an intern and resident, we always had to call the attending physicians by their last name."[22] At the time, the egalitarian Anfinsen already was an acknowledged leader in the field of protein chemistry; seven years later he would share the Nobel Prize in Physiology or Medicine. To be on a first-name basis with a future Nobel laureate was empowering to someone just starting out.

The role of preceptor was a delicate balance between providing direction and allowing the apprentice to develop independence and learn how to solve problems. Anthony Fauci admired the freedom that his mentor, Sheldon Wolff, provided to trainees: "He would give you resources, independent resources, to pursue what you needed to pursue. He had a spectacular capability of picking bright young people, pointing them in the right direction and getting out of their way." Fauci, today a seasoned scientific leader and institute director himself, continued: "That's something that is a very important trait of a mentor. He would figure out that you had what it takes, and once he figured that out, he would encourage you to do whatever you want; he would support you and, above all, he would stay out of your way."[23] Thomas Boat was given a similar level of autonomy: "When I was at NIH, I basically picked the project I did and sort of bootstrapped it."[24]

The spirit of camaraderie extended beyond the tight-knit working relationships within individual labs. Mahlon DeLong, another member of the 1968 entering class of Clinical Associates, who became a pioneer in the treatment of Parkinson's disease, described the extraordinary spirit of interaction on campus: "Of course, the NIH was an open book. You could go anywhere and talk to anybody. That was one of the real joys of the place." DeLong, who later served as a faculty member at both Johns Hopkins and Emory, felt that the NIH had no equal: "I have never been anywhere stronger than that [NIH] was. I think everyone that was there recalls that."[25]

Reaching out to be helpful to colleagues in other programs was the norm rather than the exception. Saul Rosen pointed out one of the great strengths at NIH: it was packed with experts in virtually every type of biomedical research. "No matter what new thing you wanted to try, there is someone in the next lab, upstairs, or downstairs, who has been doing it for years and may even be the world's expert."[26] A half-century later, Thomas Boat still remembered one such generous contribution to his own work: "I needed, as I recall, to do an amino acid analysis and I went to Christian Anfinsen's lab and one of the more senior investigators there basically gave me access and helped me figure out how to do it, how to interpret it, etc."[27] Jesse Roth characterized the Clinical Center as follows: "The exchanges were very free and open . . . we kind of knew what was going on in each other's kitchen."[28]

For young physicians, many of whom lacked any research background, the experience was a complete immersion. Even the lunch hour became an opportunity to learn science, as Henry Metzger described: "We had a journal club, as far as I was a member, five days a week. People got together, had their lunch together very often, brown-bagged it and discussed science."[29] Lab groups did not confine themselves to discussing other people's work—they dissected each other's results in regular meetings. "Often, when the experiment didn't work," Jesse Roth noted, "it was actually the most exciting because it gave you data that you hadn't expected."[30]

Having grown up in New York City, Roth cultivated a certain feistiness within his lab meetings: "Everybody would provide suggestions and complaints. There would be fighting—not physical fighting, but good arguments." He continued: "Several of the guys who came from Europe—they remember their first data club and they thought that the lab was on the verge of disintegration, because guys were standing up and yelling at me or the board. 'What are you talking about?' 'How could that be?' Well, it was just a free-for-all of ideas with no insults, no scars."[31]

Beyond lab meetings, journal clubs, conferences, and attending rounds, trainees could attend formal classes. One such offering dated to the early years at NIH, when Christian Anfinsen, along with fellow senior scientists Robert Berliner and Daniel Steinberg, led an effort to expand educational opportunities for junior colleagues and trainees. As Steinberg later recalled: "Some of us, and I in particular, wanted to take advantage of the remarkable concentration of experts in the biomedical sciences at NIH and let the trainees at various levels learn from them. Also, we missed the traditions and trappings of academia."[32]

When approached by Anfinsen, Berliner, and Steinberg, Director James Shannon was cool to the idea of an in-house educational program, which might be perceived as extending beyond its research mission and competing with local academic institutions. However, initial courses were offered under the auspices of an already approved night-school program administered by the US Department of Agriculture. Within five years, that arrangement was replaced by the creation of a new non-governmental nonprofit entity, the Foundation for Advanced Education in the Sciences, Inc. (FAES). The typical evening course was an hour or two once per week for a semester. Topics ranged from emerging scientific subjects, such as medical genetics, to an introduction to medical history.[33] Such courses were optional, and not all Associates chose to participate, but those who did typically found them to be an important part of their training experience.

Henry Metzger described the value of the evening program: "It included a substantial didactic component so that many of us whose premedical training had not been all that rigorous in terms of physical chemistry, mathematics . . . [and] organic chemistry, had a chance to at least get some further training in those areas. It wasn't like getting a PhD, but at least one became familiar with a little bit more [of] the approaches and methodologies."[34] Alan Schechter believes that "FAES . . . made the NIH much more like a research university than is true for almost any government research laboratory." Still, Schechter feels that the value of the evening courses extended beyond the educational content. As an Associate, the FAES classes enabled him "early on to get to know personally many of the then current or future leaders of NIH."[35]

In addition to formal classes, Anfinsen helped establish a series of informal evening seminars. About fifteen to twenty advanced-level seminars, using a group participatory format rather than the FAES lecture format, were offered at a time. Modeled after the tutorial system at Oxford University, seminars were led by scientific experts who guided Associates' readings and discussions in various areas. Alan Schechter described a seminar taught by Anfinsen and colleague David Davies in which "eight or ten of the associates worked together to build these molecular models and we learned a great deal about the principles of protein structure from building these models."[36]

Although Director Shannon had concerns about mission creep at the NIH, the scientists there—most of whom came from university settings—felt an affinity for the collegiate culture. Donald Fredrickson, who later served as NIH director, described it thus: "We never thought we were a government institution for one minute." He added: "We were so close and we were such a large part of the academic community that we really just considered ourselves part of that."[37]

To some extent, the NIH campus enjoyed the best of both worlds. As a federal entity it received generous financial support from the US government, and simultaneously it was shielded from the bureaucratic processes of other agencies. Unlike research faculties at universities who had to compete for grants to fund personal scientific efforts, NIH scientists had stable and predictable research funding for the laboratories. As Saul Rosen described: "When I was a senior investigator, I was insulated budgetary problems to a certain extent by my branch chief and then by the Scientific Director of my Institute [NIAMD]. . . . Except for the fact that on a couple of occasions it would have been nice to have a sexy piece of equipment that I wasn't able to get right away—maybe I had to wait some years because of budget priorities."[38]

The relative freedom that NIH staff and trainees enjoyed was apparent even in their manner of dress. Unlike colleagues at the National Naval Medical Center across the street, Commissioned Officers in the Public Health Service at NIH dressed in civilian clothes. "I never had a uniform," Donald Fredrickson recalled. "We were not disloyal to the Public Health Service—we would wear a uniform if we needed to. There was always someone whom we could borrow one from."[39] Harry Kimball was typical of the trainees: "Most of the Clinical Associates never had uniforms. I never had a uniform. However, we did have a rank. It was a Navy Lieutenant Commander." This middle rank is equivalent to the rank of major in the US Army. Kimball explained: "We had all of the rights and privileges of regular service people. We'd go to commissaries, but we didn't salute or anything."[40] The pay Clinical Associates received, though still modest, was a big step up from the paltry wages that they earned as residents.

Clinical Associates enjoyed other privileges, one of which was shared office space where they could work and interact. At least in some institutes the size of the desk mattered, according to Jesse Roth:

> They converted one patient room into an office for the young physicians, so the young physicians were all in one group. When they got there, they were each allowed to order a desk for themselves. Having been at fancy hospitals, like [Columbia] Presbyterian or Mass General, where the little desk they had at the hospital was just a sliver, they all went to get themselves a desk. They went to the surplus property guy at NIH and each would come back with an enormous desk . . . and this room that the physicians had was entirely consumed by these desks.[41]

Working at super-sized desks, Associates developed friendships that were sustained over many years. Tony Fauci, who also entered as a Clinical Associate in 1968, characterized these relationships:

There is a certain pride and good feeling about people who have shared
that very special experience at NIH. . . . Bob Lefkowitz is a very, very
prominent scientist [and subsequent Nobel laureate]. . . . Harold Varmus is a Nobel Prize winner now. . . . Mike Brown is a Nobel Prize winner. . . . All four of us were here together when we were Clinical Associates and that bond of being here together in the same year of 1968—the
class of 1968—you feel a very special bond with these people.
. . .

So, when we talk about things, not infrequently in the conversation
comes out the fact that we were in the same class together at the NIH.
So, it's an important feeling to have been part of a class . . . it's really
more of an *esprit de corps* that you have.[42]

Clinical Associates have fond memories of their days at NIH, maybe
because many could finally catch their breath after clinical residencies.
As Bob Lefkowitz recounted: "For me, it was a real treat to actually have
time to spend with my kids, which I hadn't had before—literally, from
the day the first was born when I was in medical school."[43] Fellow Clinical Associate Thomas Boat had a similar experience: "My wife would
not infrequently, especially when the weather was nice, drive the kids
over and we would have lunch on the lawn outside the Clinical Center.
And she would sometimes get somebody to sit and she would come over.
There were tennis courts and she and I would play tennis on the NIH
Center grounds."[44] However, the come-and-go atmosphere disappeared
three decades later following the bombing in Oklahoma City of the Alfred P. Murrah Federal Building on April 19, 1995, and the September
11, 2001, terror attacks. Based on a 2002 report by the Office of Inspec-
tor General, strong security measures were implemented across all government installations, including NIH. Eventually, an eight-foot-tall
fence was erected around the perimeter of the campus, and entry was
controlled through guarded access points.

Back in the less security-conscious days of the 1960s, however, the
NIH had an open-door policy. For those whose tastes ran to the arts,
there were opportunities not typical of most scientific or governmental
organizations. A Sunday afternoon chamber music series was founded
in 1968 by the biochemist Giulio Cantoni. A refugee from Italy during

World War II, Cantoni was a flautist and a personal friend of the conductor Arturo Toscanini. Using the vehicle of the FAES, Cantoni and his cofounder, the pianist Paola Saffiotti (wife of staff scientist Umberto Saffiotti), were able to arrange funding for ten performances each year, which were open to the public and delivered in the sold-out 500-seat auditorium at the Clinical Center.[45] Launched three years before the opening of the Kennedy Center in Washington, the NIH chamber music series quickly earned a reputation as one of the area's prime venues for classical music. Through his relationship with Toscanini, Cantoni "was able to get musicians on the way up before you couldn't afford them."[46] Even preeminent artists such as Rudolf Serkin and Isaac Stern graced the stage of the Clinical Center. The series continued for four decades; after 9/11 it was moved off campus for security reasons.

When reflecting back on their years as Clinical Associates, most alumni view the experience as a defining period in their lives. One such alumnus was Robert Gallo, who arrived at NIH in 1965 and remained for three decades; he is best known for his pioneering research in the 1980s on the human immunodeficiency virus. Gallo summed up his years as an Associate: "It was a dreamland for me."[47] And so it was for most of the former Clinical Associates who worked, studied, and played on the NIH campus during those brilliant years.

PART II

MENTORS AND APPRENTICES

CHAPTER 6

NIH'S FINEST HOUR

Nirenberg Cracks the Genetic Code

This chapter describes the cracking of the genetic code by Marshall Nirenberg, who later would become Joe Goldstein's NIH mentor. The story begins with a two-page article published in 1953 in which the scientists James Watson and Francis Crick first describe the structure of DNA.[1] Watson, all of twenty-three years old, was a research fellow and had completed his PhD less than three years earlier. Crick, a dozen years older, was still in graduate school (World War II had interrupted his studies). Working together at the Cavendish Laboratory, a physics research unit at Cambridge University, the two junior colleagues pieced together a variety of sources of information to develop their proposed double helix configuration in which the four nitrogen-rich nucleotide base building blocks were paired up in two separate combinations. Each pairing was composed of a single-ringed molecule with a partner double-ringed molecule. One permissible pairing was the smaller thymine

(T) with the larger adenine (A). The other acceptable pairing was the smaller cytosine (C) with the larger guanine (G).

Their spiraling double helix structure was elegant architecturally, but equally important it suggested an efficient means by which DNA could be copied. In a separate paper published in the same journal five weeks later, they described their replication model. In concise prose, Watson and Crick indicated that the two strands could be separated so that: "Each chain then acts as a template for the formation on to itself of a new companion chain, so that eventually we shall have two pairs of chains, where we only had one before. Moreover, the sequence of the pairs of bases will have been duplicated exactly." In this article, the authors also wrote the following prescient statement: "It follows that in a long molecule many different permutations are possible and it therefore seems likely that the precise sequences of the bases is the code which carries the genetical information."[2]

The use of the term "code" in reference to the language of biological inheritance was a tip of the scientific hat to Erwin Schrödinger. The 1933 Nobel Prize–winning physicist published a best-selling book in 1944 titled *What Is Life?*. His slim volume was based on a series of lectures he delivered the prior year at Trinity College in Dublin. Even before DNA was known to be the molecular vehicle for carrying genetic information, Schrödinger proposed that there must be a "code-script" that programs "the entire pattern of the individual's future development and of its functioning in the mature state."[3] Schrödinger identified chromosomes as the site of this code-script. In unveiling his vision in advance of any hard data, he acknowledged: "This is a fantastic description, perhaps less becoming a scientist than a poet."[4]

Later, Watson would credit Schrödinger for stimulating his interest in how inheritable traits are passed from generation to generation. In his words: "The notion that life itself might be perpetuated by means of an instruction book inscribed in a secret code appealed to me."[5] Once it became clear that DNA within chromosomes was the source of these instructions, there was an obvious mathematical conundrum. DNA is written in a four-letter alphabet. The information from DNA is used to direct the manufacture of proteins—the blue-collar workers of cells responsible for, among other things, their structure, movement, communication, defense, and digestion. Proteins are constructed from basic components called "amino acids" that line up, one after another, like cars in a long railroad train. There are twenty different core amino acids, and while the length of a human protein can vary widely, on average there are slightly fewer than 500 amino acids in a human protein.

The arithmetic challenge, therefore, is that the alphabet of DNA has just four letters, whereas the alphabet of proteins has twenty letters. Clearly, a single nucleotide base, with only four options, cannot on its own fully specify one of the twenty amino acids. Even two nucleotides together could create only sixteen unique combinations (four for the first letter multiplied by four for the second letter). At a minimum, it would take at least three nucleotides in a molecule of DNA to have enough possible combinations to account for all twenty amino acids. With three bases, there would be sixty-four possible unique combinations (four for the first letter multiplied by four for the second letter multiplied by four for the third letter). Crick credits the physicist George Gamow with suggesting, not long after the famous DNA structure article appeared, that each amino acid was coded by a triplet of adjacent bases. Gamow's theoretical model of how the amino acids were assembled into protein utilized skeletal cavities in the DNA double helix as a physical template. And though Gamow's speculation about the mechanical process was wrong, he deduced correctly that triplets of DNA bases were needed for coding the twenty amino acids.[6]

Gamow's model of DNA serving as a structural template for protein assembly was at odds with experimental evidence from nearly fifteen years earlier. In 1939, the Swedish geneticist Torbjörn Caspersson and his American colleague Jack Schultz, working together at the Karolinska Institute in Stockholm, made an important discovery. They found that protein production in rapidly growing cells was distant from the central command center in the cell's nucleus, where DNA is concentrated.[7] The assembly plant for proteins was in the cell's hinterlands, where there was an ample supply of DNA's chemical cousin, RNA. Within a year of the DNA structure paper, Watson and his colleague Alexander Rich, then at the California Institute of Technology, speculated on the respective roles of DNA and RNA. In their words: "DNA could control RNA synthesis [production], with RNA responsible for protein synthesis."[8]

Interestingly enough, this paper was sponsored by Linus Pauling, who that same year would be selected to receive the Nobel Prize in Chemistry and who had been a leading competitor to Watson and Crick in solving the structure of DNA.

The interest in RNA, its structure, and how it contributed to building proteins led several leaders in the field to form a social and scientific fraternity. Founded in 1954, it was an exclusive band of bookish brothers limited to just twenty members—the exact number of amino acids. Each member had a nickname related to one of the amino acids—Watson was "Proline" and Crick was "Tyrosine." The clique dubbed itself the "RNA Tie Club," and the members were presented with a bespoke necktie in black wool featuring an RNA helix embroidered in green and yellow. Each also received a gold tiepin with the three-letter abbreviation for their assigned amino-acid moniker.[9]

What the RNA Tie Club may have lacked in fashion sense was more than offset by sheer intellectual firepower. Eight members would go on to win Nobel Prizes. Many of the leading genetics researchers of the era were tapped, although there were some surprising omissions, such as Pauling and the future Nobel Prize winners Maurice Wilkins, Jacques Monod, and François Jacob. Truth be told, it was as much a drinking society as a scientific club, but the initiates were imbued with a Knights of the Round Table–type of bravado, assuming that advances in understanding how RNA worked were likely to come from within their membership.

Among those excluded from a seat at the table was a twenty-seven-year-old graduate student at the University of Michigan named Marshall Warren Nirenberg. Born in New York City on April 10, 1927, Marshall was the second child of Harry and Minerva Nirenberg. Harry had enlisted in the US Army during World War I. After the Armistice, Harry joined his father's shirt manufacturing business, from which he gained a comfortable income.

Marshall's happy and active childhood was interrupted when, at age nine, he contracted rheumatic fever and was bedridden for a year. During his convalescence, Marshall was tutored at home, and he occupied his spare time with reading. In part motivated by a desire to provide Marshall with a more temperate environment to restore his health, the family relocated the following year to Orlando, Florida. Long before it became a family theme-park destination, Orlando was a quiet, rural backwater. The Nirenbergs purchased and operated a dairy farm, and Marshall spent his free hours in the swampland near their home. He was fascinated by the diverse flora and fauna and was known to capture snakes, including venomous ones, fearlessly and, injudiciously, hide them in a sack under his bed.[10]

Marshall's immersion in the natural world was invigorating, speeding his recovery and fostering a lifelong curiosity about biology. He became an avid collector of butterflies and spiders, even contributing specimens of arachnids to the American Museum of Natural History. His amateur hunting and gathering was supplemented with instruction by biologists who came to the area during World War II to teach jungle survival skills to US Army pilots from the nearby base.[11]

Nirenberg enrolled at the University of Florida in 1945. He was hardly a stellar student, graduating with many C's and even a few D's. His undistinguished academic performance notwithstanding, Marshall worked as a teaching assistant in comparative anatomy and managed to graduate in three years. For a couple of years thereafter, he worked for his father as a salesman; bored by the work, he returned in 1950 to the University of Florida to pursue a master's degree in zoology. In graduate school, unlike his college years, he was focused and earned high marks. He continued to work while in school, serving as a research assistant conducting biochemical studies at the university's nutrition laboratory. Marshall's thesis project took his childhood insect collecting to a stratospheric level by amassing 10,000 specimens of small, mothlike insects known as caddisflies.[12]

The next stop for Nirenberg was a thousand miles north, and in 1952 he undertook doctoral studies in biochemistry at the University of Michigan. In Ann Arbor, Marshall did a creditable job on his coursework, but the research project assigned to him was unpromising, so he switched midstream to another topic: how a type of cancer cell utilized certain sugars as sources of fuel. Nirenberg published three papers on this topic with his dissertation adviser, James Hogg, and was awarded a PhD in 1957.[13]

On Hogg's advice, Marshall headed to the NIH for a postdoctoral fellowship in the National Institute of Arthritis and Metabolic Diseases.

DeWitt "Hans" Stetten, the institute's associate director in charge of the in-house research program, assigned Nirenberg to work with the Yale-trained microbiologist William Jakoby. Under Jakoby's direction, Nirenberg gained skills in working with enzymes—the protein accelerators of chemical reactions within cells. Together, they published three papers; it was solid science but did not suggest either great originality or future achievement on the part of the trainee. As Nirenberg's two-year fellowship was ending in 1959, both Stetten and Jakoby were content to let Marshall head somewhere else.

Fortunately for Nirenberg, another scientist at NIH was willing to take a chance on offering him an opportunity there. Gordon "Gordy" Tomkins was a risk-taker, and as the recently appointed head of the Section of Metabolic Enzymes, he was in a position to make a gamble on Marshall. Tomkins had impeccable academic credentials: Harvard Medical School, Peter Bent Brigham clinical training, and a PhD in biochemistry from the University of California, Berkeley. Hardly a one-dimensional scholar, however, Tomkins was a free spirit who once toyed with becoming a jazz musician (and he continued to play for fun at various venues in the Washington area). Tomkins's passions were diverse, and according to Stetten "his wit and charm were ebullient and contagious. . . . He would meet an investigator doing something mundane and, in an instant, through his flights of fancy, would embellish and embroider the work until both were certain they were onto some fundamental discovery. Then Gordy would offer the person a job."[14]

For Nirenberg: "Gordon was a live wire. . . . He was probably the most articulate person I ever met in my life. . . . What he basically did best was talk to people. I found it wonderful to be able to talk to him. . . . He followed every experiment, and he knew the details of what I was doing and what other people had done as well."[15] With Tomkins's blessing and encouragement, Nirenberg—only two years out of his graduate studies and with no training in research on nucleic acids or protein synthesis—decided to pursue the unthinkable: the human genetic code. Many senior scientists thought it was a fool's errand. Nirenberg recounted one such reaction: "One night, shortly after I became an independent investigator, I walked in the corridor adjacent to my lab and saw Bruce Ames, who was then one of the best scientists at the NIH. He was working at night in his lab, so on a whim I decided to ask his advice." Nirenberg outlined his plan to Ames and recalled: "When I told him this, he looked at me. He said: 'It's suicidal to do it.'"[16]

Nirenberg understood that Ames was only trying to provide sound professional guidance: "I knew that it would take two years to get my work set up, to learn the field, to get the systems going, to just set up to be ready, to be prepared for the challenge. You are supposed to hit the ground running and have everything all set up and know exactly what you want to do. It should be productive because, in a sense, you have to prove yourself."[17] Moreover, Nirenberg knew that the competition would be fierce in a field already populated by thought leaders like the members of the RNA Tie Club. "Some of the best people in the world were working on this problem. I asked myself: 'How can one person, working alone, who has never worked in the field before, make a contribution? How could such a researcher be compared with all of the really bright people who are very experienced, who have big labs, and who are working in the field?'"[18]

With the odds stacked against him, Nirenberg drew some inspiration from an anecdote told to him by another postdoctoral fellow, John Bryant. Having just returned from Munich, Bryant worked in the laboratory of Feodor Lynen, director of the Max Planck Institute for Cellular Chemistry. Lynen had trained under the Nobel laureate Heinrich Wieland, and in 1964 Lynen himself would share the Nobel Prize in Physiology or Medicine for his work on the metabolism of cholesterol and fatty acids. According to Bryant, when he asked Lynen what he would study if he was just starting out, his response was encouraging: "That he would pick a problem that interested him, that he was really excited about, and that other people were interested in. He wouldn't worry too much about competition from other people."[19] Whether or not Lynen actually gave such advice, this tidbit of laboratory gossip was enough to embolden Nirenberg to pursue his audacious dream.

If Marshall needed a reminder of the modest assets that he was bringing to the table, he had to look no farther than his work space. "At first, Gordon put me in the instrument room because there was no other space in his section. I had a bench, one half room actually in the instrument room, but the noise of the ultracentrifuge that would be running all of the time drove me crazy, so we finally got the ultracentrifuge moved out."[20] What Tomkins could not provide in facilities he made up for in personal attention, as Nirenberg recalled: "What he [Tomkins] gave me was his time, the most valuable thing that he had, basically, and that is a rare thing. He would come around lunchtime. I can see him slouching up against the refrigerator with a sandwich in one hand, and we would talk." Nirenberg relished the give-and-take—the way that they could almost read each other's minds, finishing each other's sentences. "At night, what I would do is go home and think about the work and write down notes and get ideas. To be able to bat it back and forth with somebody else is just wonderful."[21]

Tomkins also gave Nirenberg the luxury of unpressured time to get his bearings in a new field. Marshall later expressed his appreciation: "One thing I will be forever grateful to Gordon Tomkins for is that he made me feel secure, and so I didn't publish. I published nothing in this period of almost two years. Toward the end of the two-year period, we got our first publication. I never felt threatened or bothered by my lack of publications."[22] Such freedom to explore without worrying about the scientific hangman's noose (a thin bibliography) was uncommon at the time and even more exceptional today. One would not have predicted a bright future for a thirty-four-year-old biochemist four years out of doctoral work and with fewer than ten publications to his name.

Nirenberg started by trying to determine whether protein synthesis was stimulated by DNA or by RNA. For this purpose, he chose as his experimental focus the common gut bacterium *Escherichia coli* (*E. coli*). This organism is named for the Bavarian pediatrician Theodor Escherich, who first discovered it in 1885 while studying fatal intestinal diseases in children. *E. coli* is easily isolated, grown, and maintained, so it became a favorite choice of researchers in the fields of microbiology, biochemistry, physiology, and molecular biology. Marshall was following a well-worn pathway to this bacterium.

Rather than using whole bacterial cells, however, Nirenberg chose to work with so-called cell-free extracts. By mechanically disrupting the bacterial walls, Marshall could isolate the gel-like "sap" within the cell where protein synthesis occurred. In so doing, he could exert greater control over protein synthesis, including acceleration of the rate and expansion of the amount of material produced. Working alone for about a year and a half, Nirenberg struggled to perfect the experimental system, tinkering with all of the conditions.

With the arrival of his first postdoctoral fellow, Nirenberg was able to shift into high gear. Heinrich Matthaei, only two years younger than Marshall, had a PhD in plant physiology from the University of Bonn and came to the United States on a NATO research fellowship. Matthaei's goal was to learn about protein synthesis, but arrangements fell through with his intended host at Cornell University, as did backup plans at Rockefeller University in New York and the Wistar Institute in Philadelphia. Running out of options, Matthaei traveled farther down the East Coast to Bethesda, where he learned that the only scientist working on protein synthesis at the NIH was Marshall Nirenberg. It was a twist of fate that brought the unseasoned pair of investigators together in October 1960.

Working side by side, Nirenberg and Matthaei refined the experimental system and were able to demonstrate that the addition of DNA to the protein manufacturing machinery had no effect, whereas the addition of RNA turned on the assembly process. As Marshall later remembered: "That was the first evidence that I was aware of that messenger RNA [mRNA] existed. And I jumped for joy when I saw the first experiment worked and all the controls were there and everything was in duplicate. I literally jumped for joy and let out a holler because I knew that we had found something that was exciting."[23] The publication of these findings[24] appeared on April 28, 1961. A fortnight later, two other teams, one including the future Nobel laureates François Jacob and Sydney Brenner, and the other including the future Nobelists Walter Gilbert and James Watson, reported on the isolation of mRNA (messenger RNA) in a much more prestigious and widely read journal. This important molecule would be understood as the transient liaison between the genetic information in DNA in the nucleus and the protein assembly operations in the periphery of the cell.

In an effort to see if their cell-free extract would respond to other types of RNA, Nirenberg and Matthaei found that single-stranded RNA from the tobacco mosaic virus—named after the distinctive discoloration that it causes on tobacco leaves—was an excellent candidate.

The viral RNA was a comparatively powerful stimulant for protein production. Marshall decided that he needed to pursue the tobacco mosaic virus finding, so he headed to the University of California, Berkeley, to visit Heinz Fraenkel-Conrat. The world's leading expert on this particular virus, Fraenkel-Conrat literally had taken the microorganism apart and reconstituted it. Since Fraenkel-Conrat had fully characterized the coat protein produced by the genetic material of this virus, Marshall wanted to see if his experimental system could synthesize the coat protein.

Before Nirenberg departed for the West Coast, he and Matthaei mapped out a parallel line of investigation that Matthaei would pursue in Bethesda. Rather than using naturally occurring RNA, such as that in the tobacco mosaic virus, they would explore some man-made RNAs. They started with stored material provided by fellow NIH scientist Daniel Bradley, who earlier had made the synthetic RNA for other purposes. The specimen that Bradley gave to Nirenberg was a monotonous string of the single base, uracil, lined up single file—one after another—like a column of identical soldiers. Uracil (U) is chemically similar to thymine (T), and in RNA U replaces T as one of the four key base nucleotides. The chain of U's was characterized as UUUUUUUUUUUUUU or simply as "poly-U." On May 27, 1961, at 3 a.m., Matthaei ran the experimental system using the unvarying artificial messenger. Within an hour, the boring repetitive coding template had produced a chain of amino acids that was equally unvarying—it was composed only of phenylalanine. In other words, a message that was confined to U produced a peptide characterized by only one type of amino acid: phenylalanine.

In the lonely darkness on that spring night in Bethesda, Matthaei had experienced one of the true eureka moments of molecular biology. The discovery was the culmination of five days of working virtually around the clock to determine which amino acids were incorporated into the peptide that was generated by Marshall's cell-free system using Bradley's recycled poly-U. Today, determining the amino-acid sequence in a chain is a routine, fast, and automated procedure. In 1961, however, it was a labor-intensive, manual effort. Matthaei had exhausted nearly all other possible amino-acid compositions, and phenylalanine was one of the last two amino acids that he tested.

The poly-U experiment provided the first major clue as to how a command delivered by a gene was processed by the protein assembly apparatus. To derive this insight, Nirenberg and Matthaei had tricked Mother Nature or, perhaps more accurately, adapted the tools of her trade in a creative way. By using genetic hardware evolved over eons, the two NIH scientists managed to crank out a custom-designed product from an artificial set of directions. It was simultaneously brilliant and simple. They now knew that, if phenylalanine was going to be included into a growing protein chain, one set of instructions was written with only the letter U. Of course, they didn't know how many U's were required, but some consecutive number of adjacent U's was a command for phenylalanine. It may not be the only directive for including this amino acid, but undeniably it was one such command.

Matthaei, in a state of euphoria, worked in the lab all night. Even though it was a Saturday, Gordon Tomkins arrived at nine in the morning to check on progress and became the second person in the world to learn about this breakthrough. It was fitting that Tomkins—the risk-taker who almost alone sensed Nirenberg's potential and nurtured it through two minimally productive years—learned the results before anyone else. When Matthaei called Nirenberg to inform him, the trio of insiders knew that such a momentous discovery would not remain secret for long; they were determined to present it formally rather than to have it leak out by word of mouth.

Stetten, the man who hired Nirenberg but was unimpressed by his slow start, came to understand that a star had been born in his institute. Stetten counseled his junior colleague to get the poly-U findings into the scientific literature as quickly as possible. Nirenberg recalled Stetten's advice: "'Marshall, this is going to be a very important publication.' He said: 'Write it well' when I sat down to write it, and I think that was very good advice. I also think it was good advice that he gave me to have the paper in press before leaving for Moscow."[25]

Nirenberg was referring to his traveling to Moscow for the Fifth International Congress of Biochemistry. A massive meeting with more than 6,000 attendees expected, Marshall was one of many scientists invited to present their latest work. This would be the first forum in which Nirenberg would discuss the poly-U experiment in public. Once the

secret was revealed, Stetten knew that Nirenberg's head start in cracking the genetic code would be lost, so it was important to plant the flag
in the scientific literature first.

The fastest route to publication in a leading journal would be to have
a member of the National Academy of Sciences—the preeminent organization of American scientists—submit the article to its publication
Proceedings of the National Academy of Sciences, or *PNAS*. In a practice
since discontinued, *PNAS* allowed academy members to "communicate"
articles written by nonmembers if the contribution was deemed important by the member. This process was an expedited pathway to publication, bypassing the sometimes lengthy delay that can occur during the
normal peer-review process. Established as a quality-control process,
peer review for scientific journals requires several steps. Once a scientist
submits a manuscript to a journal for consideration, the editor forwards
it to experts in the field. The reviewers—whose identities remain anonymous—provide the editor written critiques of the submission. Based
on this feedback, the editor can make one of several possible decisions.
The paper can be accepted for publication in its current form—a rare
outcome. The manuscript can be rejected because of perceived irremedi-
able flaws in the design, conduct, or interpretation of the work, or simply
because it is not sufficiently original or important. A final alternative for
the editor is to ask the author(s) to address questions and concerns raised
by the reviewers and to resubmit the article for further consideration.

The fast-track approach available at *PNAS* replaced critiques from
anonymous reviewers with the trusted judgment of a single academy
member. And though many landmark papers were published using this
process, there also was the risk that inferior work could make its way
into print. Equally important, those who had insider access to the old
boys' network of academy members had a distinct advantage in getting
their work published quickly. In the case of the poly-U experiment, the
work was groundbreaking; because Marshall worked at the NIH, he
also had access to several of the old boys.

Nirenberg's first choice to communicate the paper was academy
member Leo Szilard, a Hungarian American physicist who played
a critical role in the Manhattan Project to develop the atomic bomb.
After World War II, Szilard migrated to biological research, ultimately

spending the last few years of his life ensconced in the Dupont Plaza Hotel in Washington, DC, from whence he held forth on various matters, especially campaigning for world peace. Nirenberg came to pay homage to the great man in his makeshift office in the lobby of the hotel. Nirenberg recalled: "Szilard didn't know anything about protein synthesis, or about what I was going to tell him, so I had to start from scratch. I spent the whole day with him. . . . Everybody that would come through the lobby there would wave and say, 'Hi, Leo.'" He continued: "In between those conversations with other people, I told him what I had done and the implications of it. But after listening to me for the whole day, he said that he simply didn't have the background."[26]

Fortunately for Nirenberg, there was another potential sponsor: Joseph Smadel, a virologist who was then working as an NIH administrator, agreed to communicate the work. Nirenberg did not know Smadel personally, and Smadel had never conducted work in molecular biology, but he was an accomplished scientist who, the following year, would become a recipient of the Lasker Award—often described as America's Nobel Prize. On Thursday, August 3, 1961, just sixty-eight days after Matthaei first saw the string of phenylalanines produced, Smadel communicated two papers to *PNAS*. The articles appeared back-to-back in the October 1, 1961, issue of the journal. The first one, with Matthaei as lead author, was a nine-page description of the cell-free extract system.[27] The companion fourteen-page paper, with Nirenberg as the first author, provided an in-depth characterization of the poly-U breakthrough.[28]

The weeklong meeting in Moscow began on August 10, 1961, only a week after the two *PNAS* papers had been submitted, so the findings were not yet known beyond a small inner circle of NIH scientists. Upon arriving at the meeting, Nirenberg ran into James Watson. For those keeping score, Watson was "Proline" in the RNA Tie Club and was not particularly interested in what Marshall had to say. Although Watson did not bother to attend Marshall's scheduled presentation himself, he did deem it worthy enough to send a colleague to take notes. It was not hard to find empty chairs in the room. According to Nirenberg: "This was a talk that was in a small amphitheater, with an enormous projector—as big as a person. I gave the talk and relatively few people came to it. Almost nobody—maybe there were 25 people."[29]

Word quickly got out, however, that this relatively unknown investigator had announced a major new finding. Nirenberg's hallway encounter with Francis Crick ("Tyrosine" in the RNA Tie Club) led to an invitation to repeat the presentation. "He [Crick] said that he had been searching all over for me and was glad to see me, and he invited me to give the talk again in a large symposium that he was chairing." That session was scheduled for Tuesday, August 15, at 10:30 a.m. Nirenberg continued: "The second time I gave the paper it was a very large audience. The reception was really remarkable—fantastic. I remember Matt Meselson, who was sitting right up front. I didn't know him at the time, but he was so overjoyed about hearing this stuff that he impulsively jumped up, grabbed my hand, and actually hugged me and congratulated me for doing that."[30] Meselson, a young Harvard professor, and not a hugger by nature, was a coauthor of one of the two recent papers describing the role of mRNA.[31]

The impromptu embrace by Meselson was not necessarily a sign that the in-crowd was welcoming Nirenberg into its company. They clearly expected one of their own—the proud owner of an RNA Tie—to lead the charge in cracking the code. Nevertheless, a few months later, Francis Crick delivered a BBC radio address in which he admitted, perhaps with a stiff upper lip: "The real breakthrough in the problem is due to two young biochemists at the National Institutes of Health (at Bethesda in America) called Nirenberg and Matthaei. This August, at a Biochemical Congress in Moscow, they reported a spectacular result. . . . This result has now been repeated in labs all over the world. Moreover, other artificial RNAs can be produced and tested in the system."[32]

One of the attendees at Nirenberg's second presentation in Moscow was Severo Ochoa, who two years earlier shared the Nobel Prize in Physiology or Medicine for the discovery of an enzyme that could assemble RNA-like chains of nucleotides. Nobody in the world knew more about making artificial RNA strands than this Spanish American biochemist, who was then working at New York University. After Nirenberg finished his talk, Ochoa immediately telegraphed his lab and instructed them to replicate Marshall's experiment. From his Nobel Prize–winning work, Ochoa had a stockpile of designer-made chains of nucleotides that could be run through a cell-free protein synthesis system similar to the one that Nirenberg and Matthaei had used. In addition to the rich supply of artificial mRNA, Ochoa had a large group of scientists to assign to the effort. Marshall had Matthaei and that was it—clearly, they were punching above their weight.

The fact that Ochoa had set his sights on cracking the genetic code was made evident to Nirenberg soon after he returned to the United States. Nirenberg was invited to Boston to speak in October 1961. James Watson sat in the front of a packed auditorium, and in the middle of Nirenberg's talk Watson began flicking a newspaper impatiently, suggesting to Nirenberg that the RNA Tie Club member was not pleased with some aspect of the presentation. The most disturbing turn of events, however, came during the question-and-answer period when Peter Lengyel, an Ochoa trainee, stood up. Rather than posing a question, Lengyel proceeded to steal the limelight by sharing data produced by the NYU team. It is an understatement to describe this scene as atypical of the decorous world of science. For a scientist to travel uninvited from one city to another to present results during an invited speaker's talk is beyond the pale. Nirenberg was taken aback:

> The rumors I had heard that he [Ochoa] had synthetic polypeptides and he had found other amino acids going into protein and he was ahead of us were absolutely true. Just the fact that Ochoa would send someone to give a talk after my talk was a remarkable thing. I had never heard of anything like that. It was very depressing at that time because it was clear that they were way ahead of us in deciphering the code.[33]

Feeling defeated so soon after his key discovery, Marshall returned to the NIH to consider the options. "I felt that I had reached a crossroads here. I felt that either I would pull out and let Ochoa take it away—let him do the code—or I could really dig in and compete with him." It was a Saturday, and by chance Robert Martin, a postdoctoral fellow working under Bruce Ames, happened to be in the lab. When Marshall recounted the story of the talk in Massachusetts, Martin immediately signed up for the cause: "I'll help you. Let's look up how you make synthetic polypeptides this weekend, and Monday you can do the experiments."[34] By making and characterizing a large number of artificial

RNAs, Martin suspended his own research program for several months in order to assist Marshall. In Martin's words: "We at NIH were terribly angry with Ochoa and his colleagues for jumping in on Marshall and Heinrich's discovery."[35]

Both Ochoa and Nirenberg were invited to make presentations at the New York Academy of Medicine on November 9, 1961, only three months after the Moscow talk. Nirenberg talked about the poly-U work, but Ochoa bested him by announcing that his group had figured out not one but *eleven* coding messages.[36] Afterward, Ochoa invited Marshall to his lab at NYU, introduced the visitor to his team, and graciously served tea in the library. It was a cordial meeting but ended without any hope of collaboration. With the gauntlet thrown down, Nirenberg confessed later: "To my horror, I found that I enjoyed competing. . . . The competition stimulated me to become more focused and I accomplished far more than I would have in its absence."[37]

The battle of the labs drew the attention of other informed observers. One such insider was Rollin Hotchkiss, then at Rockefeller University and known for his work on DNA. Referring to the Soviet Union's downing of an American U-2 spy plane in May 1960, Hotchkiss quipped: "The U-2 incident started the Cold War, the U-3 incident started the code war."[38] Ochoa and his team used the same fast-track publication pathway in *PNAS* to publish their first paper on deciphering the code. They submitted the manuscript on October 25, a little more than two months after Marshall's breakthrough announcement in Moscow and about three weeks after his initial paper was published in the same journal. The Ochoa paper—the first of nine he produced on this topic—appeared in print on December 1, 1961. In this paper there were two brief, passing references to the work of Nirenberg and Matthaei.[39]

The poly-U experiment had used one of the simplest artificial RNAs—one composed of the single nucleotide base U. There were only three other single-base RNA nucleotides: one with only C, one with only G, and one with only A. At most, these four single-nucleotide chains would drive the synthesis of the monotonic chains of four amino acids. In order to go beyond these simple messages, the NIH and NYU teams needed to work with combinations of various nucleotides. The technology of the day did not permit them to determine the exact sequence of nucleotide bases in the artificial chain, but they could measure the overall proportions of components.

As previously noted, Ochoa had a big advantage when it came to artificial strands of nucleotides. He had produced many for his prior studies and had a library of them stored away in deep freezers. Nirenberg had no background in nucleotide synthesis and no cache of specimens to exploit, with only one postdoctoral fellow working alongside him. What leveled the playing field was the eagerness of Marshall's NIH colleagues to come to his aid. In addition to Martin—who had paused his own research to assist Nirenberg—others quickly signed on. A senior scientist, Leon Heppel, was key to the effort. Heppel, a physician with a PhD in biochemistry, had come to the NIH in 1942. He was one of the first biochemists to work with nucleic acids, and, like Ochoa, he had a freezer full of synthetic RNAs. Not only did he make these specimens available to Marshall, Heppel and his junior colleague Maxine Singer helped make others.

With recycled as well as made-to-order nucleotide strings, the teams could observe how varying the proportions of the component bases would relate to the distribution of amino acids inserted into the resulting products. It was a complicated exercise, but if one knew the overall mix of nucleotides in the instructions and the resulting distribution of amino acids incorporated into the products, then it was possible to begin to link the signal with the response. Fourteen months after the Moscow presentation, Marshall submitted another paper to *PNAS* summarizing results using twenty-two different artificial nucleotide coding fibers. The artificial messages included twelve separate two-base combinations (six mixtures of A and C, four combinations of C and G, and two A and G versions).

Similarly, Marshall and his team studied four different chains with various proportions of three nucleotides, all including various amounts of A, C, and G. They also examined six different artificial coding templates that had all four nucleotides at divergent levels. Assuming that the coding occurred in triplets, the NIH group could assign tentative amino-acid compositions for thirty-four of the sixty-four possible three-letter words. They also found "degeneracy" in the coding—that is to say, a given amino acid may be specified by more than one triplet. For example, the amino acid lysine appeared to be coded by four different nucleotide triplets, all of which began with two A's. To put it another way, if the first two letters of the triplets were both A's, then lysine would be coded regardless of the identity of the third letter in the message. A similar degeneracy existed for the amino acid proline, which was specified by a pair of C's regardless of what third nucleotide base completed the triplet.[40]

Although considerable progress had been made in deciphering the code using random sequences of artificial mRNA, there still were many unknowns. The experimental system allowed qualitative pattern recognition, but it lacked quantitative specificity. A great deal of inference was required, including the most basic question of how many nucleotide bases were required to specify an amino acid. The assumption that three nucleotides were required rested on theory and not on hard experimental evidence. Critically, the randomly ordered artificial messages could suggest the overall composition of the coding units but not necessarily the exact sequences of nucleotides. Nirenberg needed a new way to obtain precise answers on the size of the coding unit and the exact sequencing of bases in it.

A breakthrough came when Nirenberg's team created a second experimental system. With this new approach, they discovered that a three-nucleotide unit could link up with its matching decoding partner—transfer RNA (or tRNA)—and bind to the protein manufacturing machinery in the cell's ribosomes. The bound complex could be trapped on a filter and analyzed for its amino-acid content. In this way, a specific three-letter code could be tied directly to its corresponding amino acid.

By the time that this innovation occurred, Matthaei's two-year postdoctoral fellowship had ended. Although Marshall implored him to stay with the team, it was clear to Matthaei that, as a former trainee, he would not be viewed or treated as Nirenberg's coequal partner. Matthaei felt—with some justification—that he had contributed substantially to the effort but was not the one being invited to make presentations and take the bows. Feeling undervalued and in search of greater independence, Matthaei returned to Germany, where he was hired by the Max Planck Institute and continued to work on the human genetic code.

Although Matthaei's departure was a definite setback to the efforts at NIH, Nirenberg had a steady stream of bright trainees who were eager to join the deciphering work. One of them, who was critical to the success of the second phase of the work using the three-nucleotide binding assay, was Philip Leder. A graduate of Harvard College and Harvard Medical School, Leder arrived at the NIH in 1962 following completion of his medical residency at the University of Minnesota. When Leder joined Nirenberg's lab, the team had grown to nine people. He was assigned responsibility for developing the more precise mRNA binding assay. When they discovered that a three-nucleotide minichain was sufficient for the binding assay to work, the pathway to solving the code was clear: Nirenberg's team needed to assemble all of the sixty-four possible types of triplet in order to run them through the assay.

That was easier said than done; nobody had a freezer full of the sixty-four triplets. The team would have to cook them up from scratch—or so it seemed. Miraculously, Leder came across an advertisement in a European journal for the sale of nucleotide doublets. All of the sixteen possible doublets had been produced, and half-gram amounts were being offered at a cost of $1,500 each. The Nirenberg team ordered the entire set of sixteen, although one was confiscated in transit by US customs agents. Apparently, the white powder in the vials looked suspiciously like illegal drugs, so one vial was removed for testing. Even without the missing vial, the NIH group had prefabricated dyads to which they could separately attach nucleotides to make all sixty-four triads.

One of the trainees in the lab, Merton "Mert" Bernfield, was able to make about half of the triplets using an enzyme that could attach either a U or a C at the end of a doublet. Bernfield, an alumnus of the University of Illinois's medical school and with training in pediatrics at Cornell, negotiated a deal with Nirenberg: Bernfield agreed to do the spadework of making triplets if he was permitted to use the remainder of his time to pursue other interests. With pressure to get the triplets made as quickly as possible, Nirenberg was happy to accommodate Bernfield's request.

The other half of the needed triplets was generated by a team including Leder, Maxine Singer, and Marianne Grunberg-Manago. Singer was a former postdoctoral fellow working for Heppel who stayed on as an independent scientist. Just as Robert Martin had put his own work on

hold to help Nirenberg, Singer selflessly volunteered to assist her colleague. Grunberg-Manago was a French biochemist who was visiting
in Singer's lab at the time. In an interesting twist of fate in the small
world of nucleic acid research, she had worked previously with Ochoa
and had discovered the first enzyme capable of assembling nucleotides
into chains. At NIH, she would partner with Singer and Leder to use
that very same enzyme to construct the triplets required to best Ochoa
in the code-cracking race.

The team making the triplets fed them to Nirenberg, who, with his
two technicians, ran them through the binding assay. Nirenberg would
state later: "It was like a little factory to make these things."[41] Leder remembered the work as all-consuming: "I couldn't sleep for days at a time
because of the excitement. I must admit that it was competitive; there's
no question about that. I would go to bed thinking about the next day's
experiments and then jump out of bed in the morning and rush to the
laboratory. I stayed late at night. It was a lot of work, but the intellectual excitement was enormous."[42] The progress achieved with this new
approach was announced first at the Sixth International Congress of
Biochemistry in New York City during the last week of July 1964. Three
years after his poorly attended initial presentation of the poly-U experiment at the Fifth Congress, Nirenberg was now a headliner and reported equally stunning results. The published description of the new assay
appeared in September 1964,[43] followed by an avalanche of papers over
the next year on specific coding triplets. Recognizing that the NIH's
lead was now insurmountable, Ochoa waved the white flag and pulled
out of the coding race.

As Ochoa departed, another competitor emerged: Har Gobind
Khorana. Born in India, Khorana received a doctorate in organic chemistry at the University of Liverpool, followed by fellowships in Zurich
and at Cambridge. He had done pioneering studies on the synthesis of
small nucleotide strings, so he was well positioned to generate the triplets needed for the coding work. Khorana was able to chemically synthesize all sixty-four of the coding triplets.[44] Equally important, he was
able to create artificial RNA chains with known repetitive sequences of
nucleotides. Some of these chains had just two alternating nucleotides,
others had three in recurrent cycles, and still others had four lined up

over and over. By introducing these artificial messages into a cell-free protein synthesis system, Khorana could relate to the source messages the amino-acid sequences that were produced.[45]

Nirenberg acknowledged that the pressure he felt from Khorana was related to the new competitor's facility with producing man-made messages; in his words Khorana "was the one who devised the techniques and was a leader in the field." Nirenberg added: "It was a race to synthesize those triplets." As to Khorana's contribution to breaking the code, Nirenberg was somewhat dismissive: "Khorana came in very late in the game. He chemically synthesized the 64 triplets after we had already deciphered and had synthesized the triplets enzymatically and had identified the codons. He was a competitor at the very end, or past the end of the work. It didn't mean much at the time because we had already done it, or most of it."[46]

The scorecard for cracking the genetic code was kept on a handwritten chart that Marshall first created on January 18, 1965. At that time, more than half of the sixty-four triplets had been linked to their corresponding amino acids. Updated versions of the chart would be created over the course of the following year as new triplets and their amino-acid products were identified. Each addition was greeted with cheers of "We discovered a new one!"[47] If there was a victory lap for the coding work, it occurred at the Cold Spring Harbor Laboratory in New York—the mecca for geneticists—during the first week of June 1966. Three hundred and fifty scientists were invited to a symposium titled "The Genetic Code." Among the illuminati present were James Watson, Francis Crick, François Jacob, Jacques Monod, Severo Ochoa, and Har Gobind Khorana. In all, at least a dozen current or future Nobel laureates attended.

When he rose to give the opening presentation, Marshall may have experienced a flashback to seven years earlier when he was at this very same location taking an introductory course in bacterial genetics. Or perhaps he reflected on a visit there in June 1963, in the heat of the coding race with Ochoa, when he presented the results of the work using randomly ordered artificial messages.[48] On this day, he presented the summary of the coding assignments as determined by the triplet binding assay.[49]

The story of Marshall Nirenberg's success at cracking the genetic code is, at heart, the story of the NIH. He arrived in Bethesda with little experience, and he provided, at best, only modest early evidence of future promise. Yet, a senior scientist, Gordy Tomkins, recognized Marshall's latent potential and nurtured it. Tomkins encouraged the fledgling researcher to think boldly and to pursue an important subject. When the competition grew intense, Marshall's NIH colleagues rallied to his cause in what DeWitt Stetten—the man who hired Nirenberg but was unimpressed by his early progress—described as "NIH's finest hour." And, indeed, it was.

CHAPTER 7

BEGINNING AT TERMINATION

Marshall Nirenberg and Joseph Goldstein

As Joe Goldstein neared graduation from the University of Texas South-western Medical School, the chairman of medicine, Donald Seldin, mapped out a career development plan for the star student. The first stop was two years of clinical training at Massachusetts General Hospital, then two years of research at the NIH, capped by an additional two years of specialized training in medical genetics. This was all designed with the goal being Goldstein's return to Dallas as a faculty member.

Everything proceeded like clockwork until the unexpected occurred: the intended mentor at the NIH, Gordon Tomkins, accepted an offer to join the medical school faculty at the University of California, San Francisco (UCSF). Tomkins, the brilliant and admired biochemist and aspiring jazz musician, had been the guardian angel for Marshall Nirenberg at NIH. Long before others recognized Marshall's potential, Tomkins rescued and supported the unproven investigator. With Tomkins moving soon to the West Coast, alternative supervision would have to be arranged for Goldstein at NIH.

Plan B turned out to be Marshall Nirenberg's lab. With scores of trainees hoping to work with the man who led the deciphering of the genetic code, Joe Goldstein moved to the head of the line. It helped that Joe knew Edward "Ed" Scolnick, a Clinical Associate already in the Nirenberg lab. Scolnick had attended Harvard for both college and medical school, remaining at MGH for his residency. A year ahead of Goldstein at MGH, Scolnick was impressed by Joe's intellect and skills. As Scolnick was beginning his second year with Nirenberg, he lobbied on behalf of Goldstein: "When I asked him [Nirenberg] if my fellow Massachusetts General Hospital house officer, Joe Goldstein, could join us after Joe's original designated lab no longer existed, he willingly agreed. 'As long as you can squeeze him into your space, he can come. It sounds as if he is a very good person.'"[1]

Goldstein was shoehorned into Nirenberg's crowded lab. Being selected to work with Nirenberg did not necessarily mean that a Clinical Associate would be working on the genetic code. By 1968, when Goldstein arrived, most of the deciphering was complete—the sixty-four nucleotide triplets had all been made and analyzed in relation to the amino acids they specified. Marshall's team was now focused on a key question: When reading the message conveyed by RNA, how does the protein synthesis machinery know when to start and when to stop making a particular protein chain? This was an important inquiry, but Nirenberg's personal attention was being drawn elsewhere.

In his words: "Everything was going beautifully in the lab. I mean, I felt I could do it with one hand tied behind my back. And I was always interested in neurobiology and there were only two systems in biology where information is encoded and retrieved. The gene is one and the brain is the other. So, I decided to switch to neurobiology because I was interested in neurobiology and I didn't know anything about it."[2] This was not the first time that Nirenberg had tacked in a different direction. In 1959, he dropped his prior work on enzymes and switched to the pursuit of the genetic code. That redirection had been risky—"suicidal," in the words of Bruce Ames, an established investigator—but somehow Marshall was still standing. In fact, he was standing quite tall. Now, having virtually solved the enigma of the genetic code, he was ready for a new challenge.

Nirenberg described how he approached this fork in the road:

> For five years, I had worked as hard as I could, flat out, on the code—deciphering the genetic code. It took five years and there were people—postdoctoral fellows in my lab and collaborators who worked on it—a total of maybe 20 people deciphered the code—very much a joint project. And so, on the one hand, I gave all of the postdoctoral fellows in my lab and essentially all of my lab to one of the postdoctoral fellows who was Tom Caskey, who could lead everybody else in the field of protein synthesis. That gave me the time to explore different systems in neurobiology.[3]

Although such a shift in focus was less risky than it had been earlier, hazards remained. As Marshall later admitted:

> I didn't want to fail. When you switch fields, you give up all the things that you have established in the lab—all the methods that you have checked out, all of the information that you have been reading. . . . And you start to read new literature and to think about new problems. So, . . . it was really exhilarating to make this switch, but tough to do it because you want to be productive.[4]

The junior colleague Nirenberg had deputized to complete the coding work, Tom Caskey, was well suited to the task. Like Goldstein, Caskey was a native of South Carolina, although he hailed from a much larger hometown, the state capital of Columbia. Caskey stayed close to home to attend the University of South Carolina, then traveled up the road to Durham, North Carolina, to attend medical school at Duke University. As a student at Duke, Caskey worked for a year doing biochemistry research under the direction of James Wyngaarden. A leader in studies of metabolic diseases, Wyngaarden had spent three years as an Associate at NIH and still maintained strong connections there. Using his contacts, Wyngaarden opened doors of opportunity at the NIH for Caskey—just as he would do later for Michael Brown at MGH.

Caskey arrived at Nirenberg's lab in 1965 after two years of clinical training at Duke. "There were three or four hot laboratories at that time and I met with Marshall and it was clear that he was on to really exciting work on the genetic code. So, I came in to do the code work, I'd say about a third of the way through it and participated in developing the technologies to fill in all of the 64 positions in the [triplets]."[5] Caskey was given top billing among eleven coauthors on the paper that Nirenberg presented at the Cold Spring Harbor symposium in June 1966. That paper, delivered with Caskey in attendance, was the crowning triumph of the code race.

One of the remaining tasks in the genetic code work was to determine, as Nirenberg put it: "Is the code universal? Do higher organisms have the same genetic code [as bacteria]?"[6] Nirenberg turned to Caskey to help answer that question. As Caskey later recalled: "I was the lead scientist on the universality of the genetic code and I never thought that was very important. Marshall always said that was one of the greatest pieces of work we did. I said: 'Marshall, you're just exaggerating.' I couldn't see any other way for the code to work other than universally in all living species."[7] The team had done virtually all of the code-breaking work in cellular extracts from the bacterium *Escherichia coli*. Would the same genetic code that operated in a one-cell bacterium be found in higher-order animals? To answer this question, the Nirenberg team set up triplet cell-free binding assays in which the RNA triplets were measured separately from *E. coli*, a frog, and a guinea pig. The same basic pattern of genetic coding was observed across these selected bacteria, amphibians, and mammals. Nirenberg noted: "Small variations in the code have been found in some organisms under certain circumstances, but all organisms that have been tested . . . use the same standard code. So, this strongly suggests that the code originated very early in biological evolution—that all forms of life on this planet are derived from common ancestors and that we are all related."[8] For Nirenberg, who since childhood had been fascinated by the diversity of nature, finding a shared mode of inheritance was a powerful—almost spiritual—revelation.

When Joe Goldstein arrived at the Nirenberg lab, he was given a choice: signing up for the final phase of the genetic code work with Caskey and Scolnick, or joining Marshall in the neuroscience program. For

Goldstein, it was an easy choice, as he thought that the neurobiology efforts were "very vague. . . . I'd known Ed Scolnick well at the MGH— he was a resident of mine. He told me how exciting the genetic code work was . . . and how great it was to work with Tom. . . . So, I chose that route."[9] At that time, the final phase of the code work, appropriately enough, focused on termination of protein synthesis. The team wanted to know: When the full complement of amino acids has been added, one after another, and the protein chain is complete, what causes the translation process to stop?

For Joe Goldstein, there were some initial bumps in the road, as he recalled: "In the very beginning, for the first few months, I was sort of lost and then I found my way and . . . [the other associates] . . . were really helpful. . . . It was intense and it was a lot of fun."[10] One did not have to look far for assistance, as Caskey described: "We were jammed in like sardines and if you had two feet of bench space, you were lucky. We were moving so fast at that time and we didn't have much space—you had to make do."[11]

The intimacy of the work environment required a certain amount of tolerance among the Associates. Goldstein described Ed Scolnick as "the most mercurial of the group. He was terrific and really smart. Whenever his experiments would work, he would be the most elated person in the world, and when they didn't, he would be really down."[12] Tall and thin, Scolnick would "hover over me [Goldstein] when I'd be watching my results on the scintillation [radioactivity] counter. He would try to interpret them before I could."[13] The good-natured competitive streak in Scolnick would carry him far. He would later discover an important genetic mutation that disturbs signaling between cells leading to cancer development. Professionally, he would also serve as president of research laboratories at the pharmaceutical giant Merck.

As for Caskey, with only three years at NIH before Goldstein arrived, the junior colleague found him to be "a really good boss. He would subtly get you to work harder and harder without demeaning you or criticizing. . . . He was good about that."[14] He was so good, in fact, that Caskey would go on to identify the underlying genetic defects in a couple dozen different major inheritable diseases and would patent the DNA-based test for personal identification used by crime-solving agencies worldwide. Caskey would move from academics to industry, serving as a senior vice president at Merck and participating in the massive Human Genome Project. There were no underachievers in the Nirenberg lab.

On a day-to-day basis, Caskey was running the show as Nirenberg's attention increasingly was drawn toward his neuroscience work in partnership with fellow NIH scientist Phillip Nelson. Occasionally, Nirenberg would seek updates on the coding work from his team. Ed Scolnick recalled vividly his initiation into the reporting process to the big boss: "I remember the first time Marshall popped in and said: 'Come on in and tell me what you're doing.' And I started to say to him: 'Well, here's my data.' And he said, 'I don't want to see your data. Tell me how you did the experiment.' I'll never forget this. 'How did you do the experiment?'" Scolnick continued: "And I started to explain to him what I did, which wasn't what he wanted. He said: 'No, no, tell me from the beginning how you did the experiment.' In that meeting, he taught me how you really do science—the experimental approach; the bookkeeping. The solution books, the meticulousness with which you have to know" the reagents being used, and the order in which to add them while avoiding inadvertent mixing. "I learned more in that hour with Marshall than I had in all my prior time working in laboratories. It was eye-opening."[15]

The work that Scolnick, Caskey, and Goldstein were conducting on the termination of protein synthesis was not on the identity of the RNA coding stop signal. That had been determined already. It was known that three of the sixty-four triplets were stop signals. These triplets involved combinations of two or three different nucleotides—uracil (U), adenine (A), and guanine (G)—in specific sequences. These three stop signals were UAA, UAG, and UGA. In 1967, Mario Capecchi, a graduate student at Harvard working with James Watson, demonstrated that there was a "release factor" that removed the completed protein from the manufacturing apparatus in the cell's factory for protein production.[16]

Once the release factor had been identified, the team in Nirenberg's lab was determined to find a way to study this process in greater depth. It required the development of yet another assay, namely, an experimental system that allowed the measurement of the biological processes and products. As Caskey pointed out: "What kept Marshall ahead of the game was he kept coming up with innovative assays."[17] The first such example—and the most famous—was the cell-free system that he perfected with Heinrich Matthaei in 1961 for initially reading the poly-U artificial message and then randomly ordered strings of nucleotide message chains. The second game-changing model was the triplet binding model that he developed with Philip Leder in 1964 that facilitated completing assignments for all sixty-four RNA coding triplets. The third assay was developed with Tom Caskey beginning in 1967 and created a way to study the termination process. Years later, Caskey made it sound easy: "We developed this incredibly simple way of measuring chain termination and isolated the proteins and purified them. . . . The simplicity of the assay was what enabled us to win."[18]

Although the concept of the chain termination assay may have been straightforward in theory, developing and optimizing it required painstaking effort. As Scolnick later described:

After a year of pretty much getting nowhere in the project based upon an assay that Tom Caskey dreamed up, we had an in-road into the problem and then for a couple of months the research went really spectacularly well. We made some absolutely novel discoveries, creative discoveries, the most important of which occurred sometime in the late Summer of '68 [shortly after Joe Goldstein's arrival], which really changed my life completely in research.[19]

Scolnick went on to chronicle this eureka moment. While Caskey was on vacation, Scolnick and a technician were working to purify the release factor that Capecchi had first described. "It was late in the day and it was really terrific. We had found this termination factor." As they continued to run the purification instrument, about an hour later around dinnertime, just as they thought that they had captured all of the release factor, "there was a second peak . . . and that was completely unexpected—a really surprising result, and in looking at it, I said: 'Well, we can't go home now!'"[20] When they checked the two isolated products against the three known termination triplets, they found that one of the isolated factors recognized two of the three stop signals (UAA and UAG), whereas the second isolated factor recognized one stop signal in common (UAA) but also recognized uniquely the third stop signal (UGA).

Three decades later, Scolnick still felt the euphoria of the moment: "We knew we had really cracked the mechanism of the chain termination and that we had the factors that recognized triplets and they were proteins, not transfer RNA's which is what recognize the rest of the genetic code. We were sure it was right." With Caskey away on vacation, Scolnick elected to go straight to the top: "I called Marshall at home . . . this was pretty late, maybe eight o'clock at night—and told him what we had found. His first question was prototypic of Marshall. He said: 'Are you sure it's reproducible?' And I said: 'It's reproducible. You can tell from the data.'" He continued: "I went over to his house and showed him the data. He was just as excited as we were. We finished up pretty late and went home, and I realized at that point that I could never not do research. The excitement—the high involved with that discovery was so great that it was like being addicted to something."[21]

The rush of adrenaline quickly became a rush to publication, and on August 17, 1968—only six weeks after Goldstein arrived at NIH—his colleagues submitted a manuscript on their finding of not one but *two* separate protein release factors that responded to one shared and two separate stop signals.[22] The article appeared in print on October 1, 1968. About two weeks later, on Wednesday, October 16, 1968, an even bigger announcement occurred: three American scientists (Robert Holley of Cornell University, Har Gobind Khorana of the University of Wisconsin, and Marshall Nirenberg of the NIH) were selected to receive the Nobel Prize in Physiology or Medicine for their interpretation of the genetic code and its function in protein synthesis. At the age of forty-one and hardly more than a decade after completing his doctoral degree, Marshall had been tapped for the highest recognition in scientific discovery.

"When I received a call from Stockholm, at first I thought that the boys in the lab were playing a trick on me—were having fun," recalled Nirenberg.[23] Although his protégés in the lab were not averse to a good joke, they were just as surprised as their boss. As Caskey relived the events years later: "It was a fantastic day. I had come in early to work, which was my habit, and somehow I had missed the radio announcement;

so I was working in the lab when my wife, Peggy, called and said that she had heard on the news that Marshall had been awarded the Nobel Prize for his work on the genetic code. So, immediately the word spread."[24]

In preparation for Nirenberg's arrival on campus, the team prepared a clever banner that they hung in the hallway: "UUU are Great MARSHALL." It was, after all, the poly-U experiment that had catapulted Nirenberg onto the international stage as the front-runner in the genetic code race. "Eventually, Marshall came to the laboratory about mid-morning, and we were, of course, celebrating and having a good time laughing and joking with him when about that time the formal phone call came through. . . . We were drinking champagne out of beakers," Caskey said with a smile.[25] The symbolism was perfect—Nirenberg receiving the official call in his crowded laboratory surrounded by his team of bright and dedicated associates.

As might be expected, a whirlwind of activities ensued, beginning with an official press conference so that the NIH leadership could acknowledge publicly the first scientist on the Bethesda campus to win a Nobel Prize. Nirenberg would be followed by four other recipients: Julius Axelrod (1970), Christian Anfinsen (1972), Carleton Gajdusek (1976), and Martin Rodbell (1994). Not only was Nirenberg the first, he was by far the youngest (Axelrod, Anfinsen, and Gajdusek were all in their fifties when selected, and Rodbell was almost seventy). Even when compared with other scientific superstars, Nirenberg's major recognition occurred very early in his professional career.

Once the official NIH press conference was over, the remainder of this momentous day became a family affair. Marshall and his wife and fellow NIH scientist, Perola Zaltzman Nirenberg, hosted the lab at their Bethesda home. "I can remember being at his house with everybody so excited and with little kids running around, and Perola hosting this disjointed group of people who were just happy over the day's events." Caskey continued: "Later that evening we moved to this restaurant on Wisconsin Avenue and we had . . . a banquet that evening. Again, Marshall and Perola were there. Now, the children were gone, and it was mainly scientists that evening."[26]

After the celebratory events ended, the lab attempted to return to normal, or at least as close to normal as possible under the circumstances. The team of Caskey, Scolnick, Goldstein, and colleagues redoubled their efforts to delineate the process of termination of protein synthesis. Within five months they submitted another publication on this topic. This paper, unlike its predecessor on the two release factors, did not list Nirenberg as a coauthor, although he communicated it to the journal and was acknowledged by the authors for his contributions. This was not an act of modesty on Nirenberg's part, although even after winning a Nobel Prize he remained a remarkably humble person. Rather, this likely was a calculated decision to avoid any perception that he was the intellectual force behind the work and that his four junior colleagues were only following his lead. By sitting on the authorship sidelines, he was offering a vote of confidence in the independence of the team of associates he had assembled. With Goldstein as the second author, the team identified a new component, with the characteristics of a protein, that was a "stimulatory" factor for the rate at which the finished proteins were unbound by the two previously identified release factors.[27]

This paper, published in May 1969 (not quite a year after Goldstein joined the lab), laid the groundwork for the first manuscript that Goldstein would prepare as lead author. Four decades later, the former trainee still remembered the intimidating experience of crafting a paper with Marshall Nirenberg: "Tom [Caskey] and I would go through many drafts and then we would have a scheduled meeting with Marshall after he read the paper. That required going in about every day to say: 'Have you read the paper?' Finally, he had read the paper. Then, we all sort of wished we had not gone in, because when we got the paper, there were marks in black ink, in blue ink, in red ink—like he had read it three times." He continued: "In fact, I can specifically remember his saying the first time: 'Tom, I'm really surprised at you. You've been through this with me. Then, he looked at me and said: 'This is your first time, so you're off the hook, but go read the papers of Arthur Kornberg, Earl Stadtman, and Maxine Singer.' Those are the people that he mentioned."[28]

It would have been easy, and perhaps expected, for Nirenberg to refer his trainees to his own papers, many of which were considered instant classics. But instead of holding himself up as a paragon of scientific writing, he pointed to other current or former NIH scientists that he admired. Kornberg, who worked at NIH for more than a decade, had won a Nobel Prize in 1959 along with Severo Ochoa, earning him the moniker "the Emperor of Enzymes." Stadtman, who spent his entire career at NIH and won the National Medal of Science, was known for his rigorous approach, described with reverence on campus as "the Stadtman Way." Singer, another recipient of the National Medal of Science, was Nirenberg's collaborator on the genetic code work. Together they were something of a dream team of scientific writing, and Nirenberg was secure enough to point his trainees to their publications rather than to his own.

After many drafts, Nirenberg finally was content with the Goldstein paper, and on November 7, 1969, he communicated it to the *Proceedings of the National Academy of Sciences*. It was published four months later. This contribution expanded their earlier identification of the stimulatory factor. They purified it and assured that it was distinct and different from other proteins involved in the translation process. Then, they identified its likely role in assisting with the recognition of the coding stop signal.[29]

Before the end of his two-year fellowship, Goldstein would produce two more papers as lead author. In one, he demonstrated that the UAA stop signal that had been studied in bacterial systems similarly terminated protein synthesis in mammalian cell extracts, specifically those derived from the cells of a rabbit.[30] In the other paper, published a month later, Goldstein and Caskey showed that there were three distinct steps in the cell-free model of termination of protein synthesis.[31] During his time at NIH, Goldstein was the lead author on three papers and a coauthor on three others. This is an unusually high rate of productivity and reflected favorably on Goldstein's strong work ethic and the exceptional support structure of colleagues. All these articles were published in high-impact journals, as would be expected of a lab of such international stature.

In addition to learning how to craft a scientific paper, Goldstein later identified two other aspects of his training in the Nirenberg lab that served him well. As a mnemonic, he referred to these lessons as the "Three *P*'s":

1. **Purification**—the process of cleansing proteins from the many contaminants in biological systems.[32] He had spent much of his fellowship working on isolating the stimulatory protein. In order to obtain a pure sample of this protein, it had to be separated out laboriously from the sea of other compounds, including the myriad of other proteins, in the experimental system. In the days when Goldstein was learning the process, removing contaminants was a tedious, multistep exercise. The purification of biological molecules typically involved exploiting unique characteristics such as size, electrical charge, and ability to dissolve in various reagents. Progress was monitored by measuring the amount of material and its biological activity. Charting these parameters gave the trainee a sense of the importance of quantitative assessment in the laboratory. For a scientist, no skill is more critical than precision and accuracy in measurement.

2. **Poly-U**—the classic experiment that had launched Nirenberg, and the community of molecular biologists, on the path to deciphering the genetic code. In Goldstein's words: "Great discoveries come from imaginative experiments."[33] Although it is advantageous to gain an initial insight into how a biological phenomenon can be studied, it is equally important to get all of the variables—temperature, acidity, added ingredients—just right. This is the reason that Nirenberg wanted to know, in exquisite detail, how Scolnick had performed his experiments, starting from the very beginning rather than with the data produced. Every aspect of the design and execution of an experiment is crucial, down to the details of composition, source, and characteristics of the reagents deployed.

3. **Papers**—alluding to lessons learned as to how to write clearly, accurately, and precisely. Even the framing content of the captions on figures and tables must convey to readers exactly what was done and what was observed. The main points of the article should be evident by perusing these descriptors, and Goldstein has taught his own students the importance of constructing "legendary legends" in their publications.[34]

With a laugh, Goldstein added: "If you master these three P's, with a little luck, the fourth P will come—prizes."[35] He had the rare privilege of sitting in a ringside seat when his mentor won the highest honor in science—a Nobel Prize. To witness such an event is inspiring, but like Nirenberg himself, Joe Goldstein did not set this as a goal or expectation. Both mentor and apprentice—whose discoveries, in turn, would be groundbreaking and celebrated—retained remarkable modesty and a soft-spoken reserve. For both of them, it is probably fair to say that winning prizes was at best a pleasant sidelight, if not an actual distraction, from their true aspiration, which was to understand basic biological processes.

It was Nirenberg's style to treat everyone with respect—from technicians who worked alongside him for decades, to trainees, to colleagues, and even to competitors. Caskey illustrated this quality by comparing Nirenberg with his other admired mentor, James Wyngaarden, his research adviser at the Duke University School of Medicine. Speaking of Wyngaarden, Caskey said: "I always had great respect for him, but he was the professor." In contrast: "Marshall Nirenberg was my collaborator. I mean, that's a different attitude and Marshall developed and encouraged that attitude."[36]

Had Goldstein learned nothing but the catechism of the Three *P*'s during his two years at NIH, it would have been time well spent. However, there was another dimension to his work that proved important to his future as an investigator. In addition to working in the lab purifying and analyzing proteins, he was obligated to care for patients treated at the NIH Clinical Center. Admittedly, the bedside work occupied a modest portion of his time, which he estimated at about 20 percent, and it was required only during his first year. The amount and type of patient care for Clinical Associates varied by institute, and for Goldstein, working in the National Heart Institute, his principal task was to admit patients, and "if you found anything [abnormal], you'd have to do a typical work-up," he noted. "I guess that's why they probably liked people [Clinical Associates] from the MGH and Columbia and places like that who had good clinical training. If you found anything that was unusual, you had to alert the investigator who was responsible for the patients." He added: "You were there basically if an emergency came up."[37]

Unlike the PhD researchers, such as Nirenberg and Earl Stadtman, who were engaged in very basic laboratory studies, the NIH scientists studying these patients were physicians. Some of the era's superstars in clinical research were on the NIH staff. One such example was Frederic "Fred" Bartter. A graduate of Harvard Medical School, Bartter undertook clinical training at MGH. He was recruited to the NIH in 1951 and would head the Endocrinology Branch of the Heart Institute. Bartter is most associated with the hereditary syndrome that he first described in 1962 and that bears his name. In this condition, patients have a disorder of kidney function that gives rise to diminished blood levels of potassium and, to a lesser extent, chloride.[38] Bartter studied a range of diseases while at NIH, including hormonal disorders and associated metabolic alternations.

Cholesterol is a waxy compound needed by the body to help protect nerves, produce hormones, and build the defensive walls of cells. Lipoproteins are clever packages in which cholesterol and other water-hating molecules are encased within a water-friendly envelope to facilitate transport within aqueous solutions, such as blood. Lipoproteins come in several flavors, of which two have gotten the most public attention. One is high-density lipoprotein (HDL), the so-called good cholesterol, because it removes circulating blood cholesterol by transporting it to the liver, where it is broken down into bile salts. The other is low-density lipoprotein (LDL), the so-called bad cholesterol, because it can be deposited into clogging plaques within arterial walls, including those of the heart, thereby reducing the flow of oxygen-carrying blood to the tissues. Donald Fredrickson was known for identifying patients with inherited aberrations in metabolism of lipoproteins and lipids.

One of the early examples of these genetic disorders arose in 1959 when a five-year-old boy named Teddy Laird came to the attention of scientists at the NIH Clinical Center. Teddy lived on Tangier Island in Chesapeake Bay and, like many children during that era, had his tonsils removed to prevent recurrent infections. Unlike other children, however, Teddy's tonsils were very large and orange in color. Examination under a microscopic indicated that the tonsils were loaded with deposits of cholesterol. In 1960, Fredrickson and Teddy's NIH doctor traveled to Tangier Island to see if they could find the condition in any other residents. Only Teddy's sister had the telltale swollen, orange tonsils, and examination of the blood of the siblings revealed that they both lacked almost any HDL. The NIH team discovered more modest reductions in

HDL among Teddy's parents and other relatives. They named the condition Tangier Disease, concluding that it was a rare, inherited disorder.[39]

Fredrickson studied many other patients with abnormal lipoprotein
levels, including families who, like those on Tangier Island, appeared to
have inherited disorders of cholesterol metabolism. One such patient
was admitted by Joe Goldstein to the NIH Clinical Center. She was a
seven-year-old girl who had first experienced angina on exertion at the
age of three. Angina is a squeezing type of pressure in the chest that
occurs when the heart muscle is not getting enough oxygen, usually because of a blockage in one or more heart arteries. This condition typically occurs in people in their fifth decade of life or older. To observe
it in someone who was barely old enough to enter elementary school
was startling. When Goldstein first met her, the patient could not walk
across her hospital room without experiencing chest pain. Even more
disturbing, this young girl had suffered a heart attack at age six. As if
this was not a tragic enough story, she had a brother two years older who
had the exact same condition. Given the severity of their symptoms and
underlying illness, both children were hospitalized at the NIH Clinical
Center on an essentially permanent basis.[40]

Goldstein's patient had a different lipoprotein problem than was seen
in Tangier Disease. The siblings had total cholesterol levels about eight
times the normal amount for children their ages. The excess was almost
entirely in the form of LDL (the bad cholesterol). The surplus of cholesterol circulating in her blood was being deposited in her arteries, including her heart arteries, giving rise to angina and heart attacks. When the
doctors tried to reduce cholesterol in her diet, even lowering it to zero,
there was no reduction in the amount of cholesterol in her blood.[41]

Today, there are treatments that could be used to lower her LDL cholesterol and address blockages of heart arteries, but in 1968 physicians
did not have much to offer. At the time, the use of leg veins to surgically
bypass blocked heart arteries was just being introduced for adults. An-
gioplasty—the use of catheters with attached balloons to snake into the
areas of blockage and flatten the obstructing plaques—was more than
a decade away from introduction in the United States. Moreover, statin drugs—powerful LDL-lowering agents—would not be developed
and approved for human use by the Food and Drug Administration

until 1987, almost two decades into the future. Goldstein's patient did not have time to wait for the development of these new treatments; her blockages were already present and placing her at very high risk of a potentially fatal heart attack.[42]

As was his custom during his residency, Joe Goldstein told Mike Brown about the little girl with sky-high cholesterol and the advanced heart disease. The occurrence of the disorder, known as familial hypercholesterolemia (see discussion in chapter 13), within siblings strongly suggested an underlying genetic cause. The parents of these children had elevated LDLs as well, but only about twice the normal level. The excess LDL in the parents was sufficient to place them at high risk for heart attacks, but not until adulthood. The parents had a milder form of the condition because they each had only one defective copy of the gene. This single-copy gene defect frequency varied by population, but on average it occurred in about one in 500 persons. The severe form of the disease, as manifested in the siblings, required having two defective copies of the gene—one inherited from each parent. This was a much less common situation, occurring on average about once in a million persons. So, even a doctor who specialized in treating cholesterol disorders might never see one of these severely affected children. The siblings had come all the way from Houston to the NIH Clinical Center because it was the world leader for diagnosing and studying inherited cholesterol abnormalities.

Since they first met in Boston during clinical training, Goldstein and Brown had developed a shared zeal for understanding disease processes at a much more fundamental level. Why were some people affected with a particular condition while others went unaffected? What was the underlying biological problem? In the case of the little girl from Texas, did she have such an overload of LDL cholesterol because her body produced too much? Was there some uncontrolled stimulation for the production system for LDL cholesterol? Alternatively, was there a failure of the normal "off-switch" that stops production of LDL cholesterol when it gets too high? If production was not elevated, was she somehow failing to eliminate LDL cholesterol appropriately? Or was there yet some other possible explanation? In 1968, even the gurus in the field—those who would define the entire classification scheme for inherited disorders of lipoproteins—did not have a clue.

As Joe Goldstein prepared to leave NIH for the next phase of his training (a fellowship in medical genetics at the University of Washington), he would not forget the young patient with familial hypercholesterolemia that he treated at the Clinical Center. Somebody had to figure out what was causing her to experience such devastating illness. Why not him?

CHAPTER 8

FOLLOWING THE RIGHT PATH

Earl Stadtman

For Earl Stadtman, a life in science began in fertile soil or, more precisely, in the pursuit of fertile soil. As a teenager during the Great Depression, Stadtman earned pocket change doing yard work for homeowners in San Bernardino, California. Located about sixty miles east of Los Angeles on the iconic Route 66, San Bernardino was one of the anchor cities, along with Ontario, Redlands, and Riverside, of the so-called Inland Empire, ruled by Emperor Orange, which was introduced into local agriculture in the late nineteenth century. In this semiarid climate of sunny, dry summers and cool, moist winters, citrus farming (and before that cultivation of grapes) was made possible by irrigation systems fed by local aquifers. The fine, friable, sandy loam soil around San Bernardino had good drainage and was ideal for orange groves.[1] Navel[2] and Valencia[3] oranges brought prosperity to the region, or at least to the growers, well into the twentieth century. When Stadtman was a teenager in San

Bernardino, the town was surrounded by more than sixty square miles of orange groves.

Even with favorable growing conditions, Stadtman's yard-work clients wanted to get a competitive edge on their neighbors. They asked him about soil additives that might be used to improve lawns and plants. After hearing the same question again and again, the enterprising Stadtman saw a business opportunity. His plan was to go to college and study soil science, then set up a soil-testing laboratory in order to analyze samples and advise customers on which fertilizers to use. After graduating from high school, he dutifully enrolled in San Bernardino Valley College in 1937, finishing two years later.

Using money saved from mowing lawns and a loan from their sister, Stadtman and his brother each paid the $27.50 registration fee for enrollment at the University of California, Berkeley. The loan was sufficient for them to buy textbooks, but it was not enough money to pay for other expenses, so both brothers got jobs working in a boardinghouse that had twenty student residents. Earl washed dishes three times a day, and as if his hands were not immersed in enough soapy water, he also got a job washing glassware in a university laboratory, earning about $40 a month. Between cleaning jobs, he also took classes, one of which included soil microbiology taught by Horace Albert "H. A." Barker.[4] Barker, not yet thirty-three years old, was a junior faculty member, having joined the Agricultural Experiment Station of the university in 1936.

A native of Oakland, California, Barker was an outdoor enthusiast, and his fascination with the natural world attracted him to his undergraduate major (biology). He graduated from Stanford University in 1929 and stayed there for graduate studies, initially biology and then biochemistry. He was awarded a PhD in 1933 and was accepted as the first postdoctoral fellow of an assistant professor named Cornelius Bernardus "C. B." van Niel. A Dutch microbiologist, van Niel trained at the famed Delft Microbiology Laboratory and in late 1929 came to California to work at Stanford's Hopkins Marine Station.[5]

At the Hopkins Marine Lab, Barker was introduced to the "Delft School" scientific approach that van Niel had learned. Dutch investigators focused on what they described as microbial ecology, meaning the study of how various environmental characteristics, such as the presence or absence of oxygen, influence organisms that live in a particular setting. The primary focus of the Delft research was the biochemical pathways that allowed bacteria to adapt to their surroundings.[6] Barker was so impressed by van Niel's laboratory and pedagogical skills that he decided to undertake a further year of training under van Niel's Delft professor, the renowned biochemist Albert Kluyver.

Kluyver, whom van Niel characterized as "the Master," was the founder of the field of comparative microbiology and spent his career studying the metabolic processes of bacteria. In 1926, with colleague Hendrick Donker, Kluyver advanced the radical proposition of "*die Einheit in der Biochemie*" (Unity in Biochemistry). In essence, Kluyver and Donker proposed that basic biochemical processes in cellular metabolism are similar across species.[7] Kluyver expressed the theory memorably in a dictum: "From the elephant to the butyric acid bacterium—it is all the same!"[8] During his year working under Kluyver, Barker initiated work on aspects of bacterial metabolism that would become the template for the rest of his career. He adopted the methods of his second Dutch mentor for measuring the amounts of materials on which the bacteria fed and the products of their consumption.[9] Barker made his own contributions to that effort by painstakingly isolating two previously unidentified bacteria. Later, he named one of these new organisms *Clostridium kluyverii* in honor of his mentor.[10]

When Barker returned to the United States, he took a position on the faculty at the University of California, working as a soil microbiologist at the Agricultural Experiment Station.[11] As it turned out, Barker was in need of a technician, and Stadtman, then a senior, was selected to help with various activities such as growing cultures. Stadtman graduated in 1942, and as he was preparing to leave, his soil physics professor, Dr. Geoffrey Bodman, asked Earl if he had learned anything in his coursework there. Stadtman replied that his goal had been to learn how to test soil to advise clients on choosing fertilizers, but, expressing some dismay, he learned that it was a fool's errand. Without missing a beat, the professor replied: "Well, Stadtman, if you learned that, then your time here has not been wasted."[12]

Stadtman attempted to enlist in the United States Navy, but the overworked and underfed candidate was rejected when he failed to meet the weight requirement. After a year of conducting topographic work for a military access road across Alaska, Stadtman returned to Berkeley; Barker hired him in 1943 to work on a government-funded project related to the war effort.[13] In addition to studying dried apricots (see note 13 above), he published his first five scientific papers describing, among other things, the effects of temperature,[14] moisture,[15] oxygen,[16] and sugars[17] on the deterioration of dried fruits.

There was another fortuitous byproduct of the apricot work: while working in the Food Technology Department in 1943, Stadtman met Thressa "Terry" Campbell. Two years younger than Earl, Terry was assigned to the same department to work with a bacteriologist named Reese H. Vaughn, an expert on food spoilage. Stadtman mistook Terry for a new dishwasher and asked her out to dinner. She accepted the offer, and it was only later that evening, as they dined in San Francisco, that he learned the truth: not only was she a research assistant, she also had a master's degree. Reflecting back on that first date, Terry recalled that her dinner companion was "intimidated."[18]

Working in the all-male bastion of soil microbiology, Terry Campbell relied on the skills of self-sufficiency and resiliency that she developed early in life. A native of upstate New York, her father's sudden and unexpected death when Terry was only eleven years old left the family farm in financial uncertainty during the depths of the Great Depression. Despite such challenges, Campbell went on to graduate from high school as the valedictorian of her class at sixteen. She won a New York State Regents Scholarship to attend Cornell University, where she majored in microbiology and graduated in 1940. She remained at Cornell for graduate work in microbiology and nutrition, completing a master of science degree in 1942. She decided to pursue doctoral studies at the University of California, where a chance laboratory encounter led to a dinner date and, later that year, to a marriage with Earl Stadtman.

The newlyweds undertook their doctoral studies with Barker. Terry's project involved the study of methane gas production from two different types of bacteria. Not only did she investigate these bacteria; she actually discovered them in samples that she dug up from the heavily polluted black mud in San Francisco Bay. This was not a pleasant task, as the mud flats produced hydrogen sulfide—also known as "sewer gas" due to its distinctive rotten-egg stench. As unwelcome as this aroma may have been, for Terry Stadtman, searching for anaerobic bacteria—those that survive only in the absence of oxygen—there was no more idyllic scent. The oxygen-hating microbes that she studied were producers of methane gas. Methane is a colorless, odorless gas discovered by the Italian physicist Alessandro Volta (which he collected from Lake Maggiore in northern Italy for study and later characterized as "inflammable air native of marshes").

The role of bacteria in producing methane was discovered in 1906 by Nicolaas Louis Söhngen, the first doctoral degree recipient at the Delft School of Microbiology.[19] The most common environmental setting in nature for bacterial generation of methane is where organic material is decomposed in oxygen-deficient settings, such as underwater or in solid-waste landfills. In addition, methane-producing bacteria thrive in the digestive tracts of many animals, especially ruminants, such as cows. (Extraction of fossil fuels has become a major contributor to atmospheric methane, which now is recognized as a potent greenhouse gas, estimated to account for about a quarter of man-made global warming.)

One of the methane-producing bacteria that Terry Stadtman discovered was unique in that the only organic material that it could digest was formate, a salt of the simplest of all organic acids, with only one carbon atom. Stadtman and Barker named this new, fast-growing, self-propelling bacterium *Methanococcus vannielii* in honor of C. B. van Niel, Barker's mentor and a pioneer in the field of methane-producing bacteria.[20] The other bacterium that Terry Stadtman isolated from the black mud of San Francisco Bay had an aroma that only a discoverer could love. This organism produced putrescine and cadaverine—chemicals aptly named for their rancid smells. Stadtman later named this organism *Clostridium sticklandii* after Leonard Hubert Stickland, a biochemist at Cambridge University. Although it may seem off-putting to have one's name associated with such a foul-smelling organism, Stickland identified the chemical reactions used by certain *Clostridia*, including this one, to break down amino acids for energy.[21] Terry and Barker published four research papers from her dissertation research on methane-producing bacteria.

While Terry Stadtman concentrated on methane-producing bacteria, her husband worked with Barker on another topic altogether. Barker had offered to allow Stadtman to write up his work on dried apricot deterioration as a dissertation, but Stadtman was not looking for the easy way out. He wanted to experience a full apprenticeship under Barker, so he decided to study *Clostridium kluyverii*, the bacterium that Barker had isolated from the canals of Delft and named after his mentor there.[22] Barker had conducted prior studies that demonstrated the ability of *Clostridium kluyverii* to use simple chemical building blocks to construct more complex molecules. Specifically, this anaerobic bacterium could attach the two-carbon compound ethanol to the two-carbon salt molecule acetate to construct fatty acids with short chains of carbon atoms.

One of the innovative aspects of Barker's work was that the process of assembling the two-carbon fragments together was followed using radioactively labeled molecules. Radioactive isotopes were not yet available to most biochemists, but Barker had an important advantage: he was working at the University of California, Berkeley, which had established a Radiation Laboratory.[23]

Barker's initial work with carbon-14 focused on the genesis of fatty acids from basic molecular building blocks in a three-step process.[24] He characterized this process in a paper published jointly with both Terry and Earl Stadtman.[25] Despite training at the same time with the same mentor and working for more than a half-century in adjacent laboratories, Earl and Terry Stadtman would publish only three papers together. This trio of joint papers came from a combined portfolio of more than 550 scholarly contributions. Perhaps in part because they maintained separate and distinct yet parallel research interests and identities, Terry and Earl Stadtman enjoyed a happy marriage of more than sixty years.

When necessary, wife and husband were quick to support one another. An early example was Earl's doctoral work. The experimental system he used to measure the production of fatty acids was cumbersome. The process of growing, maintaining, and studying intact microorganisms was tedious and time-consuming. Earl's entire approach was redirected after the Stadtmans' visit to Terry's alma mater, Cornell University.

There, Terry's former undergraduate adviser, the biochemist Irwin "Gunny" Gunsalus, had been working with cell-free experimental systems to study vitamin B6 in bacteria.[26]

Gunny invited Earl into his lab to demonstrate how bacterial cell suspensions could be dried and then ground up to release enzymes for study. Upon returning to Berkeley, Stadtman successfully implemented Gunny's technique with Delft bacteria. With Barker, Stadtman published an initial paper describing how these cell-free extracts were made.[27] Then, in rapid succession, five more publications followed up on the mechanisms of fatty-acid generation and decomposition. The fact that the enzymes worked, even in the absence of the structure and function of a living bacterium, defied the expectations of many microbial biochemists and opened up opportunities for studying many other metabolic processes.

When Terry and Earl Stadtman completed their doctorates in 1949, they bid a sad farewell to their mentor, Barker. In search of further training opportunities, they found postdoctoral positions in two different laboratories in Boston. Earl received an Atomic Energy Commission fellowship to work in the Biochemical Research Laboratory at Massachusetts General Hospital. The laboratory was headed by Fritz Lipmann, a native of Königsberg, the capital of East Prussia. Born at the turn of the twentieth century, Lipmann completed a medical degree in Berlin, followed by a doctorate in chemistry supervised by Otto Meyerhof, who four years earlier was a corecipient of the 1922 Nobel Prize in Physiology or Medicine. Meyerhof was thus honored demonstrating that muscles, in order to fuel their work, consume oxygen and sugars and produce lactic acid as a byproduct. Not long before receiving the Nobel Prize, Meyerhof was denied the position of chair of physiology at the University of Kiel due to the rising anti-Semitism in Germany. Meyerhof was hired into a temporary position at the Kaiser Wilhelm Institute, where Lipmann, also Jewish, served for four years as his assistant.

At the time, the Kaiser Wilhelm Institute was a mecca for biochemists, with Meyerhof and four other future Nobel laureates in Physiology or Medicine (Otto Warburg, 1931; Hans Krebs, 1953; Fritz Lipmann, 1953; and Severo Ochoa, 1959). Such an assemblage of medical research talent at a single moment in time would occur in very few places (a couple of which will be discussed in later chapters). Following his time with Meyerhof, Lipmann secured a post with Albert Fisher at the Kaiser Wilhelm Institute before joining the Carlsberg Foundation's Biological Institute in Copenhagen. Seven productive years in Copenhagen came to an abrupt end with Adolf Hitler's rise to power, and in 1939 Lipmann escaped Europe for the United States, going first to Cornell Medical School, then to Massachusetts General Hospital.

In 1941, Lipmann wrote a landmark paper on the role that high-energy phosphate chemical bonds play in driving many physical activities, including muscle contraction, as well as biochemical reactions, such as the manufacture of proteins and other large biological molecules.[28] A few years later, Lipmann discovered and later named an important molecule, Coenzyme A (CoA).[29] Enzymes are molecules, usually made of proteins, that speed up biochemical reactions, including virtually all metabolic processes. Occasionally, an enzyme needs a helper molecule, or coenzyme, to support its activity.[30]

Earl Stadtman recalled his days there with affection: "In his [Lipmann's] opinion, the most important thing was to maintain a good environment in which all of the individuals that participated in the research had a familial feeling and liked and interacted socially and scientifically with one another. I have always listened to that. I have always adhered to that."[31]

While Earl Stadtman was working with Fritz Lipmann (who three years later would win the Nobel Prize in Physiology or Medicine for his discovery of Coenzyme A), Terry Stadtman pursued her postdoctoral fellowship under the direction of Christian Anfinsen, at the time a thirty-three-year-old assistant professor of biological chemistry at Harvard Medical School. Born in a steel town in western Pennsylvania, Anfinsen moved with his family to Philadelphia as a young boy. He remained in the area to attend Swarthmore College on a scholarship, where he was a football player whose athleticism and rugged good looks made him popular on campus.

Anfinsen graduated with a BS in chemistry in 1937. Two years later, he completed a master's degree in organic chemistry at the University of Pennsylvania. He was then awarded a fellowship to study enzymes at the Carlsberg Laboratory in Copenhagen. Anfinsen arrived there in 1939, around the same time Lipmann was seeking safe harbor in America to escape the threat of Nazi occupation. Anfinsen himself was forced to cut short his stay in Copenhagen when the Germans invaded Denmark in April 1940.[32]

Upon returning to the United States, Anfinsen enrolled in the doctoral program in biological chemistry at Harvard Medical School. With timetables for higher education going into overdrive to meet workforce skills for the war effort, Anfinsen completed the PhD in short order. He was put to work on a government-sponsored antimalaria research campaign. This was critical to the success of military operations in the South Pacific, where American troops saw high rates of debilitating malarial infection.[33]

After the war, Anfinsen undertook a fellowship at the Medical Nobel Institute in Stockholm, where he studied methods to purify and characterize enzymes and other proteins. This fellowship was conducted under the direction of Hugo Theorell, a leading figure in enzyme research. Theorell had worked with Otto Warburg at the Kaiser Wilhelm Institute in Berlin, two years after the latter was awarded the 1931 Nobel Prize in Physiology or Medicine. Warburg and Theorell isolated a "yellow enzyme" from yeast—one of the first enzymes to be fully characterized—with its distinctive golden color attributable to a component derived from vitamin B2.[34]

Having studied under Theorell for a year, Anfinsen returned to Harvard in 1948, where he began to organize his own research program. Terry Stadtman arrived for her postdoctoral fellowship a year later, when Anfinsen was still establishing his own research agenda. Terry's project involved the metabolism of cholesterol, and for this purpose she chose to work with another soil-derived bacterium. This microbe was Nocardia, which requires oxygen for its survival, unlike the anaerobic bacteria that she had investigated with Barker. Terry was interested in trying to identify compounds that served as stepping-stones along the path to creating steroid hormones. Unfortunately, cholesterol was broken down into final products, so she was unable to identify any intermediates. However, her efforts did not go entirely unrewarded, as an enzyme involved in cholesterol degradation was identified and purified, leading to its later use in the clinical measurement of cholesterol levels.[35]

Terry's year in Anfinsen's lab allowed her to refine important skills for working with enzymes and proteins. Even more important, when Anfinsen was recruited to head the Laboratory of Cellular Physiology and Metabolism at the newly created National Heart Institute, Anfinsen in turn offered staff positions to both Terry and Earl Stadtman. By today's standards, it may not seem remarkable to recruit a two-career couple. In 1950, however, husband-and-wife recruitments were highly unusual. In fact, most universities had rules prohibiting a married couple from being recruited into a single department in order to avoid perceived or real potential favoritism.

Individually, the Stadtmans had offers of faculty positions from several universities, but as a couple there were no such offers. One frank assessment came from Thorfin Hogness, who directed the Institute of Radiobiology and Biophysics at the University of Chicago, where Earl was being recruited. In response to Earl's request for a faculty appointment for Terry, Hogness wrote: "If your decision is to be based upon simultaneous academic staff appointments for both you and Mrs. Stadtman, it may mean that you are closing your opportunities for an academic career, since I believe that the policy of the University of Chicago in this regard is no different from that of most other universities."[36]

The NIH was not encumbered by such barriers, and as early as 1938 the bacteriologists Jerald Wooley and Bernice Eddy, both already employed at NIH, were married and remained on staff. After Earl and Terry Stadtman were recruited by Anfinsen in 1950, they were followed in quick succession by Marjorie and Evan Horning, Martha Vaughn and Jack Orloff, and Barbara Wright and Herman Kalckar. The four female scientists worked in a shared room within Anfinsen's laboratory, because even with an enlightened employment policy the social norms of the day frowned on any appearance of consorting in the workplace. When the future NIH director Donald Fredrickson first arrived in 1953 as a Clinical Associate, he was assigned to work with Marjorie Horning on cholesterol metabolism. Reflecting back nearly a half-century later, Fredrickson quipped: "I was there with four women and I thought all the scientists at NIH were women."[37]

Anfinsen and his team set up shop in NIH Building 3, which, as its numerical designation would suggest, was one of the original six buildings built on the campus. Constructed in 1938, the roughly 50,000-square-foot Georgian-style brick building included three floors, two basements, and an attic. In 1947, just three years before the Stadtmans arrived, Arthur Kornberg was recruited to set up the Enzyme and Metabolism section at the National Institute of Arthritis and Metabolic Diseases. A dozen years later, Kornberg would be chosen as the corecipient of the 1959 Nobel Prize in Physiology or Medicine for his work on how DNA is replicated.

A year after Kornberg arrived, James Shannon was appointed director of the research program on the NIH campus, and he stocked Building 3 with a dream team of superstar researchers. Shannon had directed the federal government's malaria research program at New York University during World War II. When he came to NIH a few years later, he brought his New York brain trust with him. Among the recruits were Bernard Brodie and Robert Berliner. Brodie would go on to win the prestigious Lasker Award. Berliner would be appointed as deputy director of science before leaving to become dean of the Yale University School of Medicine. Brodie, in turn, recruited his former malarial research colleague, Julius Axelrod, as a technician. Perhaps the most overqualified technician in history, Axelrod would go on to complete his PhD en route to being named as the corecipient of the 1970 Nobel Prize in Physiology or Medicine for his work on neurotransmitters.

With the addition of Anfinsen in 1950 (who two decades later would share the Nobel Prize in Physiology or Medicine), Building 3 hosted three future laureates among the staff. The egalitarian culture that led to the early recruitment of married couples also prevailed in the case of religious affiliation. Many of the first recruits—including Kornberg, Brodie, Berliner, and Axelrod—were Jewish, and Anfinsen converted to Judaism later. At a time when Jews still faced discrimination at universities, the NIH meritocracy was open to all serious researchers regardless of their religion.

The growth rate of new programs at the NIH during the early days was almost meteoric, and sometimes scientists were recruited even before work spaces were ready. In Earl Stadtman's words: "When we arrived here, we were supposed to be in the basement, and there were no labs in the basement at that time. So, we were farmed out, and in this building

. . . about half of the first floor belonged to Kornberg." Even though the Stadtmans were in a different institute, Kornberg welcomed the new colleagues into his space. "He made available a temporary laboratory for us to work in on his floor," Stadtman recalled with appreciation.[38]

The camaraderie in Building 3—both personal as well as professional—was cherished by all who worked there in the early 1950s. Five decades later, Axelrod described the working environment: "There was nothing like being around such great scientists—future scientists. . . . It was a wonderful experience for me. And we all worked freely—we knew what we were doing. We exchanged ideas."[39] Such a free and open sharing of information may seem to be the natural consequence of mixing together so many bright people. And even though science is an inherently social enterprise, individual investigators traditionally are rewarded for their unique contributions to knowledge. A premium is placed on being the first to make a discovery. There is no glory in finishing second. So, not surprisingly, scientists can be reluctant to share their best hypotheses and latest results. Informal sharing of information and ideas, such as Axelrod described, tends to be the exception rather than the norm.

What, then, gave rise to the distinctive culture of openness that permeated the early days of Building 3 and the NIH campus more generally? To some extent, the modest scale of the enterprise created a comparatively high-contact environment. At the time, there were only six buildings on the NIH campus (compared with roughly ninety today). In the early 1950s, it was possible for a scientist to be on a first-name basis with most of the other NIH investigators, even those in other institutes. In addition, the close proximity of the labs, even after the massive Clinical Center opened in 1953, enhanced opportunities for hallway conversations and impromptu consultations.[40]

This was the ethos that greeted the Stadtmans when they began working at NIH. Amazingly, of the nineteen scientists who worked in Building 3 at the time, fifteen (including both Stadtmans) would be elected into the prestigious and highly selective National Academy of Sciences.[41] Though this group was destined for future success, most NIH researchers were just starting out in their careers at the time; the Stadtmans were the youngest (thirty and thirty-one years old), Kornberg was thirty-two, Anfinsen was thirty-four, and Axelrod was the elder statesman at thirty-eight.

Terry Stadtman began her work at NIH continuing the cholesterol studies she started with Anfinsen in Boston. Fairly quickly, however, she was drawn back to researching the oxygen-hating bacteria she discovered in San Francisco Bay. Working with *Clostridium sticklandii*, she focused on how the bacterium consumed the six-carbon chain amino acid lysine. She discovered that vitamin B12—also known as cobalamin because it contains the mineral cobalt—was essential for the enzymatic breakdown of lysine.[42] In studying the degradation of glycine, a simpler two-carbon amino acid, Terry discovered that energy was conserved by the concurrent formation of a chemical that could store the power created.[43]

While exploring glycine metabolism, Terry observed that the activity of three proteins was essential to the process. One of these proteins was available only when the chemical element selenium was in the growth media. Through extensive studies, Terry was able to demonstrate that this protein contained selenium—one of the first such enzymes to be described.[44] Further investigation of the composition of this protein lead her to identify the amino acid selenocysteine,[45] a chemical cousin of the known amino acid cysteine, with the substitution of a selenium atom for a sulfur atom. Selenocysteine was the twenty-first amino acid to be discovered and the first since William Cumming Rose, a biochemist working at the University of Illinois, discovered threonine four decades earlier.[46]

While Terry was working on vitamin B12 and selenium-containing proteins in her workhorse bacterium, Earl, in addition to his postdoctoral studies with Lipmann on Coenzyme A, extended his doctoral work on fatty-acid metabolism. He demonstrated that he could re-create in a test tube the biological reactions of Coenzyme A accepting a two-carbon building block.[47] All he had to do was mix together the basic chemical ingredients along with the enzyme that he had discovered with Barker and—voilà—the two-carbon fragment was hitched successfully to the coenzyme.

In the early years, the fellows in Earl's lab were exclusively basic scientists, not physicians. The first physician to train with him was Roy

Vagelos. The son of Greek immigrants, Vagelos grew up in New Jersey, majored in chemistry at the University of Pennsylvania, and graduated from the Columbia University College of Physicians and Surgeons in 1954. After two years of clinical training at Massachusetts General Hospital, he was accepted as a Clinical Associate at NIH. Nearly six decades later, he still retained vivid memories of his interview with Stadtman: "Earl was very soft-spoken, but as he spoke, he became more excited about his work. Even though I didn't really follow what he was saying, I ended up asking to work in his lab. He said: 'You know, I've never worked with an MD.' I replied, 'Well, I have never worked with a PhD. So, why don't we give it a try?'"[48]

Stadtman affirmed his skepticism about taking on a physician trainee: "Quite frankly, I was only a young PhD myself at the time, but I didn't have much confidence in the possibility that a physician could do the kind of work we were doing."[49] Vagelos remembered Stadtman's continuing reservations: "Every few weeks, he would ask me if I thought I had made a mistake, but we worked together."[50]

In a tribute to Earl written many decades later, Vagelos wrote to his former teacher: "You were personally working on a microbial propionic acid fermentation. You explained the reactions you were studying, put my hands on a Beckman DU spectrophotometer and walked me through its operations. Of course, you were following an enzymatic reaction that you described to me." Vagelos continued: "Then you stepped back and said, 'Now you take over.' I falteringly took over. We worked together initially. . . . Within a short time you moved to another project, leaving the short chain fatty acid project with me."[51]

This generous act—passing along a productive line of investigation to a junior colleague—was the type of nurturing behavior that endeared Stadtman to scores of trainees. For Vagelos, it was the start of a professional path that would take him from a decade at NIH to academia and eventually to leadership of a major pharmaceutical company. And it all resulted, as he said to Stadtman, because: "You made it possible by handing over your main research project to me and moving to another challenge."[52]

A redirection in Earl Stadtman's scientific interests resulted from a sabbatical year that Terry and he spent in Europe in 1960. During the first half of the sabbatical they engaged with Feodor Lynen's laboratory in Munich, where Earl discovered a further role of the vitamin B_{12} coenzyme. Lynen, an expert in cholesterol and fatty-acid metabolism, would be named as the corecipient of the 1964 Nobel Prize in Physiology or Medicine. Lynen was the second Nobel laureate with whom Earl worked (slightly more than a decade after Earl's fellowship with Lipmann in Boston).

Stadtman spent the second half of his sabbatical year in the lab of Georges Cohen at the Pasteur Institute in Paris. There, Earl worked on an enzyme involved in the conversion of the amino acid aspartate to each of three other amino acids—lysine, threonine, and methionine. The biochemical sequence by which aspartate is transformed into the other amino acids begins with a common first step, but then it branches off into separate paths leading to different end products. Working with Cohen and his colleague Gisèle Le Bras, Earl was able to identify in the bacterium *Escherichia coli* at least two different versions of the enzyme that expedites the initial common step. The story became even more intriguing when the investigators discovered that specific versions of the enzyme were controlled by each of the different end products. For example, when enough lysine was made, lysine turned off the lysine-generating enzymatic pathway. Similarly, when sufficient threonine was manufactured, threonine shut down the threonine-generating pathway.[53] This self-controlling, multitasking enzyme system was both elegant in its design and complex to decipher.

Upon returning to NIH, Earl accepted a new postdoctoral fellow who had trained at the University of Washington under the respected microbiologist Helen Whiteley. The trainee was Clifford Woolfolk, who came to Earl's lab hoping to continue pursuing his work on the aspartate branched metabolic pathway. Earl was uncomfortable working on that topic: "I told him: 'Well, you know, that's really Georges Cohen's problem. I don't want to become a competitor with him in that field. If you want to work on a branched metabolic pathway, then you'll have to find another enzyme.'" Stadtman continued: "I suggested that he go to the library and look up metabolic pathway charts . . . and come up with suggestions of enzymes that were involved in not one but several metabolic pathways. Also, I told him that it had to be an enzyme whose activity could be readily measured."[54]

Woolfolk came back to Stadtman with three possible choices, and they started working on that which was easiest to measure. Unfortunately, they could not demonstrate any evidence of end-product control of the enzyme's activity, so they moved to the next enzyme, glutamine synthetase. They studied this enzyme from the same bacteria—*Escherichia coli*—used for aspartate metabolism studies. Glutamine synthetase assists in the conversion of one amino acid—glutamate—into another amino acid—glutamine. This transformation occurs through a chemical combination of glutamate with ammonia, using a high-energy phosphate compound as fuel for the reaction. Glutamine, in turn, is a source of nitrogen for the manufacture of various other biological molecules. The regulation of glutamine synthetase is critical to a host of cellular processes.

This was unlike the aspartate metabolism pathways that Earl studied during his sabbatical in Paris. Whereas there were multiple different versions of the key enzyme—each separately controlled by a different end product—for glutamine synthetase there was only a single instance of the enzyme. The brilliance of the glutamine synthetase control mechanism was that none of the multiple different end products could completely shut down the enzyme's activity. Each of the products had a partial effect, but only when they all acted in concert were they able to turn off the enzyme completely. Woolfolk and Stadtman referred to this collective control system as "cumulative feedback inhibition."[55]

When Woolfolk accepted a faculty position at the University of California, Irvine, Stadtman needed someone to pursue glutamine synthetase work. The heir to that effort arrived under somewhat humbling circumstances. Henry Kingdon was then a Clinical Associate who had been selected to work with Roy Vagelos. But Vagelos departed to become chair of the Department of Biological Chemistry at Washington University in St. Louis, and Kingdon was left without a supervisor. He had driven to Bethesda with his wife and two daughters; he arrived with little cash in hand. One trainee advised Kingdon to talk with Stadtman about the predicament—which he did with some embarrassment.

Stadtman immediately reached into his pocket and gave the young trainee $50. Ever generous, Stadtman agreed to take Kingdon under his wing to work on the glutamine synthetase project.[56]

The supply of the purified enzyme that Woolfolk had prepared was running low, and Kingdon's first task was to cook up a new batch. He followed the recipe Woolfolk recorded dutifully, but to Kingdon's chagrin the newly isolated enzyme did not manifest the same pattern of end-product inhibitions that Woolfolk reported. How was it possible that the same purification process could result in two different patterns of biological activity? Had Woolfolk incorrectly specified the purification process? Had he been mistaken in his observations about the enzyme's inhibition profile? Had Kingdon not followed the purification procedures correctly? The failure to replicate Woolfolk's earlier work was disheartening and concerning.

Here is Kingdon's version of the story, as retold to Stadtman: "So one day as I was stomping around having a temper tantrum, I complained that Cliff [Woolfolk] must have been wrong; you [Stadtman] said, 'No, Clifford was very careful.' So I said, 'All right, I'll go ahead and look into it if you want, but I feel like I'm doing control experiments that Cliff should have done in the first place.' (I was not famous for my graciousness!)"[57]

The team explored literally every possible explanation for the disparate results. They confirmed that both enzymes had the same amino-acid composition, and they also ruled out any differences related to purification procedures, storage, or measurement technique. After months—and no stone unturned—Stadtman and Kingdon were able to show that differences in how the bacteria were grown and harvested were responsible for the discrepant results. Again, in Kingdon's words: "You [Stadtman] stuck by Cliff (you knew him and I didn't), and you were patient enough with my rantings and ravings to get me focused enough on the task at hand."[58]

Daniel Atkinson, a biochemistry faculty member at the University of California, Los Angeles, described Stadtman's work on glutamine synthetase as: "Probably the most productive source of information and concepts regarding mechanisms of regulation of metabolic processes."[59] In 1979, President Jimmy Carter recognized Stadtman's contributions by awarding him the National Medal of Science. A dozen years later, the Houston-based Robert A. Welch Foundation presented its annual award for advancing chemistry jointly to Stadtman and the future Nobel laureate Edwin Krebs.

The quality of science produced in Stadtman's lab was matched by the caliber of excellence within the learning environment that Earl and Terry cultivated. Together they served as mentors for more than a hundred scientists. A dozen of their former trainees would be elected to the National Academy of Sciences. One of Stadtman's trainees was Stanley Prusiner, who went on to win the 1997 Nobel Prize in Physiology or Medicine. Prusiner credited Earl with introducing him to several important aspects of scientific inquiry. "First," according to Prusiner, "Earl taught me how to do simple experiments." A second lesson was: "When you get a result, you have to prove it five, six, seven, eight different ways, not just one."[60]

Another Stadtman trainee was the fellow NIH scientist Ira Pastan, who would go on to mentor the future Nobel laureates Robert Lefkowitz and Harold Varmus. In a tribute written to Earl, Pastan recalled bringing his experimental results to his adviser:

> After we finished going over the results, you [Stadtman] sat quietly for a minute or two and I thought we were finished. But then you began to explain what might be going on and what all the possibilities were, and there were many I had not considered. . . . As a result, I frequently tell my postdocs the following: "The data are trying to tell you something but you must pay attention."[61]

The way in which Stadtman prepared trainees for publicly presenting their findings also made a lasting impression on Pastan: "We rehearsed until it was perfect. 'Make it clear,' you said. 'Explain why the experiment was done, how was it done, what the results are and what they mean.' I cannot count how many times I have done that with my [own] postdocs."[62] Skills in written communication also were finely honed in Stadtman's lab. Prusiner, the future Nobel laureate, remembered the writing lessons he acquired from his mentors: "Earl and Terry taught me how to write manuscripts. They taught me how to state the results clearly and offer every reasonable interpretation. They taught me to state in the discussion of a paper what is known and what is uncertain, or to quote Earl, 'remains to be established.'"[63]

Another NIH trainee who benefited from Earl's mentorship was Michael Brown. For him, the route to Stadtman's lab was delayed by a slight detour.

CHAPTER 9

IN EARL'S COURT

Earl Stadtman and Michael Brown

In May 1966, when Mike Brown was a senior medical student and applied for the Clinical Associate program, he listed biochemistry, studying protein structure and function, and how enzymes work as his preferred experiences at NIH. His goal was to pursue a career in academic medicine, focusing on teaching, patient care, and research on metabolic diseases. Brown applied to several different NIH institutes and interviewed with a number of lab chiefs. At the end of the interview process, he had to rank-order his preferences among the labs. The form had thirteen lines for identifying selections; for good measure, below the last line, Brown added a fourteenth and a fifteenth choice.

Labs also ranked their choices among candidates, and the two rank-order lists were compared to find the best possible matches. If no lab ranked a candidate high enough, that person would not make the cut. Mike Brown indicated as his fourth choice Jesse Roth, who ended up matching with Bob Lefkowitz. Brown's sixth choice was Ira Pastan, who ended up matching with Harold Varmus. All the way down at number fourteen, Mike Brown wrote in "Leonard Laster." If it had not been for Leonard Laster, Brown recalled with a laugh, he "would have been in Vietnam treating jungle fever."[1]

Leonard Laster was a native of New York City who, like Bob Lefkowitz, graduated from the highly selective Bronx High School of Science. In 1944, at age fifteen, he entered Harvard College and, by the end of freshman year, had taken enough prerequisites to apply to medical school; if admitted, he would have been only nineteen years old at graduation. In Massachusetts, the minimum age to earn an MD degree was twenty-one, so Laster was deferred. A couple years later, he was admitted to Harvard Medical School, completing both his bachelor's and medical degrees within six years, graduating just shy of twenty-two in 1950. Like Mike Brown, Laster did his internship and residency at Massachusetts General Hospital.

At MGH, Laster learned about exemption from the Doctor Draft for those serving as a Clinical Associate at the NIH; he interviewed and was accepted into the program. He later recalled one of his mentors at Harvard telling him: "'Go down and spend two years there and get out. It's going to be a boondoggle; it's going to be government-run; it's going to be a waste of money.' He said that the government would have been wiser to give the money to Harvard instead of building the Clinical Center [at NIH]."[2] Quite the contrary, Laster found the experience as a Clinical Associate to be exhilarating: "The Modern era of medicine was born there in that time. It was an extraordinarily exciting time and it was a demonstration of the benefits to people that come from juxtaposing . . . basic research and clinical care. . . . It was Camelot!"[3]

Laster left Camelot for one year for Boston, where he trained in gastroenterology under Franz Ingelfinger, head of the Evans Memorial Department of Clinical Research at Boston University Medical Center. Laster and his fellow trainees were referred to as the "Fingerlings"; professor Ingelfinger would later serve for a decade as editor of the prestigious *New England Journal of Medicine*. Upon completing his fellowship, Laster returned to NIH, where he became head of the Genetic and Gastrointestinal Disease Branch. In that capacity, he was responsible for a fourteen-bed clinical research service that was run by his two Clinical Associates.

Although grateful for being selected as one of these fellows, Mike Brown was curious about why Laster had picked him. Five decades later, Brown recalled: "After I was there for a little while I asked him [Laster]: 'You know, the other 13 labs didn't choose me. Why did you choose me?' He said: 'Well, I was in the audience when you gave that talk on the restrained rats. I thought that was kind of cool what you did. The fact that you actually wrote a formula and you could explain things.'"[4] Laster was referring to the talk that Brown had delivered as a senior medical student to a gastroenterology subsection of the meeting of the Federation of American Societies for Experimental Biology in Atlantic City. The FASEB conference attracted thousands of attendees, but Brown was a complete unknown, presenting self-analyzed data from a summer research project. His talk attracted fewer than a couple dozen, but one attendee—a perfect stranger—would find the work sufficiently interesting to bring him to NIH later. Brown added: "I tell this story to students all the time because no matter how trivial the project seems at the time, if you think a little bit about it, you can find something interesting . . . and who knows, maybe it will be beneficial."[5]

Another fortuitous situation arose when Franz Ingelfinger, by that time editor of the *New England Journal of Medicine*, invited his former trainee, Laster, to write a three-part review article on a type of cell in the small intestine that is critical for food absorption.[6] This was the second opportunity for Laster to prepare such an extensive review for the *Journal*. The previous instance was a three-part set of articles he wrote with Ingelfinger in 1961, before Ingelfinger became editor. This time, Laster chose to share the opportunity with his fellows, thereby getting them to do the grunt work of reviewing the literature, as well as the writing. In return, the trainees would be able to buff up their own credentials with three papers in a very high impact publication. Indeed, it is rare for physicians-in-training to have one paper, much less three, published in the *New England Journal of Medicine*. The excitement of this accomplishment was somewhat diminished for Brown by the fact that he did not get top billing on any of the publications. The first author on all three was fellow trainee Jerry Gardner, Brown's medical school classmate at

Penn (and, before that, an All-America guard on the 1962 University of Kansas basketball team). Gardner would go on to become chief of the Digestive Disease Branch at NIH. Brown and Gardner got along well, even if Brown would have liked to outscore the former Jayhawk guard on at least one of their joint papers.

In reality, while the coup of three *New England Journal of Medicine* papers was a résumé-builder, it was not the main thrust of Brown's work with Laster. Laster was the lead gastroenterologist (a specialist in digestive diseases) at NIH. The range of medical disorders that Laster and his Clinical Associates studied was astounding. One patient was about thirty years old and had a rare hereditary disease characterized by the inability to absorb fats. Certain vitamins, namely A, D, E, and K, are described as "fat-soluble" because they dissolve in organic liquids and are absorbed and transported in the body in parallel with fats. People who have difficulty absorbing fats, therefore, are susceptible to deficiencies of fat-soluble vitamins. A shortage of vitamin A can lead to many problems, but one of the first to appear is night blindness.

This particular patient was hospitalized permanently at the NIH. As Brown remembered:

> He was relatively healthy, but when his body was depleted of vitamin A, he would develop night blindness. So, what they would do was they would give him a massive dose of vitamin A orally. Even though his absorption was poor, it was good enough to restore his night vision. Then, they would put him on a regular diet where he would not have [supplementary] vitamin A, and every week they would measure his night vision and figure out how long it took for him to go night-blind again. That's how they knew what the half-life of vitamin A is in the body. It would take months—literally months—for him to become vitamin deficient.

By today's standards, such a study—in which an effective treatment exists but is delayed solely to see when a patient's symptoms returned— would be unlikely to be approved. Organizations known as Institutional Review Boards have been created to ensure that the rights and welfare of human research subjects are protected. The mandate to safeguard the

welfare of human subjects was codified in federal law in 1974, with principles and standards developed by a national commission whose report
was published in 1978.[7] Interestingly, one of the eleven members of that
commission was Donald Seldin—Joe Goldstein's former mentor at the
Southwestern Medical School of the University of Texas.

Mike Brown recalled other memorable encounters on the wards of
the NIH Clinical Center in 1968: "There was a young girl . . . who was
hospitalized there. Somebody had . . . measured this enzyme sulfite oxidase. To this day, I don't know what that enzyme does." As it turns out,
sulfite oxidase is involved in the final step of metabolizing sulfur-containing amino acids in food by adding an oxygen atom to the sulfite
molecule. An inherited deficiency of this enzyme results in an extremely
rare and fatal condition involving neurological and cognitive disorders.
This condition is so infrequent that only a couple dozen cases have been
reported in the medical literature. The patient at the Clinical Center,
one of the first such cases to be described, developed gastrointestinal
bleeding, so the doctors studying her wanted Brown to determine the
source of the bleeding. Brown wondered: "Was the bleeding caused by
sulfite oxidase deficiency? So, I go there and I try to look at the chart."
Before examining the patient, a consulting specialist almost always reviews the background information in the medical record to become familiar with the history and presentation. Brown continued: "They say:
'Well, you can't see the chart.'"

For a consultant to be denied the opportunity to read the patient's
medical record is a bit like asking a trail guide for directions after putting a blindfold on her. When Brown asked why the chart was top secret,
the reply was: "Well, we haven't published the paper yet." In mounting
frustration, Brown responded: "Well, yeah, but how am I going to tell
whether this is due to sulfite oxidase deficiency without knowing anything about it?" To which the retort was: "Just tell us where the bleeding
is coming from." As it turned out, the patient with this rare fatal genetic
disorder had the not-so-unusual problem of hemorrhoids.[8]

This episode provides a vivid, if somewhat disturbing, illustration
of how the routine business of caring for patients can collide with the
scientific interests of those studying them. Then, as now, investigators
were rewarded professionally for being the very first to describe a clinical

condition. The NIH Clinical Center was a magnet for patients with mysterious and unusual medical conditions. The doctors there specialized in figuring out and describing the underlying abnormalities. The hope, of course, was that the knowledge gained in studying these patients would lead to new and better treatments for the patients at the Clinical Center and beyond. The essence of this relationship was well described by Harvey Alter. A leader in the field of hepatitis research, Alter was a former Clinical Associate who returned as head of the Transfusion Medicine Department around the time of Mike Brown's days at the Clinical Center. In Alter's words: "Both you and the patients know that you're here to find out what's wrong, to study many patients, and to publish the results. So both patients and physicians come in with a totally different perspective than in a regular hospital. The ability to do studies depends upon the patients' confidence in the people taking care of them."[9]

An example of how breakthroughs can occur in unexpected ways at the Clinical Center dates to Christmas 1968. Six months into his service, Brown was caring for a girl in her late teens who had what would be described today as an acquired immunodeficiency syndrome. She was highly susceptible to infections, one of which was a bacterial overgrowth of her small intestines, leading to malabsorption and general bodily wasting. The malabsorption is what brought her case to Laster's attention and to Mike Brown's care. She also suffered from long-standing infections of her lungs and other organs, but her condition rapidly deteriorated when she acquired influenza during a widespread outbreak. Her respiratory symptoms became so severe that she had to have a breathing tube inserted.

"So, now she is on a respirator," Brown recalled. "There was no intensive care unit, so she is on a respirator in a bed on a regular ward at NIH. I had to take care of her." He continued: "I will never forget one evening she developed a pneumothorax [an air collection between her lung and chest wall that impedes lung expansion] . . . but there was nobody else around, so I had to insert this chest tube to re-inflate her lungs." Brown continued: "During the course of this she became anemic and so I gave her a unit of fresh blood—a couple of units of fresh blood. It seemed to improve her—her infection seemed a little better and her fever was down a little bit.[10]

"As she didn't need the red blood cells anymore, I said: 'Let me try some plasma [the non-cellular fluid part of blood that contains proteins, enzymes, and antibodies].' So, we gave her a unit of fresh plasma . . . and so after a couple of weeks of these plasma infusions, she got enormously better . . . all of the infections were gone," he explained. "I said: 'Wow, there is something going on here. . . . So, I kept giving her these infusions. So, Laster comes by and says: 'I don't understand this . . . what is the plasma doing? Are we helping her or not?'"[11]

Laster decided that they needed an opinion from an outside expert. One of the acknowledged leaders in the field of immunology at the time was Robert Good. A survivor of polio, Good was a pediatrician with a PhD in anatomy who served on the faculty of the University of Minnesota. Earlier that same year, Good led the team that performed the first bone-marrow transplant for siblings who were not identical twins. Good came to NIH, and Brown presented the history of what had transpired with the care of this patient with an acquired immunodeficiency. A half-century later, the interaction is still imprinted in Brown's memory: "Bob Good says: 'You're killing this girl.' I said: 'What are you talking about? She is much better. She is walking around, talking, laughing. She has gained weight. She looks terrific,'" as Brown explained it. "He [Good] said: 'She will get hepatitis from this plasma, People with immunodeficiency always die when they get hepatitis. You keep giving her plasma, she is going to get hepatitis.' So, he absolutely said to stop the plasma infusions."[12]

On Good's advice, Laster instructed Brown to discontinue plasma treatments. Hoping to find a compromise, Brown offered a suggestion: they could minimize the risk of an inadvertent fatal infection by collecting plasma from a single healthy known donor who led, in Brown's words, "the cleanest life." Laster agreed to this strategy for reducing the risk of hepatitis. As Brown recalled: "We found a person—a very dedicated person, and for the next year while I was still on [the clinical] service, every two weeks she would get this plasma infusion and she was fine. She was actually discharged and got an apartment near NIH so that she could come in every two weeks and get these infusions. And everything was terrific."

A year later, when Brown was no longer on the Gastroenterology Service, he received a phone call from the Clinical Associate who followed him in Laster's lab. It was bad news. The patient that Brown had nursed back to health with plasma infusions had contracted hepatitis. Incredulous, Brown asked: "How could she have hepatitis? She's getting plasma from this donor." To which the reply came back: "Oh no, that donor left NIH, so we switched to another donor." As it turned out, the new plasma donor worked for the NIH blood bank transporting blood products throughout the Clinical Center, so he had repeated exposure to potentially contaminated patient samples.

"So, I rush over there to see her and she didn't look so bad. She had jaundice, but not so bad. It turned out that she got through the hepatitis with no problem at all, because she kept getting this plasma and it totally restored her immune system." The real shock came almost two decades later when Brown got a call from the patient congratulating him on receiving a major award. Since the days that Brown had first given her the plasma, she had continued to receive the infusions. Now in her midthirties, she had married but did not have any children. Although she no longer suffered from diffuse infections, she had sustained permanent damage to her lungs from the recurrent pneumonias before the plasma treatments. Her only hope was a lifesaving lung transplant, which, sadly, she did not receive. Nevertheless, she never forgot the young Clinical Associate who came to her aid when the best medical minds in the country offered no hope.

When Brown was not treating night blindness, or hemorrhoids in patients with inherited metabolic diseases, or malabsorption in immunodeficient patients, he was occupied with the bread-and-butter work of the Gastroenterology Service. The Clinical Associates on this unit had two principal tasks. First, they obtained small pieces of intestinal lining from patients with various medical conditions. Second, they would set up laboratory methods to measure the level of enzymes that were suspected to be missing or abnormal in these persons. Today, the process of sampling intestinal tissue is performed by a relatively quick, safe, and routine outpatient procedure.[13] Back in 1968, the technique was much less common, in part because the equipment was comparatively bulky and primitive.[14]

Learning the technique for obtaining these biopsies was Brown's first challenge. As he recalled: "I came there with no experience. I had two years of residency; that was it. And then you become the gastroenterologist of the NIH. I knew nothing. I was being taught by the fellow who was the year ahead of me." In an example of just how small the world of medical research was: "Laster's previous fellow [Peter Loeb], the guy who had done my job the year before and was now working in the lab a second year, was from Dallas—a graduate of this medical school [the University of Texas Southwestern Medical College in the class ahead of Joe Goldstein]."[15]

Once Brown mastered the technique for obtaining the intestinal sample, his next task was to run biochemical measurements on the specimen. Often, there was a suspicion of a specific underlying abnormality because the patient was not properly absorbing or processing a particular substance. The poorly absorbed or processed material would show up in excess levels in the patient's blood or urine. With a piece of tissue in hand, one could then study the enzymes associated with the metabolism of the substance in question, hoping to find the underlying defect.

In this approach to identifying metabolic defects, Laster was sitting in the catbird seat. At the time, there weren't many ways of obtaining tissue from affected persons and normal controls, so Laster's intestinal biopsies were prized commodities. When it came to analyzing these specimens, Laster's team was operating at a disadvantage, however. Laster was not a biochemist, so the Clinical Associates often were left to their own devices to develop and refine the assays of the enzymes of interest. This is where Mike Brown ran into difficulties. In his words: "I knew nothing about how to measure enzyme activity. . . . The control was always alkaline phosphatase, which is by far the easiest enzyme in the world to measure. I couldn't get the alkaline phosphatase assay to work. It was frustrating."[16]

The situation was made only more discouraging when he would compare notes regularly with his good friend and fellow MGH resident Joe Goldstein: "Joe was working in [Marshall] Nirenberg's lab and used to drop by and tell me: 'Oh, I just ran this column and I got this enzyme off, and here is the peak of the enzyme.' Everything he was doing was going beautifully and here I am struggling to get this enzyme assay to work and there is nobody to help me."[17]

Advice about how to proceed often came from senior scientists at NIH, even in casual and informal ways. One such instance occurred while Brown was performing a medical procedure on one of the premier scientists at NIH, Gordon Tomkins. Tomkins was the NIH scientist who first saw the potential in Marshall Nirenberg and supported the future Nobel laureate. In Brown's assessment, Tomkins "was really a great, great scientist. He went on some trip and developed diarrhea, so my job was to sigmoidoscope this guy." Sigmoidoscopy is a procedure in which a doctor uses a device inserted into the patient's rectum to examine and, if necessary, sample tissue from the large bowel. In the midst of this rather intimate and uncomfortable procedure, Brown remembered: "As I am looking through the sigmoidoscope, he [Tomkins] is asking me: 'What are you working on in the lab?' 'Well, I am working on these enzymes and they are not working.' He [Tomkins] said: 'Well, why are you working for Laster?' So, while I am sigmoidoscoping him, he is telling me what is wrong with my research."[18]

In a strange twist of fate, Mike Brown had Richard Nixon to thank for learning how to do biochemical assays. After the 1968 presidential election, Nixon appointed Lee DuBridge as his science adviser. A physicist and the recently retired president of the California Institute of Technology, DuBridge was described by colleagues as "the High Priest of Science." DuBridge needed a health expert, so he called James Shannon, the director of NIH, hoping to find one. In Laster's words, DuBridge needed "a live body to fill the space because he had forgotten to hire anyone to cover medicine and medical research—which shows you how high it ranked in the political scene then." He continued: "So, Shannon said that I was going to volunteer to go down and help DuBridge for a year. And I said I would do it. . . . So, I was detailed by the Public Health Service to the President's Office of Science and Technology in 1969."[19]

When he arrived in his new position, Laster discovered that "even though every year NIH's budget had gone up progressively, especially in the Shannon years—he was a master politician—[he learned] that the Nixon gang was planning on cutting the NIH budget." So, Laster forced

his way into budget discussions that otherwise were attended by econo-
mists, who he described as "fuzzy-headed pains in the neck."[20]

DuBridge's appointment as Nixon's science adviser was short-lived.
Nixon was concerned about DuBridge's loyalty, sharing with the White
House staff that "Lee doesn't understand the process. Once a decision
is made, he [DuBridge] must be behind it." In July, Nixon informed his
inner circle of John Ehrlichman, Bob Haldeman, and Henry Kissinger
that "DuBridge has to go soon." Rather than confronting DuBridge and
firing him, Nixon chose a less direct path. He used a 1970 advisory study
that suggested that the role of the science adviser be reoriented from
policy to long-term planning.[21]

DuBridge resigned voluntarily on August 19, 1970, and was succeeded by the engineer Edward David, who lasted longer than his predecessor; but in January 1973 he also resigned, indicating "disappointment
that his advice had not been heeded."[22] With David's resignation, Nixon
closed the Office of Science and Technology and abolished the position
of science adviser. Laster remained with the office until it was shuttered,
and during Laster's absence from NIH Brown saw an opening to find
another mentor. It was unclear, however, whether he could transfer and,
if so, with whom he would work.

At this juncture, an acquaintance from the past reappeared to advise
Brown. During medical school at Penn, Brown competed for top honors
with his classmate and friend Amiel Segal. Before starting a two-year
internship and residency at Albert Einstein College of Medicine, Segal
also interviewed for a Clinical Associate position. Having published a
monograph from his studies at the Walter Reed Army Institute of Research, Segal was a desirable candidate. He was selected by a premier
scientist—the laboratory of Earl Stadtman.

Brown got an earful from his former classmate about how great
things were going for him: "He [Segal] was telling me what a terrific
scientist Stadtman was and Stadtman was known as the enzymologist
of the NIH. I wanted to learn how to work with enzymes. So, halfway
through the second year, I talked with Stadtman and he agreed to accept
me as a fellow in his lab." But "Amiel was telling me how great it was,
so that's why I switched and that turned out to be the transformative
experience of my life."[23]

Even though it was unusual to make such a swap and to do so as one's fellowship was ending, the NIH approved Brown's change of labs. Similarly, the fact that he would be moving from one institute (Arthritis and Metabolic Diseases) to another (Heart) did not raise any red flags. However, because Brown had limited time remaining in his current appointment, a supplementary fellowship was required. Stadtman, whose success with Clinical Associates was well known and respected throughout the NIH, was able to secure additional funding to support a third year for Brown.

When he arrived in Stadtman's lab, Brown was assigned to work with Amiel Segal. The project was related to the current focus of the lab. "Stadtman's big discovery at the time was [related to] the enzyme glutamine synthetase in bacteria," Brown noted, explaining that it "basically takes ammonia and converts it into glutamine." Glutamine is an amino acid with a five-carbon backbone. Glutamine plays many roles in the body, among others serving as an essential building block for proteins, as a source of energy, and as a detoxifying carrier of ammonia in the bloodstream. Glutamine synthetase (GS) is the enzyme that assists in the production of glutamine by combining another five-carbon amino acid, glutamic acid, with ammonia.

When enough glutamine has been generated, seven different chemical end products of glutamine metabolism are capable of turning off the enzyme. The fact that there are so many different inhibitors of the enzyme is unusual but not unique. What is novel about this inhibition system is that each of these end products has only a partial effect. Their ability to interfere with the normal enzyme function mounts as the number of different end products increases. The maximum level of inhibition—eliminating about 90 percent of the enzyme's activity—occurs when all seven products are present. Stadtman labeled this masterful symphony of multiagent blocking "cumulative feedback inhibition."

The question was: How do these various products inhibit GS? The answer came from the work of a previous trainee in the Stadtman lab using studies of the common gut bacterium *Escherichia coli*. In Brown's words: "Another MD, a fellow named Ben Shapiro, had made this big discovery about two or three years before I joined the lab." At that time, it was known that a necessary ingredient for inhibition was another chemical compound, adenosine triphosphate (ATP). One of the most important molecules in biology, ATP is the energy storage unit that is necessary for fueling many physiologic processes. Triphosphate refers to three phosphate groups, each of which is composed of a phosphorus atom surrounded by four oxygen atoms. Adenosine is a nitrogen-containing compound that can be converted into the building blocks of genetic material. The three phosphate groups are lined up single file and attached to the adenosine component like a wagging tail. Each phosphate group has a strong negative electrical charge. All of that negativity does not like being forced together, and the removal of just one phosphate group results in a much happier fit. When one of the phosphate triplets is detached, a burst of energy is produced and the remaining molecule, with a pair of phosphates, is known as ADP (where "DP" stands for "diphosphate").

The freed-up phosphate group then can attach to other molecules in a process referred to as "phosphorylation." Many enzymes are switched from an active to an inactive state, or vice versa, by the attachment of a phosphate group. When the phosphate entity binds to a particular amino-acid site on the enzyme, it causes a change in the three-dimensional shape of the enzyme. Depending on the circumstance, the altered shape may cause an active enzyme to become inactive, or have the exact opposite effect. In 1992, the biochemists Edmond Fischer and Edwin Krebs were corecipients of the Nobel Prize in Physiology or Medicine for their discovery of phosphorylation.[24] What made their discovery Nobel-worthy was that an estimated one-third of all proteins in humans are subject to phosphorylation, affecting how cells move, propagate, and digest fuel. Specific defects in phosphorylation of various proteins have been linked to many diseases.[25]

Stadtman's team discovered that ATP was involved in the regulation of GS—but not by using the method Fischer and Krebs described. Instead of adding and removing a phosphate group, in Brown's words: "What Shapiro figured out is that the adenosine from ATP was being attached covalently to the enzyme."[26] This was quite a surprising result—everyone had come to expect that all of the action was at the other end of the ATP molecule, but in the case of GS it was the presence or absence of adenosine and the immediate phosphate group (adenosine monophosphate, or AMP) that was flicking the enzyme's switch on and off.[27] The chemical bonding of AMP to GS—the process by which the enzyme is made inactive—was referred to by Stadtman as "adenylylation."

Unlike phosphorylation, which is a ubiquitous means of regulating physiologic processes, adenylylation is rather unusual. In fact, it took another four decades before another such example of adenylylation was found. In fact, this discovery occurred at the University of Texas Southwestern Medical School, where Joe Goldstein studied and he and Mike Brown would spend their entire academic careers. Kim Orth, a biochemist there, was studying the mechanisms by which a particular food-borne bacterium attacks and destroys its mammalian host cells. Orth and her colleagues found that these bacteria insert the biological equivalent of cellular malware into the host cell, interfering with its normal functioning. The malware operates by attaching AMP to various enzymes, leading to the cell's loss of structural integrity and eventual death. In reporting her discovery, Orth wisely chose to replace the tongue-twisting "adenylylation" with the easier-to-pronounce "AMPylation."[28]

About the time that Orth was entering first grade, Mike Brown was working on the process by which GS was switched between active and inactive forms. His predecessors in the Stadtman lab (Ben Shapiro and Henry Kingdon) identified an enzyme that was responsible for attaching AMP to GS, thereby making the enzyme inactive. Brown's task was to work on the reverse process—the removal of the AMP molecule, thereby making GS functional again. He set about the task of purifying the enzyme that is responsible for detaching the AMP molecule. One of the curious observations made before he arrived was that the removal enzyme required the presence of uridine triphosphate (UTP). A chemical cousin to ATP, UTP has the same tail of three phosphates attached to a nucleoside—in this case, uridine instead of adenosine. As Brown recalled, the lab was befuddled by a question: "Why in the world do you need UTP in order to remove an AMP from an enzyme? We had no idea."[29]

The answer to this question came as Brown was burning the midnight oil in the lab:

> Late one night, I was purifying [the enzyme that removes the AMP] and someone else was working at purifying the enzyme that attaches the adenyl [AMP]. . . . I somehow got this inspiration. I looked at the molecular weight of the removing enzyme and I realized it was the same molecular weight that the other guy was getting from the enzyme that transfers the [AMP] group. I said: "My God, it could be the same enzyme doing both reactions!" So, I took this protein and I added it to GS that didn't have adenylylation, and sure enough, it attaches the AMP group. Then I took another aliquot [portion] out of the enzyme and I pre-incubated it with UTP plus another factor. Now it had converted into an enzyme that removes the [AMP].[30]

So, the same enzyme essentially was a molecular double agent. In the absence of UTP, it activated GS. When UTP was lurking around, however, the enzyme did just the opposite—it inactivated GS.

Thus the question became: Why does UTP have to be present in order for inactivation to occur? The answer came to Brown out of the darkness that same night: perhaps UTP is somehow attaching to the activating enzyme and, in the process, converting it to its alter ego—the inactivator. "I was able to show that was the case, all in one night. I spent the whole night in the lab. Stadtman was known to come to work at about 5 or 6 o'clock in the morning—that was his thing," Brown recalled many years later. "I knew that he would be coming in a certain entrance. I remember so clearly that I was standing there. I was flipping coins up in the air and catching them, just to pass the time while waiting for him. I was just so excited."[31]

Brown continued:

> He came and I told him the story. I said: "You know, there is a whole other [chemical] reaction going on here." . . . His typical response was: "Uh huh." He didn't trust a thing that I was doing, so the next day, he comes into the lab and he says: "I have to repeat this with my own

hands." He didn't know how to use any of the modern equipment that we were using. We were using these micropipettes and he was trying to do the reaction with these big pipettes that people stopped using 20 years before. I had to teach him how to do this. Finally, he just gave up and believed me because he really thought it was too amazing.[32]

This nighttime breakthrough occurred in June 1971, the last month of Brown's third and final year at NIH. With his fellowship ending, he had made arrangements already for the next step of his career. His plan was hatched with his friend Joe Goldstein, a 1966 graduate of the Southwestern Medical School of the University of Texas. His mentor there, Donald Seldin—chair of the Department of Medicine and chief talent scout for the institution—had mapped out a six-year training plan for Goldstein that had one and only one final destination: his return to Southwestern Medical School to develop a Medical Genetics Division.

When Goldstein met Brown in Boston and they struck up a friendship based on shared interests, Goldstein became Seldin's recruiting agent. Goldstein was convinced that Brown would thrive in the intellectual environment that Seldin was building in Dallas. Brown was not such an easy mark, however. With his roots in the Philadelphia area, Brown was skeptical that he and his wife, Alice, a native New Yorker, would feel comfortable in Texas. His mind changed, however, as soon as he met Seldin in person. The encounter was etched in Brown's memory: "He [Seldin] was just the most imposing person I'd ever met. Just in terms of erudition, not only in medicine, but also in science, and [Seldin] was incredibly inspirational. So, I decided to give Southwestern a try, even though I still thought it was a Bible School."[33]

Having decided on Dallas, Brown was confronted with a dilemma: whether or not he could just drop the exciting work with Stadtman on GS enzyme regulation. In his words: "I couldn't leave—having just made this discovery—without following it up. I was incredibly excited." The thrill of the science was colliding with the practicalities of life. "Alice and I were living in this house across the street from the NIH. [This was] the first time that either one of us had lived in an actual house. We had always lived in apartments. We had rented this house, but we had given up the house and the lease was over . . . so, we had to move out of this house."[34]

Brown often gives credit to his wife for her patience and understanding, and this was one such instance:

> I told her [Alice] that we have to stay here at least through the Summer, but we had no place to live. The landlady—the owner of the house— had . . . another property that she owned. It had a big house, but it also had this little shack in the backyard. So, we moved into this little shack, which had no air-conditioning. . . . Washington [s]ummers can be pretty brutal. It was OK for me, as I was working literally 24 hours a day, but Alice had to make do. We stayed there for another two months and I got to do all of the experiments that really proved this discovery.[35]

Every extra day spent in Stadtman's lab was a treasure for Brown. His description of his mentor echoes those of other trainees:

> Stadtman was a very quiet man. You would go in and show him your data, and he would kind of nod and make a few cursory remarks and you basically wouldn't get much out of him. Then he would go home that night and the next morning you would go to see him and he already would have ten more experiments planned. . . . I never saw him excited, even when I made my big discovery. But he was so rigorous. The experiments that he would tell you to do were all designed to destroy his own hypothesis. . . . You only accept something when you have tried every way to falsify it and you fail.[36]

Brown continued:

> When you are in a lab like Stadtman's lab and the word gets out that you just made this enormous discovery, not only do you get to present it to the lab meeting, but all attention focuses on you. You become the fair-haired boy and every day Stadtman wants to know what you have done. And again, he sets up this sort of obstacle course that I had to prove so

many things in order for him to believe this [finding]. . . . The fact is, it gave me the first sense that I could be a scientist. That was . . . so important for my confidence and my ability to be a scientist.[37]

Mike Brown stayed an extra year at NIH, and then he tacked on a few bonus months. In a real sense, he was struggling to leave his teacher—the man of few words, meticulous methods, absolute integrity, and generous spirit. Their names appeared together on just three publications,[38] but the influence that Earl Stadtman had on Mike Brown would last a lifetime. Brown had worked his way up from measuring transit times in rat intestines, to sampling and assessing human intestinal tissue, to exploration of an elegant regulatory process in a complex metabolic pathway. He had gone from amateur investigator to serious scientist—and the next stop was Dallas.

CHAPTER 10

HARMONY IN HORMONES

Ira Pastan and Jesse Roth

Two NIH scientists, Ira Pastan and Jesse Roth, teamed up to attempt to answer a basic question: How do individual hormones and the specific cells they influence recognize each other? This question may seem straightforward, but in the mid-1960s nobody knew the answer. Hormones convey important calls to action, but only certain cells can carry out those specific orders. How do the hormones—produced remotely and circulating in minute amounts within the bloodstream—connect with their target cells? There must be a precise recognition process, but what does it involve? The search for an answer to such questions had its origins six decades earlier and an ocean away.

The term "hormone" was coined in 1905 by Ernest Henry Starling, a physiologist at University College in London. In a lecture before the Royal College of Physicians in June 1905, Starling, then thirty-nine years old and already an internationally recognized investigator, offered the following definition: "These chemical messengers, however, or 'hormones' [from the Greek *ormao*, meaning "excite" or "arouse"], as we might call them, have to be carried from the organ where they are produced to the organ which they affect by means of the blood stream."[1]

If the hormone is carrying a message, how does it know where to deliver it? The answer, or at least the first suggestion of a possible answer, came from a most unlikely place: the study of immune-system responses. Even before Starling first coined the term "hormone," the German medical researcher Paul Ehrlich was developing a concept that he referred to as *seitenkettentheorie*, which is a mouthful but can be expressed in English as "side-chain theory." A decade later, Ehrlich would go on to become the corecipient of the 1908 Nobel Prize in Physiology or Medicine for his contributions to understanding how the body fights infections. Side-chain theory was premised on Ehrlich's belief that cells have appendages designed to capture circulating nutrients. According to Ehrlich's model, when a bacterial infection occurs, the invading organisms or their toxins occupy these side-chains. The cells respond by cranking out more side-chains, some of which escape into the circulation, where they bind to bacteria or toxins and inactivate them. Three years after introducing his theory, Ehrlich revised the terminology, replacing "side-chain" with "receptor."[2]

While Ehrlich was pondering lock-and-key links between receptors and bacteria,[3] the English physiologist John Newport Langley was focused on dog drool. Langley had come to Cambridge as a student in 1871 and remained at the university a half-century until his death in 1925. Langley spent the first fifteen years of his career studying secretions, particularly those of the salivary glands of dogs and other animals.[4] In the course of this work, in 1878 Langley observed that two chemicals—pilocarpine and atropine—had opposite effects upon salivation. Pilocarpine stimulated secretion, whereas atropine stopped it. From his studies, Langley concluded in muted tones that: "We may, I think, without much rashness, assume that there is some substance or substances in the nerve endings or gland cells with which atropin and pilocarpin are capable of forming compounds. On this assumption, then the atropin or pilocarpin compounds are formed according to some law of which their relative mass and chemical affinity for the substance are factors."[5]

From his work on glandular secretions, Langley migrated to the study of the nervous system. In 1905, based on his observations, Langley concluded that: "We may suppose that in all cells two constituents at least are to be distinguished, a chief substance, which is concerned with the chief function of the cell as contraction and secretion, and receptive substances which are acted upon by chemical bodies and in certain cases by nervous stimuli. The receptive substance affects or is capable of affecting the metabolism of the chief substance."[6]

If Ehrlich and Langley may be thought of as the founders of cellular receptor theory, they perceived that their work, deriving from unrelated fields of study, was describing separate and distinct biological phenomena. Although Ehrlich came to accept the commonalities, Langley never did and chose not to use the term "receptor," preferring his own phrase: "receptive substance."[7]

The concept of cell receptors remained controversial well into the middle of the twentieth century. One of the most influential skeptics was the English investigator Henry Hallett Dale, who shared the Nobel Prize in Physiology or Medicine in 1936 for his work on chemical messengers in the nervous system. Seven years later, during World War II, Dale spoke at a scientific conference and offered the following perspective: "It is a mere statement of fact to say that the action of adrenaline picks out certain such effector-cells and leaves others unaffected; it is a simple deduction that the affected cells have a special affinity of some kind for adrenaline; but I doubt whether the attribution to such cells of 'adrenaline-receptors' does more than re-state this deduction in another form."[8]

Even someone who made fundamental contributions to understanding receptors thought of them more as a theoretical construct than as an actual physical entity. Raymond Ahlquist, an American pharmacologist, famously reported that there were two different types of receptors that respond to adrenaline and related compounds. Ahlquist termed these differing patterns "alpha" and "beta," respectively. Broadly speaking, activation of the alpha receptor tends to constrict blood vessels, raising blood pressure, while contracting the smooth muscles of the digestive and urinary tracts. Activation of the beta receptors, in contrast, tends to be associated with increased heart-muscle contraction and relaxation of the smooth muscle lining the airways of the lungs. Ahlquist's differentiation enabled the development of drugs aimed specifically at enhancing or blocking one or the other of these two actions.

Yet, even to Ahlquist, a receptor man to the core, the idea that actual physical entities exist to recognize chemical messengers was a step too far. As late as 1973, he wrote: "This would be true if I were so presumptuous to believe that alpha and beta receptors really did exist. There are those who think so and even propose to describe their intimate structure. To me they are an abstract concept conceived to explain observed responses of tissues produced by chemicals of various structure."[9]

Other contributors to the field offered perspectives on resistance to the idea that receptors were real entities. One was James Black, a Scottish pharmacologist who built on Ahlquist's work to develop propranolol, the first selective beta blocker. Propranolol was shown to reduce morbidity and mortality among heart disease patients, quickly making it one of the most prescribed medications. Black noted: "The only people who talked about receptors as interactive entities was a small cadre of pharmacologists who were interested in the quantitative relationship between dose and response . . . a pure idea, necessary to allow them to do the math. But they were embarrassed about it, that it was a pure invention."[10]

That was pretty much the state of thinking in 1963 when Ira Pastan met Jesse Roth at the National Institutes of Health. This pair was young—Pastan was thirty-two and Roth was not yet twenty-nine—and undaunted by conventional wisdom. A little extra motivation was provided by their boss, Joseph Edward "Ed" Rall, director of the Clinical Endocrinology Branch of the National Institute of Arthritis and Metabolic Diseases. Roth later recalled the fatherly Rall telling him: "You know Jesse, you could keep doing that [Roth's prior work]; that's a good way to go, but you know this is a special time, special place, why don't you think of the *best* thing you could possibly work on?"[11] With the gauntlet thrown down, Roth and Pastan turned their attention to the biggest question that they could think of: trying to determine whether hormone receptors truly existed or had merely sprung from the vivid imaginations of mathematically inclined pharmacologists.

Though young, Pastan and Roth brought skills and valuable experience to the task. Pastan, a native of Winthrop, Massachusetts, was born on June 1, 1931. Winthrop is located about five miles northeast of Boston. Pastan attended public schools and Hebrew school in Winthrop before being admitted to the elite, all-male Boston Latin School. Pastan attended Tufts College in Boston, settling on his real interest: biology. He was not a particularly serious student—at least until he met Linda Olenic, a Radcliffe student whose intellect and charm motivated him to improve his own academic performance. They were married in 1953 on the day he graduated from college.[12]

Pastan matriculated at Tufts Medical School, where the famed endocrinologist Edwin "Ed" B. Astwood allowed Pastan to conduct research work during the school year and summers. Astwood was known for groundbreaking work on the discovery of two drugs that could be used to treat hyperthyroidism—the excessive production of thyroid hormones. Pastan thrived in this environment, surrounded by a hub of science—even those indelicate aspects of it, like going to the slaughterhouse early in the morning to procure bovine thyroid glands for the day's experiments.

Pastan wanted to pursue his clinical training at Yale. With Astwood's influential advocacy on his behalf, Pastan was accepted in New Haven in 1957. After completing two years of clinical training, Pastan came to the NIH and was assigned to the Clinical Endocrinology Branch. There he finished up a project that he had started years earlier in Astwood's laboratory at Tufts. This work, solo-authored, involved dispersing thyroid tissue into single cells and examining their ability to function.[13] Concurrently, Pastan began a new line of research in partnership with another young investigator, James B. Field. Field was interested in how hormones affected the metabolism of sugar in various endocrine glands. Because Pastan had an interest in the thyroid gland, he and Field collaborated on the effect of a thyroid-stimulating hormone on sugar metabolism in the thyroid. It was a productive working relationship, and over the next few years Pastan and Field published paper after paper, including one that won the Van Meter Award for outstanding research on the thyroid.[14]

Nearing the end of his two-year training commitment at NIH, Pastan realized that his knowledge of biochemical analysis was insufficient for the research he wanted to pursue. A friend at NIH, Roy Vagelos, had trained with Earl Stadtman at the National Heart Institute.

Vagelos convinced Pastan to apply for a fellowship position with Stadtman. Pastan was accepted into the laboratory for a two-year term, and
the experience was transformative.

"I would say that in Earl's lab I learned how to do science," Pastan
would later recall. There, he was schooled in: "How to ask the right question, how to design experiments, how to think about my results, and
how to proceed in a very systematic step-by-step experimental way to a
final solution rather than trying to hit a home run. The run was there as
a goal, but the approach to get it done . . . [was] solving one problem at a
time, until you solve the whole problem."[15]

Pastan's work under Stadtman was a real detour from his thyroid
studies. In fact, his new area of research might have been inspired by
a quote from Ivan Turgenev's novel *Fathers and Sons*: "We sit in the
mud, my friend, and reach for the stars."[16] In Pastan's case, the mud in
question came from the Potomac River, near where George Washington chose what would become the nation's capital. Among the attributes
of the Potomac that Washington most admired was its "inexhaustible
fund of rich mud [that] can be drawn as manure."[17]

Within that same rich mud can be found bacteria that are obli-
gate anaerobes, meaning that they cannot survive in an environment
containing oxygen. One such bacterium is referred to as *Clostridium*,
named after the Greek word for "spindle" because of its rodlike shape.
Working with Stadtman, Pastan was able to isolate a previously un-
recognized strain of the bacterium. This newly described microbe was
named *Clostridium barkeri* in honor of Horace Albert "H. A." Barker,
the University of California microbiologist and biochemist who was a
mentor to Earl and Terry Stadtman.[18]

One feature of this Potomac River mud bacterium was that it required a high concentration of nicotinic acid, also known as vitamin B3,
for growth. This suggested to Stadtman's team that vitamin B3 might
be a source of fuel for this microorganism. Pastan's work focused on
identifying the products of the fermentation, or breakdown, of nicotinic
acid. Several publications resulted from these studies; more important,
however, Pastan emerged from the Potomac mud with newfound skills
in biochemical analysis that would inform how he approached research
on hormones in human beings.

When his two-year fellowship ended in 1963, Pastan was invited back to the Clinical Endocrinology Branch by Rall. Rall encouraged Pastan to team up with the newly arrived Jesse Roth. Born on August 5, 1934, Jesse was the middle of three children raised in an Orthodox Jewish household in Brooklyn's Borough Park neighborhood. His father sold wholesale children's and women's wear to mom-and-pop stores. Roth attended a Jewish day school, where he spent mornings in bible and Talmud studies, followed by secular classes in the afternoon.

Preparing for college, Roth sat for the highly competitive daylong examination for the New York State Scholarship. Roth won a scholarship, but one of the stipulations of the $1,400 award was that it had to be spent on tuition at a New York–based institution. He selected Columbia because it was an Ivy League school close to home. When he arrived at Columbia, however, he had a rude awakening. As he later recalled: "I got to Columbia and they were kicking sand in my face—the kids that had gone to private school, the kids that had gone to Stuyvesant or Bronx Science—we were just nowhere anyway like those guys. . . . That first year was a struggle; but the second year, we were picking up speed, and by the fourth year we were really doing it."[19]

Although he did not get into his preferred medical schools, he did well enough to be accepted at a number of others. The Albert Einstein School of Medicine was opening at Yeshiva University. Roth took a chance on this new school, and in September 1955 he joined fifty-five other students as part of the inaugural class. While in medical school, Roth conducted a project on the thyroid.

Luck, in the form of personal advocacy, interceded again when it came to selecting an internship and residency. The faculty at Einstein "used their influence and connections to try and match us to the right places. We felt we were placed; we weren't just applying. And I got into . . . one of the best ones in the country at Washington University—Barnes."[20] The faculty was outstanding, including the husband-and-wife team of Carl and Gerty Cori, who shared the Nobel Prize in Physiology or Medicine in 1947 for their work on how the body metabolizes sugars.

The team that the Coris built at Barnes created a rich environment to learn endocrinology. Exposed to this group of brilliant hormone experts, Roth was inspired to pursue further training in that area. Like

Pastan, he was attracted to the program at Yale, but the fellowship slots there were filled by internal candidates; late in his final residency year, Roth was left without a pathway for further training. Again, luck intervened as the chair of internal medicine at Einstein, Irving London, happened to be invited to Barnes Hospital to give a talk. Roth met with this leader from his alma mater to discuss his situation. When asked where he might want to go, Roth mentioned the laboratory of Dr. Sol Berson at the Bronx Veterans Administration (VA) Hospital. As it turned out, London knew Berson and suggested that Roth make an inquiry about a position. Within a few days a most unexpected letter arrived from the Bronx VA Hospital. Berson wrote: "I just got a letter from Dr. London; he says that I should take you. You're on."[21]

This would have been a golden opportunity even if Roth had a tall stack of other offers on the table. Solomon "Sol" A. Berson and his research partner, Rosalyn "Ros" Sussman Yalow, were in the early stages of major discoveries that would revolutionize modern medicine. Working in a VA hospital in the Bronx, they were still somewhat unknown inside elite research universities. Berson was born in New York City on April 22, 1918, the eldest of three children. He was educated in public schools, where he became a gifted violinist, as well as a chess prodigy. At age twenty, Berson graduated from City College of New York with a bachelor of science degree. He wanted to study medicine and applied to twenty-one schools but was turned down by every one—another victim of religious quotas. Rejected and dejected, Berson applied to graduate school and was admitted to New York University, where he earned a master of science degree in 1939 and remained there as an anatomy instructor for dental students. In 1941, NYU admitted Berson to medical school; that was followed by a year of internship at Boston City Hospital and then two years in the United States Army. Upon discharge, Berson pursued additional training in internal medicine at the Bronx VA Hospital.[22]

His partner Ros (pronounced "Rahz") Yalow was born on July 19, 1921, in the Bronx. Neither of her parents finished high school, and her mother's dream was that Ros would become a teacher. Even at the age of eight, however, the headstrong Yalow had set her sights on becoming a scientist—despite the fact that science was virtually an all-male fraternity. At Walton High School, a prestigious all-female public school in the

Bronx with more than 6,000 students, her early interest in mathematics migrated to chemistry. She was inspired by reading Eve Curie's 1937 best-selling biography *Madame Curie*, about her double Nobel Prize–winning mother. Yalow went on to Hunter College, the all-female, public, tuition-free sister school to City College of New York; there she became the college's first physics major.

Yalow graduated with high honors and wanted to continue studies in physics, but even with a strong academic record the odds were stacked against her. She applied to a number of graduate programs and was rejected by every one. A letter that her supervisor at Hunter College received from Purdue University was remarkably candid and probably expressed the reality at other schools as well: "She is from New York. She is Jewish. She is a woman. If you can guarantee her a job afterward, we'll give her an assistantship." As with Berson, Yalow needed to find an alternate path and settled on employment as a secretary at the College of Physicians and Surgeons at Columbia University, where she worked for the biochemist Rudolph Schoenheimer. Having escaped his native Germany during the rise of the Third Reich, Schoenheimer was one of the first scientists to use radioactively labeled compounds to study metabolic processes. Ros Yalow thus had a front-row seat to work that would inspire her own use of radioisotopes.

The US entry into World War II opened a door of opportunity for Ros; many potential male students were drafted into the military, leaving graduate schools struggling to fill classes. In 1941, Yalow was admitted to the graduate program in physics at the University of Illinois on the condition that it would have no responsibility to secure a job for her afterward.

Within the College of Engineering, there were 400 teaching fellows and faculty; Ros Yalow was the only woman. There was no attempt to hide the gender bias: she was a straight-A student, but when she received an A-minus in a laboratory course the chair of the physics department reportedly said that it affirmed that women could not shine in such work. Nevertheless, Yalow persevered and received her master of science in nuclear physics in 1941 and her doctorate two years later.

Yalow's first job was a teaching position at Hunter College. But she wanted to pursue research and needed a different setting to do so. Dr.

Edith Quimby, a medical physicist on the faculty at the Columbia University College of Physicians and Surgeons, allowed Yalow to volunteer in her laboratory. Equally important, Dr. Quimby introduced Yalow to Dr. Bernard Roswit, who was developing a radioisotope service at the Bronx VA Hospital. Starting as a consultant in 1947, then transitioning to a full-time staff position in 1950, Yalow developed the radioisotope laboratory and started planning a research agenda.

Within months of her arrival, it became clear to Yalow that her skills in physics needed to be coupled with someone who could bring complementary knowledge and expertise in clinical medicine. She sought the advice of Dr. Bernard Straus, chief of medicine at the hospital. Straus had just the right person for her: Solomon Berson, who Straus characterized as "the brightest physician that I have ever trained." Straus arranged an initial meeting for the physician and the physicist. Yalow later declared: "After half an hour, I knew he was the smartest person I had ever met." Berson, equally inspired, withdrew from his earlier acceptance of a job offer in Massachusetts and signed up with Yalow.[23]

When they met, Yalow was twenty-nine years old and four years out of doctoral training, with minimal research experience and virtually no background in medicine. Berson was thirty-two years old, fresh out of his medical residency and lacking any research experience or knowledge of radioisotopes. On the basis of their youth and inexperience, it would be charitable to characterize their chances of success as a long shot. Yet both had overcome bias and obstacles through hard work, and they had synergistic skills, undeniably brilliant minds, mutual respect for one another, and determination.

They shared a cramped office with two identical desks facing each other. They kept the office door closed and enjoyed the privacy for planning and conducting research without distractions. The closeness of their interaction paid quick dividends, and they published papers on three different topics within the first year. More than 200 hundred joint papers would follow, many of which were important contributions, but two in particular were game-changers.

The first was a paper published in 1956, resulting from a study of how quickly insulin made with radioactive iodine was removed from the bloodstream. Radioactive isotopes were used as markers for hormones and other biological materials because the radiation could be easily measured, allowing investigators to determine exactly where the labeled materials were located and how much of it was present. In contrast to earlier methods, the use of radioactive materials was very sensitive, allowing measurement at levels much lower than imaginable before. For work with hormones, which circulate in miniscule concentrations, one needed a technique that could measure mere traces of the chemical messengers.

Berson and Yalow used this technology to investigate how quickly insulin was removed from the blood of patients. They compared diabetics who had been treated previously with insulin to diabetics with no prior insulin treatment and to healthy controls. Going into the project, and based on the prevailing wisdom, Berson and Yalow fully expected that the diabetic patients would see faster removal of insulin from their systems. It was suspected that diabetic patients had heightened activity of an insulin-destroying enzyme, resulting in the accelerated removal of insulin.[24] What Berson and Yalow actually found was that diabetics who had not received insulin treatment previously cleared the radioactively labeled insulin at a rate similar to that of nondiabetic patients. So, diabetes per se was not affecting the rate of insulin removal. What did seem to affect the rate of insulin removal was whether or not the person had previously been treated with insulin—slowing it down if there was prior exposure.[25]

What could be going on here? The hypothesis Berson and Yalow advanced was that persons with prior exposure to insulin developed antibodies, which would then bind to the radioactive insulin and delay its removal. Many scientists considered this to be heresy, as the prevailing wisdom was that something as small as insulin—a peptide molecule— could not stimulate the creation of antibodies. Antibodies were thought to occur only in response to much larger invading entities, such as bacteria.[26] Only after Berson and Yalow reluctantly agreed to change the term "antibody" to "binding globulin" in the title would Stanley Bradley, editor of the *Journal of Clinical Investigation*, agree to accept and publish it.[27] Berson and Yalow went on to prove that these binding globulins were, as they had proposed originally, antibodies.

Berson and Yalow spent the next several years experimenting with antibodies made by a variety of animal species against insulin from an equally diverse range of sources. In this process, they discovered that the antibodies made by guinea pigs against insulin from pigs had a strong cross-reaction against human insulin. This finding led Berson and Yalow to develop one of the most important technologies of modern medicine: radioimmunoassay (RIA).[28] "Radio" refers to the use of radioisotopes as markers; "immuno" relates to the antibodies used to bind to the material of interest; and "assay" means an approach to measuring the material. Radioimmunoassay is a clever technique used to measure minute amounts of circulating materials in the body. It can and has been applied to a range of materials, not just insulin and other hormones.[29]

Yalow would go on to win the Nobel Prize in Physiology or Medicine in 1977 for developing the RIA for hormones.[30] Tragically, Berson had died of a heart attack five years earlier, just before his fifty-fourth birthday. Nobel Prizes are not awarded posthumously, so Berson was not a corecipient, but Yalow was quick to acknowledge her partner's contributions in her Nobel lecture.[31]

Jesse Roth arrived in the Berson-Yalow lab in 1961 just as the RIA, in his words, "took the field by storm." Even as they were reshaping basic tools that would transform the field of endocrinology, Yalow and Berson worked in a relatively modest and protective environment. Roth later recalled: "Yalow and Berson spent 85 percent of their time doing bench research. It was fun coming into the lab to work shoulder-to-shoulder with these people. We could see them as often as we wanted for as long as we wanted. It was like a tutorial."[32]

Another new fellow, Seymour Glick, started just prior to Roth's arrival. Glick was assigned to develop an RIA for growth hormone (GH). Also known as somatatropin, GH is secreted by the pituitary gland and has a wide variety of effects. Among other impacts, GH strengthens bones, builds muscle mass, and grows internal organs.

Glick later recalled his first day in the Yalow-Berson laboratory: "I remember following them around. They didn't walk; they ran. Everything was on the run and I was running around all morning. And here comes 12:00 P.M. to 1 P.M. And nobody eats; I'm starving—dying of starvation."[33] As it turned out, Berson and Yalow kept snacks in their office so that they did not have to break for lunch and could remain in perpetual motion. Working at such a frenetic pace and with the tailwind of their insulin RIA behind them, Yalow and Berson fully expected to develop the GH assay quickly, maybe even before their two new fellows arrived. Berson and Yalow made little progress on the GH RIA before taking a long-planned summer break in Europe.

Glick started at the beginning of July 1961, and Roth joined him soon afterward. Berson and Yalow encouraged their new trainees to pursue a tag-team approach, saying: "You know we have been successful, much more successful as partners than we could have been as two individuals, so we encourage you to try and form a partnership."[34] Prior to starting in the lab, Roth reached out to his new colleague. As Glick recalled: "One evening, he [Roth] called me up and said: 'You know we're going to be working together; let's get to know each other,' and he knocked on my door, and we became very, very close."[35] The newly consummated partnership had to withstand a year and a half of false starts and dead ends before they achieved a reliable assay. A half-century later, Glick still remembered the frustration: "There were times we thought that we would never get there—and this was with Berson and Yalow's help, working day and night, every single day."[36]

Once Glick and Roth refined the GH RIA, they began to search for stimuli for release of this hormone. What they found was a shock to themselves and to the field of endocrinology. In Glick's words: "We did a whole lot of tests, and when we found that insulin hypoglycemia [low blood sugar] produced a rise in growth hormone, that was like hitting the jackpot. That was a real breakthrough because people had not anticipated that growth hormone was a kind of hormone that was involved in moment-to-moment regulation. Growth hormone was assumed to be for growth—a slow moving kind of hormone."[37] Roth, with his usual irrepressible, if not entirely data-driven, enthusiasm, said: "Ninety percent of what's known now about growth hormone, we learned in about four months in the Spring of 1963."[38]

Glick presented the results to the scientific community at the prime-time Friday-morning plenary session of the fifty-fifth annual meeting of the American Society for Clinical Investigation in Atlantic City, New Jersey. Roth characterized the audience response in terms more typically associated with Broadway musicals than with scholarly talks: "It brought the house down. So, we were stars—young stars—overnight."[39] Many in the crowd assumed that the breakthrough really was attributable to the senior scientists—Berson and Yalow—but Berson was quick to give credit where it was due: "No, no. The boys did that." The team rushed to get the results into print in a series of highly cited articles,[40] and as Glick recalled: "Within the next year, we were invited everywhere. We were on the circuit. Everybody invited us. We received job offers."[41]

Roth had arrived at NIH in 1963, and having perfected his partnership skills with Glick, he was primed for a similar pairing with Pastan. Together, they planned to combine their talents—Pastan's newfound expertise in biochemistry, and Roth's recent success with RIA—to tackle the question of whether hormone receptors truly existed or were simply theoretical constructs. For Pastan and Roth, this was not an academic question but a very practical matter. In Roth's words: "In July 1963, we posed the question: 'How does the cell know insulin is there? How does a thyroid cell know that TSH [thyroid stimulating hormone] is there? And he [Pastan] working on the thyroid, and me, working on insulin, were limping along together, creating the concepts, and creating the tools."[42]

Most endocrinologists "assumed that hormones were like vitamins; they would go into the cell, they would find the enzymes, and then the combination of the hormone with the enzyme would do what it's supposed to do," explained Roth. This model simply did not make any sense to Pastan and Roth. "Let's say insulin gets into a muscle cell, and the muscle cell starts to take up glucose; how does the muscle cell know that insulin is there? The muscle is being bathed with ten million different molecules, and only one of them is insulin. How does it know the insulin is there?"[43]

According to Roth: "That is what got us to say: 'There must be something there that's really recognizing insulin from everything else'; and we thought: 'Well, that must be . . . the receptor.'" With this guiding belief, Pastan and Roth started to hunt for where such a specific hormone receptor might be located. The focus began inside the cell. After searching in vain, the research partners became convinced that they were looking in the wrong place. "We started to play around with it," Roth recalled, and "it's clear that it was on the cell surface. That was a surprise to everybody." "When you do research, the first thing you have to do is convince yourself that you are right," Roth confided, "and then you have to figure out how to convince the world that you are right."[44]

Within two or three years, Roth and Pastan grew increasingly confident in their findings, and their original paper on the subject appeared in 1966. This publication focused primarily on the effect of TSH on slices of thyroid tissue, with similar, but much more limited, observations on the effect of insulin on skeletal muscle.[45] Pastan and Roth showed that the hormone effect was preserved even after the medium outside the cell was depleted of hormone. This finding suggested—but certainly did not prove—that the hormone was attached in some way to the effector cell. When an antibody or a digestive enzyme was added to the medium, however, the hormonal activity was eliminated. This observation implied that the hormone attachment must be on the cell surface, as the antibody is too large to cross the cell's protective outer layer.

Roth later characterized this initial experimental system as "relatively crude." It was submitted on behalf of Roth and Pastan to the *Proceedings of the National Academy of Sciences* by James Shannon, director of NIH. Even in such a high-impact journal, the paper went largely unnoticed by the research community.

Had they lived long enough to see it, one can only wonder how Paul Ehrlich and John Langley would have greeted this initial experimental evidence in support of their belief in receptors (Ehrlich) and receptive substances (Langley). Unfortunately, it took more than a half-century for their independent yet reinforcing concepts to be supported by preliminary evidence in a test-tube model. Pastan and Roth now were eager to take the next steps: isolate an actual hormone binding receptor and demonstrate its connection to the hormone's biological activity.

CHAPTER 11

PRIEST AND PROPHET

Jesse Roth, Ira Pastan, and Robert Lefkowitz

A half-century after Jesse Roth interviewed Bob Lefkowitz for a Clinical Associate position at NIH on July 1, 1966, Roth recalled their interaction in detail. Without question, Lefkowitz was a bright physician. He had graduated from Bronx High School of Science, followed by Columbia University, then Columbia University College of Physicians and Surgeons, and he was about to start an internship at Columbia-Presbyterian Hospital. At each step, Lefkowitz excelled in record speed. Roth's interviewee was only twenty-three, about three years younger than the typical medical school graduate. He even looked the part of a studious geek, with closely cropped dark hair and heavy horn-rims.

The quality of Lefkowitz's résumé was obvious, but Roth understood it at a much more personal level. He had grown up in New York City and attended Columbia University, where he competed with alumni from Bronx Science. Roth was also aware from personal experience that religious prejudices and quotas persisted at elite universities. To be admitted to and succeed at an Ivy League school, Jewish students had to be at the top of their class. With all of this in mind, Roth knew that the fidgety candidate was very smart. But Lefkowitz had no prior research experience. Although he was not unique among Clinical Associate applicants in this regard, it was almost as if Lefkowitz had gone out of his way to avoid doing research. During medical school, for example, when given opportunities to dirty his hands in a lab, Lefkowitz chose instead to undertake more advanced clinical electives.

During his interview, Lefkowitz had a hard time concentrating. With his internship starting that very same day, Lefkowitz had arranged for another trainee to cover him while he traveled to Bethesda for interviews at NIH. Bob was known and trusted at Columbia-Presbyterian from his days there as a medical student. Confident that Lefkowitz could handle the pressure, the program director assigned him to start on an especially busy clinical service: the public patient wards. Even before Lefkowitz was scheduled to start, he spent a week learning about the patients for whom he would be responsible. His well-rehearsed start as an intern now was disrupted inconveniently by the interviews at NIH. He was trying his best to keep his head in the game in Bethesda while not wanting to be perceived as shirking his patient-care responsibilities back in New York. Frequent glances at his wristwatch revealed a growing anxiety about getting back to New York in time.

Roth described the scene: "The interview was kind of funny because he [Lefkowitz] was trying so hard to focus and trying so hard to put on the research persona, but he kept losing his focus. . . . So, it . . . almost could have been a good comedy routine of the two of us."[1] For Roth, it was the first chance to pick his own trainee, so he was just as eager to make the best match possible. Prior trainees had been chosen by the institute and assigned to Roth, but now he had earned the right to select his own fellow. It was a limited privilege, however, because he knew that the more senior scientists would have first choice in the selection process. "I was low on the list among the mentors that were competing for talent as I was a new, hardly known kid."[2] With a laugh, Roth described both Lefkowitz and himself as the "ugly ducklings" of the selection process, getting paired together once all of the attractive swans had been matched up.[3]

When Lefkowitz applied to the NIH Clinical Associate program, his ultimate career objective was to become a physician on a university faculty. As he stated in his application, he aspired to a job that would allow him to divide time between teaching and research. In order to prepare for these pursuits, or at least the scientific portion of it, Lefkowitz planned to learn the basic skills needed to conduct research during his two years at NIH. Roth asked questions to try to determine how serious Lefkowitz was about a research career. When Lefkowitz responded that he wanted to be an academic physician, dividing his time and energies between teaching, patient care, and research, Roth grew impatient. As Lefkowitz remembers the exchange: "He [Roth] really dressed me down. . . . He said: 'You can't do all that. Either you're going to do research or you're going to be a clinician, but you can't do all that—it's not going to happen.'"[4]

As he departed the NIH campus, Lefkowitz was convinced he had struck out in all the interviews. He was told very directly by Donald Fredrickson at the National Heart Institute that an applicant who lacked any research experience had no chance of being selected in his institute. "Next to that, I would say Roth was the most discouraging," Lefkowitz confided. "So, when I got home, I told my wife . . . 'It was really bad. I'm not at all sure I'm going to get a spot offered.' Which meant basically, I was going to Vietnam. I said that the two worst were Fredrickson and this guy, Roth, who really read me the riot act." He continued: "Sure enough, two weeks later you get a call. And I got a call from Jesse saying that I'd matched to his lab. I almost fell over."[5]

Lefkowitz was accepted just as Roth and Pastan were putting the finishing touches on their initial paper on hormone binding to cell surfaces. Not surprisingly, the project assigned to Lefkowitz, which he would begin two years later when his fellowship started, was an extension of this work. Roth and Pastan had identified presumed binding of thyroid stimulating hormone on the surface of thyroid cells and suggested binding of insulin on the surface of muscle cells. These initial results, based on a relatively crude experimental system, defied the prevailing dogma that hormones entered cells in a fairly nonselective way and then triggered a chain of events that led to specific actions. The conventional wisdom was that the entire process of hormone action occurred inside the target cell. In Roth's words: "At that time, people thought that hormones went inside cells. . . . So, there was no need for a receptor because each set of enzymes would bind insulin or bind the hormone and they didn't need a uniform recognition system."[6]

The work that Lefkowitz undertook with Roth and Pastan would challenge that presumption. "When Bob came in '66, we had done some of our early experiments and had started to shape up . . . a real strategy—a pretty detailed strategy." Two years later, when Lefkowitz started his work, it was still a risky project, as Roth explained:

We didn't know at that time in 1968 when he came, were we able to bring the pieces home. We had been working on pieces, but would it all come together? Each one had their significant risks. In addition, Ira and I both were speaking about receptors as we were formulating things in public spaces, and we didn't get any resonating responses. I could remember a lot of times going to talk and I would have a mix of things to talk about and when I talked about receptors, I would say much of the time I didn't get any response.[7]

Roth remembered their shared apprehension: "We were nervous on two counts. As we were piecing the pieces together, would it all come together? And secondly, was the scientific community prepared to embrace it . . . would the scientific community treat us as heroes or just ignore us?"[8]

Even though Roth had an ultimate goal of studying insulin and Pastan had worked on thyroid hormone, they chose to launch the hormone receptor work on a different target: adrenocorticotropic hormone (ACTH). Also known as corticotropin, ACTH is a thirty-nine–amino acid molecule secreted by the pituitary gland. The pituitary is a diminutive body, oval in shape, reddish-brown in color, and about the size of a pea. It is hidden away on the underside of the brain, just behind the nasal passages and cradled within a saddle-shaped bony cavern. The pituitary dangles by a slender, funnel-shaped stalk from the hypothalamus, an almond-sized part of the brain that monitors and regulates the body's internal environment.[9]

What the pituitary lacks in size, it more than makes up for in power within the body. In fact, it has been described as the "master gland," because the hormones that it secretes control many other components of the endocrine system, including the thyroid, the adrenals, the ovaries, and the testes. The anterior (front) lobe, which constitutes about three-fourths of the gland, is the source of six different hormones. Among the anterior pituitary hormones is growth hormone, for which Roth and his research partner, Seymour Glick, with their bosses Sol Berson and Ros Yalow, had developed a radioimmunoassay to measure its presence and helped to study its function. Another anterior pituitary hormone is thyroid stimulating hormone, for which Roth and Pastan had identified cell-surface binding on thyroid cells. A third hormone secreted by the anterior pituitary is ACTH.

ACTH stimulates the cortical (outer) part of the adrenal gland, causing release of cortisol.[10] Cortisol is a steroid hormone that helps the body deal with impending stress or danger. Cortisol acts on many organ systems, increasing the production of glucose, the body's sugary fuel, in order to assure that there is a ready source of energy for muscle action. Cortisol also raises blood pressure and reduces inflammation and has many other important effects.

As he was completing his work with Yalow, Berson, and Glick, Roth participated in the development of the first radioimmunoassay for ACTH,[11] and this initial RIA was relatively insensitive for a variety of reasons. First, ACTH typically circulates in the blood at very low levels, which vary by time of day and other factors. Second, it was difficult to make antibodies to ACTH, because the hormone tended to disappear quickly from the circulation and, while present, stimulated the release of cortisol, which suppressed the immune response. Nevertheless, the original RIA was adequate for the investigators to characterize ACTH levels in patients with a variety of conditions where the hormone level in blood was high, including excessive pituitary secretions, adrenal insufficiency, and during the stress of surgery. Four years later, around the time that Roth, Pastan, and Lefkowitz were launching their search for

ACTH receptors, Berson and Yalow, working alone, produced a more sensitive RIA for this hormone.[12]

Another key preparatory step for studying ACTH receptors was to develop an in vitro (or tissue culture–based) model for assessing the hormone-related biological activity of the cell. For this purpose, Pastan and Roth, working with NIH colleague O. David Taunton, used a mouse adrenal tumor that was known to be sensitive to ACTH, producing adrenal steroid hormones under its influence. The investigators developed an extract of the tumor that contained cellular membranes. When ACTH was added to the extract, the initiation of biological activation was measurable. These observations suggested that hormone binding to the receptor and the production of downstream hormonal effects were connected. It was unclear, however, whether this was a direct relationship or, alternatively, was indirect and mediated through some other factor(s). Most important, Pastan and Roth now had a working laboratory prototype that could be used for subsequent investigations. As they wrote in their paper on this topic: "The partially purified particulate system described here, by reason of its sensitivity, simplicity, and stability, should provide a useful tool in characterizing further the steps between hormone binding and enzyme activation."[13]

As the developers of this "useful tool," they had an enviable lead in the effort to link hormone binding to cellular activity. Moreover, they were convinced that their findings were not just a test-tube curiosity; rather, their work "with the isolated particles can be reasonably extrapolated to events *in vivo*."[14] That is to say, the same processes they observed in the test-tube model would be the basis for ACTH stimulation of normal adrenal cells in living animals, including humans.

Working on ACTH was a pragmatic choice. This hormone was readily available in a pure form. It also had a known chemical composition. Moreover, it was well known which parts of the ACTH structure were essential for its biological activity. This allowed Roth and Pastan to target the placement of the radioactive iodine labeling marker on a location that would not interfere with the hormone's function. For all these reasons, the interaction of ACTH with adrenal tissue was a good place for the team to focus their early hunt for hormone receptors. As Roth noted, however: "The system we developed with Bob was not our primary goal. Our primary goal was really the insulin receptor. We did the ACTH receptor because we knew we could do it faster and we could prove the principle" that hormone receptors exist.[15]

Most endocrinologists at that time would have scoffed at the supposition there is a one-size-fits-all mechanism for initial hormonal interaction with the different cells that they impact. The orthodoxy was that each hormone interacted with its effector cells in a unique manner. Adherence to the one-hormone/one-mechanism concept made a lot of intuitive sense, as the pairings of individual hormones and their effector cells were so specific as to suggest unique modes of interaction. Roth recalls the team's mind-set: "We were already thinking that the rules were going to be simple and so switching from TSH to insulin to ACTH didn't bother us. We were overconfident that that wasn't going to be a barrier."[16]

Now, the stage was set for the work that Bob Lefkowitz would undertake with his two mentors. As he recalled:

My last day at Columbia was June 30, 1968. I was on the private [patient] service—Harkness Pavilion. . . . I had been busy—up all night . . . God knows how many admissions on the private service. . . . Whenever I got off—let's say 8 a.m.—I went down to the call room—stripped off my whites, threw them in the laundry basket; dressed, went down, and exited the medical center from the main entrance . . . where my then-wife, Arna, was waiting in our blue Dodge Dart, with our two little boys in the back seat. The trunk was all loaded up. Our [household] goods had already been picked up. I got in the car . . . and off we went to Washington. And, the very next day, July 1, I reported for duty.[17]

When Lefkowitz arrived at the NIH, Roth was away for at least a week, so Lefkowitz was welcomed to Room 8N246 on the eighth floor of the Clinical Center by Pastan and an avuncular senior investigator, Saul Rosen. Lefkowitz was assigned work space in Pastan's laboratory, literally ten feet away from Pastan himself. The space was tight—Pastan had two rooms, each about 260 square feet. Roth's lab was just a few doors down the hall, so the trio worked in close proximity.

Roth and Pastan mapped out the research strategy together, with Pastan leading the tissue culture/biological activity portion, and Roth leading the RIA/hormonal measurement component. The plan involved several key tasks for Lefkowitz. One was to successfully attach radioactive iodine to ACTH without interfering with the hormone's biological activity. As Roth explained, this was often a delicate procedure: "They [labeled hormones] were often a little bit damaged and didn't behave so well. And they surely didn't retain their biological activity. So, when we started doing the receptor, we had to devise a mechanism for labeling at very high specific activity, because we thought we needed that, and at the same time, not injure the molecules so that it wouldn't bind to the receptors."[18]

After attaching the radioactive iodine without adversely affecting the binding, Lefkowitz had to separate out the radioactively labeled ACTH from the unlabeled hormone. Then, he had to isolate cell membranes that contained the receptors. Finally, he had to demonstrate binding and activation of the hormone's effects on the effector cell. It was a logical and clear strategy. Of course, nobody had ever attempted such an effort before, and Lefkowitz was stepping into a research lab for the first time in his life. Other than that, what could go wrong?

Looking back years later, Lefkowitz admits: "It was just brazen gall that you would think that you could do that." Regarding his preparation for the task, he acknowledged: "I didn't have a PhD. I wasn't a biochemist. I wasn't anything—I was a physician."[19] Aside from Lefkowitz, nobody else was surprised that he did not hit a home run on his first at-bat in the lab. For someone at the top of his class since childhood, speeding through the best academic institutions, this was a rude awakening. Reflecting back, Lefkowitz acknowledged that he did not react well to the frustration. "It was painful. The first year was an unmitigated failure. In fact, I was used to a great deal of success. This really set me back on my heels."[20]

The initial impasse—the cause of so much struggle—was to demonstrate that the attachment of the radioactive iodine did not interfere with the biological activity of the ACTH. As Lefkowitz described: "When you do the radio-iodination, or even the cold iodination [add non-radioactive iodine], you want to use the gentlest possible conditions. So, only a tiny fraction becomes iodinated." Dividing out the radioactive from nonradioactive ACTH was a challenge: "How the hell are you going to separate two molecules of an approximate molecular weight of 3,500, which differ by one atom? . . . So, I spent a year trying to do that. . . . Today, it would be pretty straightforward with some of the methods that are available. But, at the time . . . that's what drove me nuts."[21]

Roth remembers spending two-hour sessions with Lefkowitz each week, just to keep the trainee's spirits afloat.[22] Meanwhile, Lefkowitz was counseled by the kindhearted Saul Rosen: "The difference between a really successful scientist and an average scientist is that for the average scientist, maybe 0.5 to one percent of his experiments work. For an absolutely fabulous scientist, it could be as high as two percent."[23] As a floundering Clinical Associate, Lefkowitz discounted that advice as a thinly veiled attempt to prop up his deflated ego. Only later, after a lifetime of experience as a researcher, would he conclude that those estimates may be "an optimistic view."

The lack of progress in the lab, and the emotional toll it was taking on Bob, came to a head about five months into the project when he and his family traveled to his parents' home in New York City for the Thanksgiving holiday. An only child, Lefkowitz was very close to his father. The elder Lefkowitz, Max, was an accountant and knew nothing about medicine or research, but he was a good listener and knew his son well. After hearing about Bob's unhappiness with his repeated failures in the laboratory, Max told his son: "Look, you always wanted to be a doctor. You'll fulfill your military requirement there at the NIH. Just get through it and then you'll go back to your clinical training and go on with your career as a cardiologist."[24]

These words were just the salve that Bob wanted and needed. When the holiday ended, Lefkowitz returned to Bethesda and followed his father's advice. He began applying for residencies and fellowships to commence after his two-year obligation at the NIH was completed. This father-son agreement became a blood oath when Max Lefkowitz died suddenly and unexpectedly just a few weeks later. The Thanksgiving counseling session was the last conversation that Bob would ever have with his father. "That deeply affected me in several ways," Lefkowitz remembered, "but one of the strangest ones was that I always felt that I had made a pact with him. We had a plan—I was going to pursue my clinical training and that's where I would go."[25]

Lefkowitz recalled the shock of learning about his father's untimely passing and the spontaneous offer of help provided to him by fellow Clinical Associate Harold Varmus: "I was in clinic on December 17, 1968, when I got a call from my mother that my father just died suddenly of a heart attack. I was in a carpool at the time, so I had no way of getting home. I had not driven that day. I remember walking next door, banging on Harold's office door and asking him to come out for a minute." Lefkowitz continued: "I said: 'My father just dropped dead.' So, he was the very first person I shared that information with. And I said: 'I've got no way of going home.' Just like that, he said: 'I'll drive you.' And I remember Harold driving me back to my townhouse so that I could load the family up and drive to New York."[26]

At a time of overwhelming grief, his father's enduring legacy was to unburden Bob of the pressure to succeed in research. If things did not go well in the lab, so what? This was just a temporary detour on the road back to clinical medicine for Lefkowitz, and if it wasn't a particularly productive diversion, at least Lefkowitz had met his obligation to Uncle Sam. Anything beyond that was just icing on the career cake. He decided to put in the effort in the lab, but he did not see any future in all the other activities available to Clinical Associates. When it came to the formal courses and informal tutorials that were offered: "Unlike my brethren, I did not [participate].... I basically did the research work and went to all the conferences in our branch.... We had grand rounds every week of some sort and speakers and that kind of stuff. But, I didn't take advantage of the very rich stuff that was there." Reflecting on why the avid student in him did not resurface, he speculated: "I'm just projecting back in time—one of the reasons might be that after six months of that failure, I was probably convinced that I wasn't going to be a scientist, so what the hell. I don't need all this crap."[27]

At the time of the crushing loss of his father, Bob could take some consolation in the opportunity to develop a deeper relationship with his own children. "For me, it was a real treat to actually have time to spend with my kids, which I hadn't had before—literally, from the day the first was born when I was in medical school. So, basically, it was time with my family and work. That was it." As to his routine: "I basically worked long hours during the week and probably half a day on Saturday. But, no, I was not one of these guys who was always there working. Because ... I had the family and it was literally the first time I was getting to be a parent. So, I really prized my private time."[28]

Freed from his own high (and perhaps unrealistic) expectations for success in research, Lefkowitz could calm down and let his own cortisol levels drop from anxiety-induced peaks. This is not to suggest that the work got any easier or that the frustrations disappeared, but at least he could cope better with them. He continued his experiments, making nominal progress into his second year. Then, his 1 percent chance for success kicked in. With Pastan's help, Lefkowitz obtained adrenal tissue and prepared an extract of membrane fragments in order to conduct binding studies. Under Roth's guidance, he was able to label ACTH with radioactive iodine in two forms while still preserving the hormone's function. He eventually navigated around the roadblock of separating out the labeled and unlabeled forms of the hormone. With the necessary tools in hand, Lefkowitz began testing the ability of the radiolabeled hormone to bind to the adrenal extract. He also measured the response of the extract in producing the next step in hormonal action. As results began to come in, Lefkowitz had data that required interpretation, so he consulted with his two mentors.

"Jesse [Roth] was the most enthusiastic, charismatic guy I ever came across," Lefkowitz says with a smile. "When you showed him a result, no matter how trivial, he was hanging from the ceiling. And that was great—I loved him, but he was totally non-critical. He would look at it and in the fullness of time, the result could have been dribble or it could have been important, but his reaction was always the same."[29]

Roth's exuberance was diametrically countered by Pastan's measured response and critical assessment. In Lefkowitz's words: "I would go to Jesse [Roth], show him my result and he would . . . talk about Nobel Prizes—whatever. I'd go to see Ira [Pastan]—same result I'd show him. He'd look at it and he'd say: 'You're trying to interpret that? Did you do this control?'" When the inevitable answer came back—"No"—Pastan would ask him if he had done another control, and again the reply would come back negative. The consultation would end with Pastan's deflating conclusion: "You can't interpret this at all. This is nonsense." Lefkowitz still recalls: "I would go away with my tail between my legs."[30]

Although the conflicting messages from the two mentors might have been confusing on one level, they provided Lefkowitz with a sense of balance that he would take forward into his later work. He needed Roth's infectious enthusiasm to bring him through the dark days of repeated failures. But, as a newly minted investigator, Lefkowitz required Pastan's rigor and skeptical mind-set. One did not have to be a psychoanalyst to see parallels between the styles of the two mentors and those of Lefkowitz's parents. Like Roth, Max Lefkowitz had a nurturing persona, with unbounded warmth and devotion to his beloved son. Rose Lefkowitz, an elementary-school teacher, demonstrated many of the same attributes that Pastan displayed: an appreciation for discipline, integrity, and high performance. These counterbalancing expectations, ingrained in Lefkowitz since his childhood, became the touchstones for his development as a scientist.

As with Lefkowitz's parents, Pastan and Roth shared a special bond. In describing Roth, Pastan uses glowing terms: "Incredibly imaginative, articulate, brilliant person." In reflecting on Roth's style, Pastan insightfully points to early educational experiences. "Jesse was trained as a Talmudic scholar and has what I call a Talmudic way of thinking. Several other scientists I know were trained that way—[it is] a very logical way of putting everything together. Often it is right, sometimes it is wrong, but it is always very logically constructed. Jesse is a very useful person to talk to and to discuss experiments with."[31]

Pastan views his own approach, shaped by Earl Stadtman, as a contest between competing interpretations of results. "Earl never formally told me this, but there is this type of philosophy where you have a thesis," he said, "and then you have an anti-thesis, and then you synthesize it all together. So, there has to be an element in doing experiments of saying: 'Is that really true? You know, maybe it's not true, and maybe, I can do an experiment to try to show it is not true.' So, I am quite focused in doing research that way."[32]

Without judging one approach superior to the other, Pastan contrasted his detail-oriented method to the big-picture perspective invoked by Roth. "He [Roth] liked interesting hypotheses ... [what] Jesse was saying was: 'If this is true, then that is true, and maybe we ought to be doing something else.' It is a little more global."[33] Without question, the broad view that Roth adopted was influenced by his two mentors, Sol Berson and Roz Yalow. With admiration, he notes that they "were miracle people. . . . They were self-taught. They taught themselves research."[34] As outsiders, they were less bound by traditional thinking and approaches. With the RIA, they invented a brand new technology. Rather than focusing narrowly on one problem or one application, they pursued a broad agenda. In so doing, they became archetypes for what Pastan described as "global" investigators.

Drawing on his boyhood studies in Jewish day school, Roth contrasted what he characterized as the "priestly" approach with the "prophetic" tradition. In the priestly school of thought, as practiced by the acolyte, Pastan, and the High Priest, Stadtman, each advance is an orderly and reasoned extension of prior findings. In contrast, the prophetic mode, as typified by Berson and Yalow, and their pupil Roth, involves leaps of original and imaginative insights, often minimally grounded in prior observation. "The giants come from the prophetic tradition," Roth asserted.[35] Roth, a tall man who cast a long shadow, clearly felt at home emulating the titans of the prophetic camp.

So while it may not have been obvious in the interview process, Lefkowitz had lucked into the good fortune of being trained by a prophet *and* a priest. They approached research in two fundamentally different but complementary ways. Pastan favored an empirical, methodical, test–assess–retest, incremental process. Roth followed a more deductive path, beginning with broad, abstract concepts and then designing experiments to test specific instances. Remarkably, these two collaborators drew strength from each other. Roth—the animated, wisecracking New Yorker—and Pastan—the reflective and analytical Bostonian—together were able to tackle a big challenge that required both approaches.

The prophet and priest were still relatively young when they were supervising Lefkowitz. In 1968, Pastan was thirty-seven and Roth was thirty-four. Although Lefkowitz, at twenty-five, was about three years younger than most Clinical Associates, there still was a relatively modest age gap between the two mentors and their trainee. Roth recalled that, as a young supervisor, the nature of his interaction with fellows was particularly close: "There was a comradery that was that of . . . the gang of guys on the block. We were a great team." Later in his career, the dynamics evolved: "As the age spread started to grow, they became more respectful, more restrained . . . the later ones were more like children, whereas the earlier ones were more like kid brothers. It had that kind of intense, joyous participation."[36]

To Lefkowitz, the decade or so between his own age and that of his two mentors seemed like a much larger gap. "I thought that Jesse and Ira were like senior faculty . . . to me, they were like old guys." He recalls his discussions with these "senior citizens": "I would talk to both of them and I'd get different ideas on what to do, almost invariably," he said. "Then, I'd make up my own mind. Either I'd choose which of the two pathways was more productive or I'd work out a merged experiment that would incorporate elements of both. So, again, every time I think back to it, I think: 'Boy, I was so fortunate to have the two of them,' and two such different guys." Lefkowitz added that his mentors had a hands-off approach to supervision: "They were there when I needed them, but otherwise, 'you figure it out for yourself.' . . . I like that mentoring style, but it requires enough maturity on the part of the trainee to know when you need help." As to the process of seeking guidance, Lefkowitz noted: "We didn't have any regular reporting time or anything like that. I worked and when I had something to show them, I'd show them. I would generally show it to both and I would always show it to both separately. Every once in a while, we'd all get together."[37]

Roth, like his own mentors, Berson and Yalow, was in perpetual motion. Lefkowitz laughingly recalled trying to keep pace with the lanky, fast-moving Roth:

> I remember often he'd be standing outside the lab and I'd say: "Jesse, I need to talk with you about something." He'd say, "Come on—let's walk and talk." He wouldn't stand still long enough to actually talk to him. So, we'd go heading off down this long corridor to wherever he was going. I'd literally have to take two steps to his one. I'm not short, either. We would walk and talk. You'd be breathless by the time you got to wherever the hell you were going.[38]

The team had to tackle two key issues. First, they had to demonstrate that, once labeled, the radioactive iodine-hormone retained its biological

function. Second, they had to show that the labeled hormone was binding to receptors and not to other parts of the cell. They went on to establish the strength of binding in a musical chairs–type study, in which the
labeled hormone had to compete for receptor sites and biological activity
with unlabeled hormone and its derivatives of various potencies. This is
the same basic principle underlying the RIA technique.

In short, Lefkowitz had built on the earlier rudimentary study of
Pastan and Roth concerning cell-surface binding of hormones. With
the ACTH model, they had a much more rigorous and quantitative
measurement of biological activity and a definitive assessment of hormone-receptor specificity. It passed the test demanded by a sign that
Roth kept behind his desk: "In God We Trust; All Others Must Show
Their Data."[39] Having convinced themselves that they had demonstrated
the presence of specific, high-affinity ACTH receptors on the surfaces
of responsive adrenal cells that, when bound to a hormone, could trigger
the biological actions of ACTH, they were ready to convince the rest of
the scientific community.

Lefkowitz had never written a scientific paper before, and his first
attempt was, in his words, "painful": "I would go to his [Roth's] apartment and we would literally write together. . . . We would sit there with
a pad and we would compose. . . . It was obsessive. The number of drafts
was beyond belief."[40] When Roth finally was happy with the paper, it
was passed along to Pastan for his input. According to Lefkowitz, Pastan
served "more in the editorial role. My sense is that he [Pastan] would
tone things down and say: 'You can't say that.' He was an editor."[41] Finally, when all three coauthors were happy with the manuscript, they
opted for the prestigious *Proceedings of the National Academy of Sciences.*
The paper was communicated on their behalf by James A. Shannon, who
only a few months earlier had stepped down as director of NIH. The
submission occurred on December 22, 1969—almost exactly a year after
the premature death of Max Lefkowitz and less than eighteen months
after Bob's arrival at NIH. The eight-page paper appeared in print
in March 1970, with Lefkowitz as the first author, followed by Roth,
Pastan, and, between them, William Pricer, the senior technician who
had assisted in the work.[42]

With a functioning experimental system in place, Lefkowitz was able to generate several additional publications[43] as he wrapped up the research fellowship. Roth remembers the series of publications as coming quickly: "Bang, bang, bang—three more on ACTH—different aspects of it."[44] As Lefkowitz described: "There was another in *Science* applying it in trying to develop an assay that you could use to actually detect ACTH levels in patients. Then the third one was in *Nature*."[45] Lefkowitz was batting three-for-three in some of the most respected medical journals. A half-century later, with the perspective of a lifetime of dealing with journal editors, Lefkowitz confessed: "It is so amazing when I think back, that my first three papers—I thought nothing of it at the time because no journal was anything to me—that my first three papers were in *PNAS*, *Science*, and *Nature*." Lefkowitz admitted: "The one in *Nature*—it wasn't a big deal—it had to do with some calcium requirements for hormone activation, but not for binding. No great shakes, in retrospect. It's just that receptors were so new then. You could've published anything."[46] The trifecta of ACTH receptor publications also served as a harbinger of what was to come in Lefkowitz's career. To date, he has produced an almost unheard-of 900 scientific publications, including eighty-five in the *Proceedings of the National Academy of Sciences*, thirty-nine in *Nature* journals, thirty in *Science,* and a half-dozen in the *New England Journal of Medicine*, as well as many more in other prestigious journals.

After a year and a half of frustration, Lefkowitz was now a published author of paradigm-shifting studies. Although the earlier paper by Pastan and Roth had received limited attention, in the intervening years the scientific world had warmed up to the idea of cell-surface receptors, and the ACTH papers were generating a buzz of excitement. Nobody could have been more surprised than Lefkowitz himself. At age twenty-seven, less than two years into his research career, he was part of a major discovery, and in that process he became hooked on science. As he would later reminisce: "The idea caught fire in my imagination that you could do this."[47] Elsewhere, he described the emotional impact of making a new finding: "Once you experience the exhilaration of knowing that you know something in that moment that nobody else knew, even if it is very small in its import, it is very seductive."[48]

Although the bulk of the time that Lefkowitz spent at NIH was devoted to laboratory research, as with other Clinical Associates he also had patient-care responsibilities. These involved a half-day per week in an endocrinology clinic and, separately, a couple of months each year on the in-patient service. The patients for whom he cared were referred because of special interests from the NIH scientists. "Jesse's claim to fame was that when he was a fellow with Berson and Yalow, he developed the first radioimmunoassay for growth hormone. Now, he was running a study, which would become the definitive study of acromegalics."[49] The term "acromegaly" is derived from the Greek *akron*, meaning "extremity," and *megas*, meaning "big." The name of this condition refers to the tendency of affected persons to have enlarged bones in their hands, feet, and face. It is an uncommon disorder that may develop insidiously in middle-aged adults when the pituitary gland produces too much growth hormone. The NIH Clinical Center was one of the few places where these patients were being studied at the time, so Lefkowitz saw more than his fair share: "I worked up probably more acromegalic patients during that time than 99 percent of endocrinologists see in their lifetime," he said. "They [patients with acromegaly] had a big, beefy hand that I just learned to recognize.... Twice in my clinical career, after that, I was able to make a diagnosis of acromegaly previously unsuspected by everybody else who saw the patient, just by shaking their hand."[50]

The call schedule was not particularly burdensome: "The every-fifth night that you were on call was great because nothing ever happened. So, you'd work in the lab," he recalled. "It was a good excuse to work late. Even the two months that you were on service . . . new patients—they were all elective—so they'd arrive in the morning. By early afternoon, you were done. You'd make your rounds, so you had the rest of the day to work in the lab."[51] When Clinical Associates were called for an emergency, it might not be the type of urgent situation one would find in a busy teaching hospital. Lefkowitz laughingly recalled one such episode:

> My beeper went off one night. I called the operator and she said something like: "Is this Dr. Lefkowitz?" I said: "Yes." She said: "Are you the

Officer of the Day?" and I said: "Yes, I am." She says: "Code Yellow." I said: "I don't know what that means." She said: "You're the Officer of the Day. You are supposed to know this." I said: "Well, I don't know it and if you don't tell me, I can't help you." She said: "Okay, I'm not supposed to tell you this, but it means animals loose ... animals loose in the building." I pictured like a stampeding herd of God-knows-what.[52]

With that image bringing a smile to his face, Lefkowitz continued:

I said: "Can you tell me the location?" She said: "Yes, it's on the ninth or tenth floor of the Clinical Center." I said: "Okay, what am I supposed to do?" She said: "I don't really know, but you probably should go up there." So, I go up to the ninth or tenth floor and it's late at night and all locked up. I see a light, so I go into a lab and there's a guy there. I said: "Did you report the animals loose in the building?" He said: "Yes, I did." I said: "What's going on?" He said that he was working with some mice and two of them jumped off the thing and he can't find them. I said: "Well, can I help you look for them?" And he said: "Sure." So, we looked around for a while, but never found them.[53]

With his credentials in Code Yellow established, Lefkowitz was offered and accepted an appointment to further his clinical training in cardiology at Massachusetts General Hospital. As he recalled: "Even though the [ACTH] project was then working and Jesse tried significantly, in my recollection, to get me to stay, I had already committed myself to go to Mass General. And frankly ... I was so burdened down by all of the failure that I wasn't all that sorry to be leaving it all behind and moving on to something new."[54] The surprise would come a few months later while immersed in clinical work: he would realize just how much he missed the thrill of scientific discovery.

With the departure of Lefkowitz, Roth continued the hormone-receptor work with a series of talented Clinical Associates. After identifying insulin receptors in an experimental system using liver cells, he entered a period of remarkable productivity, both in the lab and in translating the basic research findings into studies of human patients. As Roth described: "We were very lucky. The receptor stuff became fabulous . . . the receptors were just pouring [out] good things . . . we were getting invited to meetings everywhere to talk about receptors."[55] One of the aspects that Roth most cherished was the expansion of the concepts and methods from work on insulin to many other hormones: "In those days, there was fluidity, like the Renaissance—Ah! The boundaries didn't hold; the ideas spread!"[56]

Among the Clinical Associates who joined Roth in the receptor work was C. Ronald "Ron" Kahn, who later would emerge as a leader in endocrinology, eventually becoming president and director of the Joslin Clinic, a renowned diabetes center in Boston. Another trainee—one of the few African Americans at NIH during that era—was James Gavin, who would go on to assume leadership roles at Howard Hughes Medical Institute and the Morehouse School of Medicine. Yet another Clinical Associate who worked with Roth was Jeffrey Flier, whose career would lead to becoming dean of the faculty of medicine at Harvard University. One of Roth's greatest legacies was his ability to judge, attract, and develop talent—"the guys on the block," as he had described them: some guys—some block!

As for Pastan's path forward, his horizons were expanding in other directions. And though he remained engaged with the receptor work for a few years, he would forge a research partnership in a different area of investigation. That is another story altogether, which we discuss in the next chapter.

Clinical Center, National Institutes of Health. Undated. Courtesy of the Office of NIH History and Stetten Museum, the National Institutes of Health, Bethesda, MD.

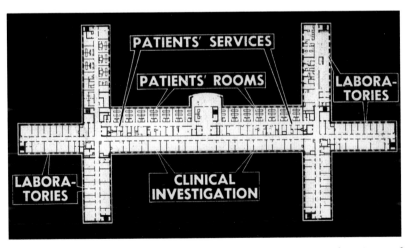

Architectural layout of a typical floor of the Clinical Center, National Institutes of Health, with a long corridor of patient rooms and an adjacent corridor of research laboratories. Undated. Courtesy of the Office of NIH History and Stetten Museum, the National Institutes of Health, Bethesda, MD.

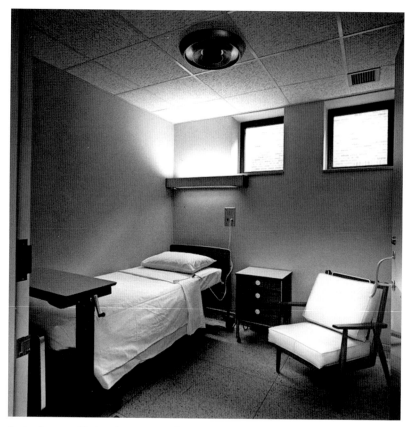

Patient's room, National Institutes of Health. Undated. Courtesy of the Office of NIH History and Stetten Museum, the National Institutes of Health, Bethesda, MD.

The
WAR goes on
more bombing
more deaths
more countries

COME help stop it

RALLY TO END THE WAR
WEDNESDAY OCT 13
Lafayette Park - NOON

you say you'll think about it — but have
questions?

MEETING TO PLAN
TO ANSWER
QUESTIONS

TUESDAY OCT 12
Wilson Hall - noon

vietnam moratorium committee at
NIH / NIMH

Rally poster, Vietnam Moratorium Committee war protest, National Institutes of Health. 1969. Courtesy of the Office of NIH History and Stetten Museum, the National Institutes of Health, Bethesda, MD.

Joseph Goldstein, photograph for Clinical Associate's application. 1966. Courtesy of the Office of NIH History and Stetten Museum, the National Institutes of Health, Bethesda, MD, and Dr. Goldstein.

NAME					*1968*	
GOLDSTEIN, Joseph Leonard		*NHI — CA*				DATE 4/18/66

P. ADDRESS **Box 178, Kingstree, So. Carolina**
M. ADDRESS ~~5319 Fleetwood Oaks Dr., Apt. 256, Dallas, Texas~~

DOB	CITIZENSHIP	APPLIED FOR	APPLIED TO
4/18/40	US	Ca-RA-SA	**NHI, NIAMD**

SCHOOL **M.D. '66, Univ. of Texas Southwestern Medical School**
INTERNSHIP ✓ **'66-67, Int. Med., Mass. Gen. Hosp., Boston, Mass.**
RESIDENCY *67-68 —* " " " " "

INTEREST **Full-time career in academic medicine in field of internal medicine. As a faculty member in a department of int. med. I would anticipate that my major activities would include teaching and basic medical research. My investigative interests will probably be in the field of intermediary metabolism.**

EXPERIENCE SOUGHT AT NIH. **.the basic biochemical trng. & background that will prepare me to carry out independent investigations in some aspect of**

HONOR SOCIETIES **AOA; Phi Beta Kappa; Omicron Delta Kappa (inter. metab.**

ACTIONS	L.I.	APP. SENT	CO. ST.OP. 4/19/66
	REJ.	APP'T.	CORD APP:

O.P. ACTION

NIH-106-6
Rev. 9-65   **NIH ASSOCIATE INFORMATION AND STATUS RECORD**

Joseph Goldstein, Clinical Associate application card, National Institutes of Health. April 18, 1966. Courtesy of the Office of NIH History and Stetten Museum, the National Institutes of Health, Bethesda, MD, and Dr. Goldstein.

Marshall Nirenberg in research laboratory, National Institutes of Health. Undated. Courtesy of the Office of NIH History and Stetten Museum, the National Institutes of Health, Bethesda, MD.

"UUU ARE GREAT MARSHALL" [Nirenberg] banner hung in hallway on the day of the Nobel Prize announcement, National Institutes of Health. October 16, 1968. Courtesy of the National Library of Medicine, Bethesda, MD.

House staff, Massachusetts General Hospital, Boston; Michael Brown (*row 2, second from right*) and Joseph Goldstein (*row 3, far left*) are among the resident physicians present. 1967. Courtesy of Drs. Brown and Goldstein.

NAME **BROWN, Michael Stuart** *NIAMD - Laster* *1968* DATE 5/6/66

P. ADDRESS ~~269 Harvard St., Cambridge, Mass. (As of 6/1/66)~~ *Please see*
M. ADDRESS ~~4242 Spruce St., Phil. Penn. 19104 (Until 6/1/66)~~ *letter*

DOB	CITIZENSHIP	APPLIED FOR	APPLIED TO **NCI, NHI, NIAMD, NINDB**	*for later*
4/13/41	US	CA,RA,SA		*(over)*

SCHOOL **M.D. Univ. of Penn. Scho. of Med.** *new address*
INTERNSHIP **1966-67 Mass. General Hosp., Boston 02114 - Medicine**
RESIDENCY *'67-68* " " "

INTEREST **Research, teaching & practice in metabolic disease.**
Academic care er, concentrating on research into biochemical
mechanisms and their application to disease states.

EXPERIENCE SOUGHT AT NIH **Extension & deepening of background in biochem.,**
especially enzyme kinetics, protein structure & mechanisms of (over)

HONOR SOCIETIES **Phi Beta Kappa, Alpha Omega Alpha**

ACTIONS	L.I.	APP. SENT	CO.ST.OP. *5/10/66*
	REJ.	APP'T.	CORD) APP:

O.P. ACTION *NIAMD - Metabolic Disease Br.*
CA

NIH-106-6
Rev. 9-65   NIH ASSOCIATE INFORMATION AND STATUS RECORD

SEEK AT NIH: heredity - and the methods by which these are
elucidated.

New address - per letter in folder
    Michael S. Brown, M.D.
    c/o Mr. Harvey Brown
    155 West 68th Street
    New York, N. Y.

Michael Brown, Clinical Associate application card, National Institutes of Health.
May 6, 1966. Courtesy of the Office of NIH History and Stetten Museum, the National
Institutes of Health, Bethesda, MD, and Dr. Brown.

Clinical Investigations' class photograph, National Institute of Arthritis and Metabolic Diseases (NIAMD), National Institutes of Health; Michael Brown (*row 2, third from right*), Robert Lefkowitz (*row 3, third from right*), Harold Varmus (*row 4, third from right*), and Ira Pastan (*row 2, fourth from left*) are among the investigators present. December 1968. Courtesy of the Office of NIH History and Stetten Museum, the National Institutes of Health, Bethesda, MD.

Earl Stadtman in research laboratory, National Institutes of Health. Undated. Courtesy of the Office of NIH History and Stetten Museum, the National Institutes of Health, Bethesda, MD.

Harold Varmus as a medical student prepares for a fellowship at a mission hospital in India. Columbia University, College of Physicians and Surgeons. *Stethoscope* 20, no. 5 (May 1965): 7. Courtesy of Archives and Special Collections, Health Sciences Library, Columbia University.

Harold Varmus, medical school graduation photograph. Columbia University, College of Physicians and Surgeons yearbook, 1966, p. 79. Courtesy of Archives and Special Collections, Health Sciences Library, Columbia University, and Dr. Varmus.

ultimately to devote to it; an opportunity to learn to use research tools; a chance to become more deeply involved in any one of several areas of interest than has been possible at school, so that I may, for the first time, begin to formulate concrete experimental plans of my own.

96 Haven Ave.
Apt. 45
Presbyterian Hosp.

Harold Varmus, Clinical Associate application card, National Institutes of Health. March 25, 1966. Courtesy of the Office of NIH History and Stetten Museum, the National Institutes of Health, Bethesda, MD, and Dr. Varmus.

Medical house staff, Columbia Presbyterian Medical Center; Harold Varmus (*row 3,
far left*) and Robert Lefkowitz (*row 1, seated, far left*). 1967–1968. Columbia University,
College of Physicians and Surgeons. Courtesy of Archives and Special Collections,
Health Sciences Library, Columbia University, and Dr. Varmus.

Investigators in research laboratory, National Institutes of Health; Jesse Roth (*standing, far left*) and Ira Pastan (*standing, far right*) are among those present. Undated. Courtesy of the Office of NIH History and Stetten Museum, the National Institutes of Health, Bethesda, MD, and Dr. Pastan.

Robert Lefkowitz with his eldest son, David. Columbia University, College of Physicians and Surgeons yearbook, 1966, p. 94. Courtesy of Archives and Special Collections, Health Sciences Library, Columbia University.

Classroom, College of Physicians and Surgeons; Harold Varmus (*row 2, far left*) and Robert Lefkowitz (*row 2, second from left*) are among the students present, with Professor Kneeland, "Differential Diagnosis." Columbia University, College of Physicians and Surgeons yearbook, 1966, p. 34. Courtesy of Archives and Special Collections, Health Sciences Library, Columbia University.

Robert Lefkowitz, medical school graduation photograph. Columbia University, College of Physicians and Surgeons yearbook, 1966, p. 72. Courtesy of Archives and Special Collections, Health Sciences Library, Columbia University.

NAME **LEFKOWITZ, Robert Joseph** *NIAMD - Roth* *1968* DATE 3/28/66

P. ADDRESS **1565 Odell St., Box 62, NYC**

M. ADDRESS

DOB	CITIZENSHIP	APPLIED FOR	APPLIED TO **NHI, NIAMD**
4/15/43	**US**	**CA-RA**	

SCHOOL **M.D. '66, Columbia Univ. Col of Phys. & Surgeons**

INTERNSHIP ✓ **'66-67, Med., Presbyterian Hospital, NYC**

RESIDENCY **'67-68, Med., "**

INTEREST **Academic Medicine. After 2 yrs. at NIH I would return to a Univ affiliated Hosp. & obtain further residency (subspecialty Metabolism etc & lab. training. Qualify for Amer. Board of Int. Med. Then spend my time in teaching and research.**

EXPERIENCE SOUGHT AT NIH **Opportunity to obtain training in research methods hile availing myself of the resch. opportunities for didactic lectures, etc. on basic science**

HONOR SOCIETIES **Phi Beta Kappa; AOA**

		APP. SENT	CO-6T.OP 3/28/66 bjects.
ACTIONS	L.I.		
	REJ.	APP'T.	CORD APP:

O.P. ACTION

NIH-106-6
Rev. 3-65   NIH ASSOCIATE INFORMATION AND STATUS RECORD

Robert Lefkowitz, Clinical Associate application card, National Institutes of Health. March 28, 1966. Courtesy of the Office of NIH History and Stetten Museum, the National Institutes of Health, Bethesda, MD.

CHAPTER 12

OVERCOMING REPRESSION

Ira Pastan and Harold Varmus

While knee-deep in his pursuit of hormone receptors with Jesse Roth, Ira Pastan entered a partnership with another young NIH scientist, Robert "Bob" L. Perlman. A former Associate, Perlman came to NIH in 1965 for a two-year commission when he was not quite twenty-seven, after completing a medical degree and a doctorate in biochemistry from the University of Chicago. He also had two years of clinical training in pediatrics at Bellevue Hospital, the large public facility in New York. Despite his meteoric trajectory, Perlman was uncertain about what he wanted to do professionally.

As a child, Perlman had considered becoming a rabbi; early in his college years, he toyed with the idea of pursuing philosophy, ultimately selecting medicine because most of his friends were headed in that direction. In medical school, Perlman found a role model in the famed biochemist and pediatrician Albert Dorfman, under whom Perlman also completed his doctoral dissertation.[1]

For a peripatetic soul like Perlman, one could not have found a more understanding supervisor than Harold Edelhoch.[2] Perlman described Edelhoch: "Very generous about letting me sort of look around to see what else I was interested in and pursue other things in my spare time."[3] One of his fellow travelers on this journey was Ira Pastan, with a lab down the hall. Pastan, still a junior member of the Clinical Endocrinology Branch, was seven years older than Perlman and had his own thyroid-related research interests plus collaborative work with Jesse Roth.

Perlman had the opportunity to observe Pastan at the branch's weekly journal club, where newly published papers were discussed. "People would present papers and really dissect them and criticize them and tear them apart in a way," Perlman recalled. "It was a wonderful learning experience for new people entering the field, like myself. I remember being impressed at Ira's critical skill in doing that."[4] One paper that stirred attention was by Earl Sutherland and his student Richard Makman at Case Western Reserve University.[5] This paper was published in 1965 and featured surprising observations. The head-scratching aspect was a chemical messenger that Sutherland and his colleagues had discovered as a key component of hormone action in animal cells that also was present in the lowly gut bacterium *Escherichia coli*. Prior to this study, it was presumed that the molecular components of the sophisticated systems needed to run hormonal signaling between cells would not be found in a single-cell organism like a bacterium.

The hormone communication system that Sutherland first described would lead to his selection in 1971 as the winner of the Nobel Prize in Physiology or Medicine. His work demonstrated that a molecule known as cAMP (cyclic adenosine monophosphate) acts as what Sutherland characterized as a "second messenger," transferring the initial signal from a hormone and then launching a cascade of steps needed to generate the appropriate biological action. Although discovered only later, the initial message is not transmitted directly by the hormone, because it cannot cross the cell's protective surface membrane. Instead, the message is conveyed by the binding of the hormone to a cell-surface receptor—the very same entities that Pastan and Roth were trying to isolate and purify. The bound hormone then triggers the second messenger, cAMP, located inside the cell membrane, to bind to and activate an enzyme. The enzyme then turns on effector proteins, which, depending on the hormone and effector cell pairing, determine the resulting biological activity. For example, in fat cells, the hormone epinephrine enhances the breakdown of fats, whereas in liver cells epinephrine has a completely different effect: increasing the availability of consumable sugar.

Pastan and Perlman had the opportunity to hear directly from Sutherland about the finding of cAMP in *E. coli*. Pastan was coteaching a course on hormone action to NIH Associates. In Pastan's words:

> As a treat in the course, we invited a special lecturer, Earl Sutherland, who had never been to NIH before, and we asked the students to read his papers and then we met together. We did not realize until we invited Earl, and he came, that he had also had a student named Makman use his assay for cAMP in *E. coli*. Makman had shown that *E. coli* contained cAMP and its levels were regulated by glucose.[6]

The study by Makman and Sutherland raised intriguing questions. What was cAMP doing in single-cell organisms in the first place? And why was the level of cAMP in bacterial cells dependent on how much glucose—a simple sugar—was present? "Oh, my goodness," Pastan recalled thinking, "that would be interesting to study!" For Pastan, part of the attraction to studying cAMP in bacteria was that he "got into the field a little late; everyone was already studying cAMP action in animal cells. . . . I decided I would work in bacteria."[7] There was no compelling reason to jump into a new research area—he already had a successful collaboration with Jesse Roth on hormone receptors. In fact, it might be argued that it was risky for Pastan to divide his energies between two separate lines of research. "So, there was a huge conflict for me as to what to do, because both were extremely interesting."[8] As it turned out, the reward for taking on this parallel effort would be well worth the risk.

A great deal was already known about how *E. coli* controls the enzymes needed for digesting various sugars as sources of fuel. The preferred energy source for this bacterium (and most others) is glucose, because it is widely available and easily digested. When glucose is not available, however, *E. coli* can make a dietary substitution and feed instead on the milk sugar lactose. When there is a plentiful supply of glucose, the bacterium does not need to produce the enzymes for lactose digestion. Only when glucose is out of stock does *E. coli* need to rev up its lactose metabolism machinery. The way in which *E. coli* turns on and off the lactose-processing enzymes was the subject of the 1965 Nobel Prize in Physiology or Medicine awarded to François Jacob and Jacques Monod of the Pasteur Institute in Paris, along with their colleague André Lwoff.

Between 1958 and 1961, Jacob and Monod conducted a series of experiments on gene regulation in *E. coli*. This work began at the dawn of molecular biology, a mere five years after James Watson and Francis Crick first described the structure of DNA. Monod was an old-school biochemist whose work had demonstrated that the enzyme *E. coli* needed to break down lactose was more plentiful when lactose was present. Jacob was a geneticist who studied how viral genes operated within the bacterial cells they invaded. The combination of their knowledge, and the integration of observations from these two different systems, led to their proposal of a generalizable model of gene regulation.

Jacob and Monod proposed that a set of genes worked together to allow *E. coli* to utilize lactose. In 1960, they referred to a collection of coordinated genes as an "operon" (from the French *opérer*, meaning "to effect").[9] The set of genes that controlled lactose consumption was named the "lac operon." In the absence of lactose, the lac operon was turned off (or repressed), so no gene products (enzymes needed for lactose consumption) were made. In contrast, when lactose was present, the lac operon was turned on (i.e., it was "induced" or "de-repressed"), meaning that the genes were activated to produce the enzymes needed to digest this alternative food source.[10]

Fundamental to the Jacob-Monod model of regulation of gene expression is that control is exerted by an off-switch called, appropriately enough, the "repressor molecule." When a repressor protein binds to a specific site on the cell's DNA, it blocks the transcription of a specific gene or set of genes. The repressor protein can be incapacitated by an inducer molecule, such as lactose. The inducer binds to the repressor protein, thereby distorting its physical shape and impairing its ability to bind to DNA.[11] Incredibly, Jacob and Monod developed their model prior to the isolation of actual repressors or knowing the mechanisms by which they operate. It would be another five years before Walter Gilbert of Harvard University, working with the graduate student Benno Müller-Hill, isolated the lac repressor.[12] Gilbert shared the 1980 Nobel Prize in Chemistry for later work on sequencing the bases in DNA.

Back in 1967, the year after Gilbert and Müller-Hill isolated the repressor protein and two years after Makman and Sutherland found cAMP in *E. coli*, Pastan and Perlman began to wonder if there was a connection. They speculated that cAMP might overcome repression of the lac operon, allowing lactose to be used as a fuel source, even when glucose was present. Part of the appeal of exploring this topic was pragmatic. Pastan had undertaken a postdoctoral fellowship with Earl Stadtman, whose work focused on metabolism in bacteria. "Since I worked in Earl's lab," Pastan said, "I knew about growing bacteria in small and large amounts and extracting them to measure activities."[13] Beyond his relevant skill set, Pastan knew that it was a formidable topic: "There were all these exciting things going on in genetics and gene regulation and this was an opportunity to work in that area."[14] So, Pastan and Perlman jumped in together to study cAMP in *E. coli*.

Years later, Perlman had nostalgic memories of his collaboration with Pastan: "What impressed me was . . . his [Pastan's] enthusiasm and I think we both had it, but it was probably infectious and I got a lot of it from him. It was a time when we couldn't wait to do the experiments and then talk about them and then plan the next one." He continued: "It was just a heady, exciting time. . . . We would do experiments during the day and then go home and after dinner we would talk on the phone—what the results were and how to understand them and what we should do the next day." With a laugh, he recalled: "My wife said that we were like two teenage girls who wanted to talk on the phone all day long. It was just a very exciting and intense collaboration."[15]

When Pastan and Perlman added cAMP to the bacterial preparation, within a matter of minutes they observed increased production of the enzyme of interest: beta-galactosidase. This enzyme assists in breaking the two-sugar molecule of lactose into its equal component simple sugar parts—galactose and glucose. Because bacteria need simple sugars to use as fuel, beta-galactosidase activity is the key to making lactose a bacterial energy source.[16]

For Perlman:

> The first results of showing that cAMP did increase the synthesis of beta-galactosidase was as much of an "Aha!" moment as I have ever had. We worried about how cAMP was going to get into the cells, whether the experiments were going to work, but we just put it [cAMP] in, and it did work, and that was enormously exciting and then much of the rest of the work was more carefully documenting it and then trying to work out the mechanisms by which it acted. But the original phenomenon was what was exciting.[17]

Pastan and Perlman wrote up their findings and quickly discovered that some journal reviewers did not share the same excitement about the "Aha!" moment. According to Perlman: "There were publication setbacks because our initial papers were rejected and we were very despondent about that."[18] The reason that journals originally refused publication was that the upstart investigators at NIH were challenging established dogma about gene regulation. "There were people who studied this phenomenon of catabolite repression for a long time and the model that they had was just completely the opposite of what we had." Perlman continued: "Because of the work of Jacob and Monod, the idea was that genes were regulated by repression. Genes were turned off by repressors. The whole concept of catabolite repression was that when cells were growing on glucose, there were some unknown molecules that accumulated that repressed the expression of these genes."[19] The genes in question were those of the lac operon, and they coded for enzymes, like beta-galactosidase, that were needed for the consumption of lactose. "When the cells ran out of glucose, these repressors were degraded and decreased in concentration and then the gene was expressed because of the de-repression. What we were saying was: 'No, it is induction and activation of transcription' and that was just contrary to the prevailing models of how genes were regulated."[20]

In other words, the orthodoxy held that there was only one way in which gene expression was controlled. As yet undefined factors were assumed to prevent particular genes from being expressed, thereby blocking production of the enzymes for which these genes coded. Only when these unidentified blocking agents, or repressors, were removed would the genes be transcribed and the corresponding enzymes produced. Pastan and Perlman were suggesting that the expression of genes could be controlled in a completely different way. They proposed that cAMP was exerting its effect not by blocking repression but rather by stimulating gene expression. Eventually, journal editors were persuaded, leading to publication of several papers on the topic in prominent journals.[21]

The progress in studying gene regulation led Pastan to redirect his research efforts in 1967. Although he would maintain a partnership with Jesse Roth on hormone receptors, he decided to discontinue his own work on thyroid hormones. In place of thyroid studies, Pastan threw himself into work he had launched with Perlman. One person caught off his guard by this sudden switch was Harold Varmus.

A year earlier, Varmus interviewed for a Clinical Associate position at NIH. Interested in the emerging fields of molecular biology and genetics, Varmus had a full day of meetings with the heads of many leading labs at NIH. As an English major, Varmus did not have the traditional science pedigree that most interviewers were seeking. One of the senior investigators, Jacob Robbins, chief of the Clinical Endocrinology Branch at NIAMD, decided to play matchmaker. He thought that Varmus might find a connection with Ira Pastan. Robbins knew that Pastan, who was selecting his own Clinical Associate for the first time, would not have the pick of the litter. So, by linking Varmus up with Pastan, both might come out ahead.

Recalling the selection process, Pastan said: "It was very hard to distinguish among the people you interviewed and I was young . . . I wasn't much older than many of the people [who were applying to be Clinical Associates]. . . . And I had very little experience in interviewing anybody."[22] As to what made Varmus an appealing candidate, Pastan added: "Part of the reason that I ranked him high, in addition to his outstanding grades and the fact that I enjoy people who have diverse backgrounds, was that he had been an English major at Amherst. He had been the editor of the paper and had a master's degree in English, and my wife was a writer." As Pastan observed: "Harold was bright and quick and you could talk to him about anything—that was an additional plus that probably pushed him slightly over the other ones."[23]

And as Varmus later confessed, he had ranked more established labs higher, but when he was paired up with Pastan, "this outcome could not have been more fortunate."[24] In the intervening two years, Varmus would complete his medical residency at Columbia-Presbyterian Hospital alongside fellow trainee and medical school classmate Bob Lefkowitz. Absorbed in the work of caring for patients, Varmus had little time to contemplate the research that he would be undertaking at NIH. In the middle of his clinical training, he received a call from Ira Pastan out of the blue with unexpected news. Using words that must have sounded like Greek to Varmus, Pastan described his late-breaking results with Perlman: "We've found that cAMP reverses catabolite repression of the lac operon of *E. coli*."[25] As a result, Pastan explained that he was dropping the thyroid research that Varmus was expecting to begin the following year.

As Varmus hung up the phone to return to caring for his sick patients, his head was spinning. He had no idea why Pastan was so excited about this new research direction. In fact, he had no idea what Pastan was even talking about. The seminal work of Jacob and Monod on gene regulation was less than a decade old, and the resulting Nobel Prize was awarded to them while Varmus was a medical student, so it had not yet filtered into the medical school curriculum.

When things quieted down on the wards that evening—and still in shock from his conversation with Pastan—Varmus headed to the hospital's library to try to figure out what was meant by "cAMP," "catabolite repression," and "lac operon." It was a self-taught crash course in gene regulation, but it was enough to give him an understanding of what he would be investigating at NIH. What he could not learn from reading in the hospital library was how one actually goes about conducting research experiments. As a novice investigator, he had a rude introduction to laboratory work when he arrived at the Clinical Center in July 1968. On his very first day, he managed to contaminate a sink with radioactive material, ruin an experiment, and demonstrate his ignorance of routinely used chemical reagents. It was an inauspicious start, and Varmus claims that his new boss needled him with a rhetorical question: "Now remind me why I took you in the lab."[26]

In truth, Pastan dismissed these early struggles that Varmus and his fellow trainee, Bob Lefkowitz, encountered as they started their research work: "The first year is pretty tough for everybody. You are in a new field with new techniques and you do not know the background—you don't know the field. It's very hard to get started. I always tell someone . . . it is going to take a year . . . to learn the field and learn the techniques and figure out how to do things."[27]

Harold Varmus was tasked with answering a question: Does cAMP boost the production of the lactose-metabolizing enzyme (beta-galactosidase) by increasing the amount of RNA that is transcribed from the relevant lac operon gene that codes for this enzyme? The difficulty in answering is that even a simple, single-celled organism like *E. coli* has thousands of genes. The RNA transcribed by a single gene, or a few genes, is easily lost in a sea of RNA produced by the multitude of other genes. Was there a way to separate out the weak signal of the RNA of interest from the loud background noise of the remaining RNA?

The process of isolating and measuring RNA for beta-galactosidase was complicated and took quite some time for the team to optimize. The first thing they needed was a source of *E. coli* genes. For this, Pastan, Perlman, and Varmus had a friendly lab assistant in the form of a virus that had invaded an *E. coli* previously and snipped out the bacterial genes of interest. The virus (or "phage," as bacteria-invading viruses are known) preserved the bacteria genes that it appropriated from *E. coli* by splicing them into its own DNA. In this way, the phage became a not-so-innocent carrier of the bacteria genes, unsullied by the presence of the remaining thousands of other *E. coli* genes.

Now that Perlman, Pastan, and Varmus had secured an uncontaminated source of bacteria DNA, they could use it as bait to catch the corresponding RNA produced by *E. coli*. For this purpose, the team used a clever technique referred to as "molecular hybridization." It has several steps, beginning with separating the double-helical strands of DNA obtained previously from the viral thief and pulling them apart (also called "denaturing"). Then, the unpaired strands are affixed to a special filter paper so that the single filaments cannot reattach to each other. Unable to get back together, the divorced DNA strands then look for an alternative partner, which they can find when bathed in a solution containing matching RNA. The DNA hooks up to corresponding segments of RNA, much like a highly specific molecular Velcro.

In order to succeed, Perlman, Pastan, and Varmus needed a method to measure the amount of RNA that was captured in these highly specific DNA-RNA pairings, or hybrids. This was accomplished by growing *E. coli* in media containing radioactively labeled uridine—one of the nucleosides that the bacterium uses to build RNA. The resulting RNA made from these "hot" building blocks can be quantified by the amount of radioactivity that is measured using an instrument that operates like a Geiger counter.

Putting the entire process together, the team used the phage's stolen *E. coli* lac operon DNA as a specific snare for the radioactive RNA products transcribed by the bacteria under conditions of varying levels of cAMP and sugars. With the test system functioning, they demonstrated that adding a lactose metabolite to the bacteria increased the transcription of RNA by the genes that allowed lactose metabolism. When they added glucose, as they expected, the level of the lac operon gene transcription fell precipitously. Finally, when they also included cAMP, the level of transcription was more than restored to the amount observed before glucose was added. Their hypotheses were confirmed: glucose (the repressor) and cAMP (the activator) both were operating, albeit in different directions, on the transcription of the lac operon genes.

For Varmus this was an important outcome: "The hybridization assays that Ira and I developed allowed me to enjoy my first eureka moments. I could accurately measure the amount of the lac operon RNA in a bacterial cell."[28] He would later add: "Things like measuring amounts of RNA are so trivial now that students would laugh at my finding this an emotional experience. But to be able to say: 'The gene is off in this cell, and the gene is on in that cell'—that's pretty thrilling. And I knew the questions that I wanted to answer could be answered; I had an assay that was really clean."[29] With these methods, he was able to demonstrate something that nobody had observed before. That is, cAMP helped bacterial cells utilize lactose as fuel by increasing the amount of RNA transcribed so that more of the necessary digestive enzymes could be produced. cAMP was acting as an on-switch for gene expression.

Having experience working with many trainees over subsequent decades, Ira Pastan put his observations about his first handpicked Clinical Associate, Harold Varmus, into perspective: "It took him almost no time to figure out what the important thing was to do and to get it done. He can . . . figure out what the core [of a problem] is and how to deal with it very efficiently. He doesn't get sidetracked. He's not chatty. He identifies it and gets it done. I don't think I've worked with anyone ever who has the skills that Harold has."[30]

For Varmus—the former English literature major who had not stepped into a research laboratory until a year earlier and, even then, did so primarily as an alternative to serving in Vietnam—it was a revelation that he had a talent for conducting research. He recalled the feeling: "This is stuff I can do. Once I got the hang of it, I felt powerful. I could do things. I saw a question and I could answer it. Things moved incredibly quickly, and I just didn't have any failures."[31]

In September 1969, the team was ready to publish its findings. Pastan instructed his trainee to prepare the first draft of a paper. Once an initial manuscript was in hand, Pastan would suggest edits and improvements, expecting multiple revisions and many teachable moments. When tasked with preparing the first version of the cAMP/lac operon transcription paper, the English major in Harold Varmus resurfaced quickly. Pastan recalled that Harold "went home and he wrote it in a weekend and he could really type and he brought in this almost perfect paper. I couldn't believe it." Continuing, Pastan noted that: "He [Varmus] liked writing before he went into science. . . . If you read Harold's papers or hear him talk, it is a little different—a little more literary."[32]

Varmus shared equally fond memories of his first research writing assignment: "Once I learned the established rituals for organizing a scientific paper—title, abstract, introduction, methods, results, discussion—the writing itself was a pleasure. Clear exposition. Grammatical rectitude. Some nice turns of phrase to give the manuscript some class. I did not have to be taught this part of the process."[33] An example of the "nice turn of phrase" in this paper was "scant definitive information has been forthcoming,"[34] which is so much more appealing than the pedestrian but oft-encountered "little is known about this topic."

Another manner in which research findings are communicated to other scientists is by presentation at a meeting. It just so happened that a meeting was organized on the topic of the lac operon at the Cold Spring Harbor Laboratory around the time that Varmus obtained his initial experimental results. The Cold Spring Lab, which came under the direction of the Nobel laureate James Watson the year before, could assemble a premier group of handpicked attendees. The star-studded invitation list included the Nobel Prize winner and codiscoverer of the lac operon, Jacques Monod, and the future Nobel laureate and discoverer of the lac repressor, Walter Gilbert. Within the intimate confines of the private campus on the tony North Shore of Long Island, the meeting convened on Monday evening, September 1, 1969, with Monod delivering opening remarks, followed by a session chaired by Gilbert. The meeting continued with morning and afternoon sessions all week.

Pastan was assigned two times to speak—one on each of the final two days of the conference. Pastan was an outsider to the exclusive club of molecular geneticists, and these talks would provide him an opportunity to establish himself with the cognoscenti. Rather than basking in the limelight alone, however, he chose to allow his colleagues—including Varmus—to present as well. This was an exhilarating moment for a physician who only a couple of years earlier was teaching himself about the lac operon through late-night reading at the Columbia-Presbyterian Hospital library. Team Pastan scored a major victory that week: Repression was not the whole story on gene regulation; activation of genes also could occur.

As often is the case in scientific research, new findings may answer one question while raising many others. In this situation, Varmus and his mentor demonstrated that cAMP was involved in stimulating transcription of the lac operon genes, but as Varmus himself might have written, "Scant definitive information on the mechanism of cAMP action has been forthcoming." It is one thing to demonstrate that cAMP has a boosting effect on lac operon gene expression, but it is quite another to show how it exerts that effect. In short order, they provided further insight.

A subsequent paper, submitted as Varmus was preparing to complete his appointment, suggested that cAMP did not act alone. A protein that Perlman and Pastan had just identified[35] and labeled "cAMP receptor protein" (CRP) was shown to be an essential partner to cAMP in activating transcription.[36] Later work would show that this protein is involved in the regulation of more than a hundred genes in *E. coli*, mostly involved in the digestion of sugar fuels. When cAMP is present and bound to CRP, the protein's structure is altered, allowing it to bind to specific regions of DNA where it can control transcription. The cAMP-CRP complex can increase the initiation of transcription, as exemplified by its effect on the lac operon. Elsewhere, the cAMP-CRP duo can inhibit initiation, and in still other cases, the bound combo impedes the termination of transcription.[37]

In reflecting on the discovery of the role of cAMP and CRP on gene transcription, particularly in the early days when their interpretations were questioned, Perlman credits Pastan with teaching him: "That you have to have the courage of your convictions and continue to pursue your ideas, even if they are unpopular and met with resistance. It is not enough to be smart and creative. . . . There is a certain amount of intellectual courage, or personal courage, that is required to go against the grain."[38] For Pastan, the dogged pursuit of a new theory about how genes are controlled brought him recognition and, not surprisingly, recruitment by a number of leading universities. As he later recalled: "When we discovered cAMP was important in gene regulation, that was a big deal and I was invited everywhere. And one of the jobs I was invited to consider was at Stanford."[39]

Despite the attraction, Pastan was not packing his bags quite yet for Palo Alto. When he returned to Bethesda, Pastan explained to Mort Lipsett, his tennis partner, that he had decided not to uproot his family. Still, he felt constrained in his current work situation: "I like all of the people, but I'm the youngest and I now have two [laboratory] modules and I will not have more until someone leaves and no one is going to leave." On the spot, Lipsett (an endocrinologist working in the National Cancer Institute) volleyed back: "I thought you were happy where you were . . . but if you're not, why don't you join my group and I'll give you six modules and two technicians and three fellows and an office, and whatever you want."[40] It was a dream offer for Pastan. Game—set—match.

Still, Pastan was apprehensive about a switch in research focus to cancer, which he saw as still in an early stage of development. Fortunately, Lipsett was reassuring, according to Pastan: "He [Lipsett] said, 'You can do the same thing you are doing and you don't need to change anything.'"[41] With that promise in hand, Pastan agreed to relocate his lab, including Varmus, to the National Cancer Institute. He did not have to move far: the trip started on the eighth floor of the Clinical Center and ended two stories higher.[42]

These personnel shifts illustrate a number of signature elements of the NIH at the time. First, resources were not distributed uniformly across the various institutes. Cancer research was in a growth mode, with abundant space and ample funding compared with other institutes. Second, the administration at NIH did not restrict the movement of investigators from one institute to another. In academic settings, such "poaching" of talent often is frowned upon, but at NIH there was a greater sense of shared purpose. Third, in transitioning from an institute on metabolic diseases to one on cancer, Pastan was not required to change his research agenda. He was exploring basic mechanisms of gene regulation, and these were understood to have potentially wide applications, including for cancer causation. The disease-oriented titles of the NIH institutes were not interpreted by the campus leadership as boundary markers for areas of investigation. Fourth, changing institutes did not mean that Pastan could not continue to collaborate with his former colleagues in Arthritis and Metabolic Diseases. The collaborative environment at NIH allowed, and even encouraged, building bridges between investigators in different areas, made easier at the time by their close proximity within the same building. This would become more of a challenge, albeit not an insurmountable one, as the NIH grew, with greater physical separation between the institutes.[43]

For Harold Varmus, there were questions about the next steps. During his time as a Clinical Associate, he had the opportunity to take classes on a variety of topics taught by NIH experts in their respective fields. Two courses had a particularly strong influence on him. One was taught by John Bader, a University of Rochester–trained microbiologist who undertook two years of postdoctoral work at the California Institute of Technology before joining the NIH staff in 1962. Bader was a pioneer in research on viruses whose genetic information was coded in RNA (rather than in DNA).

In his course, Bader introduced Varmus to a concept developed by Howard Temin, a virologist at the University of Wisconsin. Temin proposed (even though scant definitive information had been forthcoming) that these RNA viruses had their genetic information translated into DNA, creating a new entity that he termed a "provirus." The DNA of the provirus then could be incorporated into the DNA of an infected animal cell, leading to subsequent replication of the viral DNA. This theory was highly controversial at the time because it violated, or at least appeared to violate, the "Central Dogma of Molecular Biology"—the first and second commandments of molecular biology as laid down by Francis Crick in 1958: "Thou shalt transcribe genetic information from DNA into RNA" and "Thou shalt translate genetic information from RNA into protein." Temin was accused of profaning these commandments by suggesting that viral RNA could be transcribed into DNA. As we will see later, he would go on to demonstrate that RNA viruses do indeed disobey the first commandment, leading to Temin's selection as a corecipient of the 1975 Nobel Prize in Physiology or Medicine.

The second class that captured Varmus's attention was taught by Michael Potter, a University of Virginia–trained physician who came to NIH in 1954 and emerged as a leader in the field of tumor biology. His early claim to fame—for which he would later receive the Lasker Award in 1984—came from studies showing how injecting mineral oil into the bodies of mice could create solid tumors that produced massive quantities of various antibodies. Potter lectured on the known causes of cancer about five years after the first Surgeon General's report on smoking and health. There was a growing body of evidence pointing the finger at a variety of agents, such as chemicals, radiation, and viruses. Of particular interest to Varmus was how certain RNA viruses can cause cancer—a phenomenon observed in many species. It was plausible, perhaps even likely, that these and other agents acted by damaging the integrity of the cell's genetic material. At the time, however, the mechanisms of gene derangement were sealed in a seemingly impenetrable black box.

The lectures on cancer at NIH were eye-openers for Varmus; he had learned little about the subject in medical school or during two years of clinical training. Treatment for cancer at the time entailed a brutal assault that often produced collateral damage. The literary soul in Varmus was stirred a few years earlier by a leading cancer specialist at Columbia, John Ultmann, who described cancer therapy by invoking words appropriated from Shakespeare: "Diseases desperate grown, By desperate appliance are relieved, Or not at all" (*Hamlet*, Act 4, Scene 3).

Varmus had an up-close and personal view of such desperation. Shortly after he arrived at NIH in 1968, his mother, then in her late fifties, was diagnosed with breast cancer that already had invaded the regional lymph nodes. "We had no idea why she had breast cancer, whether there was a genetic component, whether she'd been exposed to something environmental; it was disturbing [not knowing] whether this was a spontaneous thing that couldn't be predicted."[44] She had her breast and lymph nodes surgically removed, as well as both her adrenal glands (a treatment then used for hormonally dependent cancers), in addition to chemotherapy. "She was well for a year or two after breast surgery, and then it turned up in her bones and other places and there was no way to control it."[45]

Varmus decided that he wanted to focus on cancer and, in particular, on how infection with viruses might give rise to cancer in animal cells. "You infect a cell and the cell changes its behavior; nothing could be more dramatic than that," he said. "And that was a very attractive notion because all of us who had watched cancer develop in our friends and family members, or had taken care of cancer patients on a hospital ward, saw this as one of the great mysteries—why should a normal cell suddenly go crazy and outgrow the surrounding cells and ultimately kill the patient?"[46]

Sigmund Freud, the great teller of medical tales and whose work Varmus admired in graduate school, might have suggested that there was a link between his mother's illness and his decision to dedicate himself to the study of cancer. Varmus resists the notion that his career choice arose from subconscious drives, but he does acknowledge that her malignancy, and the sledgehammer approach then used to treat it, reinforced for him the need to gain a better understanding of cancer.[47]

When Varmus started contemplating job opportunities, the trainee felt a strong pull westward. He had visited friends in the San Francisco area and, like many tourists, fell in love with the city and its surrounding environment. There were several excellent research labs in California with interests in this area. He decided to roll the dice and start at the top with Renato Dulbecco. A virologist at the Salk Institute in La Jolla, California, Dulbecco would win a share of the Nobel Prize in Physiology or Medicine in 1975, along with the renegade Howard Temin and David Baltimore (see chapter 15), for his work on how the genetic material from DNA tumor viruses is incorporated into the genome of infected cells. Dulbecco turned down Varmus sight unseen, with the disappointing news delivered on two separate occasions through his administrative assistant. With no luck in sunny Southern California, Varmus continued his job search up the coast.

In Northern California, there were two apparent options. The first was to work with William Robinson, of Stanford University, who was a leading figure in research on hepatitis, later implicating it as a cause of liver cancer. Varmus found Robinson "not inviting," so he opted to meet with the other prospective Bay Area employer. At the University of California, Berkeley, Varmus interviewed with Harry Rubin, a veterinarian who was an expert on an infectious agent known as Rous sarcoma virus, or RSV (see discussion on Francis Peyton Rous in chapter 15), which causes cancer in chickens. Varmus found the meeting with Rubin to be off-putting when the senior RNA tumor virologist openly criticized the Central Dogma–challenging the work of Temin, who also happened to be one of his former trainees. Equally concerning to Varmus, Rubin displayed "a surly attitude toward molecular explanations of cell behavior."[48] It was clear that Rubin would not be a good fit for Varmus, but the visit was not a waste of time. Rubin suggested to Varmus that he make inquiries with a newly constituted group of virologists at the Medical School of the University of California, San Francisco, across the bay.

As UCSF reached its centenary in the 1960s, it was in the midst of a rapid transformation into one of the nation's leading academic health sciences centers. This unprecedented growth was spurred by the vision of the University of California System president Clark Kerr. An economist and former chancellor of the flagship campus at Berkeley, Kerr pushed for academic excellence across the entire system. At UCSF, this initiative symbolically rose to great heights in the form of paired glass towers, Health Sciences East and West, designed to accommodate the growth of the research program. In 1966, the adjacent towers opened on the Parnassus campus, less than a mile from the Haight-Ashbury district, then home to Janis Joplin, the Grateful Dead, the Jefferson Airplane, and many other countercultural icons.

When Harold Varmus showed up unannounced on the UCSF campus, he hunted around the three-year-old, fifteen-story Health Science East building until he located the fourth-floor labs of the small cadre of researchers that Rubin had mentioned. Among this group were two former NIH scientists: Leon Levintow and one of his erstwhile Clinical Associates, Michael Bishop. Levintow was recruited to UCSF's medical school in 1965 in the midst of Bishop's two-year NIH training period. The two friends would reconnect three years later when Levintow offered Bishop a faculty position in San Francisco. Bishop arrived in 1968 at the exact same time that Harold Varmus was starting as a Clinical Associate at NIH.

From the very first conversation with Levintow, Bishop, and their colleague Warren Levinson, Varmus felt at ease with the UCSF virologists. They were young and hungry and worked together as a team, meeting regularly and pooling resources such as staff, equipment, and trainees. Looking to add to their crew and finding Varmus an attractive addition, Bishop offered him a position as a research fellow to commence a year later. So, an impromptu visit to the West Coast resulted in the best of all possible worlds for Varmus: a welcoming new home in a fascinating city with friendly and supportive comrades. Harold Varmus felt like he had come home.

PART III

FOUR LAUREATES

CHAPTER 13

THE TEXAS TWO-STEP

Goldstein and Brown

When Joe Goldstein completed his appointment as a Clinical Associate in Marshall Nirenberg's laboratory, he was not quite ready to return to the University of Texas Southwestern Medical School as a faculty member. The chairman of medicine in Dallas, Donald Seldin, had mapped out a six-year professional development plan for Goldstein. The first two years were spent in clinical training at Massachusetts General Hospital. The next two years were devoted to acquiring research skills at NIH. Now, the finishing touches would be two years focused on the study of medical genetics. The ultimate destination for Goldstein—carefully orchestrated by Seldin—was to return to Dallas to establish a medical genetics program there.

Goldstein would learn medical genetics from one of its shining lights, Arno Motulsky. Known as the "Father of Pharmacogenetics," Motulsky pioneered work on how responses to medications can vary according to a person's genetic constitution. In 1957, at the University of Washington in Seattle, Motulsky founded one of the first academic divisions of medical genetics. His.path to the Pacific Northwest was both harrowing and inspiring.

Born on July 5, 1923, in a small town in Germany, Motulsky was raised in a family of shopkeepers. Their comfortable livelihood was threatened by Adolf Hitler's rise to power. In May 1939, a few weeks shy of his sixteenth birthday, Motulsky, along with his mother, brother, and sister, boarded the ocean liner *St. Louis* in Hamburg headed for Cuba. The Motulskys and the more than 900 fellow passengers, mostly Jewish, sought refuge from Nazi persecution. Upon arrival in Havana, the passengers were denied entry. In what would become known as the "Voyage of the Damned," the ship was blocked from landing in the United States and Canada as well. Rebuffed in North America, the *St. Louis* returned to Europe, where the passengers were given asylum in a handful of countries. The Motulskys ended up in Brussels, Belgium, until the Nazis overran the country a year later. Motulsky was classified as an enemy alien and was moved to a series of internment camps, eventually securing a visa to enter the United States. He departed from Lisbon, Portugal, in June 1941, ten days before his eighteenth birthday—an age limit that would have barred his transit through Spain to board the ship in Lisbon.[1]

Separated temporarily from the rest of his family, who escaped to Switzerland, Motulsky was reunited with his father in Chicago. Working in a hospital laboratory by day to support himself, Motulsky earned a graduate equivalency diploma and then enrolled in premedical courses in the evening. He enlisted in the United States Army at age twenty and was sent to Yale to complete premedical courses, returning to Chicago to attend medical school at the University of Illinois. After graduating in 1947, he undertook clinical training at Michael Reese Hospital in Chicago. When the Korean War broke out, he and other discharged physicians that the US Army had educated during World War II were recalled to service. Motulsky worked for two years in the blood diseases lab at Walter Reed Hospital in Washington, DC, and in 1953, upon discharge from the military, he accepted a faculty position at the University of Washington School of Medicine, which had been in operation for only seven years. Motulsky arrived in Seattle the same year that Watson and Crick proposed the structure of DNA. At the time, most medical schools had little instruction in genetics, and few faculty members had expertise in this area. The creation of the Division of Medical Genetics at the University of Washington would place Seattle on the leading edge of this emerging discipline.[2]

When Joe Goldstein arrived in Seattle to work with Arno Motulsky, he could not forget one of the patients he had treated at the NIH Clinical Center. That six-year-old girl already had suffered a heart attack and could not walk across her hospital room without experiencing chest pain. Her brother, a few years older, had the same life-threatening disorder. This condition was first described more than three decades earlier by Carl Müller in Norway. He reported seventeen families, comprising seventy-six individuals, 90 percent of whom had heart disease. These patients had elevated levels of cholesterol in their blood and had visible fatty deposits underneath their skin, especially around the joints. Müller observed that this hereditary condition was passed on equally to both male and female offspring, if either parent was affected.[3] This disorder became known as familial hypercholesterolemia (FH), which means literally that it occurs within kindreds and is characterized by high levels of cholesterol in the blood. Working in Lebanon, another researcher, Avedis Khachadurian, demonstrated that there are two forms of FH.[4] The more common type, with milder manifestations, occurs among persons who have inherited an abnormal gene from just one parent. About one in 500 persons is affected with this condition, demonstrating cholesterol levels about two to three times normal and heart attacks beginning to occur in early adulthood. The other form of FH is much rarer (about one in a million persons) and arises when an individual inherits a defective gene from both parents. As with the six-year-old patient Joe Goldstein treated at NIH, in this situation the cholesterol levels are eight to ten times higher than normal and heart disease is evident in childhood.

If there is a Public Enemy No. 1 among biological molecules, cholesterol is the primary culprit that many people would identify. Perhaps to their surprise, however, cholesterol actually is essential to human existence—it plays many critical roles in bodies and indeed all animals. It is a waxy substance that is a major component of the protective membranes that surround animal cells. The flexibility of these membranes— in contrast to the rigid structure of cell walls in plants—facilitates the ease of movement that is key to animal survival. Additionally, cholesterol plays vital roles in many bodily functions, from the generation of vitamin D and steroid hormones, to the digestion of foods (especially fats), to the insulation of long nerve fibers.

How did this essential molecule, cholesterol, come into such public disfavor? The story goes back more than two centuries to cholesterol's discovery in France. It was first isolated and purified from gallstones, leading to its naming from the Greek *chole* (bile) and *steros* (solid). Not long thereafter, also in France, cholesterol was discovered circulating in the blood.[5] It was not until the early twentieth century that the relationship between cholesterol and heart disease began to emerge. The medical term for hardening of the arteries is "atherosclerosis," which derives from the Greek *atheros* (gruel) and *sclerosis* (stiffening). In 1910, the "gruel" within these plaques in hardened arteries was shown by the Nobel Prize–winning German chemist Adolf Windaus to be packed with cholesterol.[6] In Russia, the pathologist Nikolai Anitschkow fed rabbits cholesterol, producing atherosclerosis, thereby establishing an experimental link between excess consumption of cholesterol and its deposition in arteries.[7]

Just after the end of World War II, major advances in cholesterol research began to occur in the United States. At MGH, Paul Dudley White, widely recognized as the founder of modern cardiology, would lead a study revealing that elevated blood cholesterol was one of several risk factors for heart attacks in young adults. Shortly thereafter, John Gofman, a physician with a PhD in chemistry at the University of California, Berkeley, separated out two principal entities for transporting cholesterol in blood—low-density lipoprotein (LDL, or "bad cholesterol") and high-density lipoprotein (HDL, the "good cholesterol").[8] Gofman went on to demonstrate that heart attack patients have an excess of LDL, hence its "bad" label.[9] The role of LDL is to transport cholesterol in the blood, delivering the waxy substance to cells to use for membrane construction and other purposes. In addition to exhibiting high levels of LDL, heart attack patients also have low levels of HDL, hence its "good" reputation. HDL also is a transporter for cholesterol in the blood; during that process it picks up cholesterol from tissues and delivers it to the liver, where it can be degraded and eliminated from the body.

Why does the body need cholesterol transporters in the first place? A packaging system for cholesterol is required, similar to the physical properties that prevent oil from mixing with water: the oily molecules that form cholesterol will not dissolve in the watery environment of the blood. The cholesterol transporters effectively wrap cholesterol molecules in a more water-friendly envelope so that they can be shipped around the body. An LDL particle is about the size of a small virus—a million of them lined up single file would be about an inch long. The central core of the spherical LDL particle is stuffed with about 1,500 molecules of cholesterol, bathed in a fatty marinade. The covering of the LDL particle is composed of water-friendly molecules that keep the transported material dissolved in blood. Children with the double dose of FH—abnormal genes passed along from both parents—have such high blood cholesterol levels that the excess amounts get unloaded into visible collections underneath the skin, and similar deposits clog their arteries, including those of the heart. When clots form within these narrowed arteries—as happens during a heart attack—oxygen-carrying blood cannot get through, and the oxygen-starved tissue, such as heart muscle, dies. Persons who have the more common, single-dose gene defect of FH tend not to have the visible cholesterol deposits, but over time their higher-than-normal LDL levels result in "gruel" in their arteries that puts them at risk for heart attacks.

When Joe Goldstein first saw his six-year-old patient with FH at the NIH Clinical Center, investigation of this disorder was limited to affected kindreds, and in fact little was known about the prevalence of this condition in the general population. Together with Arno Motulsky and Edwin Bierman, a clinical-research leader at the University of Washington, Goldstein designed a study to help answer that question. The team identified thirteen hospitals in the Seattle area that cared for almost all patients with heart attacks. During an eleven-month observation period, nearly 1,200 heart attack survivors were identified, from which 500 were selected for study, plus nearly twice as many comparison subjects.

From these populations, Goldstein and colleagues demonstrated that heart attack survivors had elevated cholesterol and triglyceride levels when compared to controls.[10] They went on to examine family members of heart attack survivors with high cholesterol or triglyceride levels. Triglycerides are fats that are found in the blood. The sixteen FH families in this study had an overall fivefold excess of elevated cholesterol levels among 132 relatives. However, triglyceride levels among FH family members did not differ from controls. The surfeit of cholesterol within these kinships was accompanied by at least one family member in seven with the hallmark fatty deposits under the skin. Among siblings of heart attack patients, half had excess blood cholesterol levels, without a gender differential (as expected from the inheritance pattern observed elsewhere). Investigators estimated the frequency of the single-copy FH defect among heart attack survivors as 4 percent under age sixty and slightly less than 1 percent aged sixty and older. They estimated frequency among the general population to be between one in 500 and one in 1,000 persons.[11]

While Goldstein was conducting this community-wide study of FH—more than a full-time undertaking—he managed to find spare moments to learn a new lab skill. As he reminisced: "My office in Seattle was right next to this guy named Stanley "Stan" Gartler. He was one of the few people in the world in that period of time doing good work in human fibroblasts." The main active cell of connective tissue, fibroblasts are large and flat, with long, spindly projections. The appeal of using fibroblasts in lab experiments was clear: unlike cells from internal organs, they were obtained easily from a small skin sample with minimal risk. Fibroblasts also reproduce quickly and can be maintained in cell culture and had been used to demonstrate metabolic defects in a variety of hereditary diseases. As Goldstein later pointed out, however: "This was the [seventies] and it was very hard to grow human fibroblasts. I sort of nestled my way into his [Gartler's] lab and he let me work with one of his technicians, so I learned how to do skin biopsies and how to start cultures, and so forth."[12]

Once again, Goldstein was apprenticed to a master. Stan Gartler was fearless, having flown combat missions in a B-26 bomber during World

War II. He returned to the United States to complete college, followed by graduate school in genetics at the University of California, Berkeley. After a five-year postdoctoral fellowship at Columbia University, Gartler was recruited back to the West Coast by Motulsky. Gartler became a founding member of the medical genetics unit at the University of Washington. In 1965, he used a genetic marker to demonstrate that tumors arise from a single cell or, at most, a few cells—a major insight into cancer development.[13] A couple years later, Gartler stunned the community of scientists working with tissue cultures when he used the same genetic marker to demonstrate that eighteen purportedly independent cell lines in wide use were all contaminated with HeLa cells.[14] This cellular imposter was the tenacious cultured cervical cancer cell line once familiar only to experimental scientists. (More recently it has received widespread attention from the best-selling book *The Immortal Life of Henrietta Lacks*; her name is the source of the acronym "HeLa.") Gartler recognized—to the chagrin of many colleagues—a critical point: investigators who used contaminated cell lines were unknowingly studying a different cell type. In the near term, Gartler's conclusion consternated his colleagues, but in the long term it served to promote improved standards of practice in tissue-culture work.

From Gartler, Goldstein "learned the 'ins and outs' of culturing human fibroblasts and other cell types. . . . Stan was a wonderful and generous teacher."[15] They published five papers together, impressive enough in two years but for the fact that Goldstein published another five papers with Motulsky, grabbing attention for his careful delineation of the genetics of nonfatal heart attacks. Goldstein, modest to a fault, confessed with a wry smile: "I was really a dynamo in those days."[16]

Back in Bethesda, Goldstein's fellow wunderkind, Mike Brown, added an additional year to his commitment to NIH when he transitioned from one lab supervisor (Leonard Laster) to another (Earl Stadtman). The bonus time with Stadtman—working on the regulation of the bacterial enzyme glutamine synthetase—proved so productive that Brown and his wife, Alice, extended their stay in Bethesda a few months. Eventually he had to honor his commitment to join the faculty at the University of Texas Southwestern Medical School. Sold on the opportunity in

Dallas by Joe Goldstein and his professor there, Donald Seldin, Brown managed to convince his skeptical wife that they would stay only one year. Mike and Alice Brown—Northeast natives—harbored a somewhat dim view of what life might be like in Dallas. Brown had declined an offer in San Francisco (more to Alice's liking), yet he knew Dallas was the more shaky ground with Alice. One year at UT Southwestern, however, would lead to a lifetime.

Brown set up shop at UT Southwestern in 1971, a year before Goldstein would return. As Brown described: "The fact that I came here and had a year before Joe was extremely important. . . . Joe had already been recognized as a genius here, as a medical student. So, if we had come together, then everybody would have thought that I was just on his coattails."[17] Brown launched an ambitious project—he wanted to isolate and purify a critical enzyme used by the body to produce cholesterol. In mammals, cholesterol comes from two sources: the diet, and internal production. The principal sites of cholesterol manufacture in the body are, first and foremost, the liver, and second, the intestines, with smaller amounts produced in the skin, muscle, and other tissues.

The biochemical pathway leading to cholesterol generation starts with a two-carbon molecule and, after many steps, ends up with the finished product—a twenty-seven-carbon structure composed of four interlocked rings. One of the critical early rate-limiting steps involves the enzyme HMG-CoA reductase. This interested Brown because he and Goldstein had speculated that children with FH had a defect in the regulation of this enzyme. Normally, it is programmed to decrease cholesterol production when there are high levels circulating in the blood. If this control mechanism was lacking in FH patients, as Brown and Goldstein suspected, their liver cells would continue to manufacture cholesterol even when it was overabundant.

Brown had learned how to isolate and purify enzymes under Earl Stadtman at NIH and thought he could procure HMG-CoA reductase in pure form. This might seem to be overoptimistic: even the German biochemist Feodor Lynen, who discovered the enzyme and shared the 1964 Nobel Prize in Physiology or Medicine for this work, had been unable to purify it. The challenge was that the enzyme is bound to a membrane within the cell, which held on to it tenaciously. Brown recalled his former mentor's reaction to hearing about the proposed project:

> When I told Stadtman that was what I was going to do, that's the only time I have ever heard him laugh. He just broke out and said: "Wait a second. You're going to do something that this other guy—this great biochemist—says is impossible? You're going to do it?" And I said: "Yes, sir." Well luckily, I stumbled onto a method and I was able to at least remove the enzyme from the membrane and partially purify it.[18]

Brown was fortunate to work with experienced colleagues who supported his initial efforts.[19] Brown could not have found a better environment for working on HMG-CoA reductase. He was able to grind up rat livers and release the membrane-bound HMG-CoA reductase by adding a snake venom, then stabilize the enzyme by adding a pinch of salt. He submitted the enzyme isolation methodology for publication, with senior faculty colleagues John Dietschy and Marvin Siperstein (considered to be a guru in cholesterol) as coauthors.[20]

Not only had Brown accomplished what a Nobel laureate thought could not be done; he did it in a little more than a year. "The Department here had such an interest in that enzyme and the whole cholesterol work," Brown said, "so, I got an opportunity to demonstrate to them that I could do something on my own. They gave me my own laboratory, and when Joe came [back to Dallas], he had his own laboratory."[21]

Mike Brown's success in purifying the elusive enzyme was not the only big news at UT Southwestern in 1972. Joe Goldstein, who Brown described as being "known as the brightest medical student that they had ever seen and will ever see again," had returned to campus. "He was already very well known, and his return to Dallas was very much anticipated."[22] Goldstein's sterling reputation was burnished by his recently completed study in Seattle on the genetics of cholesterol and triglyceride disorders.

With both of their careers moving forward independently, Brown and Goldstein were content to pursue separate research agendas. "To begin with," Goldstein explained, "our labs were geographically separate."[23]

Brown noted: "This idea of uniting the two labs—that was never in the plan. We wanted to collaborate on one project dealing with children with high cholesterol, but other than that, the plan was to have separate laboratories."[24]

Brown described his colleague's independent work:

> Joe's main project was to figure out how estrogen worked . . . nobody knew anything about how steroid hormones worked in those days. There is this observation that if you take an immature male chicken, a rooster—it has to be immature and it has to be male—and if you inject estrogens, it stimulates the liver to produce these huge amounts of lipoproteins and the plasma becomes milky and fills up with lipids. So, he thought this was a great way to figure out how estrogens work—it must be turning on some gene in the liver. So, that was his main project.[25]

Clearly enjoying the story, Brown continued:

> The problem was that you had to have these little immature chicks that were male and nobody can tell the difference between a male and a female chick. Farmers hire these specialists who come in and will sort their chicks for them, because they only need one rooster and lots of hens. So, Joe had to hire this guy, an old farmer, to come in, and he ordered two dozen chicks to tell him which ones were male and which ones were female. Sometimes, the chickens would get out and Joe was chasing them down the hall. It was really a mess.[26]

In between Goldstein's fugitive fowl and Brown's rodent chopped liver, the friends found time to join forces on a question that had haunted them since their days at NIH: What type of gene defect could cause a preschooler to have an LDL level ten times higher than normal, resulting in life-threatening artery blockages? "We did it because it was a puzzle—to try to figure out why these children had such high cholesterol levels," Brown acknowledged. While focusing on this rare genetic problem, Goldstein and Brown hoped that their research would have much broader implications. "We felt that if we could understand why these children had such high cholesterol levels, that it might help us understand why garden variety high cholesterol occurs."[27]

Brown and Goldstein brought their complementary skills to their work together on FH. In Seattle, Goldstein had learned the art of tissue culture from Stan Gartler. Brown had demonstrated his proficiency in working with enzymes—skills he perfected under the watchful eye of Earl Stadtman at NIH. Their working hypothesis, according to Brown: "There was a defect in the HMG-CoA reductase enzyme—this allosteric enzyme [one that is involved in biological control and regulation] that should be inhibited by cholesterol, and that the patients had a mutation in the enzyme itself that prevented it from being turned off by cholesterol."[28] The obvious tissue type to use to examine HMG-CoA reductase activity would be liver cells, where most of the action is located during cholesterol production. However, obtaining specimens of liver tissue from patients with FH and healthy control subjects would be logistically and ethically problematic. In Seattle, Goldstein worked with fibroblasts—much easier to obtain from small skin biopsies—and a number of other genetic defects had been demonstrated in these connective tissue cells. Because other investigators had shown that cholesterol could be produced and regulated in cells other than the liver, Brown and Goldstein crossed their fingers that human fibroblasts would work for HMG-CoA reductase as well.[29]

Goldstein and Brown demonstrated that enzyme activity could be measured in cultured normal fibroblasts and that it was suppressed when cells were bathed in serum containing cholesterol. When they removed the serum (and, thus, the cholesterol), the normal cells cranked up the HMG-CoA reductase activity as expected. If they then added back LDL, the enzyme's activity in normal cells plummeted again. Curiously, if they added back HDL instead of LDL, there was no observed change in the activity of HMG-CoA reductase. In other words, the enzyme was not being switched off by cholesterol in any form; this was particular to cholesterol in LDL particles. Brown and Goldstein also noted that even miniscule amounts of LDL could suppress the enzyme. In other words, HMG-CoA reductase was both highly specific to LDL cholesterol and exquisitely sensitive to changes in LDL concentrations.

This combination of high specificity and high sensitivity would prove important in the ultimate characterization of the underlying biological process.

Once they established how normal fibroblasts respond to LDL, Goldstein and Brown were ready to test cells from a patient with the double-dose form of FH (mutations inherited from both parents). Unlike the days at NIH, they no longer had a ready source of patients with this once-in-a-million condition. Then, lightning struck: "At that moment, the telephone rings," recalls Brown. The call was for the cholesterol guru, Siperstein, and was placed by a pediatrician in Denver. As Brown described: "The secretary answers the phone and this is the most amazing thing. If she hadn't done this, I don't know what would have happened." He continued: "She said: 'I'm sorry, Dr. Siperstein is away in Switzerland. He's on a sabbatical in Geneva, but he has a young associate, Dr. Brown. Would you like to speak to him?' 'Okay.' She didn't have to say that he had a young associate. Nine times out of ten, a secretary would say: 'I'm sorry, he's not here.'"[30]

The improbable conversation continued: "So, I get on the phone and this guy tells me about a 12-year-old girl and she has this enormously high cholesterol. She's had multiple heart attacks and two days from now, Dr. Starzl is going to do an operation in her abdomen and he will have access to her liver and he will do a liver biopsy." He continued: "He wanted Dr. Siperstein to come up there and take this liver biopsy and measure the rate at which it was producing cholesterol."[31] Dr. Thomas Starzl had recently been appointed chair of surgery at the University of Colorado. Starzl performed the first successful liver transplant in 1967 and was a leader in the development of donor-organ preservation and drug treatments to prevent immune system rejection of transplants in recipients.

Starzl was convinced that patients with FH simply were producing too much cholesterol. He hoped to demonstrate excess output by measuring cholesterol generation from a piece of surgically removed liver tissue. There was one problem, however: whatever level of cholesterol production the patient's liver yielded, there was no way to determine whether it was high, low, or perfectly normal. There were no reference values to compare against, as normal persons do not have their liver biopsied to measure cholesterol production. Even though a liver measurement would be uninterpretable, however, a fibroblast measurement was just what Mike Brown needed to compare against the normal cells that Joe Goldstein and he had characterized.

Brown was not about to let the opportunity pass. Trying to contain his excitement, he replied: "'I know all of the methods of Dr. Siperstein. I can do that, but all I want is a piece of the skin from the incision,' because that is the way we had gotten the fibroblasts. He said: 'I am sure Dr. Starzl would have no objection to that.'" Brown continued: "And I said: 'By the way, what operation are you doing?' He said: 'Dr. Starzl won't let me tell you that.' I said: 'What are you talking about?' He said: 'Dr. Starzl said that I'm not allowed to tell you the operation.'"[32] The secrecy had eerie echoes of Brown's days at the NIH Clinical Center. As a gastroenterology fellow, he was asked to find the source of bleeding in a teenage girl with sulfite oxidase deficiency. When Brown asked to review her medical records to learn the medical history and prior workup, he was denied access because investigators had not yet published their findings. Once again, the willingness of investigators to share information was impeded by the fear that they might get scooped by a colleague. Not in a position to dissent, Brown acquiesced to the need-to-know terms of engagement.

The patient in Denver, referred to by her initials, J. P., came to medical attention at age three because of the characteristic fatty deposits under her skin. J. P. had a blood cholesterol level that was nearly ten times normal, with the excess confined to an elevation of LDL. Both her parents had cholesterol levels two times normal, and her mother had suffered a heart attack at thirty-one. A diagnosis of FH was made—her parents having the milder single-gene defect form, with J. P. experiencing the more severe double dose of defective genes.

Between her diagnosis and the time of surgery nine years later, J. P. had undergone a variety of dietary and medical interventions, with little or no reduction in her cholesterol level, except when she was fed solely through an infusion into her veins. Six months before surgery, she began to experience chest pain; a cardiac catheterization revealed a poorly functioning heart valve and widespread blockages in the arteries of her heart. About one month prior to surgery, J. P. experienced a heart attack.

With her life-threatening heart disease and lack of response to any other therapy, Starzl and his team attempted a rather heroic operation—the one that he had been reluctant to reveal to his colleagues in Dallas. The procedure, developed for treating liver failure, involved shunting blood away from the diseased organ. This dramatic procedure was based on treatment for another type of inherited defect in the liver. When this liver bypass was performed, patients' elevated cholesterol levels plummeted. There was no evidence that a liver shunt would work for FH patients as well, but no other treatment was effective. Time was running out for J. P.[33]

On March 1, 1973, Starzl and his team successfully performed the liver shunt operation. During the procedure, Starzl took liver specimens to examine under the microscope and for Brown to assess cholesterol production. Most important for Brown, however, he was provided a skin specimen that he could take back to Dallas to grow fibroblasts in tissue culture. J. P. recovered from the surgery, and her cholesterol levels indeed did drop to about half the preoperative amounts. The fatty deposits under her skin began to disappear, and her chest pain subsided. Her heart arteries still had blockages, and about a year and a half following surgery she died suddenly and unexpectedly—presumably from heart disease. Undeterred, Starzl performed the same operation on two other FH patients with the severe form of the disease over the next two years.[34] Eventually, he reported on a dozen patients treated with the liver shunt.[35] When more effective nonsurgical management became available, the liver shunt for FH would become a historical curiosity. Starzl would go on to develop a world-famous organ transplantation program. His patient J. P., a pioneer in her own right through her willingness to undergo an experimental procedure and donate tissue, made a contribution to medical research that endured long after her all-too-brief life.

When Mike Brown returned to Dallas with the sample of J. P.'s skin, it took several weeks for the fibroblasts to grow out in the tissue culture. Finally, Goldstein and Brown were ready to compare the HMG-CoA reductase activity they had measured previously in normal fibroblasts to the enzyme activity in a patient with the double-defect form of FH. The fateful experiment happened on a day when Mike Brown was scheduled to deliver a talk in Atlantic City, New Jersey, at the meeting of the Federation of American Societies for Experimental Biology. This is the same annual meeting where, as a senior medical student seven years earlier, he had presented the results of his study of intestinal motility in rats. His first talk largely went unnoticed, with the important exception of Leonard Laster, whose favorable impression secured an appointment for Brown as a Clinical Associate at NIH.

Back in Dallas, Joe Goldstein and his technician, Suzanna "Suzy" Dana, were studying J. P.'s fibroblasts. As Suzy recalled: "I was there when the results were coming off and it looked like: 'Hey, you know, something's happened here and it looks good.' I thought it was kind of interesting, but I didn't realize the significance of it." Goldstein described the eureka moment when he first saw the results: "The amazing finding was that when the cells were grown with lipoproteins in the serum, there was about a hundred or two-hundred-fold increase in the cholesterol synthesis enzyme [HMG-CoA reductase] from the girl [J. P.] who had the familial hypercholesterolemia compared with the normal individual. It's very rare that you see a difference like this."[36] The presence of lipoproteins in the serum had turned down cholesterol synthesis in normal fibroblasts, but in J. P.'s cells the cholesterol manufacturing was surging along, apparently blind to the sea of lipoproteins outside the fibroblasts.

Goldstein's reaction, as reported by Suzy Dana, was hardly the characteristic understated, genteel Southern demeanor for which he was known on campus: "Dr. Goldstein came back and was looking at the results and was just bouncing off the walls and was saying: 'Do you know what this means? Do you know what this means?' And I kept saying: 'Well, yeah, it looks like it worked.'" Without Mike Brown present to join in the excitement, Goldstein sought out the next best celebrant: "I ran into Dr. Seldin's office."[37]

It was all too fitting that Seldin was one of the first to know about the startling result. It was Seldin who had carefully mapped out Joe Goldstein's professional development, opening the doors for his protégé at both MGH and NIH. Had Goldstein not been admitted to those institutions, he might never have met Mike Brown. By offering faculty appointments to both Goldstein and Brown, Seldin had created the opportunity for them to collaborate. Perhaps most important, he nurtured the Brown-Goldstein partnership by treating the rising stars as equals in every respect.

As for Brown, in a time before cell phones, text messaging, and email, he remained quietly in the dark about the discovery for several hours. As Brown recounted the event: "When I got back to my hotel I had a message that said: 'Call Joe Goldstein at this number.' So, I get Joe on the phone and he says: 'You can't believe the experiment.' I said: 'What are you talking about?' He said: 'Suzy, the technician, came in and showed me the data." He continued: "It's unbelievable—I mean, the patient's cells have an activity of the enzyme that's a hundredfold above normal. I really questioned her. There's no question that she did the experiment right, but maybe it's some fluke. Of course, we have to repeat it, but if it's real, we have an incredible discovery.'"[38]

Brown did his own version of bouncing off the walls:

I ran out on the Boardwalk and I'm really so excited. I bump into some friends of mine who had been fellow residents at MGH and a couple of them were actually in Fredrickson's laboratory at NIH [whose patient with FH was the one that first stimulated Goldstein and Brown to want to understand this disease]. We all go out for beers together—it is late in the evening. We are sitting there drinking beers . . . but I didn't dare tell them because, first of all, nothing is true unless you repeat it, and it could have been an artifact.[39]

Brown is not by nature a secret-keeper, and it must have been apparent to his colleagues that something was brewing, but somehow he managed to keep his own counsel. Brown wasted no time returning to Dallas, however, flying back the next morning.

The finding with J. P.'s fibroblasts was so striking that Brown and Goldstein wanted to rush it into print. The problem was that they had observations—albeit striking ones—on only a single FH patient. Senior colleagues cautioned them that it would be premature to extrapolate solo results to the universe of FH patients—they needed data from more patients. This was not an easy assignment. J. P. had virtually fallen out of the sky. Where were they going to find other patients with this rare disorder? The hunt would take them nearly a thousand miles north, across the Canadian border, to a physician named Jean Davignon at the Institut de Recherches Cliniques de Montréal. The frequency of FH in the province of Québec is about twice that observed elsewhere, likely deriving from a gene defect among some of the original seventeenth-century French settlers and perpetuated over generations within inbred communities.[40]

When approached by Goldstein about obtaining skin samples from patients with FH, Davignon agreed readily, so Brown and Goldstein— who were at yet another meeting in Atlantic City—hopped on a shuttle from New York to Montréal. As they deplaned in Montréal, "there was this band playing and all of these corsages and flowers," Goldstein recalled. "We decided: 'How did everybody know that we were coming here to get this great material?'"[41] Unbeknownst to the two intrepid researchers, the shuttle was celebrating an anniversary, so the festive greeting was not in honor of their great contribution to medical science. Without further musical accompaniment, Brown and Goldstein retrieved the skin samples from two patients, a ten-year-old boy, L. L., and a twenty-three-year-old woman, A. C. Returning to Dallas, the partners grew fibroblasts from the two new donors and repeated the experiment.

The rhythm of their work became the organizing force in the lives of Brown and Goldstein, even when other circumstances might have dictated otherwise. In the midst of this frenzied period, on June 1, 1973, Mike Brown's wife, Alice, went into labor with their first child. Years later, Alice laughingly recalled her husband's antics: "I was at Saint Paul's Hospital, which is just across the street from the lab. He would come in, see how I was doing, run back to the lab." Likely in somewhat stronger terms than the following, she told him: "You can spend one day at the hospital!" Mike Brown's version provides slightly different color commentary:

Right in the middle of that [initial discovery] my wife decides to have our first baby. So, she's in labor . . . and she has a breach delivery and it's a tough delivery. By the time the pediatrician comes, the baby is okay and she's okay, and everything is fine. I get to leave the hospital. It is now around one o'clock in the morning. So, what do I do at one o'clock in the morning? I go to Joe's apartment so that we can plan the experiments for the next day. That's the God's honest truth.[42]

Even the pouring rain was no deterrent—the research show must go on!

When Brown and Goldstein tested the fibroblasts from L. L. and A. C., they found the same phenomenon observed with the cells from J. P.: there was no decrease in cholesterol production when bathed in serum with lipoproteins. With this confirmation in hand, Brown and Goldstein wrote up their findings for publication. Wanting to get published quickly, they opted for the *Proceedings of the National Academy of Sciences*. On June 20, 1973, Brown's NIH mentor, Earl Stadtman, an academy member, communicated the article on their behalf; it was published four months later.[43]

At this point, Goldstein and Brown knew that HMG-CoA reductase was not shutting off as it should, but they did not know why the normal regulatory mechanism was failing. They suspected that it was not a structural aberration in the enzyme itself but rather "a hitherto unidentified gene whose product is necessary for mediation of feedback control by lipoproteins."[44] What could this other gene product be? Brown and Goldstein worked nonstop to try to figure it out. "We started this system where we planned every experiment the day before," Brown explained. "So, we'd get the results of the experiment in the afternoon and then we would plan the experiment for the next day. And we had a system where every experiment could be completed within a day."[45]

As the diurnal cycle of planning, executing, and analyzing together became routine, Goldstein and Brown gave up their separate independent projects. "This partnership sort of gradually developed—it didn't happen overnight," Brown explained. "As we began to be more and more comfortable working together—literally planning the experiment together; sitting over a pad and planning the next day's experiments and arguing over exactly how to do the experiment. As that developed, we realized that there was no way that either of us could take individual credit for anything that happened."[46] According to Brown, the pair "made the formal acknowledgment that if I said something brilliant on a Thursday, it was probably because Joe had said something equally brilliant on the Tuesday and had planted the idea." He continued: "We decided that since everything is a give-and-take, it is impossible to credit ideas to either one of us. We said: 'Okay, we're not going to do that. Whatever comes out of the lab is Goldstein and Brown, Brown and Goldstein.'"[47] The conjunction of the two names became so inseparable that others began referring to the pair as "Brownstein."

Together, Goldstein and Brown attacked the challenge of exploring the type of gene defect that could lead to a failure of normal control mechanisms on cholesterol synthesis. Within a year, they demonstrated that the genetic defect was not in the HMG-CoA reductase enzyme itself, which shut down appropriately in FH patients' fibroblasts when cholesterol was added directly, rather than in the form of lipoproteins. The problem appeared to be a specific inability of LDL to gain access into the cell, where it could unload its cholesterol cargo and thereby dial back the enzyme activity.[48]

So, Brown and Goldstein started focusing on the mechanism by which LDL crossed the protective cell membrane. They labeled LDL with radioactive iodine and noted that it bound tightly to the cell membranes of normal fibroblasts. When they attempted the same thing with fibroblasts from patients with the inherited double dose of FH (now numbering five people with the addition of two more affected six-year-old girls), there was no binding of LDL to cell membranes. Goldstein and Brown interpreted these findings as reflecting an apparent "interaction of LDL with a physiological 'receptor,'" but they noted that the "molecular mechanism by which binding leads to suppression of synthesis of HMG-CoA reductase molecules is not yet known."[49] Further studies suggested that this highly specific cell-surface binding was necessary for bringing LDL into the cell, where it could be chemically degraded and also ratchet down the manufacture of cholesterol. Their conclusions were beginning to sound much more firm: "We believe that the primary genetic abnormality in familial hypercholesterolemia resides in a gene whose product is necessary for the production of a high affinity cell surface receptor for LDL."[50]

Brown and Goldstein were convinced that LDL receptors existed, but others were not so easily convinced. In 1974, only a handful of cell-surface receptors were recognized, and most involved the specialized communication systems for hormones, as Bob Lefkowitz had demonstrated with his mentors at NIH, Jesse Roth and Ira Pastan. When Goldstein and Brown submitted the LDL receptor paper, the journal editor sent it to experts for independent scientific appraisals. One of the reviewers wrote back a summary assessment: "It is my considered opinion that publication of this paper with its incomplete observations would not serve medical science—neither would it earn credit in the long run for its authors."[51] Fortunately, the editor, Eugene P. Kennedy, took a more favorable view, and a revised version of the paper was accepted. Over time, its significance was recognized so widely that it would become a classic.

Mike Brown pointed out that the opinions of others mattered less to them than their own judgment on their work: "It wasn't necessary for us to impress the world; we were trying to impress each other."[52] They also could depend upon each other for moral support. As Brown described: "When one of us has been feeling down, when things just aren't going well, almost invariably the other will pick them up. Having two people really does propel you over the rough spots."[53]

In pursuing their work together, Mike Brown and Joe Goldstein brought different but complementary perspectives. As Brown recalled years later:

> In the old days, when we used to work in the laboratory, we would frequently have to go to a microscope to look down at the cells. . . . If I were the first one, I would dial it up to the highest magnification, so I could see the details in the cells. And then Joe would walk up to the microscope and immediately dial down to the lowest magnification, so he could see the whole pattern of the cells. That illustrates a difference in the way we tend to think.

Joe Goldstein added: "If you look at high power, you see a lot of details, but you also miss the big picture. If you look at low power, you see the big picture, but you miss the details."[54] Together, they were able to master both viewpoints.

As former reporters and editors of student newspapers, Brown and Goldstein were very serious about their approach to writing. Brown described an exacting process: "We would argue about a single word. We would be writing along and I would say something and Joe would be writing it down and then he'd stop and he'd say some word—he'd want to change that word and I would say: 'Joe, we're not trying to get every detail right now. We're trying to get just the broad picture.'"[55] Their authorship style—modeled after their NIH mentors, Nirenberg and Stadtman—is marked by accuracy, clarity, and precision.

In working together so closely, Goldstein and Brown learned how to avoid the pitfalls of a partnership. In Goldstein's words:

> There are two occupational diseases of collaboration. One is astigmatism—that's when the two partners do not see eye-to-eye. We argue all the time about details, but if you don't see eye-to-eye on the big picture, then it will never work. Then, the second is ego-titis. If two people have big egos, they often do clash, especially when one of them will end up with a bruised ego more than the other.[56]

Brown framed the elements of successful collaboration in slightly different terms:

> A partnership like this requires that one of the partners, and only one, is a saint. If neither of them is a saint, then they are going to be fighting constantly. If both of them are saints, they'll be too nice to each other and nothing will get done. So, if it can't be two saints and it can't be no saints, the only other possibility is one saint. And I'm not a saint.[57]

Brown continued:

> Of course, we disagree on lots of small things, but we work them out. What makes it so fantastic is that when Joe disagrees with me, I may react violently to begin with. But, I realize that he is a smart fellow, he has a good track record, and he must have a reason for his opinion. And that happens vice versa. So, in the end, we always come together. We respect the opinion of the other.[58]

Once they established the existence of a specific LDL cell-surface receptor, Brown and Goldstein next turned to exploring the process by which the bound LDL enters the cell and is processed. They determined that the captured LDL remains on the cell surface for a relatively short period—less than ten minutes on average.[59] Within an hour, the ingested LDL is broken apart, its protein digested completely, leaving cholesterol in the cell.[60] The rapid ingestion of receptor-bound LDL was determined to occur through a clustering of the receptors within protein-coated pits in the cell membrane. The pits are pinched off from the rest of the membrane, carrying the receptors and bound LDL into the cell, where the lipoprotein is digested.[61] Once relieved of their cargo of LDL, the emptied receptors are recycled, heading back to the cell's surface, where they are reintegrated into the membrane in order to bind more LDL.

Goldstein and Brown would go on to purify the LDL receptor using cells taken from the adrenal cortex of cows.[62] With determination, they were able to clone and sequence the LDL receptor cDNA (complementary DNA) and its gene. The encoded receptor protein is composed of nearly 850 amino acids, a task that technological advances would make much simpler today. The binding end of the receptor is located on the outside of the cell and contains many negatively charged amino acids that attract the positively charged amino acids of the major protein on the surface of the LDL particle. Toward the other end of the receptor protein is a sequence of twenty-two water-resistant amino acids that span the cell membrane, followed by a sequence of fifty amino acids that anchor the receptor on the inside of the cell.[63] Interestingly, the LDL receptor appears to be assembled from a series of segments that are similar to portions of other proteins with completely different biological functions.[64] Deploying these same component parts in various physiologic processes allows an economy in production of proteins, as if it had been designed by an efficiency expert.

Brown and Goldstein began to catalog the various mutations of the LDL receptor gene that can give rise to FH. They discovered quickly that there were many ways in which the finely tuned system could go awry. The most common problem was a failure to produce the LDL receptor altogether. Other types of defects discovered included the inability of manufactured receptors to migrate to the cell's surface; receptors that reached the cell surface but failed to bind LDL; and receptors that bound LDL but did not cluster in pits for ingestion into the cell.[65]

The inventory of inherited gene defects in the LDL receptor now numbers 1,700-plus and continues to grow as more affected individuals are studied.[66]

In focusing on the rare instances of doubly inherited gene defects in FH, Brown and Goldstein had elucidated the intricate mechanisms for controlling cholesterol levels. This information would prove to be invaluable when paired with research under way halfway around the world. In Tokyo, Akira Endo, a biochemist working at the Sankyo pharmaceutical company, was screening 6,000 fungal compounds to find inhibitors of cholesterol production. He identified a compound (initially labeled "ML-236B"), derived from a penicillium mold that grows on oranges, that blocked HMG-CoA reductase activity in rat livers. Brown and Goldstein became aware of Endo's work because a computer search revealed a Japanese publication in which Endo had cited the research in Dallas on cholesterol regulation. Brown and Goldstein wrote to Endo in 1977 requesting a sample of ML-236B to test in their experimental system. Endo graciously obliged; when added to normal human fibroblasts, the fungal compound, also known as compactin, inhibited cholesterol synthesis powerfully. Brown and Goldstein published these findings jointly with Endo.[67]

Having observed that compactin decreased the production of cholesterol, Goldstein and Brown wondered whether it would also boost the number of LDL receptors in order to bring more cholesterol into the cell. They had a connection to another pharmaceutical company, Merck Sharp & Dohme, through its head of research, Roy Vagelos. Like Mike Brown, Vagelos had worked as an NIH Clinical Associate under the direction of Earl Stadtman. Merck had discovered another fungal compound that inhibited cholesterol production. This molecule, mevinolin, was provided to Goldstein and Brown, who served as consultants to Merck. When tested in experimental dogs, mevinolin (later renamed "lovastatin") increased the production of LDL receptors in liver cells, thereby diminishing the circulating LDL in the animals.[68] Nevertheless, Merck hesitated to develop lovastatin as a human therapeutic agent because of initial concerns about potential harmful effects.

When Vagelos was elevated to head Merck, Ed Scolnick was recruited to fill the vacancy in the research program. Scolnick, another former

NIH Clinical Associate, had helped Joe Goldstein gain an appointment in Marshall Nirenberg's lab. The Merck team decided to test lovastatin in clinical studies, and the drug was shown to be effective in reducing LDL levels in persons with the single-dose form of FH[69] and in persons who had elevated cholesterol without any known hereditary predisposition.[70] Merck applied to the US Food and Drug Administration for approval of lovastatin in November 1986. In September 1987, the product, under the brand name "Mevacor," was given the green light, opening up an entirely new class of drugs for managing high cholesterol. This class—known as statins—includes some of the most widely prescribed drugs in the United States. More than one-third of all adults are considered to be candidates for treatment, and more than half of those eligible actually receive the drugs. In retrospect, work that Brown and Goldstein initiated decades earlier to understand a rare genetic disorder led to insights that today are helping to prevent illness in tens of millions of people.

Even before the first statin drug was approved, there was growing recognition that advances in understanding the cholesterol metabolic pathways was going to transform health and health care. Brown and Goldstein were honored with the Canada Gairdner Foundation International Award (1981) and the Albert Lasker Award in Basic Medical Research (1985). It was not a great surprise, therefore, when they were contacted about another prestigious award. The pair was in Boston to deliver the keynote address at a symposium hosted by the Massachusetts Institute of Technology. In the early morning hours of Monday, October 14, 1985, Mike Brown was awakened by a telephone call to his hotel room. "I pick it up and it's a woman's voice and she says: 'Is this Dr. Brown?' And I said: 'Yes,' in a very groggy voice. 'Well, how do you feel?' And I said: 'What are you talking about?' She said: 'How do you feel? What's your reaction?' I said: 'I'm sorry, I don't know what you're talking about.'" He continued the story: "She said: 'I'm calling from the Reuters News Service in Washington and it's just come over the wire that you and your colleague, Dr. Goldstein, will share the Nobel Prize.'"[71]

A few hours later, the host of the MIT meeting, Dr. David Baltimore, who had won a Nobel Prize in Physiology or Medicine himself exactly a decade earlier, raised a glass of champagne to toast the latest inductees into that exclusive club. There is some symmetry in the fact that Goldstein and Brown learned of their selection for the Nobel Prize in the city where they first met nineteen years earlier. They had come full circle, but their work together was based in Dallas, where Mike Brown had long outstayed his commitment to his wife, Alice, of a one-year sojourn. The annual media frenzy that surrounds the announcement of the Nobel Prize was starting, as Goldstein recalled: "*The New York Times, The Wall Street Journal*, all had scientific correspondents in Boston. They all wanted interviews." Brown added: "One of the people said: 'When are you going to come out and make a statement?' And I said: 'Well, we don't want to do anything in Boston. We did all our work in Texas and we want to go home to Texas.'"[72] After a brief press conference, the honorees took the first flight back home to Dallas and the institution that had supported them under the careful orchestration of their academic patron, Donald Seldin, along with their faculty colleagues, friends, and family.

By the time Brown and Goldstein appeared at a hastily called press conference at an auditorium on campus late that afternoon, the skies over Dallas were darkening with a threatening thunderstorm. The weather could not dim the spirits of the standing-room-only crowd inside who gave the pair a rousing ovation when they entered, immediately surrounded by a gaggle of reporters and photographers. After patiently answering questions from the media, Goldstein was asked what he planned to do the following day. Without hesitation, he responded: "Tomorrow should be a day like any other day. We'll get back to the laboratory, back to what we're doing." Then, with an impish grin, he added: "Actually, I suppose tomorrow will be a little different."[73] In reality, Goldstein's initial response was more accurate. According to their then junior colleague, David Russell: "The atmosphere didn't change a bit, and in fact, the Prize was announced on a Monday and there were some celebrations. . . . On Tuesday, we had a group meeting and you couldn't tell that anything had happened. There was absolutely no change in the environment of the labs. People went about their business; there were all these experiments yet to be done."[74] Indeed, the greatest legacy of Brown and Goldstein may be the more than 150 graduate students and fellows who trained with them, including five who were elected to the National

Academy of Medicine and one (Thomas Südhof) who went on to win his own Nobel Prize.

Mike Brown, aged forty-four, and Joe Goldstein, aged forty-five, were remarkably young to become Nobel laureates—a decade and a half younger than the average for contemporary recipients in Physiology or Medicine. They were thirteen years into their professional partnership. As Russell noted: "It was a time when findings in the laboratory were increasing at an exponential rate." That productivity would continue unabated for years or, more accurately, for nearly five decades and counting. In one of the longest—if not the longest—sustained scientific partnerships in history, Joe Goldstein and Mike Brown demonstrated the power that can accrue when two brilliant minds are brought together in perfect balance.

CHAPTER 14

ADRENALINE RUSH

Lefkowitz and the Serpentine Journey

Honoring the pact that he sealed with his father on Thanksgiving 1968, Bob Lefkowitz departed NIH at the end of June 1970 to return to clinical training. The agreement between father and son was forged when Bob was struggling to cope with an early lack of progress in the research lab. The unfamiliar weight of disappointment was lifted from his shoulders when his father, Max, suggested that Bob focus on his original goal of becoming a practicing physician. When a few weeks later the elder Lefkowitz died suddenly and unexpectedly, Bob was devastated and felt duty-bound to follow through on the plan that they had developed together. His application to Massachusetts General Hospital for a senior residency and cardiology fellowship was accepted; the future path was settled—or at least that is the way it appeared at the time.

What neither father nor son could have anticipated is that, within a year, the research project that had been such a frustration at NIH would become a great success. Under the guidance of his mentors Jesse Roth and Ira Pastan, Lefkowitz was able to create a binding assay for adrenocorticotropic hormone and its cell-surface receptor. At a time when many leaders in the field still doubted the very existence of receptors (or, as Lefkowitz likes to say, "receptahz," exaggerating his residual Bronx accent), the work of Lefkowitz and his two mentors was a major breakthrough. Quite unexpectedly, Bob Lefkowitz discovered that he could not only conduct research, he could do it at a very high level. He also found the thrill of discovery to be intoxicating.

Although Lefkowitz was offered the opportunity to remain at NIH and continue working there, he had given his word to his father as well as to MGH—and he was not backing out of those commitments. He began a senior residency in Boston on July 1, 1970, with six months of required rotations through the emergency department and various specialty consultation services. As Lefkowitz later characterized his mindset: "I threw myself into the clinical work with my usual fervor. But something was missing. For the first time in several years, I had no data. I was like a junkie who needed a fix."[1]

The withdrawal symptoms were so intense that Lefkowitz was willing to break the MGH house rules to get an illicit dose of data. Because senior residents were compensated from clinically generated funds, they were strictly prohibited from spending time doing research. Fully aware of this prohibition, Lefkowitz simply could not resist the temptation to immerse himself again in designing and conducting experiments. During the final six months of his senior residency, Lefkowitz arranged with Edgar "Ed" Haber to work in his laboratory. Haber, a Jewish native of Berlin, escaped from Nazi Germany with his family, arriving in New York in 1939. Haber was an undergraduate at Columbia University and then attended its College of Physicians and Surgeons—the same path Lefkowitz would follow a decade later. After a residency at MGH, Haber was appointed as a Clinical Associate at NIH, working with the biochemist Christian Anfinsen. The work that Haber undertook with Anfinsen revealed that the sequence of amino acids in a protein dictated its three-dimensional structure and, thus, its biological activity. In 1972, Anfinsen would share the Nobel Prize in Chemistry in part for this work.

Haber returned to MGH in 1963. A year later, at thirty-two years old, he was appointed chief of the Cardiac Unit. When Lefkowitz joined him six years later, Haber was engaged in research on a complex system involving the regulation of the body's fluids, electrolytes, and blood pressure. One of the compounds key to this network is the steroid hormone aldosterone, which is produced in the adrenal glands and influences how the adjacent kidneys conserve the mineral sodium and, along with it, water. With his focus on aldosterone, Haber wanted Lefkowitz to apply his recently acquired skills to working on this molecule.

Lefkowitz had a different idea. Despite the gap in their seniority, he had no hesitancy about expressing his preference to his new boss. Lefkowitz was not particularly interested in aldosterone because it does not require a receptor on a cell's surface in order to gain entry. Unlike ACTH—a large protein molecule that is blocked by the cell's protective outer layer—aldosterone is a small, uncharged molecule that can swim across the cell's protective membrane entirely on its own. Once inside the cell, aldosterone binds to a receptor and involves a completely different activation process than the one that he had studied at NIH. Lefkowitz preferred to continue his focus on cell-surface receptors, albeit choosing one that was of particular relevance to cardiology. With what would be described in his old Bronx neighborhood as "chutzpah" and elsewhere as "temerity," Bob Lefkowitz told Haber that he didn't want to work on the lab's favorite hormone—aldosterone.

As an alternative, Lefkowitz proposed to study the so-called beta adrenergic receptor. Named for their responsiveness to adrenaline—the body's messenger of impending danger—adrenergic receptors are located in a range of anatomic sites, including the heart, lungs, blood vessels, intestines, and muscles. In 1948, Raymond Ahlquist, a pharmacologist working at the Medical College of Georgia, found that various organs responded differently to stimulation by adrenaline and related compounds. He proposed that there were two different types of adrenergic receptors, which he labeled "alpha" and "beta." The alpha adrenergic receptors are located in blood vessels and, when stimulated, cause a narrowing of the arteries, which results in higher blood pressure. Beta adrenergic receptors include those in the heart, which, when stimulated, produce heightened force and rate of contraction. Another subtype of beta adrenergic receptor is located in the lungs; when triggered, it relaxes the tension around airways, allowing greater inspiration. This latter type also is found in the blood vessels of muscles, where activation enhances blood flow, bringing more fuel to feed their work.

Even a pioneer in the field such as Ahlquist—whose work paved the way for understanding how various organs respond to the chemical messenger adrenaline—thought of receptors as a type of virtual reality. He wrote that he was not "so presumptuous as to believe that alpha and beta receptors really do exist. There are those that think so and even propose to describe their intimate structure. To me, they are an abstract concept conceived to explain observed responses of tissues produced by chemicals of various structure."[2] Ahlquist wrote this disclaimer in 1973, three years after Lefkowitz proposed to study these mythic entities. Ahlquist hardly was alone in his skepticism about receptors as physical entities; many, if not most, pharmacologists held similar doubts.

It is all the more remarkable (and much to his credit) that Ed Haber was willing to let Bob Lefkowitz make his case for studying the beta adrenergic receptor. Lefkowitz, still a neophyte in science but with growing self-confidence, built his arguments around both the patient-care relevance and the investigative rationale for studying these receptors. From a clinical perspective, beta adrenergic receptors had appeal because Dr. James Black, a Scottish physician and pharmacologist, had developed a drug, propranolol, that blocked beta adrenergic action on the heart. Marketed under the brand name "Inderal," this so-called beta blocker proved to be useful in treating patients with heart-related chest pain, high blood pressure, certain irregularities of heart rhythm, and those recovering from heart attacks. Approved by the Food and Drug Administration in 1966, propranolol became the first of many beta blockers in widespread clinical use. For launching this important domain of drug development, Black shared the 1988 Nobel Prize in Physiology or Medicine.

As Bob Lefkowitz was choosing a research topic, propranolol and its fellow beta blockers were all the rage in cardiology circles. In addition to being a hot topic clinically, beta adrenergic receptors had caught the fancy of the research world. Earl Sutherland, a physician and biochemist working at Case Western Reserve University in Cleveland, studied the process by which adrenaline caused liver cells to convert stored sugar into a form that could be readily used to feed the body in an emergency. Sutherland discovered that the initial messenger, adrenaline, acted through a second messenger in order to break down the sugar reserves. This second messenger, referred to by its chemical composition as "cyclic AMP," was involved in the ACTH receptor that Lefkowitz had studied at NIH, so working on another cyclic AMP–linked hormone receptor was appealing. The timing could not have been more opportune—a year after Lefkowitz proposed to work on the beta adrenergic receptor, Sutherland won the Nobel Prize in Physiology or Medicine for his discoveries about the process by which adrenaline works through its second messenger. The receptor itself had not been characterized, so Lefkowitz could fill in an important gap in the understanding of how the initial signal is translated into downstream effects.

Finally, there was a purely practical motivation for Lefkowitz to work on the beta adrenergic receptor. Unlike ACTH and many other large molecule hormones, adrenaline and related messengers and blockers were small molecules. Many of the natural messengers had been isolated, and a growing number of man-made messengers also were available. Lefkowitz could rely on the existing inventories of these compounds rather than having to create them himself. With his clinical, scientific, and pragmatic reasons mustered, Lefkowitz succeeded in convincing Haber to let him pursue this line of research.

Less clear was whether Lefkowitz could pull off a stealth research experience when he was supposed to be doing clinical work. For a while, the illicit laboratory work went undetected by the authorities. Haber's laboratories were located in a basement underneath the historic Bulfinch Building—outside of the sight and mind of the clinical leadership. Unfortunately, the clandestine efforts were unmasked by a cold winter storm. In order to avoid the frigid night air, Daniel "Dan" Federman, the residency director, decided to walk through a tunnel to his parked car. The tunnel ran adjacent to Haber's lab, and by pure chance—and to their mutual surprise—Federman encountered Lefkowitz in the hallway holding an incriminating rack of test tubes in his hands.

"Lefkowitz, I heard rumors that you were doing research," Federman declared, with a finger wagging in the resident's embarrassed face. "See

me in my office tomorrow." When the appointed hour of judgment arrived the next day, Lefkowitz was alarmed to see that Federman was
not alone—he had invited the chair of the Department of Medicine,
Alexander "Alex" Leaf, to join him. This suggested that a misdemeanor
was being elevated to a felony. As Lefkowitz was preparing himself for a
stern lecture and punishment, he was relieved to learn that he would receive only a mild reprimand; even more remarkable, no prohibition was
delivered about refraining from research in the future. This was MGH,
after all, and the powers that be prided themselves on being a leading
training ground for researchers. It simply was not in its institutional
DNA to lower the boom on an aspiring young physician-scientist.[3]

Lefkowitz continued his research through the remainder of his senior residency and the subsequent two years of his cardiology fellowship.
Contrite from his earlier episode of playing hooky from patient care, he
met all of the clinical obligations of the fellowship, but his energy increasingly migrated to the lab, where he continued to work with Haber.
It appeared that he had made a breakthrough on developing a binding
assay measuring the beta adrenergic receptor, but further assessment revealed that he had not succeeded in capturing the true receptor—that
feat would require the development of new technical methods.

As his cardiology fellowship was nearing completion, Lefkowitz began to consider his options for further employment. For someone who
had been educated in the Ivy League and never lived south of Bethesda,
Maryland, the likely hunting ground for jobs would be in the venerable
academic institutions of the Northeast. Indeed, Harvard was interested
in retaining him. The departmental leaders, undeterred by his history
of playing hooky from clinical electives, invited Lefkowitz to serve as
a chief resident for a year, followed by appointment as a junior faculty
member. This would have been the simplest path, but a trip to Durham,
North Carolina, created a bump in the road. Andrew "Andy" Wallace,
chief of cardiology at Duke University at the time, recalled the circumstances: "I remember the key recruitment visit was around the Duke–
North Carolina football game in November of 1972. It was a beautiful
day. You couldn't have asked for better conditions to recruit someone
who was going to face the New England winter."[4]

Wallace was joined in the recruitment effort by James "Jim" Wyngaarden, chair of the Department of Medicine at Duke. Wallace wanted a young faculty member in his division with the type of research pedigree that Bob Lefkowitz possessed. "I had pretty much determined that cardiology needed a couple of people who would foster insights into the molecular biology side of cardiovascular disease," Wallace explained. This was an easy sell to his boss, Wyngaarden, who was a respected physician-researcher who, a decade later, would be appointed director of the NIH. Wallace, a former Yellow Beret himself, had heard Lefkowitz speak at an American Heart Association meeting and was convinced he had found just the right man to help build the research arm of his division.[5]

The initial offer from Duke included a $24,000 starting salary, which at that time was very respectable compensation for a first-time faculty member. Lefkowitz, never really believing that his future lay in a Southern university endowed by a tobacco baron, kindly rejected the proposal. Not easily dissuaded, Wallace and Wyngaarden upped the ante, raising the salary to $32,000, and asked Lefkowitz to name his other requirements. Feeling that he had nothing to lose because he was going to remain in Boston anyway, Lefkowitz countered with the almost unthinkable. He requested that he be appointed as an associate professor with tenure, bypassing the usual and customary rank of assistant professor entirely. Moreover, the award of tenure typically is reserved for faculty members who have demonstrated substantial and sustained contributions for a half-dozen years or more. In proposing these terms, which he himself later described as "outrageous," Lefkowitz fully anticipated that the Duke team would stop distracting him from his true future at Harvard.[6]

To his amazement, Lefkowitz was given a thumbs-up by Wallace and Wyngaarden. In addition, he was promised $75,000 of start-up funding for his research lab, as well as support for a fellow and a technician and a princely allocation of 1,500 square feet of research space in a brand-new building. By contrast, the offer at Harvard literally involved the conversion of a supply closet in Haber's lab into bench space that could barely accommodate two persons working side by side.[7] Contrasting his two offers was like comparing an apple to a bushel of oranges—Harvard was relying heavily on the prestige of its name and storied tradition in order to attract an up-and-comer onto its faculty. At the time, Lefkowitz thought, "Duke was a young institution. But it was a decent institution, and the offer was just so non-comparable with what Harvard was offering that I said: 'This is it. I gotta go for it.'"[8]

Others around him were less convinced. "A lot of people said: 'How can you go to Duke?' Even my in-laws at the time." Mimicking the New York accents of his relatives, Lefkowitz recalled their bewilderment: "'Whadddaya crazy? You're at Hawvaad.'"[9] Lefkowitz admits that it was a gamble on his part, but his new employers also were taking a long shot that Lefkowitz later described as a "gutsy move." He credits Wyngaarden with the ability to identify rising stars and bet on their future potential. "He [Wyngaarden] had this amazing feel for people right at the beginning of their careers. He had this wonderful ability to pick talent. It's one thing to hire some famous professor and bring in the talent that way. But that's not what they were doing. They saw a bright young man, who seemed to be starting to make a name for himself, and they placed a bet."[10]

At the time, and even in retrospect, wagering that Bob Lefkowitz would win the beta adrenergic receptor jackpot was a leap in the dark. With eminent leaders in pharmacology questioning whether receptors even existed as physical entities, Lefkowitz had spent more than two years unsuccessfully searching for the beta adrenergic receptor. His first task was to develop a method for binding a radioactively labeled messenger to the receptor. After two years of frustrated attempts in Boston, Lefkowitz and his team solved this problem within a year after arriving at his new labs at Duke. Things were looking up for the high-priced recruit, but considerable challenges remained. For starters, the receptors were contained within cell-surface membranes and had to be extracted carefully, without impairing their biological activity. Even if one could extract them, the adrenergic receptors were present in very minute quantities. For every 200,000–300,000 protein molecules in a cell membrane, only one would be the desired beta adrenergic receptor.[11]

The solution to the first challenge—namely, removing the receptors from the cell-surface membranes—came after testing a variety of biological detergents that allow the separation of the water-loving components, such as the protein of the receptor, from the water-intolerant fatty parts of the cell membrane. After unsuccessful attempts with some of the commonly employed biological detergents, Lefkowitz and his team eventually found the perfect agent. Thanks go to the foxglove plant, whose leaves are well known as a source of the heart medication digitalis. The seeds of the foxglove plant contain a soapy compound known as digitonin. When applied to cell membranes, digitonin binds to the cholesterol and related compounds, thereby creating holes in the membrane, with a consequent loss of structural integrity. Lefkowitz and his postdoctoral fellow, Marc Caron, were able to demonstrate that, when red blood cells from frogs were treated with digitonin, beta adrenergic receptors could be separated and remained biologically active.[12]

Once the receptors were detached from the cell-surface membranes, there still was the task of purifying them for study while continuing to maintain their biological functioning. Traditional methods for separating chemical compounds from one another were not sufficient for isolating the miniscule amounts of beta adrenergic receptors. Again, Lefkowitz and his team had to get creative. They used the highly sensitive and specific binding features of the receptors to grab them away from the flood of other molecules in the detergent-washed soup of cellular materials. Marc Caron chemically attached alprenolol, a beta blocker, to insoluble beads composed of a long-chain sugar called "agarose." When a solution containing the receptors was washed over the coated beads, the receptors grabbed on to the alprenolol for dear life, while all of the other molecules simply washed away in the media. Afterward, a solution containing isoproterenol—a chemical cousin of adrenaline—was applied to the coated beads, and the receptors happily jumped off the alprenolol and onto the tighter-grasping isoproterenol. The resulting wash thus was selectively concentrated in receptors—a process that could be repeated until sufficient purification was achieved. This laborious purification process was required in order to achieve the 100,000–200,000–fold increased concentration that Lefkowitz needed to perform his studies of the receptors.

Using these techniques, the Lefkowitz lab was able to identify biologically active beta adrenergic receptors from hamster, guinea pig, and rat lung tissues. These receptors were capable of binding adrenaline and other adrenergic stimulators and blockers. All were composed of a single chain of amino acids with similar sequences of the building blocks across these species.[13] The team then set its sights on the other adrenergic receptors. Ahlquist's original classification of alpha and beta adrenergic receptors had been refined over time. The alpha receptors were known to inhibit second-messenger formation and then were divided into two subgroups. The first category, alpha-1, promotes smooth muscle contraction in blood vessels that feed the skin, gut, and kidneys, reducing blood flow to those organs. The second subclass, alpha-2, lowers heart rate and blood pressure, has a sedating effect on the central nervous system, enhances platelet clumping and clot formation, and dials back the release of insulin and the breakdown of fats. Two types of beta subtypes were known then: The first increases the rate and force of heart contractions; the second relaxes smooth muscles, especially those of the airways. The initial beta adrenergic receptor isolated by the Lefkowitz lab was of this second type. A third beta adrenergic receptor was identified later and shown to be involved in mobilizing fats for energy and in relaxing the bladder muscle.

A postdoctoral fellow, John Regan, applied the isolation and purification methods that had worked so well for the beta-2 adrenergic receptors to the other known subtypes of adrenergic receptors. They were able to purify the alpha-2 adrenergic receptor from human platelets.[14] Another postdoctoral fellow, Fredrik Leeb-Lundberg, succeeded in isolating the alpha-1 adrenergic receptor from a tissue-culture cell line derived from smooth muscle cells in the reproductive system of the hamster.[15] One by one, Lefkowitz and his team systematically worked through the arduous process of isolating and purifying the members of the adrenergic receptor family. Nevertheless, some disbelievers still questioned whether the isolated and purified proteins that were obtained were the actual receptors themselves. Lefkowitz and his colleagues came up with a compelling demonstration to dispel any doubts that they were working with the genuine items. Richard "Rick" Cerione, yet another postdoctoral fellow, took the purified beta adrenergic receptors isolated from frog red blood cells and was able to incorporate them into the cell-surface membrane of red blood cells from the African horned toad. Importantly, the toad's cells had almost no beta adrenergic receptors of their own, thus if the modified cells responded to beta adrenergic stimulation, it would have to be attributable to the transplanted receptors from the frog. The team demonstrated a dose-response relationship: the more donor receptors that they added, the greater the activity in the recipient cells. They also showed that a beta-blocker drug inhibited the activity, as did intentional degrading of the receptors by heating them up to deform their three-dimensional structure.[16]

Cerione later recalled having the impression that his project was the most important one in progress within the Lefkowitz lab at the time. When he mentioned this belief to another former trainee, his colleague reported having had the same feelings about his own work. They then compared notes with other Lefkowitz acolytes and discovered that every one of them left the lab feeling that their project was the most crucial. Through his "infectious enthusiasm"—a skill that his own mentor, Jesse Roth, had deployed—Lefkowitz managed to make everyone in the lab feel valued and central to the progress of the research.[17]

Once the receptors were confirmed, the Lefkowitz lab turned its attention to the composition of the receptor protein chain. This task was formidable because of the minute amounts of receptor material available. Short stretches of amino acids from the beta-2 adrenergic receptor were identified. From the amino-acid ordering in these short chains, they could deduce the corresponding nucleotide sequences that could be used as probes to find the gene that codes for the beta-2 adrenergic receptor. In partnership with Richard Dixon, a collaborator at the pharmaceutical company Merck, Lefkowitz and a young cardiology fellow, Brian Kobilka, labored for two years to clone the beta-2 adrenergic receptor gene and, from it, obtain the translated complete protein sequence.

Kobilka was twenty-nine years old when he joined the Lefkowitz lab. A native of Minnesota, he attended the state university in Duluth and then Yale University School of Medicine. He trained in internal medicine at Barnes Hospital in St. Louis and then pursued cardiology specialty training at Duke, where he was accepted into the Lefkowitz lab (sight unseen, as Lefkowitz was away from campus during Kobilka's interviews). The partnership with Dixon at Merck allowed Kobilka the opportunity to learn molecular biology techniques. Using these acquired skills, Kobilka generated a genomic library from hamster lung DNA. From this library, the beta-2 adrenergic receptor was cloned, and the amino-acid sequence of the receptor was deduced and reported in May 1986.[18]

Lefkowitz later recalled the eureka moment of this discovery:

> We could see a particular organization to the protein where the protein chain weaved across the plasma membrane—the cell membrane—seven times, like a snake. There was only one molecule known at the time that did that . . . and that's something called rhodopsin, which is found in the retina and is the basis for how we see. It is, in a sense, a light receptor—when photons of light impinge on rhodopsin and change its conformation or shape in a way that lets it do something which is kind of analogous to what a hormone receptor does.[19]

The serpentine path of the beta-2 adrenergic receptor and rhodopsin could be inferred from regions of the protein chain that contained seven stretches of amino acids that would be most comfortable residing within the water-abhorring core of the cell membrane. This overall organizational pattern not only mirrored that of rhodopsin; there were actual similarities in the lineup of individual amino acids in these membrane-crossing zones. Why would there be such structural parallels between a hormone receptor that is involved in relaxing the smooth muscles surrounding airways of a hamster and a light receptor in the eyes of a cow? If anything, they would have been anticipated to be quite different, as the seven membrane-piercing regions of rhodopsin—first discovered a few years earlier—until then were assumed to be distinguishing features of light-sensitive proteins.

The answer to this puzzle resided not in the role that these molecules play within the body but rather in the way that they execute their functions. The initial insights came from work undertaken by an NIH staff scientist, Martin "Marty" Rodbell, whose laboratories were located just down the hall from where Bob Lefkowitz worked as a Clinical Associate. Rodbell was interested in how the hormone glucagon interacted with its receptor on the surface of rat liver cells. Glucagon is a protein hormone that is produced in the pancreas; when released into the bloodstream, it causes the liver to chop up stored sugar into small, consumable fuel units. Rodbell discovered that the nucleotide, guanosine triphosphate (GTP), a molecule that provides energy for certain chemical reactions, could cause glucagon to separate from its receptor. Along with his colleague Lutz Birnbaumer, Rodbell published a series of papers[20] on this work shortly after Bob Lefkowitz departed the NIH to begin his cardiology fellowship.

Rodbell went on to discover that the binding of glucagon to its receptor led to the generation of GTP, which in turn activated a protein that became known as the "G protein" (a merciful shorthand for "guanine nucleotide-binding protein"). Borrowing jargon from the emerging field of computer sciences, Rodbell referred to the G protein as the principal component of the "transducer" serving as the communication link between the "discriminator" (the receptor) and the "amplifier" (downstream cellular activities) through Sutherland's second messenger, cyclic AMP. The year after Lefkowitz arrived at Duke, the Rodbell lab went on to make a GTP-like compound and showed that the nucleotide acted as a stimulant for cyclic AMP activity. Strikingly, the signal transduction worked in a variety of cells from a range of animal species, with an equally broad spectrum of hormones. This was an early indication of the fact that many different receptor systems may act through a common mechanism of signal transduction.[21]

The G protein story was picked up by Alfred "Al" Gilman, a physician-scientist who was also a Yellow Beret under Marshall Nirenberg's tutelage, overlapping with Joe Goldstein's time there. Gilman left NIH in 1971, just as Rodbell's initial GTP studies were being published. Gilman joined the faculty at the University of Virginia and, with the postdoctoral fellow Elliott Ross, began a series of experiments that demonstrated that a protein, which would be called Gs (for "GTP-binding and cyclase stimulation"), bound GTP and then stimulated the biological response through activation of cyclic AMP.[22] The work of Rodbell and Gilman was recognized as being of great importance, and in 1984 they shared the Canada Gairdner Foundation International Award with, among others, the future Nobel laureates Harold Varmus and Mike Bishop. Rodbell and Gilman were entering the stratosphere of the scientific elite.

Meanwhile, researchers at Stanford working on the signal transduction from light stimulation of rhodopsin identified a molecule, transducin, that had a similar GTP binding function as the G proteins.[23] Gilman, having moved to the University of Texas Southwestern Medical School, went on to demonstrate that transducin and the G proteins were structurally similar.[24] So, by the time that Kobilka and Lefkowitz found the protein sequence similarities between the beta-2 adrenergic receptor and rhodopsin—their eureka moment—they immediately wondered: "My goodness, maybe all of these receptors are going to look like that [cross the cell membrane seven times]."[25] Within a year, they had cloned the gene for the beta-1 adrenergic receptor[26] and the alpha-2 adrenergic receptor,[27] both of which showed the same organizational features of the seven membrane-spanning regions. The following year, they cloned the last adrenergic receptor then known—the alpha-1 version—and, once again, the same sequence pattern appeared.[28] The more data that they amassed, the more that their initial hunch appeared to be on target. Rather than being a fingerprint for light-sensing proteins, the seven-transmembrane weaving pattern was a more general feature of all receptors that were coupled to a G protein.

As investigators elsewhere sequenced other G protein–coupled receptors, the same organizing configuration was seen again and again. It was becoming incontrovertible that this serpentine arrangement was a universal feature of G protein–coupled receptors. Moreover, the number of such receptors seemed to be exploding exponentially. Today, nearly a thousand G protein–coupled receptors are known to exist in humans, and these entities are involved in biological signaling ranging from vision, to smell, to hormones, to neurotransmitters. Importantly, these receptors are frequent targets for pharmaceutical intervention, accounting for more than a third of all drugs currently on the market. So, the initial focus of Bob Lefkowitz on beta adrenergic receptors unexpectedly opened up a panoramic window onto a host of other receptors and treatment interventions.

The family of G protein–coupled receptors expanded so rapidly that proteins that fit this pattern could be identified by gene sequences without knowing the specific hormone or other messenger that binds to it or what its function might be. These known protein sequences with unidentified roles became known as "orphan receptors." Lefkowitz and his team identified one of the first orphans. It had a structure so close to that of the beta-2 adrenergic receptor that they assumed it must be its close relative—the beta-1 receptor. They were confounded, however, when they tested its binding with adrenaline-like compounds and found it to be a misfit. Not long afterward, they discovered that it was a receptor for the neurotransmitter serotonin, which is involved in mood and sleep regulation, digestion, and a host of other roles. So, this receptor was matched up with its biological family very quickly and moved out of the orphanage.[29]

Having established the ubiquity of the sevenfold membrane-crossing schema, Lefkowitz and Kobilka turned to studies of how the structural components related to the biological activity of the receptors. They noted strong similarities in the amino-acid sequence of the beta-2 and alpha-2 adrenergic receptors. They knew that the beta-2 type triggers the generation of cyclic AMP through the activation of the stimulatory G protein, Gs. By contrast, the alpha-2 adrenergic receptor depresses the production of cyclic AMP by activation of the inhibitory G protein, Gi. By mixing and matching stretches of the amino acids from the alpha-2 and beta-2 proteins, they created a series of proteins with differing combinations of parts. For example, a couple of the man-made combinations had mostly alpha-2 components but with small stretches of beta-2 material. Surprisingly, these artificially constructed receptors led to cyclic AMP generation, implying that the essential elements needed for Gs activation were conserved in these small inserts located within the third loop inside the cell. From these studies and the work of other labs, it was possible to determine that coupling to G proteins occurs at the receptor zones adjacent to the plasma membrane inside the cell. The binding to the hormone, in contrast, occurs in the receptor zones that cross the cell membrane just outside the cell.[30]

While the hard work of relating structure to function was taking place, Lefkowitz became intrigued by another aspect of receptor behavior that is referred to as "desensitization." This process occurs when a receptor is persistently stimulated by a hormone; at first, the signal is transduced with the resulting biological response, but after a few minutes the biological response diminishes, even if the hormone is still present.

Lefkowitz wondered: What mechanism could cause the overstimulated receptor to dial back its response? A postdoctoral fellow, Jeffrey "Jeff" Stadel, desensitized beta adrenergic receptors from the red blood cells of turkeys by overstimulation with an adrenaline-like compound. He discovered that the desensitized receptor was altered by the chemical attachment of a phosphate group.[31] Subsequently, a graduate student, Jeffrey "Jeff" Benovic, was able to identify the enzyme responsible for attaching this desensitizing phosphate group. The Lefkowitz team called this enzyme the "beta adrenergic receptor kinase."[32] The term "kinase" is the formal name for an enzyme whose job it is to add phosphate groups to specific other molecules. The Lefkowitz team demonstrated that their kinase had a similar structure to an independently discovered phosphorylating enzyme for rhodopsin.[33] Eventually, a total of seven such kinases would be identified, and virtually all G protein–coupled receptors were regulated by one of these enzymes.

In the process of isolating their first receptor kinase, the Duke team discovered that, as they purified the enzyme, rather than strengthening the desensitizing effect it appeared to weaken. Lefkowitz speculated there must be some essential partner to the kinase that was being squeezed out by the enzyme purification process. Eye researchers found such a cofactor for rhodopsin kinase, which they named "arrestin." When Lefkowitz secured a sample of arrestin and applied it to his team's model system, he found that it restored the desensitizing effect. Because arrestin is confined to the eye, it could not be the actual cofactor for the beta adrenergic receptor kinase, but it likely was a close chemical relative. Once the gene for arrestin was cloned, the Lefkowitz lab used it to clone a similar compound that was the actual partner to their own lab's kinase. They labeled this cofactor "beta-arrestin"[34] and later discovered a second such beta-arrestin.

The body of work produced by Bob Lefkowitz and his colleagues over the first two decades of his career is astounding. He isolated and purified multiple adrenergic receptors; demonstrated their biological functionality; sequenced the protein chains of the receptors; revealed the ubiquitous nature of the serpentine membrane-crossing organization of the G protein–coupled receptors; identified the regions of the receptor that were associated with messenger binding and cellular signal transduction; and discovered desensitizing enzymes and their oblig-atory cofactors, the arrestins. By any measure, these were impressive achievements indeed, and Lefkowitz was recognized with the Canada Gairdner Foundation International Award in 1988 and was awarded many other honors. When the Nobel Prize in Physiology or Medicine was announced on October 10, 1994, for work on "G proteins and the role of these proteins in signal transduction," Bob Lefkowitz seemed to be an obvious recipient. The Nobel rules permit up to three recipients, but in this instance, only two were named: Martin Rodbell and Alfred Gilman. The omission of Lefkowitz—whose discoveries were numerous and fundamental to understanding how G proteins work—was difficult to understand. Looking back, Lefkowitz admits his feelings: "That was very tough," adding "I would love to know the story some day." Because the Nobel rules require that nominations and committee appraisals re-main confidential for fifty years, Lefkowitz was left to speculate on why he failed to make the cut: "My best assessment was that I had some en-emies somewhere, colleagues who—they [the Nobel Committee mem-bers] confer broadly about the prize—and I think if somebody damned me, you know, some evaluator who maybe I had crossed swords with at some point . . . who knows?"[35]

A decade later, the Nobel Prize in Physiology or Medicine was award-ed to Richard Axel and Linda Buck for "their discoveries of odorant receptors and the organization of the olfactory system." The receptors were a major part of the G protein–coupled receptor family, and while Lefkowitz never worked on receptors for smell, he may have felt that his contributions to related work were being overlooked again, whether intentionally or unintentionally. And even though the Nobel Prize re-mained elusive, others were bestowing honors on him, including the In-ternational Shaw Prize in Life Science or Medicine and the Presidential Medal of Science, both presented to Lefkowitz in 2007.

Reconciled to being a Nobel bridesmaid, Bob Lefkowitz was sleep-ing soundly on the morning of Wednesday, October 10, 2012, when the telephone rang. Wearing his customary earplugs in bed, Lefkowitz was blissfully unaware of the persistent ringing. Roused from sleep—not by the telephone but rather a friendly elbow from his wife—Lefkowitz an-swered the call, which turned out to originate in Stockholm. He was informed that he had been selected along with his former fellow, Brian Kobilka—who had gone on to his own successful career at Stanford University—to receive the Nobel Prize. The Nobel Committee in Sweden had another surprise for Lefkowitz: rather than being recognized in Physiology or Medicine, the pair of physicians had been awarded the Nobel Prize in Chemistry.

Awarding the Nobel Prize in Chemistry was part of the Nobel Committee's recent trend of honoring chemical discoveries in biological systems. Although some traditional chemists may have second-guessed whether the honored work was truly within the field, Kobilka's work at Stanford included the tedious and detailed mapping of the three-dimensional chemical structure of the beta adrenergic receptor—a type of scientific pointillism in which every constituent atom is placed in its appropriate location. Together, the work Lefkowitz and Kobilka performed spanned an unusually broad range of fields—from pharmacology, to biochemistry, to molecular biology, to computer modeling, to chemistry. Shoehorning that work into any single field would not do it justice. Still, Lefkowitz and Kobilka would be the first to admit that they were not trained as chemists and did not think of themselves as such. One of the award's quick defenders was the medicinal chemist Derek Lowe, who admonished skeptical colleagues: "Biology isn't invading chemistry—biology is turning into chemistry. . . . So, my fellow chemists, cheer the hell up already."[36]

While the chemistry world adjusted to the news of the latest Nobel laureates, one can only wonder how Rose Lefkowitz, Bob's departed mother, might have felt about his achievement. A perfectionist to the core, Rose sought to instill humility in her son by reminding him when he won various academic awards: "It's not the Nobel Prize."[37] Finally, it was indeed the Nobel Prize. Bob's Uncle Henry was an easier sell. More than a decade before his Nobel Prize was announced, Lefkowitz received a call from Henry, who in a heavy Yiddish accent exclaimed: "Bobby, I'm so excited you're becoming so famous. When you get called from Scotland, I'm going with you." At first bewildered by the reference to "Scotland," Lefkowitz figured out that his geographically challenged relative was referring to the Nobel Prize. "I told Uncle Henry, 'Oh, you mean Stockholm.'" Without missing a beat, his uncle replied: "Scotland!

Stockholm! What's the difference? I'm coming with you."[38] Unfortunately, Uncle Henry did not live to make the trip to Stockholm—or Scotland for that matter.

There is little question that the five-decade pursuit of adrenergic receptors by Lefkowitz and his colleagues was a daunting journey. In an interview conducted a year before the Nobel Prize was announced, Lefkowitz confessed:

> When I look back now on the nature of the challenges and scientific problems I took on at the beginning of my scientific career, I think "Wow, if I had any idea how difficult that was going to be, I doubt that I would have started down that path." But at the time I was filled with optimism and confidence that we could ultimately reach our goals. I guess there is nothing quite like the chutzpah of youth.[39]

The Nobel Prize is conferred for scientific discoveries, but if there was a comparable recognition for scientific mentorship, Bob Lefkowitz would have been an excellent choice as well, having trained more than 200 graduate students, cardiologists, and postdoctoral fellows. The devotion of these trainees—current and former—to their mentor was on full display when about half of them showed up to celebrate Bob's sixtieth birthday in 2003. "Most of the leaders in the GPCR [G protein coupled receptor] field trained in my laboratory," Lefkowitz noted with obvious pride. "To me, that fact goes beyond any of the science, and I think the reason I've been successful at mentoring is this enthusiasm and passion I bring on a daily basis to the shared endeavor. I'm very interactive. I spend my days whipping my students and fellows into the same kind of frenzy as I'm in."[40]

Elaborating on the importance of hunger for the work, Lefkowitz points out: "The word enthusiasm is derived from the Greek and literally means 'a god within.' And so it is, since true enthusiasm for what we [physician-scientists] do—a very real passion for new knowledge—is a very empowering trait. It confers the ability, or rather, the willingness, to tackle difficult and challenging problems."[41] At the same time, Lefkowitz acknowledges the role of good fortune: "I have learned that I convey to the people around me a sense that I'm very lucky and that this luck will somehow be transferred to them. When they ask why I'm so lucky, I tell them that I'm lucky because I believe that I'm lucky." He admits to looking for the same sense of optimism in others: "For some years now, I have sometimes asked postdoctoral candidates during their interviews: 'Are you lucky?' The question generally takes them by surprise. You can imagine the range of response that I get: everything from 'Yes, I'm quite lucky' to 'No, a black cloud seems to follow me around.' With whom do you think I choose to work?"[42]

Elements of the Lefkowitz mentorship style can be traced back to his own supervisors at NIH—Ira Pastan and Jesse Roth. From Pastan, he learned rigor: how to question every result, ensuring that adequate controls were performed and that the findings can be replicated. In Lefkowitz's own words: "Some of the most important values that we can inculcate in our trainees are those related to personal integrity and rigor in their science. Of course, the most effective way to transmit these values is through the day-to-day role modeling we do."[43] From Roth, Lefkowitz learned how to think boldly and see the big picture while finding excitement in every new discovery, no matter how small. Lefkowitz also shares Roth's penchant for a quick wit and a well-exercised sense of humor. In describing his comedic sensibilities, Lefkowitz noted that there is a method to his madness: "I tend to use liberal doses of humor to encourage out of the box thinking and novel associations. Seeing the joke has elements in common with seeing a previously unappreciated and unexpected association. Somehow it seems that the more I provoke laughter at these [lab] meetings, the more creative ideas flow."[44]

Not surprisingly, the scientist who spent five decades studying every aspect of a biological process would be a big believer in pursuing the line of investigation to its conclusion. As Bob Lefkowitz tells his trainees: "There are four keys to success in science. The first is focus. The second is focus. The third is focus. And you gotta figure out what the fourth one is."[45]

When the master of focus was asked to sum up his life in three sentences, he responded: "Jewish boy from the Bronx, loves to read. Dreams of becoming a doctor. And somehow turns out to be a scientist who wins the Nobel Prize."[46]

CHAPTER 15

INFECTIOUS ENTHUSIASM

Varmus and Bishop Learn Fowl Lessons

When Harold Varmus departed Bethesda in the summer of 1970 with his wife, Connie, they decided to take the scenic route to his postdoctoral fellowship in San Francisco. During this monthlong odyssey, one of their stops was the central New Hampshire town of Tilton. This small, century-old rural community was home to the Tilton School, a college preparatory institution. With students away on holiday, the school's modest campus hosted a research conference on animal cells and viruses.

A decade earlier and 130 miles southwest, Varmus had been an undergraduate at Amherst College, where he pursued a major in English literature while enduring just enough science to meet premedical admissions requirements. Now a published author—not of literary criticism but of biomedical research—he was about to glimpse his future. The conference occurred shortly after the simultaneous publication by two separate laboratories of a finding that rocked the world of viral research.

That discovery was fundamental to understanding how the group of viruses whose genetic information is coded in RNA, rather than in DNA, are able to replicate themselves. More than five years earlier, Howard Temin, a virologist at the University of Wisconsin, had proposed the so-called provirus theory. Temin speculated that the viral RNA is transcribed into a DNA copy (the provirus), which is integrated into the host cell's DNA and then is copied along with the rest of the host's genetic material. Temin based his proposal on the observation that, if replication of the host's DNA was blocked experimentally, the replication of an invading RNA virus also was halted.[1] Temin's theory was disputed by many experts in the field, including his former mentor, Harry Rubin. During Varmus's search for postdoctoral positions the previous summer, Rubin, at the University of California, Berkeley, could not suppress his disdain for the provirus hypothesis. His skepticism was based in part on the perceived weakness of evidence. Even more damning, however, was a perception that the translation of RNA into DNA violated the Central Dogma of Molecular Biology handed down by Francis Crick: genetic information was considered to travel down a one-way street from DNA to RNA, from whence it was encoded into proteins. Temin was viewed as a heretic in the eyes of many scientists.

Temin's vindication arrived on May 28, 1970, at a prominent cancer research meeting convened in Houston, Texas. There, he announced to a stunned audience that, within a virus that caused cancer in chickens, he had discovered an enzyme that converted viral RNA into DNA. The following day, Temin received a telephone call from David Baltimore of the Massachusetts Institute of Technology. Temin had first met Baltimore fifteen years earlier when, as a recent graduate of Swarthmore College, Temin served as a summer research camp counselor at Jackson Memorial Laboratory in Bar Harbor, Maine. Baltimore, then a high-school junior, had been one of his charges at the camp, only a few years after Temin himself had been a camper there.[2]

Baltimore's telephone call after Temin's triumphant announcement was both congratulatory and confirmatory. Quite independently and virtually simultaneously, Baltimore had discovered the exact same enzyme. Baltimore presented his findings for the first time to an audience of about 300 attendees at a Cold Spring Harbor Laboratory symposium a couple weeks later. The findings of Temin and Baltimore were rushed to press and published in back-to-back articles in the journal *Nature* on June 27, less than a month after Temin's initial announcement.[3] Subsequently, Crick "clarified" that the Central Dogma was never intended to preclude the possibility of RNA-to-DNA translation. The discovery of the responsible enzyme—soon to become known as "reverse transcriptase" because it runs counter to the usual direction of transcription—was momentous. Within five years Temin and Baltimore would be named as two of three corecipients of the Nobel Prize in Physiology or Medicine. (Renato Dulbecco was the third; see chapter 12.)

Back at the July 1970 summer conference in Tilton, the discovery of reverse transcriptase was big news; talks by Temin and Baltimore stole the show. Other research groups, including the team that Varmus would be joining soon at the University of California, San Francisco, were, in Varmus's words, "desperately trying to catch up, doing competent biochemistry . . . the incremental experiments that follow any huge discovery."[4] Overshadowed by the spotlight on reverse transcriptase was a presentation made by a postdoctoral fellow working with Harry Rubin at the University of California, Berkeley. Rubin, no doubt, was eating a serving of crow for his earlier disparagement of the theory of his former trainee, Temin. He could take some consolation, however, in the presentation made by his current protégé, G. Steven "Steve" Martin, who was studying the same cancer-inducing virus in chickens.

Martin had obtained a sample of the virus from Varmus's future UCSF colleagues and treated it with a chemical known to cause genetic mutations. One of the viral mutants that resulted appeared to operate as if it were controlled by a thermostat. At normal body temperatures, the virus infected cells and they became cancerous. At the feverish temperature of 106 degrees Fahrenheit, however, the virus could infect cells and replicate, but its ability to trigger cancer was lost.[5] Martin's experiment provided compelling evidence that the capacity of the virus to survive and propagate was separate from its malfeasance in producing cancer. Given that the temperature-sensitive mutant was created by attacking its RNA, the notion was advanced that the virus contained a cancer-inducing gene, or "oncogene," that was turned off in the mutant. Moreover, because Martin's altered virus was functioning perfectly otherwise, it was reasonable to assume—and was later confirmed—that the cancer gene was physically and functionally distinct from the other core viral genes. An important implication arose out of Martin's findings: the virus was not just a trigger for a malignant gene that lay dormant in the cells of the chicken. Instead, the virus was delivering to the unsuspecting host cell a time bomb to be deposited within its own genetic material. Once the viral RNA was converted to DNA by reverse transcriptase and incorporated into the DNA of the chicken cell, all hell would break loose, with anarchic genetic instructions wreaking havoc on the cell's normal control systems.

As Harold and Connie Varmus departed New Hampshire for San Francisco, it was apparent that RNA tumor virus labs across the country were quickening their pace. A year earlier, when Temin's work was still revolutionary, Varmus had been referred by an unapologetic disbeliever (Rubin) to the UCSF virologists. When Varmus made the team, he could not have foreseen the good fortune that would ensue. Whether by fate, by chance, or by intuition, he was launching his exploration of tumor viruses at just the right time, in the optimal place, and with the perfect colleagues. The secrets of these viruses had been hermetically sealed for decades, but suddenly Temin, Baltimore, and Martin had provided keys to unlocking these treasures. Nowhere was there a more energized setting for this work than California, where multiple laboratories were engaged already. Most important, Varmus had found a kindred soul— Mike Bishop—for this journey.

Writing about his relationship with Bishop, Varmus revealed that "from the first moments . . . we seemed to have been destined to work together." Although Varmus started in a subordinate role as a postdoctoral fellow, in short order the relationship evolved to one of coequal partners: "A particular intellectual camaraderie developed between the two of us during my first few years in San Francisco. As the more senior and better known, Mike had more grant money, more people already working with him, and more applications from prospective trainees. It was essential to the growth and success of our relationship that Mike was willing to share this bounty with a generous spirit."[6] Bishop reinforced this sense of parity: "Harold's arrival changed my life and career. Our relationship evolved rapidly to one of equals, and the result was surely greater than the sum of the two parts."[7]

John Michael Bishop was born on February 22, 1936, in York, Pennsylvania. He grew up in a rural town of about 400 where his father was a Lutheran minister. For the first eight years of his education, he attended a two-room schoolhouse. His high-school class was not much bigger, with about eighty students, and Bishop was one of a handful who pursued higher education. He attended nearby Gettysburg College, adjacent to the famous Civil War battleground. At this small liberal arts college affiliated with the Lutheran Church, Bishop was a chemistry major, but he found greater intellectual stimulation from courses in history, philosophy, and literature. Just as with his future colleague Harold Varmus, a life in the arts and letters appealed to Bishop before he settled on a career in medicine.

When applying to medical schools, Bishop consulted his faculty adviser about various options. With Bishop's preference for a career in academic medicine, the adviser suggested: "You should consider Harvard." As an indication of his naïveté at the time, Bishop remembered asking: "Where is that?" The only slightly more informed faculty member replied: "In Boston somewhere, I think."[8] Following that somewhat geographically challenged advice, Bishop applied to Harvard, as well as the University of Pennsylvania, and was admitted to both. Struggling to choose, he wrote the admissions dean at Harvard, uncertain of which offer to accept and requesting a campus visit to help sort things out.[9] The deal was sealed not by a trip to Boston, which Harvard arranged, but rather by an associate dean at Penn who, upon learning of Bishop's desire for an academic career, advised him to become a Harvard man.[10]

Beginning medical school there in 1957, Bishop discovered that his lack of research experience was a major impediment to his professional ambitions.[11] A more substantial research experience was stimulated by an elective course that Bishop attended the following year. This course was taught by Elmer "Pfeff" Pfefferkorn, a recent Harvard PhD graduate who had been appointed as a junior member of the faculty.[12] In Bishop's words: "From the course, I learned that the viruses of animal cells were ripe for study with the tools of molecular biology, yet still accessible to the likes of me. From Elmer, I learned the inebriation of research, the practice of rigor, and the art of disappointment."[13]

Working in Pfefferkorn's tiny lab, Bishop stole free hours away from his medical school curriculum to study an RNA virus. He learned essential skills in viral purification, radioactive labeling of amino acids, and preparing cell extracts. Nevertheless, the work did not result in publishable results; Bishop was determined to continue in the lab, even if it meant sacrificing the prescribed standard fourth-year curriculum that prepared students for subsequent clinical work. Recalling his mind-set at the time, Bishop had "decided this is what I wanted to do with a living, and why not spend the whole fourth year of medical school doing it?"[14]

During two years of clinical training at MGH, Bishop learned a great deal, but his heart was not in patient care, as illustrated by his parting gesture: "On my final day as a medical house officer, as I walked out of the emergency ward toward a different sort of future, I removed my bulky pager from my belt and, in a moment of reckless euphoria, hurled it against the wall—disabling it beyond repair."[15] The fact that he was never billed by the hospital for its destroyed property might indicate that his was not the first beeper to meet an untimely end at the hands of a departing resident.

In 1964, four years ahead of Harold Varmus, Mike Bishop headed to the NIH as a Clinical Associate in the lab of Leon Levintow. The mentor and the trainee had some similarities in their respective backgrounds. Both were natives of Pennsylvania and attended small liberal arts colleges in the Keystone State (Levintow studied at Haverford College). Both obtained their clinical education at MGH, followed by research training at NIH.[16] About a year into Bishop's appointment, Levintow accepted an offer of a faculty position at UCSF and departed NIH and his supervision of Bishop. In Levintow's absence, Bishop initially worked fairly independently, much as he had when Levintow was present. For some time, Bishop continued a long-distance consultation with his former mentor, but this gradually transitioned to local guidance from a visiting German scientist, Gebhard Koch. In 1967, Koch returned to Hamburg, and Bishop elected to join him there for a year, putting off a faculty job offer from Levintow to join him in San Francisco.

In Hamburg, only modest progress occurred on the research front, but Bishop reveled in his surroundings in Germany, soaking up the art, the architecture, and other cultural riches. The pleasures of traveling abroad soon gave way to the real-world practicalities of employment back home. In addition to the offer from UCSF, Bishop was recruited by Johns Hopkins University, a much more established institution. Bishop decided against the offer in Baltimore but explored opportunities at Harvard, where he hoped that the authorities had had sufficient time to recover from his storied record of admissions indecision, curriculum redesign, and beeper hostilities. Perhaps the recovery was not yet complete, as an offer was not immediately forthcoming, so Bishop took the bird in hand and headed west to rejoin Levintow.

When Bishop arrived at UCSF in February 1968, the school was hardly known outside California. In his mind, however, the "decision to go there was an easy one, because the opportunities involved in going seemed so much greater than those in staying [at the more established institutions]. I would have been a mere embellishment on the East Coast. I was genuinely needed in San Francisco."[17] He recalled later: "When I arrived here my lab was essentially joined with Leon's. When I wasn't at the bench, we spent a great deal of the working day talking about everything. The administration didn't know who I was or anything about me, and I think Leon had a great deal to do with convincing them when I was young and unknown that I was worth supporting."[18]

Bishop was awarded an NIH grant to extend his studies of poliovirus, but the work of a colleague, Warren Levinson, who occupied an adjacent laboratory, began to attract his attention. Levinson, who attended medical school in Buffalo, New York, migrated cross-country for a doctorate at the University of California, Berkeley, before joining the faculty at UCSF. As Bishop described: "Warren and I essentially pow-wowed together, each of us making our own contribution, and my responsibility was to get the molecular biology going any way we could. Leon really fostered that collaboration and fostered my interest in RNA tumor viruses."[19]

Levinson's virus was the same used by Temin and one (of two) used by Baltimore for the simultaneous discoveries of reverse transcription from RNA to DNA, as well as the one in which Martin demonstrated the cancer-causing gene. This virus had been a favorite of medical researchers for many decades and first came to attention in 1909 at the Rockefeller Institute (later Rockefeller University) in New York City. A thirty-year-old pathologist there named Francis Peyton Rous, just four years out of medical school, was newly appointed to the research staff. Trained in human medicine, Rous would become most famous for a feathered patient: a Barred Plymouth Rock hen brought in by her owner, a farmer on Long Island. This bird was about a year and a half old and had been healthy until about two months earlier, when a progressively enlarging mass developed within her right breast. The hen otherwise appeared strong, and Rous removed the roughly two-inch-long ovoid tumor. When slices of the tumor were examined under the microscope, Rous described it as a spindle-celled sarcoma.[20] A cancer of connective tissue, the name "sarcoma" derives from the Greek word for "flesh." This particular sarcoma would be named in honor of its discoverer, Rous.

Unfortunately for the chicken, the tumor quickly regrew, and a little more than a month later the suffering hen was sacrificed. In exploring the behavior of the cancer, Rous attempted to transplant pieces of it into other unaffected birds. He noted that the tumor was indeed transmissible, but only to birds of the same farmer's stock and, even then, only sporadically.[21] Despite the low level of transmissibility, this was still a startling finding—that a cancer could be conveyed from one animal to another of similar background. Rous then went a step further. He ground up the tumor, suspending the material in a solution that he filtered. He strained the suspension in order to remove all the cellular debris and anything the size of bacteria or larger that could not pass through a filter. When he then took the filtrate and transplanted that into other chickens, transmission occurred faster and in greater numbers over successive generations.

This experiment demonstrated that the ability of the tumor to become established and grow was not an intrinsic characteristic of the cancer cells per se but rather resided within some extrinsic factor that was too small to be seen with a light microscope and tiny enough to pass through a filter. As Rous wrote: "The first tendency will be to regard the self-perpetuating agent active in this sarcoma of the fowl as a minute parasitic organism. Analogy with several infectious diseases of man and the lower animals, caused by ultramicroscopic organisms, gives support to this view of the findings."[22] The minute parasitic organism to which Rous referred was in fact a virus, which would come to be known as Rous sarcoma virus, or RSV. The term "virus," from the Latin for "poison," had been introduced more than a decade earlier, but nobody had yet seen one. Viruses are a tenth to a hundredth of the size of bacteria and thus could not be visualized with light microscopes. (It would take nearly three decades before a virus would be visualized under a powerful electron microscope.) So, effectively working blind to the actual agent, Rous discovered the first cancer-causing virus. These findings were not embraced quickly by the scientific community.[23] It was not until the burst of interest in tumor viruses in the 1950s—spurred by developments in molecular biology and the discovery of other cancer-generating viruses—that Rous received acclaim for his discovery of the chicken sarcoma virus. In 1966, more than a half-century after his seminal work, Rous was named corecipient of the Nobel Prize in Physiology or Medicine. Other aging scientists could take heart, no doubt, from the fact that, even at eighty-seven, one's earliest work still can be recognized and appreciated.

At the pinnacle of his acclaim, however, Rous made a bold claim that others would soon disprove. In his Nobel lecture, Rous addressed the continuing enigma of the cause of cancer: "A favorite explanation has been that oncogen[e]s cause alterations in the genes of the cells of the body, somatic mutations as they are termed. But numerous facts, when taken together, decisively exclude the supposition."[24] A little more than three years after these words were spoken, Steve Martin, using the very same virus that Rous had discovered, would demonstrate that cancer causation could be attributed to an oncogene. Bishop and Varmus would go one step further to demonstrate how such oncogenes might arise.

In 1970, Varmus arrived at the "rabbit warren of interconnected windowless rooms on the fourth floor of the Health Sciences East tower at UCSF."[25] The human inhabitants of this encased labyrinth included Varmus, Bishop, Levintow, and Levinson. A fourth faculty colleague, Herbert "Herb" Boyer, a pioneer in recombinant DNA research and later a founder of the biotech behemoth Genentech, was a frequent visitor.

Boyer worked with bacteria, and his lab was physically isolated from the virology team in order to avoid any potential cross-contamination. The gregarious Boyer, large in both frame and personality, managed to escape his quarantine regularly enough to borrow equipment that never returned in the same working order. Beyond the walls of UCSF, the team had an equally convivial network of associates at other universities. Key among these confreres was Peter Vogt, a Czech American and former trainee of Harry Rubin who was then on the faculty of the University of Southern California, and Peter Duesberg, a German American chemist at the University of California, Berkeley. The members of this club met every six weeks or so to discuss their work and to share ideas.

The dialogue with Vogt and Duesberg proved important to many aspects of the work at UCSF, none more so than a few months after the arrival of Varmus. In December 1970, Duesberg and Vogt published a key study of RSV. They used ultraviolet irradiation to create viruses that could replicate themselves in host cells but did not cause cancer.[26] Unlike Martin's earlier RSV temperature-sensitive mutant, the Duesberg-Vogt–irradiated virus was incapable of causing cancer under any circumstances. In other words, Martin's version appeared to have a partially disabled cancer gene, whereas the virus studied by Vogt and Duesberg appeared to have lost the gene entirely.

The cancer-instigating gene would become known as src (pronounced "sark") because of its role in the genesis of sarcomas. The mutant that Duesberg and Vogt studied, lacking the src gene entirely, would prove to be exactly what the doctors—Bishop and Varmus, that is—ordered. The team at UCSF wanted to use molecular hybridization—the technique that Varmus had deployed so deftly at the NIH to explore the bacterial lac operon—to pry into RSV. To do so, they needed a specific probe for the cancer-causing src gene. In an elegant multistep process, Varmus and Bishop were able to accomplish that feat. First, they used the recently discovered reverse transcriptase to copy the RNA of the normal ("wild") RSV into radioactively labeled DNA. The resulting DNA, including the transcribed src gene, was sliced into small segments. Then, the fragments of DNA were allowed to pair up with the corresponding portions of RNA from the Duesberg-Vogt RSV. All the parts of the transcribed DNA from the wild virus would find a match in the mutant RNA except for the src piece. Finally, the unpaired segments of wild DNA were separated out from the remaining paired segments.[27] The development of this probe—the transcribed DNA of the src gene—was a major advance because it would serve as a tool for much of the work to come.

Although Varmus started as the junior member of the team, he was largely responsible for the conceptualization of the src probe. A brief exchange, recalled years later by Bishop, provides some insight into how his relationship with Varmus was evolving. Bishop had been invited to give a talk and consulted with Varmus about potential topics: "I said: 'I'm not sure what I'm going to talk about.' He [Varmus] says: 'Well, why don't you talk about the probe stuff?' And I said: 'Well, Harold, that was really your idea.' And he said: 'Well, you know, we're in this together. Of course you can talk about it.' I felt a little sheepish about it, but he was right."[28]

The fact that this conversation—an otherwise brief and perfunctory exchange—would persist for decades in Bishop's memory suggests that it had a particular significance for him. Certainly, the exchange speaks to his sensitivity that he not be perceived (by Varmus or anyone else) as taking advantage of his seniority to co-opt the intellectual property of his colleague. Beneath that courtesy appears to lie some uncertainty about how credit for their work should be allocated. This was still relatively early in their working relationship—the development of the src DNA probe arguably was their first impactful contribution—so it would set a precedent for how they would view their joint efforts as their working relationship matured.

The discomfort that Bishop felt in talking about the newly developed probe, even with the reassurance from Varmus that it was a truly shared endeavor, speaks to the delicate balancing act in any collaboration. As Goldstein and Brown demonstrated at UT Southwestern, a successful research partnership relies heavily on the ability of the principals to suppress their separate egos and ambitions for the common good. Even when that is accomplished, however, the environment in which the partnership operates can either nourish it or destroy it. Because universities traditionally judge faculty performance on the basis of independent effort, there is a natural tendency to try to dissect out the individual roles of the researchers.

In the case of Brown and Goldstein, the University of Texas Southwestern Medical School defied the norms, accepted that their work was indistinguishably joint, and treated both partners on an identical basis. For Bishop and Varmus—partners who did not start with equivalent status—UCSF had a greater challenge in establishing a sense of parity. For many years, as Bishop and Varmus progressed up the academic ranks, the team on the fourth floor of UCSF's Health Sciences East Building lived in what Varmus described as "nirvana." Ultimately, as we shall see, this happy balance could not be sustained indefinitely, and an insurmountable tension arose in their working relationship.

Having created the src DNA probe, Varmus and Bishop, accompanied by the French postdoctoral fellow Dominique Stehelin, began searching for the src gene in the normal cells of various bird species. The first big hit occurred on the night of October 26, 1974, while Stehelin was working alone in the lab. When running the src probe against DNA from chickens with no prior exposure to RSV, there was a match: the viral src gene had a mirror image in the normal cells of an unexposed chicken. This was the first evidence—some might say of staggering import—that an oncogene (a cancer-causing gene) might be a variant of a normal cellular gene (dubbed a "proto-oncogene").

"Where was I at the moment of magic?" Bishop asked rhetorically. "Dominique and I often shared an evening meal at a local sandwich shop, but by the time the data chattered out of the radiation detector that October evening, Dominique was alone in the laboratory, whereas I was at home and possibly in bed."[29] Having found a close relative of the src gene in chickens, the team extended their search to other birds such as quails, turkeys, and ducks. In all instances, they found the src lookalike in normal cellular DNA.

In order to determine how far back in time src may have entered the normal avian gene pool, Varmus suggested a consultation with an evolutionary biologist. Fortunately, the San Francisco Bay area is well stocked with just about every type of academic, and in this case the content-area expert was Allan Wilson. A native of New Zealand, Wilson obtained his doctorate in biochemistry at the University of California, Berkeley, and was appointed later to the faculty there. Wilson's special expertise was in demonstrating how far back in evolutionary time various species diverged, based on molecular profiles. Wilson suggested that the UCSF team explore the class of large, flightless birds known as "ratites." Among the surviving members of this primitive family of fast-running birds is the African ostrich, the Australian emu, and the South American rhea. These primitive birds were thought to have diverged from other fowl at an early point in evolutionary history and thus would be the most distant feathered cousins to chickens.

Procuring ratites for study was a bit more challenging than finding chickens. With a bit of coaxing, the Sacramento Zoo donated an emu egg to the cause. Varmus's office became the hatchery for the emu, which at birth was the size of a full-grown chicken (adult emus can reach six feet in height and tip the scales at a hundred pounds or more). The lab's new mascot proved "charming" and "delightful," and none of the intrepid src hunters had the cold-blooded detachment to dispatch their three-week-old zoo escapee. A veterinarian on campus, who had not grown attached to the emu, performed the sacrificial deed. When the emu DNA was examined with the probe and revealed a src proto-oncogene, the oversized chick gained a measure of immortality. The team had demonstrated that the src gene was conserved in normal cellular DNA from the widest possible cross-section of birds.[30] The level of preservation across evolutionary history suggested that the proto-oncogene had been present for at least 100 million years.

The nucleotide composition of the viral src (or "v-src") was not a perfect match to the various versions of avian cellular src (or "c-src"). One would expect that the closest match would be for the c-src from chickens, for that is the type of bird from which the oncogene was isolated. As the avians diverged from an evolutionary perspective, one would expect that there would be corresponding differences introduced into their genomes over time. Thus, birds that diverged from the evolutionary path toward chickens at earlier points in history—namely, the ratites—would be expected to have the least similarity in nucleotide match with the probe. Using the testing methodology available at the time—before genome sequencing was possible—the investigators explored the tightness of the match between the v-src and the c-src of various species. The tighter the match, the stronger the strands would hold on to each other and resist melting apart when heated. The team observed exactly the

progression of tight fit that one would predict from evolutionary proximity, with the delightful and charming emu demonstrating the loosest
fit. Bishop described the result: "It was beautiful. Considering the technologies that we were using, the way those melting curves tracked with
the phylogenetic distances was uncanny."[31]

Having demonstrated the proto-oncogene across the spectrum of
birds tested, the team went one step further and asked a question: Is the
viral gene present in the cellular DNA of nonavian species? Deborah
Spector, an MIT-educated molecular biologist working as a postdoctoral
fellow for Bishop and Varmus, helped to answer that question. When
the viral gene was tested against DNA from vertebrates—ranging from
salmon, to mice, to calves, to humans—homologous regions of nucleotide sequences were found. In contrast, when compared against DNA
from invertebrates such as bacteria, fruit flies, and sea urchins, no complementary regions were detected. The conservation of the genetic information across widely ranging vertebrate species led the team to conclude
that the genes "might perform some critical function," also noting that
"the nature of that function remains obscure."[32]

Some in the scientific community were dubious about whether the
genetic content of a chicken-cancer virus could be lurking in the normal cellular DNA of humans. "The discovery that Harold Varmus and
I made with the kind help of our younger colleagues broke old rules,"
Bishop explained. "In science, what a rule means is current understanding—a current view—and the reason you can break the rule is that the
current rule is not entirely correct."[33] Sometimes there was skepticism
even if old rules, some firmly established a century earlier, were affirmed.
When the vertebrate data were presented at a major scientific meeting,
for example, an unconvinced member of the audience asked: "Are you
trying to tell us that a chicken gene is also in humans?" Bishop recalled
his disbelief at the question: "I was flabbergasted by this biological
naiveté on the part of accomplished scientists. Had Darwin labored
in vain?"[34]

Once the ubiquity of c-src was demonstrated among vertebrates,
Varmus and Bishop, as well as many others, focused on the "obscure
nature" of the normal function of this gene. In order to study the protein transcribed by s-src, a method was needed to isolate and purify the

gene product. Here, the effort was aided by animals that had developed RSV tumors. In response, these animals produced antibodies to the protein coded by the oncogene.[35] The antibodies were deployed in a lab at the University of Colorado (where they were detected),[36] as well as by the team at UCSF,[37] in order to isolate and purify the src protein. Characterization of this src product by the two groups revealed almost simultaneously that it was an enzyme whose job was to add a phosphate group to other proteins. It would be learned later that the src protein is involved in normal cell-signaling and helps to regulate many biological processes, such as cell growth, shape, specialization, movement, and survival. When a mutation occurs in the proto-oncogene, creating an oncogene, the resulting enzyme runs amok, leading to derangement in cell-signaling and loss of normal control mechanisms.

An additional question was whether the phenomenon of src—a normal cellular gene being converted into a cancer-causing gene—was unique. The answer came soon thereafter when Diana Sheiness, working with Bishop, was studying another cancer-inducing bird RNA virus, MC29 (which is mercifully easier to pronounce than "myelocytomatosis virus"). Sheiness was able to identify the oncogene in MC29,[38] and she found a proto-oncogene in the DNA of various species of birds as well as in mice, cows, and salmon.[39] Other cellular proto-oncogenes were being discovered concurrently, and a consensus was needed for how to name them. Harold Varmus describes convening a self-appointed group at a Cold Spring Harbor Laboratory symposium on RNA tumor viruses in 1980: "Over several hours and beers in a room in historic Blackford Hall, we came up with most of [the] distinctive names those genes still bear today."[40] The oncogene that Sheiness worked on, for example, was named "myc," after the myelocytomatosis virus in which it was discovered. Another oncogene was labeled "ras" because it was identified in a rat sarcoma virus. The profusion of oncogenes delineated now number in the hundreds (not all of them named with the benefit of libation). The sheer volume of these cancer-progenitor genes gives testament to the many ways that the normal genome can be disrupted and lead to malignant transformation. It also serves as a tribute to the work of Bishop and Varmus, who wrote an early entry in the ever-expanding catalog of oncogenes.

The partnership that Harold Varmus and Mike Bishop established in 1970 was born of mutual admiration and respect. In Bishop's words: "I don't think we ever really had a supervisory relationship. We very quickly fell into a co-equal relationship."[41] Varmus recalled: "Mike and I increasingly recognized the synchronies of our views on scientific matters and other things, too: books, music, politics, and the people around us."[42]

Reflecting back, Bishop acknowledges the sense of fulfillment he experienced in the personal and professional chemistry he developed with Varmus: "The arrangement between Harold and myself was unusual, widely recognized as such, and much admired. We became a hyphenated self that gave its name to a social organism—the 'Bishop-Varmus' laboratory. Among my generation of biomedical scientists, I know of very few such partnerships that achieved comparable distinction."[43]

On a day-to-day basis, the partnership was manifest less in joint laboratory work, as Brown and Goldstein had displayed, than in shared guidance of others. As Varmus described:

We both maintained some semblance of laboratory work despite the other duties of faculty life, until our early forties, but it usually involved taking care of cell cultures (an essentially lonely activity) or doing a more elaborate experiment with a technician or trainee. Still, the hours we logged together were lengthy, a string of hour-long meetings in which a single student, fellow, or technician, or sometimes little groups of two or three who happened to be doing a project together, would tell us about their latest findings or failures. Then we'd all try to plan the next step or figure out what went wrong.[44]

One venue in which Varmus and Bishop would engage with colleagues and trainees was the weekly "Rous Lunch." A former postdoctoral fellow named Arthur "Art" Levinson (who later would become chief executive officer and chair of the biotechnology firm Genentech) portrayed the general tenor of these meetings as "an aggressive, a macho type of environment that most people liked." He characterized Bishop's input as "less detail oriented," whereas "Harold was: 'Boom, boom, boom, boom, neat, not neat, you left out this control, da-da-da.' He was more into the detail. Mike preferred kind of steering the ship."[45] This description of

Varmus echoes the way that his NIH mentor, Ira Pastan, was perceived: a stickler for rigor, going over each experiment with a fine-tooth comb. Varmus acknowledges these perceptions: "In the main, I am viewed as having paid the greater attention to experimental detail. Mike to the bigger picture. Those may or may not be flattering or accurate portrayals. But there is general consensus that our frequent gatherings were, in turn, good-humored, intimidating, unrelenting, productive, stimulating, and seemingly essential to our increasing productivity as a laboratory group."[46]

Another former postdoctoral fellow who later joined the faculty, Donald "Don" Ganem, compared and contrasted key attributes of Bishop and Varmus. He noted that both were voracious readers: "But the breadth of [Mike's] knowledge was truly encyclopedic. Harold's strong suit was being quick on the uptake. He instantly could grasp every ramification of something, however remote." Etched in Ganem's memories were the preparations for his regular Monday morning meeting with Varmus: "You never wanted to go in there unless you were certain you had considered every conceivable control, every conceivable implication." Ganem would spend a full day trying to identify every possible subtlety and nuance in the work of the past week. When he sat down with Varmus the next morning: "You would show him the [result], and the first thing out of his mouth would be the [idea] you had spent all day Sunday trying to generate."[47]

Bishop and Varmus cultivated a strong work ethic in the lab, as Levinson recounted: "It was pretty much flat-out science . . . people would work 90, 100 hours a week, week in and week out."[48] The productivity of the Bishop-Varmus lab was readily apparent in its publication record. Their first joint publication appeared the year after Varmus arrived, and within a couple years they were producing an admirable number of papers—roughly one every eight to ten weeks. They continued that level until the landmark article on src in normal cells appeared in 1976, leading to a six-year frenzy of work, resulting in a publication every month or so.

Varmus dates the turning point in their professional relationship to 1979, when the UCSF administration offered Bishop the opportunity to head the George Williams Hooper Foundation. Established in 1914 through a gift by Mrs. Sophronia Hooper in honor of her late husband, the foundation's endowment supported research in a wide range of bio-medical areas. A particular strength of the foundation was its support of research on infectious diseases, so a star virologist on campus—Bishop—would be a logical fit to lead it. One of the perquisites of this new role was the opportunity to occupy a whole floor of prime research space in the penthouse of the sister Health Sciences Tower.

The prestige, funding, and space that came along with the Hooper Foundation directorship proved irresistible to Bishop. He invited his collaborator, Varmus, to join him in the new digs, but Varmus was not enthusiastic about the arrangement. In his words:

> The uncomfortable sense that I was the junior member of the facul-ty partnership was made less tolerable by the prospect of a widening, rather than a lessening gap in stature. . . . Within our institution . . . the leaders (chairpersons, deans, chancellor) tended to deal with him [Bishop] as the senior partner exclusively. His elevation to an institute directorship would solidify this aspect of our relationship and make me feel even less visible within my home base.[49]

After Varmus declined the offer to move, the UCSF administration—perhaps attempting to make amends—offered him the opportunity to renovate the existing laboratories on the fourth floor of Health Sciences East once Bishop's team relocated. With improved space and the oppor-tunity to expand, Varmus found that he was looking ahead rather than over his shoulder. The collaborative bonds between Bishop and Varmus were not cut abruptly, but rather they dissolved gradually over time. They continued to supervise several trainees together and maintained regular meetings, such as the weekly Rous Lunch. Their joint publica-tions peaked in 1981, and then decreased to a more modest level for four more years, before trailing off to an occasional joint paper thereafter.

Even though their professional interaction declined, Bishop and Varmus maintained their strong personal connections. They shared in-terest in the politics of science, and both became active in that arena. Their mutual passion for literature and the arts also served as a continu-ing bond between them. In a real sense, then, the separation of their laboratories did not arise from a tension between the partners but rather from external forces rocking the boat of their voyage together. The type of balance that the University of Texas Southwestern Medical School was able to provide to Brown and Goldstein—with resources, titles, and recognitions flowing equally to both partners—was more of a challenge in San Francisco. Varmus started as a trainee in Bishop's lab. Although the dynamic between them became one of equals quickly, the institution, for whatever reason, chose not to invite the partners to codirect the Hooper Foundation.

It can be argued that the sole selection of Bishop to run the Hooper Foundation was perfectly reasonable, as he managed the role so successfully that he was later appointed to serve for a decade as the chancellor of UCSF. In fact, there is every reason to believe that, even as UCSF was transformed into one of the most respected academic health centers in the country, it was not big enough to sustain two talents and ambitions on the scale of Bishop and Varmus. Sensing greater opportunity elsewhere, Varmus later left the institution to become, in succession, director of the NIH, president of the Memorial Sloan Kettering Cancer Center, and director of the National Cancer Institute. So, both Bishop and Varmus made the rare transition from a distinguished scientific career to positions of organizational leadership—but the latter was accomplished a continent apart.

There is some irony in the fact that, even as Bishop and Varmus were drifting apart professionally, scientific recognition (always lagging a few years behind the actual achievement) still focused on their glory days of joint discovery. First came the Albert Lasker Basic Science Medical Research Award in 1982 (along with three other corecipients). Then, two years later, they were recognized with the Canada Gairdner Foundation International Award (along with five other corecipients). That same year, they swept the major prizes in cancer research. All of this served as a happy prelude to the call they received in the early morning hours of October 9, 1989, from reporters hoping to get a quote on the announcement from Stockholm that they were selected to receive the Nobel Prize in Physiology or Medicine.

Still shy of his fiftieth birthday—almost a decade younger than the average age of Nobel laureates in Physiology or Medicine—Harold

Varmus was standing on the highest pedestal in science. It was a career that almost never started: making the cut for a Clinical Associate position at the NIH by the skin of his teeth, he was selected as much for his knowledge of English literature as for his promise as a scientist. His first days in research were inauspicious. But propelled by his focus, drive, and ambition—combined with the skilled guidance of a talented young mentor, Ira Pastan—Varmus made an important contribution to understanding gene regulation. At NIH, he also learned the tools of his trade, especially molecular hybridization, which would be the key to unlocking the secrets of cancer genes. With his fellow NIH alumnus Mike Bishop, Varmus explored the genetic underpinnings of a cancer in chickens. Had their findings been confined to this poultry disease, it would have gone largely unnoticed by the scientific community. Instead, Bishop and Varmus opened the door to a more general understanding of how malignancies can arise from aberrations in normal genes—with major implications for cancer in humans. Importantly, therapeutic approaches already have been developed by targeting the protein products translated from these aberrant genes.

The English literature major in Varmus surfaced at the Nobel banquet when he read a passage from *Beowulf* and then concluded: "Unlike Beowulf at the hall of Hrothgar, we have not slain our enemy, the cancer cell. . . . In our adventures, we have only seen our monster more clearly and described his scales and fangs in new ways—ways that reveal a cancer cell to be, like Grendel, a distorted version of our normal selves."[50]

EPILOGUE

When Bob Lefkowitz won the Nobel Prize in 2012, he became the ninth former NIH Yellow Beret from the Vietnam War era to be selected for this honor. It is remarkable that such a parade of talent would arrive at any single institution within an eight-year span. Moreover, it raises the obvious question of whether any other institution can make a similar claim. Indeed, some universities have been prolific producers of Nobel laureates. Currently, Harvard leads the list with seventy-five (and counting) former attendees and graduates who have gone on to win a Nobel Prize. The University of Cambridge is not far behind, with sixty-six laureates who studied there. Columbia, the University of California, Berkeley, and the University of Chicago round out the top five. These impressive numbers lend credence to the high standards of admissions and education at these and other elite universities.

At the same time, such tallies do not in any way diminish the remarkable experience at NIH. For instance, this book focuses on less than a decade at NIH, whereas the university totals above correspond to more than a century. The student bodies at these campuses have varied in size over time but currently range from just under 15,000 (Chicago) to more than 40,000 (Berkeley). In contrast, only a couple hundred Yellow Berets arrived each year at NIH during the Vietnam War. When the size of the candidate pool of trainees is considered, it is hard to come up with an institution that can match, pound for pound, the performance of NIH during the period of the Vietnam War. But it is not impossible.

Another institute, an ocean away, has its own claim to fame as an incubator of future Nobel laureates. The Laboratory for Molecular Biology (LMB) at Cambridge University counts fifteen Nobel Prize winners among its current or former staff scientists, with another eleven among alumni, including seven former students or postdoctoral fellows. LMB is supported by the Medical Research Council, Britain's counterpart to the NIH. Initially housed in prefabricated facilities following World War II, the forerunner of the LMB quickly gained international recognition. Its reputation was built atop the work of the founders and future Nobelists Max Perutz and John Kendrew, as well as the rising stars they recruited, including the future laureates James Watson and Francis Crick, whose discovery of the structure of DNA was performed at the lab.[1]

LMB has grown over time, although its current roster (roughly 200 permanent scientists and a comparable number of trainees and visitors) is modest compared to other major research centers. Maintaining small research teams is part of LMB's competitive strategy, according to its former director, Hugh Pelham: "The trouble with large groups is that they tend to have a group philosophy, or mentality, which means you think along one line and not about the alternatives."[2] This and many other aspects of LMB culture can be traced to its first chairman, Perutz. From his perspective, one of the key ingredients in building a world-class institute was communication: "Experience had taught me that laboratories often fail because their scientists never talk to each other. To stimulate the exchange of ideas, we built a canteen where people can chat at morning coffee, lunch and tea."[3] Other efforts to promote interaction included assuring that even the most senior staff were easily accessible, offices were unlocked, and equipment was shared.

Other aspects at LMB include core funding of operations by the Medical Research Council; as at NIH, staff scientists do not have to write grants constantly in order to support their research. Rather than recruiting so-called rainmakers to hunt for money, LMB tends to target promising young investigators. Pelham described the preferred demographic for recruits: "Ideally, we'd like to hire people in their early 30s or occasionally even younger." Group leader Leo James added: "It's an environment where you're encouraged to go after the big thing instead of having to have a publication every three months."[4]

Some have characterized LMB as a Nobel factory of sorts, but former director and Nobel laureate Sir Aaron Klug takes exception to that metaphor: "In a factory you know what you're going to make. Here we plant things that grow and mature. It takes a long time." Klug explained: "The art of scientific research is to choose interesting and important problems, but not ones that are so difficult you can't solve them in a reasonable time."[5]

The British historian William Bynum pointed out that factors for success at LMB were seen in labs that dominated the world of science in earlier times. He cited several examples, starting with Justus von Liebig, whose mid-nineteenth-century lab at the University of Giessen attracted protégés from across Europe to work under the master. A preeminent scientist at the turn of the twentieth century was the Russian physiologist and Nobelist Ivan Pavlov, whose highly organized dog lab in St. Petersburg was known in its day as a "physiology factory." Pavlov's contemporary, Thomas Hunt Morgan, was credited with launching the entire field of experimental genetics in his fruit-fly laboratory at Columbia University. According to Bynum, the common denominators that bind these historical centers of excellence with the LMB include: the development of new scientific methods; innovations in training models; emergence of new fields of investigation; and, most important, charismatic leaders who could leverage these assets to full advantage.[6]

These characteristics apply equally to the NIH during the Vietnam War period. New scientific techniques were being developed, as exemplified by Marshall Nirenberg's clever approaches to deciphering the genetic code, as well as the development of hormone receptor binding assays by Ira Pastan and Jesse Roth. Without question, the Clinical Associate Training Program was a novel strategy for connecting bright young trainees with outstanding scientists. There is a clear distinction, however, in the types of trainees that LMB and the NIH Clinical Associate program attracted. The focus of training at LMB has been on PhD basic scientists rather than on physicians. None of the postdoctoral fellows at LMB who later won Nobel Prizes were physicians. Clinical Associates, by contrast, were all physicians and typically had little or no research experience before arriving at NIH.

During the final two decades of the twentieth century, more than a third of all physician winners of the Nobel Prize in Physiology or Medicine were former NIH Yellow Berets, including, among others, Goldstein, Brown, and Varmus and his corecipient and collaborator Michael Bishop. This peak of former NIH Clinical Associate winners occurred when there was an overall decline in the percentage of Nobel Prize winners who were physicians. In the 1970s, close to two-thirds of Physiology or Medicine recipients were physicians. In the following decade, there was a slight decline, but the bottom began to fall out in the 1990s, when physicians accounted for only about a third of the winners in this category. Since then, the decline has continued, with physicians accounting for only about a quarter of Physiology or Medicine Nobelists.

What accounts for the disappearing act of physicians among Nobel Prize winners? As early as 1979, James Wyngaarden, who six years earlier had recruited Bob Lefkowitz to Duke, wrote an article published in the *New England Journal of Medicine* titled "The Clinical Investigator as an Endangered Species."[7] Wyngaarden would go on to become director of NIH three years later. In his article, Wyngaarden noted a decline, after the Vietnam War era, in physicians electing to pursue research careers, and he proposed some contributing factors. Among them: uncertainty about securing research funding; decreased opportunities for research experiences during medical school; changes in clinical training requirements that discouraged research experiences; and low stipends and payback obligations that made some federal training grants unattractive.

Wyngaarden's clarion call to protect physician-scientists was echoed by others, including Joe Goldstein, who authored an entertaining piece in 1986. A year after he shared the Nobel Prize with Mike Brown, Goldstein described a condition that he referred to as "PAIDS" (Paralyzed Academic Investigator's Disease Syndrome).[8] Goldstein suggested that this condition was prevalent among medical school faculty members who were attempting to be so-called triple threats: highly admired professors who simultaneously conduct research, teach pupils, and care for patients. Goldstein pointed out that many physician faculty members lacked the basic science training and skills needed to undertake cutting-edge research; with rare exceptions, it was unrealistic to expect anyone to be simultaneously successful in the highly specialized and time-demanding worlds of the laboratory bench and the patient's bedside.

A dozen years after they shared the Nobel Prize, Goldstein and Brown published a paper they titled "The Clinical Investigator: Bewitched, Bothered, and Bewildered—But Still Beloved."[9] Borrowing their title from another famous partnership—composer Richard Rodgers and lyricist Lorenz Hart—Goldstein and Brown sang a positive refrain about the opportunity to support physicians who are interested in research careers. Their recommendations included: building endowments to protect the time of investigators from other demands; encouraging collaborative work in the promotion and tenure process; and expanding research experiences for medical students and residents.

Unfortunately, the trend toward physicians' declining interest in pursuing research careers has continued. When Goldstein wrote his article on PAIDS, one in thirty physicians in the United States reported research as their primary career activity. A quarter-century later, that percentage was sliced in half.[10] Many factors have been cited for this trend, including a preference for higher-compensated clinical work; escalating student debt; institutional pressure to spend more time in the revenue-generating work of patient care; the growing bureaucratic burden of conducting research; increased competitiveness and uncertainty in obtaining grant support; and difficulty in securing promotion and tenure.[11] Some of these disincentives reflect a long history. For example, the 1912 Nobel laureate Alexis Carrel, who developed techniques for surgery on blood vessels, once said: "I would like better to make little money in doing scientific work than a great deal in doing surgical operations."

With few physicians following Carrel's century-old prescription for taking a vow of poverty in order to pursue a research career, the unprecedented successes of the former NIH Yellow Berets are even more remarkable. What was the formula that made this program so effective in producing outstanding physician-researchers? Undeniably, the Vietnam War and the existence of an alternative to the Doctor Draft brought some of the most talented young physicians in the country to the NIH labs. The four 1968 matriculants highlighted in this book were all at the very top of their medical school classes. Still, none was a shoe-in. Joe Goldstein had the clearest path, paved as it was by his medical school mentor, Donald Seldin. Even Goldstein had a last-minute scramble, however, when his intended NIH supervisor, Gordon Tomkins, accepted a position in California and could not take on any new trainees. Not many people gain entrance to the lab of a soon-to-be-selected Nobel laureate—Marshall Nirenberg—as a consolation prize.

For the other three protagonists in our story, the NIH interviews were all nail-biters. Mike Brown improved his odds by adding extra choice lines to his matching form and was paired with someone, Leonard Laster, who was at the bottom of his extended list. Harold Varmus was matched by a junior scientist, Ira Pastan, who thought that his wife, a poet, would enjoy conversations with an English literature major. Bob Lefkowitz was admonished sternly by one of his interviewers, Jesse Roth, that the dream of being a triple threat was unrealistic—only to find out two weeks later that Roth had selected him for the Clinical Associate program. Even for individuals with sterling academic credentials, the competition for admission was so intense that they could have been rejected easily.

Another key ingredient was the quality of the mentors. Each with a different background and at very different stages of their careers, they all taught their respective trainees with dedication and skill. Much has been written about the apprenticeships of future Nobel laureates to those who have won the Nobel themselves. On the high end, Chemistry recipient Ernest Rutherford had a dozen trainees who were selected later for recognition in Stockholm. The Physics laureate Enrico Fermi had five pupils who followed him to the Nobel platform. Otto Warburg, who won the 1931 Nobel Prize in Physiology or Medicine, having previously studied under the Nobel laureate Emil Fischer, advised that: "If you wish to become a scientist, you must ask a successful scientist to accept you in his laboratory, even if at the beginning you would only clean his test tubes."[12]

Bob Lefkowitz has traced the scientific lineages of all nine former NIH Clinical Associates who went on to win Nobel Prizes.[13] Three of them, including Joe Goldstein, worked directly for a Nobel laureate, and the remaining six were only a generation or two removed from a prior Nobel Prize winner. Mike Brown worked for the National Medal of Science winner Earl Stadtman, who in turn studied under the Nobel laureate Fritz Lipmann. Lefkowitz was mentored by Jesse Roth, who had trained under the Nobel recipient Rosalyn Yalow and her colleague Solomon Berson, who likely would have shared the Nobel Prize with Yalow had he not passed away before the award was announced. Both Bob Lefkowitz and Harold Varmus worked with Ira Pastan, who was connected through Earl Stadtman to Fritz Lipmann and directly to Edwin Astwood, who shared the 1954 Lasker Basic Science Award, often seen as a stepping-stone to a Nobel Prize.

Reflecting on the importance of his own NIH role model, Mike Brown has talked about his good fortune of "coming under the spell" of Earl Stadtman. Brown described Stadtman as "a brilliant scientist and a very critical man and somebody from whom I learned to think like a scientist."[14] Elsewhere, Brown emphasized: "I think that it is really important to find a mentor who is at the cutting edge of whatever field it is—who really is looking at the future and the important questions. It doesn't matter what the field is. It's true in any field that there are a few scientists who really are thinking ahead." Brown added that a key requirement is the rigor of the mentor's approach to science—an attribute so associated with his role model that the approach was known as "the Stadtman Way." In addition to seeing beyond the horizon and operating with rigor, Joe Goldstein noted: "A mentor can teach you about self-criticism . . . rather than self-aggrandizement"[15]—lessons that he learned working as an apprentice to a remarkably modest Nobel laureate, Marshall Nirenberg. Goldstein also indicated that "Mike and I both worked

. . . in really great labs at the NIH and one thing we learned from both Stadtman's and Nirenberg's labs was to work on things that give you big changes,"[16] by which he meant large biological effects.

The lessons NIH mentors taught their young physician pupils were not about specific scientific methods. Joe Goldstein was taught more about laboratory techniques by Tom Caskey, a fellow Yellow Beret a few years ahead of him, than by Marshall Nirenberg, who was no longer working daily in the lab. What Goldstein learned from Nirenberg were lessons about strategic issues, like how to be bold in picking important research topics, how to collaborate effectively, and how to communicate scientific results with clarity and precision. Similarly, Earl Stadtman had not worked in a laboratory for some years by the time that Mike Brown arrived. When Stadtman insisted on trying to replicate with his own hands Brown's major finding on the regulation of an enzyme, the rustiness of the master's technical skills was apparent. The influence of Stadtman is present, nevertheless, in the rigor and self-criticism that guide Brown and Goldstein, who in turn have passed down these lessons to their own trainees, including Thomas Südhof, who extended the Nobel Prize lineage.

For Bob Lefkowitz and Harold Varmus, their mentors, Ira Pastan and Jesse Roth, were much younger than Stadtman and Nirenberg. Both Pastan and Roth worked in the lab alongside their trainees. Still, the skills these mentors cultivated in their Clinical Associates were less about technical mastery and more about how to choose important research questions, how to deal with frustration and disappointment, and how to remain undaunted by external criticism while harboring healthy skepticism about their own findings. Lefkowitz had the advantage of being exposed to two mentors with completely different styles—the big-picture vision of the ebullient Roth and the sober, critical dissection of results by Pastan. As with all other human activities, science is shaped by the personalities of those who pursue it—there is no single right path to success. What a privilege it was early on for Lefkowitz to be able to observe two successful role models who were almost polar opposites in temperament and approach, but who brought their skills together to solve a previously intractable problem. Lefkowitz would adopt the best aspects of both of his mentors at NIH and would go on to oversee more than 200 trainees himself, including Brian Kobilka, with whom he shared the Nobel Prize.

When Harold Varmus signed up to work with Ira Pastan, he thought he would be conducting research on thyroid hormones. It would have been easy for Pastan to focus exclusively on the highly productive work that he was beginning to pursue with Roth on cell-surface hormone receptors. They could have marched together, studying one hormone after another and their respective receptors. And Roth did indeed lead others down this fertile path of discovery. In the meantime, however, Pastan became infatuated—as Bob Lefkowitz describes, the attraction to a research topic has much in common with romantic allure—with the process of gene regulation in bacteria. Whipsawed from one presumed research topic to a completely new one, Varmus likely wondered whether he was trading in a relatively safe and productive project for one that might end up in a dead end. As it turned out, rather than entering a blind alley, Pastan and his colleague Bob Perlman opened up a whole new road. Their discovery, contrary to prior belief, that gene expression was not controlled exclusively by repression was questioned at first by others. Ultimately, their demonstration of the choreography of elements involved in gene activation led to its embrace by the established leaders in the field. Moreover, the experience that Varmus gained with the tools of molecular biology served him well in his subsequent work and led ultimately to the Nobel Prize.

Working for a Nobel laureate or other leading scientist often is seen as a door-opener for further career advancement. In the cases of the four Yellow Berets explored here, the mentors had little influence in guiding the next steps in their employment. All four trainees had the opportunity to remain at the NIH and continue their successful work there as staff scientists. In many respects, that would have been the easiest path, as they would have avoided a disruptive move and could have continued their work without the need to secure independent support. The fact that none elected to do so—each for his own reasons—says something about where they saw the greatest opportunities for further career growth. Each arrived at NIH with the ultimate goal of becoming an academic physician, and when their tours of government service were over, all headed to university environments.

For Joe Goldstein, the plan was mapped out four years earlier by his professor, Donald Seldin, in Dallas. After two years of additional medical genetics training in Seattle, Goldstein would return to his alma mater—the University of Texas Southwestern Medical School—as a faculty member. Mike Brown, persuaded by his buddy Goldstein to consider Dallas, was sold on it after he met Donald Seldin. Brown could see immediately that Seldin was someone who understood and valued basic science as the bedrock of medical education and practice. The fact that Goldstein was headed there a year later was an additional attraction for Brown, but at the time, the friends thought that they would pursue independent careers. Only later did they discover that they were destined to work side by side in pursuing the LDL receptor.

In sharp contrast to Joe Goldstein's preordained return to Dallas, Harold Varmus appeared on a virtual walkabout into a fellowship at the University of California, San Francisco. Knowing that he wanted to live on the West Coast, and with a nascent interest in viruses and cancer, Varmus explored several leading labs in California without success. On the basis of a casual referral, however, Varmus showed up unannounced at UCSF and quickly felt a kinship with the colleagues there. His success working with the former Yellow Beret Mike Bishop led to the discovery of how normal genes can become reprogrammed into cancer-causing variants.

Bob Lefkowitz, in the depths of his early discouragement about his perceived lack of progress in his NIH research, followed his father's advice to focus on clinical work once he finished his obligations in Bethesda. Only after he got to Massachusetts General Hospital did Lefkowitz discover that he actually missed getting his hands dirty with experimental data. In fact, he lusted after it so much that he was willing to sneak into the lab when he was supposed to be engaged in patient care. After he was given a green light to continue his research, it was assumed that he would remain at Harvard and build a career there. Instead—much to the surprise of his colleagues and family—he accepted an offer from Duke University that was just too good to pass up. As with Brown and

Goldstein, despite some enticing offers elsewhere, Lefkowitz remained at the same university for his entire career.

With all four Clinical Associates headed to academic jobs, it is interesting to pose a question: Was the Nobel Prize–winning work of these four Yellow Berets shaped by their projects in Bethesda? The answer is a qualified "yes," because in all cases there were connections—some admittedly more tenuous than others. For Joe Goldstein and Mike Brown, a six-year-old patient at the NIH Clinical Center who had familial hypercholesterolemia (FH) left an indelible impression on both and served as a motivation for their later work. Goldstein pursued a community-based study of FH during his medical genetics fellowship, where he additionally learned the fibroblast tissue culture techniques that he and Brown would use in Dallas. Brown applied the expertise he gained in Stadtman's lab for isolating and purifying enzymes to the FH studies in Dallas. When his mentor learned about the enzyme that Brown would try to isolate—one that had eluded a Nobel laureate—Stadtman uncharacteristically laughed at the folly of Brown's plan. Stadtman clearly saw it as a high-risk venture and dangerous to pursue at such an early stage in Brown's career. When Goldstein and Brown observed that LDL was not gaining entry into the liver cells of FH patients, they speculated that there may be a cell-surface receptor that was not working properly. Neither of them had explored receptors at NIH, but they were aware of the work that Pastan, Roth, and others were undertaking there. While scientists elsewhere were still questioning the very existence of receptors, Brown and Goldstein had a front-row seat to some of the initial discoveries.

Similarly, there was a modest connection between the work that Harold Varmus performed at NIH and the subsequent research that led to his Nobel Prize. Although he was investigating genes in both contexts, at NIH he was studying metabolic processes in bacteria, and in his later work he was studying the role of a particular cancer-causing virus in chickens. The strongest tie between the two topics was in the tools he needed to deploy to address both research topics, especially a technique referred to as "molecular hybridization." Moreover, his interest in studying cancer—a topic that had little appeal to him when he arrived as a Clinical Associate—was piqued by lectures he attended while at NIH.

Among the four future Nobel laureates, the path from NIH project to subsequent research career was the most direct for Bob Lefkowitz. With Pastan and Roth in Bethesda, he was able to create a binding assay for adrenocorticotropic hormone. When he started to do research at Massachusetts General Hospital (MGH), his supervisor, Ed Haber, wanted him to switch gears and study a steroid hormone, aldosterone, because it was the focus of his lab. Lefkowitz resisted the suggestion, because aldosterone worked in a very different manner from the protein hormone receptors that he had studied at NIH. Instead, Lefkowitz proposed, and Haber agreed, to study the receptors that control the body's fight-or-flight responses—the so-called adrenergic receptors. It was very challenging work, which continued apace when Lefkowitz departed for Duke. Among the difficulties was the fact that these receptors exist in minute quantities and were difficult to isolate and purify. Lefkowitz had to deploy all of the knowledge he gained at NIH, but he was also forced to develop entirely new approaches to solve the mysteries of these receptors. In the process, he learned that the receptors are part of a much larger class of molecules essential to many of the body's senses and functions.

It is incontestable that the Clinical Associate program launched so many remarkable scientific careers because the brightest physicians of an entire generation were channeled into a single national institution where they were schooled by premier researchers. As Bob Lefkowitz has described: "I think a huge part of it was just how smart and driven the people were. We were all programmed for success."[17] Although talent was necessary for creating this golden age, one wonders whether it was sufficient alone. Those who experienced NIH in those heady years struggle to define the exact quality of the environment that made it so special, but they tend to believe that there was something unique about the time and the place.

Jesse Roth described the level of interaction in terms that sound very similar to Max Perutz's characterization of the canteen at the LMB:

There was one big lunchroom. The guys that had clinical duties—we all ate . . . late supper together down in the cafeteria. So, it was a very, very intimate environment. It had none of the barriers that . . . separated departments or sections in medical centers. It was just one big mixing bowl. And delightfully so. Everyone knew what everyone was doing, and everybody got help from everybody else. It was just a grand bazaar of ideas and techniques.[18]

By an amazing coincidence of timing, the channeling of such a rich talent pool to NIH occurred as a major revolution was unfolding in medical research. As Harold Varmus described: "It wasn't just that we were there getting trained, but we were being trained at a time when molecular biology was truly going to transform medicine, and teach us how disease arises, and give us new tools for doing things that were unheard of in medicine. So, there was a sense of renewal in medical sciences at a place that truly had more fire power than any other place." Recalling the social currents of that time, he added: "I suppose in some sense there was a feeling that we were in grave trouble politically because of Vietnam, but there was another face to what the country was going through. Part of the good face was the growth of medical science."[19]

Another aspect that distinguished the NIH from academic medical centers at the time was its open-door policy on hiring. Although it is almost unimaginable today when two-career households are the norm rather than the exception, in the mid-twentieth century many universities had nepotism rules that prevented hiring married couples. Earl and Terry Stadtman, for example, were hired in 1950 by NIH at identical salaries after several universities refused to offer both of them faculty positions. Jewish scientists also suffered from biased hiring quotas on many university campuses. NIH had a very different history. From his arrival in 1949, James Shannon hired former colleagues from his successful World War II malaria research operation in New York City, including a number of Jewish scientists. One of these early recruits, Julius Axelrod, would go on to win the Nobel Prize in Physiology or Medicine in 1970, two years after Marshall Nirenberg, another Jewish scientist, became the first NIH Nobel laureate.

Three of the four NIH mentors and all four of the Yellow Berets portrayed in this book were born into Jewish families. Many studies have documented the phenomenon of persons of Jewish heritage being selected for Nobel Prizes much more frequently than would be expected based on their representation in the general population. During the first century of the Nobel Prize, Jewish recipients in Physiology or Medicine accounted for about one-quarter of all winners and exceeded two out of every five American laureates. In the United States, Jews account for about ten times the number of Nobel Prizes when factoring for religious background.

The heavy representation of Jews in secular intellectual pursuits was noted as early as a century ago by Thorstein Veblen, an American social theorist of Norwegian descent who was raised a Lutheran and became an atheist. In an essay titled "The Intellectual Preeminence of Jews in Modern Europe," Veblen postulated that the rise of Jewish scientists and scholars could be traced to societal changes that were under way. Increasingly freed from the isolated boundaries of traditional religious and communal life, Jews also were confronting a lack of acceptance in the gentile world. The conflict between the release from historical strictures and the marginalization by the social elite created a "wanderer in the intellectual no-man's land" who could see facts unfiltered by the dominant culture and theories of the day. Veblen contended: "The first requisite for constructive work in modern science is a skeptical frame of mind."[20]

Over the years, others have speculated on the reasons that persons of Jewish extraction have excelled in intellectual pursuits. It has been suggested, for example, that the combination of social segregation, economic specialization, and reproductive isolation over centuries in medieval Central and Eastern Europe led to genetic selection favoring verbal and mathematical traits.[21] Bob Lefkowitz acknowledged that there are sensitivities in suggesting a role of genetics, but he still believes one cannot look past heredity: "I think it was in the DNA. . . . Yes, it was in the DNA. Let's face it . . . and it is shocking to think what was lost in the Holocaust. How many other Nobel laureates or people of amazing accomplishment were lost?"[22]

Others have questioned the role of genetics,[23] and various alternative environmental explanations have been proposed. Some cite the long-standing cultural veneration of study and learning. Lefkowitz pointed to his own upbringing in that regard: "There's the nurture. In my house, I grew up reading, reading, reading. I loved books."[24] Similarly, it has been suggested that Jews have nurtured strong analytical skills in order to succeed in both religious and secular pursuits. The style of Talmudic study, using a point-counterpoint form of argumentation, has parallels to the kind of questioning of conventional wisdom that is essential to scientific discourse.[25] Mike Brown even saw a link to the stereotypical Jewish dinner-table conversation: "We [people from Jewish households] seem to be more open and more willing to get excited about things and argue. So, I think there is something about that part of the culture that helps in terms of creativity—not just in science, but in writing books and in writing musicals, or anything else. With Joe and me, it is just a constant give-and-take."[26] Above and beyond the possible influences of aspects of culture and traditions, the drivers of achievement among Jews likely are the same as they are for other groups: education and hard work.[27]

Regardless of the reasons for the aptitude for scientific excellence among people of Jewish heritage, the fact that the NIH had an open-door policy was essential in establishing many of their careers. As Jesse Roth noted:

> If you were an up-and-coming physician and you wanted to be an academic, then the medical school you were at would . . . put you in line at their institution. The Jewish guys were not being selected for that line, so they had to do other things. So, their desire, eligibility, and willingness to go to NIH were enhanced by the fact that they didn't have an opportunity at their home institution. So, even if the draft wasn't breathing down their necks, what opportunity did they have? Well, NIH was recruiting people.[28]

Roth went on to describe how training at NIH became a stepping-stone to further career opportunities:

> NIH . . . I think played an important role in the major entry of the Jews into academic medicine because they were taken strictly on the basis of talent. And if they did well at NIH and got a research program going, they were able to then get recruited by medical schools so that

they could get grants. So, I think the NIH program played a big role in accelerating the breakdown of the barriers of Jews in medicine and Jews in academic medicine.[29]

The confluence of factors that brought together such a remarkable group of NIH trainees during the turbulent 1960s not only changed their lives; it also catapulted medical research and revolutionized approaches to treating heart disease, cancer, and other leading illnesses. With such a profound and enduring impact, it is reasonable to ask whether we will ever see such a Golden Era again. In the absence of a national circumstance that focuses so much talent at one place at one time, it is hard to imagine a parallel to the Vietnam-era rush to the NIH. As already noted, over the past half-century (and counting) there has been a decline in research interest among physicians. Those who are committed to pursuing scientific careers now have many more options than were available in the 1960s.

In 1964, NIH created the Medical Scientist Training Program to support medical schools that offered joint educational programs leading to both a medical degree and a PhD. The four future Nobel laureates featured here entered medical school in 1962, before the NIH began to support MD-PhD programs. Even if these programs had been open, Goldstein, Brown, Lefkowitz, and Varmus likely would not have applied, as they lacked prior research experience and the desire to pursue research careers. By the time they arrived at NIH six years later, there were only seven NIH-funded MD-PhD programs in the country. Since then, MD-PhD programs have been developed at ninety medical schools in the United States, with about half supported by the NIH.[30] With so many different places for a physician to prepare for a research career, no single institution can be as dominant today as the NIH was during the 1960s.

If the magic that occurred at the NIH during its Golden Era cannot be duplicated in this very different day and time, we can at least learn from what it took to build a towering center of scientific innovation. First and foremost, talent must be assembled, so the rewards for participating must be clear and highly attractive. Aptitude for selection should be defined broadly: the former English literature major may have as much, or even more, potential for creativity and innovation than someone who majored in science. Selection must be based solely on the assessment of ability and not be constrained by personal characteristics, such as those related to race, ethnicity, religion, and gender.

And once trainees are recruited they must be immersed in a protective and supportive environment. They should be apprenticed to senior investigators who can pass along the key lessons of how to choose a research problem, how to design and conduct experiments with rigor, and how to interpret and communicate results with clarity and precision. Ideally, resources for supporting the work should be readily available, and investigators should be given the freedom to choose the questions that they pursue, whether or not there is an obvious connection to a particular clinical condition. Although larger size and scale can be advantageous in addressing complex scientific questions, it also can undermine the ability of investigators to rub shoulders with colleagues and learn about their work. Science is a contact sport, and researchers benefit from interactions with their peers, often informally, to share ideas and learn from each other.

Even when all of these elements are brought together—as they were during the late 1960s at the NIH—there is perhaps some additional undefinable chemistry that must be present in order to achieve such extraordinary outcomes. Whether or not there will ever be another Golden Era, we can all rejoice that one did occur and changed science and human lives for the better.

NOTES

PROLOGUE

1. P. C. Agre, "Fifty Years Ago: Linus Pauling and the Belated Nobel Peace Prize," *Science and Diplomacy* 2, no. 4 (December 2013).
2. J. F. Kennedy, "Remarks at a Dinner Honoring Nobel Prize Winners of the Western Hemisphere," April 29, 1962, in G. Peters and J. T. Woolley, comps., *American Presidency Project* (Santa Barbara: University of California, Santa Barbara, n.d.), presidency.ucsb.edu.
3. Today it is known as NewYork-Presbyterian Hospital and is affiliated with Columbia University Vagelos College of Physicians and Surgeons (renamed for Roy and Diana Vagelos) and Weill Cornell Medical College. Its two separate medical centers are Columbia University Medical Center and Weill Cornell Medical Center.
4. J. L. Goldstein and M. S. Brown, "A Golden Era of Nobel Laureates," *Science* 338 (2012): 1033–1034.
5. Goldstein and Brown, "A Golden Era."
6. The Public Health Service, or PHS, is the federal workforce dedicated to preserving and protecting the nation's health.

7. J. D. Watson, *The Double Helix: A Personal Account of the Discovery of the Structure of DNA* (New York: Atheneum, 1968).

8. H. Varmus, *The Art and Politics of Science* (New York: W. W. Norton & Company, 2009).

9. J. M. Bishop, *How to Win the Nobel Prize: An Unexpected Life in Science* (Cambridge, MA: Harvard University Press, 2003).

10. J. L. Goldstein and M. S. Brown, "The LDL Receptor," *Arteriosclerosis, Thrombosis, and Vascular Biology* 29 (2009): 431–438. J. L. Goldstein and M. S. Brown, "A Century of Cholesterol and Coronaries: From Plaques to Genes and Statins," *Cell* 161 (2015): 161–172. R. J. Lefkowitz, "Seven Transmembrane Receptors—A Brief Personal Perspective," *Biochimica et Biophysica Acta* 1768 (2007): 748–755. R. J. Lefkowitz, "A Serendipitous Scientist," *Annual Reviews of Pharmacology and Toxicology* 58 (2018): 17–32.

11. Goldstein and Brown, "A Golden Era."

12. H. Zuckerman, *Scientific Elite: Nobel Laureates in the United States* (New York: The Free Press, 1977).

13. Zuckerman, *Scientific Elite*.

14. B. F. Jones, "Age and Great Invention," *Review of Economics and Statistics* 92 (2010): 1–14.

15. K. R. W. Matthews et al., "The Aging of Biomedical Research in the United States," *PloS one* 6 (2011): e29738.

16. H. H. Garrison, B. Drehman, and E. Neu, *NIH Research Funding Trends: FY 1995–2013* (Bethesda, MD: Office of Public Affairs, Federation of American Societies of Experimental Biology, 2013).

17. H. H. Garrison and A. M. Deschamps, "NIH Research Funding and Early Career Physician Scientists: Continuing Challenges in the 21st Century," *FASEB Journal* 28 (2014): 1049–1058.

18. B. G. Charlton, "Scientometric Identification of Elite 'Revolutionary Science' Research Institutions by Analysis of Trends of Nobel Prizes, 1947–2006," *Medical Hypotheses* 68 (2007): 931–934.

19. D. Kevles, "Big Science and Big Politics in the United States: Reflections on the Death of the SCC and the Life of the Human Genome Project," *Historical Studies in the Physical and Biological Sciences* 27 (1997): 269–297.

20. R. Florida, "The Role of the University: Leveraging Talent, Not Technology," *Issues in Science and Technology* 15 (1999): 67–73.

CHAPTER 1: ANNUS HORRIBILIS

1. US Department of Defense, Office of the Historian, *Department of Defense: Foreign Relations of the United States, 1964–1968*, vol. 27, Mainland Southeast Asia, no. 53.

2.   P. Patterson, "The Truth about Tonkin," *Naval History Magazine* 22, no. 1 (February 2008): 22.

3.   Patterson, "The Truth about Tonkin," 22.

4.   J. G. Blight and J. M. Lang, *The Fog of War: Lessons from the Life of Robert S. McNamara* (Lanham, MD: Rowman & Littlefield, 2005), 87.

5.   J. C. Skipper, *The 1964 Republican Convention: Barry Goldwater and the Beginning of the Conservative Movement* (Jefferson, NC: McFarland & Company, 2016), 213.

6.   R. D. Buhite, *Call to Arms: Presidential Speeches, Messages, and Declarations of War* (Wilmington, DE: Scholarly Resources, 2003), 229.

7.   Tonkin Gulf Resolution, Publ. Law No. 88-408, 78 Stat. 384, 88th Cong. (August 7, 1964), General Records of the United States Government, Record Group II, National Archives.

8.   B. W. Tuchman, *The March of Folly* (New York: Knopf, 1984), 321.

9.   D. M. Drew, *Rolling Thunder 1965: Anatomy of a Failure* (Maxwell AFB: Air University Press, 1986), 42.

10. C. Berger, ed., and J. S. Ballard et al., *The United States Air Force in Southeast Asia, 1961–1973* (Washington, DC: Office of Air Force History, 1977), 366.

11. Drew, *Rolling Thunder 1965*, 42.

12. *Public Papers of the Presidents of the United States: Lyndon B. Johnson, 1965* (Washington, DC: Government Printing Office, 1965), Book 2, 797.

13. W. Isaacson, *Profiles in Leadership: Historians on the Elusive Quality of Greatness* (New York: W. W. Norton & Company, 2010), 138.

14. US Department of Commerce, Bureau of the Census, *Statistical Abstract of the United States: 1977*, 98th ed. (Washington, DC: US Department of Commerce, Bureau of the Census, 1977), Table 590.

15. US Department of Commerce, Bureau of the Census, *Statistical Abstract of the United States: 1977*, Table 590.

16. US Department of Health, Education, and Welfare, National Center for Health Statistics, *Vital Statistics of the United States, 1967*, vol. II—Mortality, Part A (Washington, DC: US Department of Health, Education, and Welfare, National Center for Health Statistics, 1969), Table 1-25, 1-100-1.

17. D. E. Bonior, S. M. Champlain, and T. S. Kolly, *The Vietnam Veteran: A History of Neglect* (New York: Praeger Publishers, 1984), 4–5, 18.

18. "Monitoring Media Attitudes," Roper Center, Cornell University, *Public Perspective Online* 1, no. 5 (July/August 1990): 95–101.

19. "Monitoring Media Attitudes," 95–101.

20. R. Dallek, *Flawed Giant: Lyndon Johnson and His Times* (New York: Oxford University Press, 1998), 281.

21. M. Safer, *Flashbacks: On Returning to Vietnam* (New York: Random House, 1990), 88–97.

22. D. C. Hallin, *The "Uncensored War": The Media and Vietnam* (New York: Oxford University Press, 1986), 132.

23. D. J. Smyth, *Freedom of the Press and National Security in Four Wars: World War I, World War II, the Vietnam War, and the War on Terrorism*, master's thesis in public policy (College Park: University of Maryland, 2007), 86.

24. Gallup News Service: *Americans Look Back at Vietnam War* (Princeton, NJ: Gallup, November 17, 2000).

25. M. Lorell and C. Kelley, *Casualties, Public Opinion, and Presidential Policy During the Vietnam War* (Santa Monica, CA: Rand Corporation, 1985), 66.

26. *Public Papers of the Presidents of the United States: Lyndon B. Johnson, 1967* (Washington, DC: Government Printing Office, 1968), Book 2, 1018.

27. D. F. Schmitz, *The Tet Offensive: Politics, War, and Public Opinion* (Lanham, MD: Rowman & Littlefield, 2005), 69.

28. D. D. Perlmutter, *Photojournalism and Foreign Policy: Icons of Outrage in International Crises* (Westport, CT: Praeger, 1998), 36.

29. E. Villard, *The 1968 Tet Offensive Battles of Quang Tri City and Hue* (Fort McNair, Washington, DC: US Army Center of Military History, 2008), 80–81.

30. W. C. Westmoreland, *A Soldier Reports* (New York: Doubleday, 1976), 332.

31. US Department of Defense, Defense Manpower Data Center, Office of the Secretary of Defense, *Vietnam Conflict Extract Data File* (Washington, DC: National Archives and Record Administration, April 2008).

32. *Public Papers of the Presidents of the United States: Lyndon B. Johnson, 1968–69* (Washington, DC: Government Printing Office, 1970), Book 1, 25.

33. D. D. P. Johnson and D. Tierney, *Failing to Win: Perceptions of Victory and Defeat in International Politics* (Cambridge, MA: Harvard University Press, 2006), 149.

34. M. D. Harmon, *Found, Featured, Then Forgotten: U.S. Network TV News and the Vietnam Veterans Against the War* (Knoxville: University of Tennessee Libraries, 2011), 23.

35. S. Brown, *Faces of Power: Constancy and Change in United States Foreign Policy from Truman to Obama* (New York: Columbia University Press, 2015), 199–200.

36. D. M. Shea and M. B. Harward, *Presidential Campaigns: Documents Decoded* (Santa Barbara, CA: ABC-CLIO, 2013), 63–65.

37. J. H. Willibanks, ed., *The Vietnam War: The Essential Reference Guide* (Santa Barbara, CA: ABC-CLIO, 2013), 253.

38. M. K. Honey, *Going Down Jericho Road: The Memphis Strike, Martin Luther King's Last Campaign* (New York: W. W. Norton, 2007), 1–4.

39. A. Fleming, *Martin Luther King, Jr.: A Dream of Hope* (New York: Sterling, 2008), 109–110.

40. M. Finger, *31 Hours, 28 Minutes* (Memphis: The City Magazine, April 1, 2008).

41. C. Carson and K. Shepard, *A Call to Conscience: The Landmark Speeches of Martin Luther King, Jr.* (New York: Warner Books, 2001), 201–223.

42. Finger, *31 Hours, 28 Minutes.*

43. M. P. Graves and D. Fillingim, *More Than Precious Memories: The Rhetoric of Southern Gospel Music* (Macon, GA: Mercer University Press, 2004), 144.

44. R. E. Boomhower, *Robert F. Kennedy and the 1968 Indiana Primary* (Bloomington: Indiana University Press, 2008), 135–136.

45. Boomhower, *Robert F. Kennedy and the 1968 Indiana Primary*, 135–136.

46. B. Gilbert, *Ten Blocks from the White House* (New York: Praeger, 1969).

47. A. Csicsek, "Spiro Agnew and the Burning of Baltimore," in J. I. Elfenbein, T. L. Hallowak, and E. M. Nix, eds., *Baltimore '68: Riots and Rebirth of an American City* (Philadelphia: Temple University Press, 2011), 70–85.

48. J. L. Reiff, D. Keating, and J. R. Grossman, "West Madison Street, 1968," in *Encyclopedia of Chicago* (Chicago: Chicago Historical Society, 2004).

49. "April 5, 1968: Chicago Explodes One Day after the Death of Martin Luther King Jr.," graphics.chicagotribune.com/riots-chicago-1968-mlk/index.html (updated August 16, 2018).

50. R. B. Woods, *Prisoners of Hope: Lyndon B. Johnson, the Great Society, and the Limits of Liberalism* (Philadelphia: Basic Books, 2016).

51. US Department of Commerce, Bureau of the Census, *Population Characteristics: Educational Attainment in the United States: March 1968—Detailed Tables* (Washington, DC: US Department of Commerce, Bureau of the Census, April 28, 1969), Series P-20, No. 182, Table 1.

52. US Department of Labor, Bureau of Labor Statistics, *Employment and Earnings and Monthly Reports of the Labor Force* 15 (July 1968): Table A-12, 28.

53. US Department of Commerce, *Consumer Income: Income in 1968 of Families and Persons in the United States* (1969): Series P-60, No. 66, Table 6, 21.

54. Richard Nixon, "Address Accepting the Presidential Nomination of the Republican National Convention in Miami Beach, Florida" (August 8, 1968), in G. Peters and J. T. Woolley, comps., *The American Presidency Project* (Santa Barbara: University of California, Santa Barbara, n.d.), presidency.ucsb.edu.

55. A. Miller, *On the Shooting of Robert Kennedy* (New York: The New York Times, June 8, 1968).

56. R. Angell, "Comment," *The New Yorker* (June 15, 1968).

57. E. Tscheschlok, "Long Time Coming: Miami's Liberty City Riot of 1968," *Florida Historical Quarterly* 74 (1996): 440–460.

58. F. Kusch, *Battleground Chicago: The Police and the 1968 Democratic National Convention* (Westport, CT: Praeger, 2004).

CHAPTER 2: BEST IN CLASS

1. W. W. Boddie, *History of Williamsburg* (Columbia, SC: The State Company, 1923).
2. P. Thomason, *Historic Resources of Kingstree: Partial Inventory: Historic and Architectural Properties* (Washington, DC: National Register of Historic Places Inventory—Nomination Form, US Department of the Interior, January 1, 1981).
3. U. S. Neill and H. A. Rockman, "A Conversation with Robert Lefkowitz, Joseph Goldstein, and Michael Brown," *Journal of Clinical Investigation* 122 (2012): 1586–1587.
4. P. S. Ward, *Simon Baruch: Rebel in the Ranks of Medicine, 1840–1921* (Tuscaloosa: University of Alabama Press, 1994).
5. J. Grant, *Bernard M. Baruch: The Adventures of a Wall Street Legend* (New York: John Wiley and Sons, 1997).
6. Grant, *Bernard M. Baruch.*
7. J. Goldstein, "Retiring Editor Interviews Bernard Baruch," *The Boll Weevil* (Kingstree High School, Kingstree, SC) 271 (February 28, 1958): 1.
8. H. Varmus, *The Art and Politics of Science* (New York: W. W. Norton & Company, 2009).
9. Varmus, *Art and Politics of Science.*
10. Old York Road Historical Society, *Cheltenham Township* (Charleston, SC: Arcadia Publishing, 2001).
11. D. Scott, *Remembering Cheltenham Township* (Charleston, SC: The History Press, 2009).
12. C. E. Rosenberg, *No Other Gods: On Science and American Social Thought* (Baltimore: Johns Hopkins University Press, 1997), 123–131.
13. R. Snyderman, "Introduction of Robert J. Lefkowitz," *Journal of Clinical Investigation* 121 (2011): 4192–4200.
14. "Fifty-one Groups of Apartment Buildings Will House 12,000 Families," *New York Times*, May 5, 1939, 47.
15. Robert J. Lefkowitz, in *The Nobel Prizes, 2012* (Sagamore Beach, MA: Science History Publications/USA, 2013).
16. De P. Kruif, *Microbe Hunters* (San Diego: Harcourt, 1996).
17. Snyderman, "Introduction of Robert J. Lefkowitz."
18. R. J. Lefkowitz, interview by Raymond S. Greenberg, August 16, 2017, Duke University Medical Center, Durham, NC.
19. Snyderman, "Introduction of Robert J. Lefkowitz."
20. Washington and Lee University bears the names of two famous Virginians: George Washington and Robert E. Lee. In 1796, Washington left a $20,000 endowment to a nearly fifty-year-old school previously known as Liberty

Hall Academy, renamed Washington Academy and then Washington College in his honor. Almost seventy years later shortly after the Civil War,
Robert E. Lee became the eleventh president of Washington College. He
served five years until his death at sixty-three in 1870; the college added his
name the following year. Washington and Lee produced many distinguished
alumni, including the explorer Meriwether Lewis (class of 1793); Justice Lewis Powell (class of 1929 and law school class of 1931); and Tom Wolfe (class of
1951), the author and innovator of New Journalism.

21. "Phi Eta Sigma Honor Group Adds Sophomore, 9 Freshmen," *Ring-tum Phi:
     Washington and Lee Semi-Weekly Newspaper* 592 (February 20, 1959), 1.

22. "Goldstein Wins Phi Beta Kappa Soph Award," *Ring-tum Phi: Washington
     and Lee Semi-Weekly Newspaper* 603 (March 11, 1960), 1.

23. "Sixteen Tapped for Phi Beta Kappa," *Ring-tum Phi: Washington and Lee
     Semi-Weekly Newspaper* 614 (February 28, 1961), 1.

24. "W&L Grad Wins Nobel," *Ring-tum Phi: Washington and Lee University*
     855 (October 17, 1985), 1, 4.

25. "213th Commencement Week Events Get Underway This Week," *Ring-tum
     Phi: Washington and Lee Semi-Weekly Newspaper* 57 (June 6, 1962), hdl.han-
     dle.net/11021/29107.

26. "Students Selected for 1961 Who's Who," *Ring-tum Phi: Washington and Lee
     Semi-Weekly Newspaper* 12 (October 31, 1961), hdl.handle.net/11021/29056.

27. "W&L Grad Wins Nobel."

28. "W&L Grad Wins Nobel."

29. "W&L Grad Wins Nobel."

30. Lord Amherst was appointed governor-general of British North America
     in 1760 but was recalled to England; he did not return to fight during the
     Revolutionary War. Amherst was vilified for using smallpox-contaminated
     blankets as an early form of biological warfare against Native Americans,
     but the town and Amherst College resisted attempts to change the name.
     M. Grossman, *World Military Leaders: A Biographical Dictionary* (New
     York: Facts on File, 2007), 17–18.

31. H. W. Hewlett, "Amherst's New Curriculum in its First Year," *Journal of
     Higher Education* 19 (1948): 365.

32. Varmus, *Art and Politics of Science.*

33. Varmus, *Art and Politics of Science.*

34. Varmus, *Art and Politics of Science.*

35. M. S. Brown, interview by Raymond S. Greenberg, July 27, 2017, University
     of Texas Southwestern Medical Center, Dallas.

36. Brown, interview by the author, July 27, 2017.

37. Brown, interview by the author, July 27, 2017.

38. Brown, interview by the author, July 27, 2017.

39. W. Saxon, "Gaylord Harnwell, Physicist and President of Penn, Dies," *New York Times*, April 19, 1982.
40. Brown, interview by the author, July 27, 2017.
41. Brown, interview by the author, July 27, 2017.
42. Brown, interview by the author, July 27, 2017.
43. Lefkowitz, interview by the author, August 16, 2017.
44. Lefkowitz, in *The Nobel Prizes, 2012*.

CHAPTER 3: "MY SON, THE DOCTOR"

1. M. S. Brown, interview by Raymond S. Greenberg, July 27, 2017, University of Texas Southwestern Medical Center, Dallas.
2. E. C. Halperin, "The Jewish Problem in U.S. Medical Education," *Journal of the History of Medicine and Allied Sciences* 56 (2001): 140–167.
3. D. Johnson, "Yale's Limit on Jewish Enrollment Lasted Until Early 1960's, Book Says," *New York Times*, March 4, 1986.
4. T. N. Bonner, *Becoming a Physician in Britain, France, Germany, and the United States, 1750–1945* (Baltimore: Johns Hopkins University Press, 1995), 342.
5. L. Sokoloff, "The Rise and Decline of the Jewish Quota in Medical School Admissions," *Bulletin of the New York Academy of Medicine* 68 (1992): 497–518.
6. A. Kornberg, *For the Love of Enzymes: The Odyssey of a Biochemist* (Cambridge, MA: Harvard University Press, 1989), 310–313.
7. A. Flexner, *Medical Education in the United States and Canada: A Report to the Carnegie Foundation for the Advancement of Teaching*, Bulletin No. 4 (New York: The Carnegie Foundation for the Advancement of Teaching, 1910), 326.
8. J. G. Hanna, "A Nobel Prize: Dr. Joseph Goldstein, '63, Honored for Medical Research," *Alumni Magazine of Washington and Lee* 60 (1985): 2–7.
9. J. L. Goldstein, interview by Raymond S. Greenberg, June 5, 2017, University of Texas Southwestern Medical Center, Dallas.
10. M. J. Mooney, "The Father of Dallas Medicine," *D Magazine* (October 2013).
11. Hanna, "A Nobel Prize."
12. S. Schenker, "In Memorium: Burton Combes, M.D.," *Hepatology* 59 (2014): 1655–1656.
13. Goldstein, interview by the author, June 5, 2017.
14. CPCs originated at Harvard Medical School six decades earlier as a new way to educate medical students. In contrast to the many hours of traditional lectures, which medical students then and now found soporific, the CPC borrowed the case-history method used at Harvard Law School. N. L. Harris and R. C. Scully, "The Clinicopathological Conferences (CPCs)," in D. N.

Louis and R. H. Young, eds., *Keen Minds to Explore the Dark Continents of Disease* (Boston: Department of Pathology, Massachusetts General Hospital, 2011).

15. "Dr. David Seegal of Columbia Dies," *New York Times*, July 27, 1972 [no author].

16. P. E. Dans, "David Seegal: Ic Ne Wat and Other Maxims of a Master Teacher," *Pharos* (Autumn 2014): 5–8.

17. J. Interlandi, "Fighting the Cancer War," *Columbia College Today* (May/June 2007).

18. Brown, interview by the author, July 27, 2017.

19. Brown, interview by the author, July 27, 2017.

20. Brown, interview by the author, July 27, 2017.

21. Brown, interview by the author, July 27, 2017.

22. Brown, interview by the author, July 27, 2017.

23. Brown, interview by the author, July 27, 2017.

24. Brown, interview by the author, July 27, 2017.

25. Brown, interview by the author, July 27, 2017.

26. "The Chemistry of Discovery," *Duke Magazine* (November 5, 2012) [no author].

27. R. J. Lefkowitz, telephone interview by Raymond S. Greenberg, October 9, 2017.

28. M. M. Poen, "National Health Insurance," in R. S. Kirkendall, ed., *The Harry S. Truman Encyclopedia* (Boston: G. K. Hall & Co., 1989), 251.

29. "Medicare Is Launched into Shambles," *Life* (September 3, 1965): 52B-58 [no author].

30. R. Evans and R. Novak, "Inside Report: Medicare Crisis," *Herald Tribune*, March 3, 1966.

31. J. Q. Young, S. R. Ranji, R. M. Wachter, C. M. Lee, B. Niehaus, and A. D. Auerback, "'July Effect': Impact of the Academic Year-End Changeover on Patient Outcomes: A Systematic Review," *Annals of Internal Medicine* 155 (2011): 309–115.

32. U. S. Neill and H. A. Rockman, "A Conversation with Robert Lefkowitz, Joseph Goldstein, and Michael Brown," *Journal of Clinical Investigation* 122 (2012): 1586–1587.

33. Goldstein, interview by the author, June 5, 2017.

34. Goldstein, interview by the author, June 5, 2017.

35. J. L. Goldstein and M. S. Brown, interview by Adam Smith, December 10, 2012, Stockholm, for NobelPrize.org and Nobel Media AB, nobelprize.org/prizes/medicine/1985/goldstein/interview.

36. W. Lovejoy, telephone interview by Raymond S. Greenberg, October 20, 2017.

37. Lefkowitz, telephone interview by the author, October 9, 2017.

38. Lovejoy, telephone interview by the author, October 20, 2017.

39. Lefkowitz, telephone interview by the author, October 9, 2017.

40. Lovejoy, telephone interview by the author, October 20, 2017.

41. H. Varmus, interview by Raymond S. Greenberg, October 4, 2017, Weill Cornell Medical Center, New York, NY.

42. Lefkowitz, telephone interview by the author, October 9, 2017.

CHAPTER 4: YELLOW BERETS

1. US Department of Commerce, Bureau of the Census, *Vietnam Conflict—U.S. Military Forces in Vietnam and Casualties Incurred: 1961 to 1972*, Table 590, in *Statistical Abstract of the United States, 1977* (Washington, DC: US Department of Commerce, Bureau of the Census, 1980).

2. US Department of Commerce, Bureau of the Census, *Statistical Abstract of the United States, 1977*, 98th ed. (Washington, DC: US Department of Commerce, Bureau of the Census, 1977), no. 589, 369.

3. D. L. Anderson, *The Columbia Guide to the Vietnam War* (New York: Columbia University Press, 2002), 56.

4. R. P. Saldin, *War, the American State, and Politics since 1898* (New York: Cambridge University Press, 2011), 193.

5. Editors of Boston Publishing Company, *The American Experience in Vietnam: Reflections on an Era* (Minneapolis: Zenith Press, 2014), 177.

6. L. A. Eldridge, *Chronicles of a Two Front War: Civil Rights and Vietnam in the African American Press* (Columbia: University of Missouri Press, 2011), 51–52.

7. R. A. Cooper, "Medical Schools and Their Applicants," *Health Affairs* 22 (2003): 71–84.

8. A. E. Cowdrey, *The Medic's War: United States Army in the Korean War* (Washington, DC: United States Army Center of Military History, 1987), 12–29.

9. T. R. Goethals, "Americans First," *New England Journal of Medicine* 243 (1950): 896–897.

10. Public Laws Enacted during the Second Session of the Eighty-First Congress of the United States, 1950, Chapter 939, 826–828, loc.gov/law/help/statutes-at-large/81st-congress.php.

11. Cowdrey, *The Medic's War.*

12. F. B. Berry, "The Story of 'The Berry Plan,'" *Bulletin New York Academy of Medicine* 52 (1976): 278–282.

13. L. B. Balsam and A. DeAnda, "Historical Perspectives of the American Association for Thoracic Surgery: Frank B. Berry (1892–1976)," *Journal of Thoracic and Cardiovascular Surgery* 142 (2011): 253–256.

14. F. B. Berry, "How the Berry Plan Got Started," *Medical Times* 98 (1970): 104–106.

15. US Department of Defense, Office of the Assistant Secretary of Defense (Health and Medical), *Information Bulletin: Armed Forces Reserve Medical Officer Commissioning and Residency Consideration Program* (Washington, DC: US Government Printing Office, 1959), 1–10.

16. F. Mullan, *Plagues and Politics: The Story of the United States Public Health Service* (New York: Basic Books, 1989), 224.

17. J. E. Ransdell, "The National Institute of Health," *Radiology* 18 (1932): 942–947.

18. M. K. Klein, *The Legacy of the "Yellow Berets": The Vietnam War, the Doctor Draft, and the NIH Associate Training Program* (Manuscript) (Bethesda, MD: NIH History Office, National Institutes of Health, 1998), 1–33.

19. B. S. Park, "The Development of the Intramural Research Program at the National Institutes of Health after World War II," *Perspectives in Biology and Medicine* 46 (2003): 383–402.

20. T. J. Kennedy, *James Augustine Shannon, 1904–1994: A Biographical Memoir* (Washington, DC: National Academies Press, 1998), 9.

21. T. J. Kennedy, "James A. Shannon and the Beginnings of the Laboratory of Kidney and Electrolyte Metabolism of the National Institutes of Health," *Kidney International* 55 (1999): 326–333.

22. R. L. Bowman, quoted in Park, "Development of the Intramural Research Program," 392.

23. B. J. Culliton, "NIH Policymaker: A Fundamentalist Takes the Number Two Spot at NIH," *Science News* 95 (1969): 263–264.

24. Kennedy, "James A. Shannon and the Beginnings."

25. National Institutes of Health, Clinical and Professional Education Branch, *Appointment of Associateships for 1967 at the National Institutes of Health* (Public Health Reports) 80 (1965): 370–371.

26. A. S. Fauci, interview by Victoria A. Harden, March 7, 1989, Office of History, National Institutes of Health, Bethesda, MD.

27. J. Scipioni, "Meet the Most Powerful Doctor in America," Fox Business, June 10, 2015, foxbusiness.com/features/2015/06/11/meet-most-powerful-man-in-us-medicine.html.

28. E. Marshall, "N.I.A.I.D's Anthony Fauci," *Science* 292 (2001): 1990.

29. H. R. Kimball, interview by Melissa K. Klein, July 16, 1997, Office of History, National Institutes of Health, Bethesda, MD.

30. P. McNees, *A Brief History of the Clinical Center: Selections from Building Ten at Fifty* (Bethesda, MD: National Institutes of Health, 2003).

31. National Institutes of Health, Office of Research Information, "News from NIH: New Class of 101 New Physicians Join NIH Research Training Programs" (Bethesda, MD: National Institutes of Health, July 1963).

32. D. S. Fredrickson, interview by Melissa K. Klein, July 8, 1998, Office of History, National Institutes of Health, Bethesda, MD.

33. Fredrickson, interview by Melissa K. Klein, July 8, 1998.

34. Klein, *Legacy of the "Yellow Berets."*

35. Association of American Medical Colleges, *2016 AAMC Data Book* (Washington, DC, AAMC, 2016), 41, Table B-12: "U.S. Medical School Women Enrollment and Graduates."

36. J. A. Kastor, *The National Institutes of Health, 1991–2008* (New York: Oxford University Press, 2010), 23.

37. S. Khot, B. S. Park, and W. T. Longstreth, "The Vietnam War and Medical Research: Untold Legacy of the U.S. Doctor Draft and the NIH 'Yellow Berets,'" *Academic Medicine* 86 (2011): supplemental digital content, download. lww.com/.../ACADMED_86_4_2011_01_21_KHOT_202393_SDC1.pdf.

38. A. Fauci, interview by Sandeep Khot, July 17, 2001, Office of History, National Institutes of Health, Bethesda, MD.

39. National Institutes of Health, Clinical and Professional Education Branch, *Appointment of Associateships for 1967.* H. Metzger, interview by Melissa K. Klein, June 10, 1998, Office of History, National Institutes of Health, Bethesda, MD.

40. Khot et al., "The Vietnam War and Medical Research."

41. "The NIH Looks for Research Associates," *Medical World News*, February 22, 1974.

42. M. MacPherson, "Dan Quayle and the Vietnam Question," *Washington Post*, August 19, 1988.

43. G. Lardner and L. Romano, "At Height of Vietnam, Bush Picks Guard," *Washington Post*, July 28, 1999.

44. "Editorial Opinion: Bill Clinton's Vietnam Test," *New York Times*, February 14, 1992.

45. Kimball, interview by Melissa K. Klein, July 16, 1997.

46. B. Seger (under the attribution D. Dodger), "Ballad of the Yellow Beret," performed by the Beach Bums. Produced and arranged by Doug Brown and the Omens (Detroit: Are You Kidding Me Records, 1966).

47. B. Sadler and R. Moore, "Ballad of the Green Berets" (New York: RCA Victor, Catalogue No. 47-8739, 1966).

48. "Obituaries: Barry Sadler, 49, Balladeer, Dies," *New York Times*, November 6, 1989.

49. R. Adler, "Screen: 'Green Berets' as Viewed by John Wayne: War Movie Arrives at the Warner Theater," *New York Times*, June 20, 1968.

50. A. S. Fauci, interview by Melissa K. Klein, July 16, 1998, Office of History, National Institutes of Health, Bethesda, MD.

51. Fauci, interview by Melissa K. Klein, July 16, 1998.

52. Kimball, interview by Melissa K. Klein, July 16, 1997.

53. Kimball, interview by Melissa K. Klein, July 16, 1997.

54. Fredrickson, interview by Melissa K. Klein, July 8, 1998.
55. C. Garnett, "NIH-NIMH Vietnam Moratorium Committee Reunites for Posterity," *NIH Record* 58, no. 2 (January 27, 2006): 586.
56. Garnett, "NIH-NIMH Vietnam Moratorium Committee," 586.
57. Garnett, "NIH-NIMH Vietnam Moratorium Committee," 586.
58. F. D. Roosevelt, "Dedication of the National Institute of Health," October 31, 1940, cited in M. Lyons, *70 Acres of Science: The National Institute of Health Moves to Bethesda* (Bethesda, MD: DeWitt Stetten, Jr., Museum of Medical Research, National Institutes of Health, 2006), 48–50.
59. B. Spock, quoted in "A Wrap-Up on the Washington, DC Moratorium," recorded in Washington, DC, broadcast on WBAI, and distributed by Pacifica Radio Archives, 1969), October 15, 1969 (North Hollywood, CA: Pacifica Radio Archives, Number: BB3743., 1969), 7–12.
60. United States House of Representatives, *Concurrent Resolution 175: Code of Ethics for Government Service*, 72 Stat. B12 (Washington, DC: United States Congress, July 11, 1958). E. E. Dennis and W. L. Rivers, *The New Journalism in America* (New Brunswick, NJ: Transaction Publishers, 2011), 166–167.
61. D. Reiss, quoted in Garnett, NIH-NIMH, 587.
62. Z. Hostetler, quoted in Garnett, "NIH-NIMH Vietnam Moratorium Committee," 588.
63. Garnett, "NIH-NIMH Vietnam Moratorium Committee," 586.
64. United States House of Representatives, *Concurrent Resolution 175*.
65. B. M. Babior, quoted in Park, "The Development of the Intramural Research Program."
66. Klein, *Legacy of the "Yellow Berets."*
67. Khot et al., "The Vietnam War and Medical Research."

CHAPTER 5: CAMPUS LIFE

1. F. Keefe, quoted in K. Honey, "True Dedication to Clinical Research: The Clinical Center of the National Institutes of Health Receives the 2011 Mary Woodard Lasker Award for Public Service," *Journal of Clinical Investigation* 121 (2011): 3778–3781.
2. National Institutes of Health, *NIH Factbook: Guide to National Institutes of Health Programs and Activities*, 1st ed. (Chicago: Marquis Academic Media, 1976), 88.
3. Masur had good reason to use these two hospitals as prototypes. Both were opened less than a decade earlier and were among the first to focus on the care of patients with long-term, chronic conditions, with Memorial serving as a dedicated cancer hospital. In addition, the patient care at these hospitals was complemented by state-of-the-art research laboratories. At Memorial,

its affiliated, brand-new, thirteen-story research building was the Sloan-Kettering Institute, funded by two former General Motors executives, Alfred P. Sloan and Charles F. Kettering. At Goldwater, during World War II, a 100-bed research unit was created for the study of antimalarial drugs, a celebrated program that was overseen by James A. Shannon, MD; he later became director of the research program at the National Heart Institute and eventually became NIH director.

4.   J. Roth, telephone interview by Raymond S. Greenberg, May 30, 2017.

5.   Roth, telephone interview by the author, May 30, 2017.

6.   G. R. Edgerton, *The Columbia History of American Television* (New York: Columbia University Press, 2002), 103.

7.   H. Truman, quoted in J. I. Gallin, "The NIH Clinical Center and the Future of Clinical Research," *Nature Medicine* 17 (2011): 1221–1223.

8.   "Revolutionary Center for Medical Research Dedicated," *New York Times*, July 3, 1953.

9.   "Revolutionary Center for Medical Research Dedicated."

10. In 1953, the NIH consisted of the following seven institutes: National Cancer Institute, National Heart Institute, National Microbiological Institute, National Institute of Dental Research, National Institute of Mental Health, National Institute of Arthritis and Metabolic Diseases, and National Institute of Neurological Diseases and Blindness.

11. US Department of Health, Education, and Welfare, Office of Information, National Institutes of Health, *The National Institutes of Health Almanac* (Washington, DC: US Department of Health, Education, and Welfare, 1970).

12. NIH, *The National Institutes of Health Almanac* (1970).

13. P. McNees, "An Abnormal Reunion," *The Scientist* (March 1, 2008).

14. McNees, "An Abnormal Reunion."

15. R. J. Lefkowitz, interview by Raymond S. Greenberg, August 16, 2017, Duke University Medical Center, Durham, NC.

16. Roth, telephone interview by the author, May 30, 2017.

17. Lefkowitz, interview by the author, August 16, 2017.

18. S. Rosen, interview by Melissa K. Klein, July 23, 1997, National Institutes of Health, Bethesda, MD.

19. T. F. Boat, telephone interview by Raymond S. Greenberg, June 27, 2017.

20. A. Schechter, interview by Sandeep Khot, July 23, 2001, National Institutes of Health, Bethesda, MD.

21. H. Metzger, interview by Sandeep Khot, July 30, 2001, National Institutes of Health, Bethesda, MD.

22. Schechter, interview by Sandeep Khot, July 23, 2001.

23. A. Fauci, interview by Sandeep Khot, July 17, 2001, Office of History, National Institutes of Health, Bethesda, MD.

24. Boat, telephone interview by the author, June 27, 2017.

25. M. R. DeLong, telephone interview by Raymond S. Greenberg, July 19, 2017.

26. Rosen, interview by Melissa K. Klein, July 23, 1997.

27. Boat, telephone interview by the author, June 27, 2017.

28. Roth, telephone interview by the author, May 30, 2017.

29. Metzger, interview by Sandeep Khot, July 30, 2001.

30. Roth, telephone interview by the author, May 30, 2017.

31. Roth, telephone interview by the author, May 30, 2017.

32. R. McManus, "FAES Marks 50th Year at NIH," *NIH Record* 61 (August 7, 2009).

33. Schechter, interview by Sandeep Khot, July 23, 2001.

34. Metzger, interview by Sandeep Khot, July 30, 2001.

35. McManus, "FAES Marks 50th Year at NIH."

36. Schechter, interview by Sandeep Khot, July 23, 2001.

37. D. S. Fredrickson, interview by Melissa K. Klein, July 8, 1998, Office of History, National Institutes of Health, Bethesda, MD.

38. Rosen, interview by Melissa K. Klein, July 23, 1997.

39. Fredrickson, interview by Melissa K. Klein, July 8, 1998.

40. H. R. Kimball, interview by Melissa K. Klein, July 16, 1997, Office of History, National Institutes of Health, Bethesda, MD.

41. Roth, telephone interview by the author, May 30, 2017.

42. H. R. Kimball, telephone interview by Melissa K. Klein, July 16, 1997, Philadelphia.

43. Lefkowitz, interview by the author, August 16, 2017.

44. Boat, telephone interview by the author, June 27, 2017.

45. D. Ginsberg, "Chamber Music Series' 40 Years of Concerts Ends on a Wistful Note," *Washington Post*, April 5, 2008.

46. I. Oransky, "Giulio Cantoni," *The Lancet* 366 (2005): 888.

47. R. Gallo, interview by Sandeep Khot, August 7, 2001, National Institutes of Health, Bethesda, MD.

CHAPTER 6: NIH'S FINEST HOUR

1. J. D. Watson and F. H. C. Crick, "Molecular Structure of Nucleic Acids," *Nature* 171 (1953): 737–738.

2. J. D. Watson and F. H. C. Crick, "Genetical Implications of the Structure of Deoxyribonucleic Acid," *Nature* 171 (1953): 964–967.

3. E. Schrödinger, *What Is Life?* (Cambridge, UK: Cambridge University Press, 1944).

4. Schrödinger, *What Is Life?*

5. J. D. Watson, A. Berry, and K. Davies, *DNA: The Story of the Genetic Revolution* (New York: Alfred A. Knopf, 2017).

6.   F. Crick, *What Mad Pursuit: A Personal View of Scientific Discovery* (New York: Basic Books, 1988).

7.   T. Caspersson and J. Schultz, "Pentose Nucleotides in the Cytoplasm of Growing Tissues," *Nature* 143 (1939): 602–603.

8.   A. Rich and J. D. Watson, "Some Relations Between DNA and RNA," *Proceedings of the National Academy of Sciences* 40 (1954): 759–764.

9.   L. E. Key, *Who Wrote the Book of Life? A History of the Genetic Code* (Stanford: Stanford University Press, 2000).

10.   F. H. Portugal, *The Least Likely Man: Marshall Nirenberg and the Discovery of the Genetic Code* (Cambridge, MA: MIT Press, 2015).

11.   Portugal, *The Least Likely Man*.

12.   Portugal, *The Least Likely Man*.

13.   Portugal, *The Least Likely Man*.

14.   J. D. Stetten, ed., *NIH: An Account of Research in Its Laboratories and Clinics* (Orlando, FL: Academic Press, 1984).

15.   M. Fry, *Landmark Experiments in Molecular Biology* (London: Academic Press, 2016), 427.

16.   Portugal, *The Least Likely Man*.

17.   M. Nirenberg, interviews by Ruth Roy Harris between September 20, 1995, and January 24, 1996, National Institutes of Health, Bethesda, MD [2008] (hereafter "Harris Interviews").

18.   Nirenberg, Harris Interviews.

19.   Nirenberg, Harris Interviews.

20.   Nirenberg, Harris Interviews.

21.   Nirenberg, Harris Interviews.

22.   Nirenberg, Harris Interviews.

23.   M. W. Nirenberg, *A Conversation with Marshall Nirenberg, Summer 2009* (Bethesda, MD: Office of the Director, National Institutes of Health, 2009).

24.   H. Matthaei and M. W. Nirenberg, "The Dependence of Cell-Free Protein Synthesis in *E. coli* upon RNA Prepared from Ribosomes," *Biochemical and Biophysical Research Communications* 4 (1961): 404–408.

25.   Nirenberg, Harris Interviews.

26.   Nirenberg, Harris Interviews.

27.   J. H. Matthaei and M. W. Nirenberg, "Characteristics and Stabilization of DNAse Sensitive Protein Synthesis in *E. coli* Extracts," *Proceedings of the National Academy of Sciences* 47 (1961): 1580–1588.

28.   M. W. Nirenberg and J. H. Matthaei, "The Dependence of Cell-Free Protein Synthesis in *E. coli* upon Naturally Occurring or Synthetic Polyribonucleotides," *Proceedings of the National Academy of Sciences* 47 (1961): 1588–1602.

29.   Nirenberg, Harris Interviews.

30.   Nirenberg, Harris Interviews.

31. S. Brenner, F. Jacob, and M. Meselson, "An Unstable Intermediate Carrying Information from Genes to Ribosomes for Protein Synthesis," *Nature* 190 (1961): 576–580.

32. F. H. C. Crick, "Cracking the Genetic Code," in *Frontiers of Knowledge Series*, no. 256 (British Broadcasting Corporation, January 22, 1962).

33. Nirenberg, Harris Interviews.

34. Nirenberg, Harris Interviews.

35. R. G. Martin, "A Revisionist View of the Breaking of the Genetic Code," in DeWitt Stetten, ed., *NIH: An Account of Research in Its Laboratories and Clinics* (Orlando, FL: Academic Press, 1984).

36. P. Lengyel, "Memories of a Senior Scientist: On Passing the Fiftieth Anniversary of the Beginning of Deciphering the Genetic Code," *Annual Review of Microbiology* 66 (2012): 27–38.

37. M. Nirenberg, "Historical Review: Deciphering the Genetic Code—A Personal Account," *Trends in Biochemical Sciences* 29 (2004): 46–54.

38. Lengyel, "Memories of a Senior Scientist."

39. P. Lengyel, J. F. Speyer, and S. Ochoa, "Synthetic Polynucleotides and the Amino Acid Code," *Proceedings of the National Academy of Sciences* 47 (1961): 1936–1942.

40. O. W. Jones and M. W. Nirenberg, "Qualitative Survey of RNA Codewords," *Proceedings of the National Academy of Sciences* 48 (1962): 2115–2123.

41. Nirenberg, Harris Interviews.

42. R. Mukhopadhyay, "A 'Mad Race to the Finish': A Conversation with Philip Leder on the Genetic Code Experiment That He Began 50 Years Ago," *American Society for Biochemistry and Molecular Biology Today* (February 2012).

43. M. W. Nirenberg and P. Leder, "RNA Codewords and Protein Synthesis. I. The Effect of Trinucleotides Upon the Binding of sRNA to Ribosomes," *Science* 145 (1964): 1399–1407.

44. R. Lohrmann, D. Stöll, H. Hayatsu, E. Ohtsuka, H. G. Khorana, "Studies of Polynucleotides: LI. Synthesis of the 64 Possible Ribotrinucleotides Derived from the Four Major Ribomononucleotides," *Journal of the American Chemical Society* 88 (1966): 819–829.

45. S. Nishimura, D. S. Jones, E. Ohtsuka, H. Hayatsu, T. M. Jacob, and H. G. Khorana, "Studies of Polynucleotides: XLVII. The *In Vitro* Synthesis of Homopeptides as Directed by a Ribopolynucleotide Containing a Repeating Trinucleotide Sequence. New Codon Sequences for Lysine, Glutamic Acid and Arginine," *Journal of Molecular Biology* 13 (1965): 283–301.

46. Nirenberg, Harris Interviews.

47. C. Moffatt, "Deciphering the Genetic Code: A 50 Year Anniversary," *Circulating Now* (Bethesda, MD: National Library of Medicine, January 21, 2015).

48. M. W. Nirenberg, O. W. Jones, P. Leder, B. F. C. Clark, W. S. Sly, and S. Pestka, "On the Coding of Genetic Information," *Cold Spring Harbor Symposium on Quantitative Biology* 28 (1963): 549–557.

49. M. Nirenberg, T. Caskey, R. Marshall, R. Brimacombe, D. Kellogg, B. Doctor, D. Hatfield, J. Levin, F. Rottman, S. Pestka, M. Wilcox, and F. Anderson, "The RNA Code and Protein Synthesis," *Cold Spring Harbor Symposium on Quantitative Biology* 31 (1966): 11–24.

CHAPTER 7: BEGINNING AT TERMINATION

1. E. Scolnick, "Marshall Nirenberg, 1927–2010," *Cell* 140 (2010): 450–451.

2. M. Nirenberg, *A Conversation with Dr. Marshall Nirenberg, Summer 2009* (Bethesda, MD: Office of the Director, National Institutes of Health, 2009).

3. Nirenberg, *A Conversation.*

4. Nirenberg, *A Conversation.*

5. C. T. Caskey, telephone interview by Raymond S. Greenberg, June 2, 2017.

6. Nirenberg, *A Conversation.*

7. Caskey, telephone interview by author, June 2, 2017.

8. Nirenberg, *A Conversation.*

9. J. L. Goldstein, interview by Raymond S. Greenberg, June 5, 2017, University of Texas Southwestern Medical Center, Dallas.

10. J. L. Goldstein, quoted in F. H. Portugal, *The Least Likely Man: Marshall Nirenberg and the Discovery of the Genetic Code* (Cambridge, MA: MIT Press, 2015).

11. Caskey, telephone interview by author, June 2, 2017.

12. Goldstein, quoted in Portugal, *The Least Likely Man.*

13. Goldstein, quoted in Portugal, *The Least Likely Man.*

14. Goldstein, quoted in Portugal, *The Least Likely Man.*

15. E. Scolnick, interview by Franklin H. Portugal, December 11, 2012, quoted in Portugal, *The Least Likely Man.*

16. M. R. Capecchi, "Polypeptide Chain Termination *In Vitro*: Isolation of a Release Factor," *Proceedings of the National Academy of Sciences* 58 (1967): 1144–1151.

17. Caskey, telephone interview by author, June 2, 2017.

18. Caskey, telephone interview by author, June 2, 2017.

19. E. Scolnick, interview by Gretchen A. Case, June 24, 1998, Oral History Project, NCI Laboratory of Molecular Biology, Merck Laboratories, West Point, PA, and Bethesda, MD.

20. Scolnick, interview, NCI Oral History Project.

21. Scolnick, interview, NCI Oral History Project.

22. E. Scolnick, R. Tompkins, T. Caskey, and M. Nirenberg, "Release Factors Differing in Specificity for Terminator Codons," *Proceedings of the National Academy of Sciences* 61 (1968): 768–774.

23. Nirenberg, *A Conversation*.

24. C. T. Caskey, interview by Ruth Roy Harris, 1995, National Institutes of Health, Bethesda, MD.

25. Caskey, interview by Ruth Roy Harris, 1995.

26. Caskey, interview by Ruth Roy Harris, 1995.

27. G. Milman, J. Goldstein, E. Scolnick, and T. Caskey, "Peptide Chain Termination. III. Stimulation of *In Vitro* Termination," *Proceedings of the National Academy of Sciences* 63 (1969): 183–190.

28. J. Goldstein, presentation at "A Tribute to Dr. Marshall Nirenberg," October 2, 2010, National Institutes of Health, Bethesda, MD.

29. J. Goldstein, G. Milman, E. Scolnick, and T. Caskey, "Peptide Chain Termination. VI. Purification and Site of Action of S," *Proceedings of the National Academy of Sciences* 65 (1970): 430–437.

30. J. L. Goldstein, A. L. Beaudet, and C. T. Caskey, "Peptide Chain Termination with Mammalian Release Factor," *Proceedings of the National Academy of Sciences* 67 (1970): 99–106.

31. J. L. Goldstein and C. T. Caskey, "Peptide Chain Termination: Effect of Protein S on Ribosomal Binding of Release Factors," *Proceedings of the National Academy of Sciences* 67 (1970): 537–543.

32. Goldstein, presentation at "A Tribute to Dr. Marshall Nirenberg."

33. Goldstein, presentation at "A Tribute to Dr. Marshall Nirenberg."

34. Goldstein, presentation at "A Tribute to Dr. Marshall Nirenberg."

35. Goldstein, presentation at "A Tribute to Dr. Marshall Nirenberg."

36. Caskey, telephone interview by author, June 2, 2017.

37. Goldstein, interview by the author, June 5, 2017.

38. F. C. Bartter, P. Pronove, J. R. Gill, and R. G. MacCardle, "Hyperplasia of the Juxtaglomerular Complex with Hyperaldosteronism and Hypokalemic Alkalosis. A New Syndrome," *American Journal of Medicine* 33 (1962): 811–828.

39. D. S. Fredrickson, P. H. Altrocchi, L. V. Avioli, D. S. Goodman, and H. C. Goodman, "Tangier Disease," *Annals of Internal Medicine* 55 (1961): 1016–1031.

40. M. S. Brown, *Origins of a 40-Year Partnership* (Cambridge, UK: University of Cambridge, Nobel Prize Inspiration Initiative, Nobel Media AB, 2014), nobelprizeii.org/videos/michael-brown-cambridge-lecture.

41. Brown, *Origins of a 40-Year Partnership*.

42. Brown, *Origins of a 40-Year Partnership*.

CHAPTER 8: FOLLOWING THE RIGHT PATH

1. J. G. Holmes, H. W. Marean, N. P. Neill, A. S. Root, A. T. Sweet, and W. E. McLendon, *Soil Survey of the San Bernardino Valley, California*

(Washington, DC: US Department of Agriculture, Government Printing Office, 1905).

2.   C. Lee, "The History of Citrus in California," *California Country* (March/April 2010).

3.   D. Karp, "Valencia Oranges, under Siege in California, Fight to Survive," *Los Angeles Times*, July 5, 2013.

4.   E. R. Stadtman, An Oral History Conducted on February 13, 2001, by Buhm Soon Park [interview no. 3] (Bethesda, MD: National Institutes of Health, 2001).

5.   Built in 1892, Stanford's Hopkins Marine Station, near Monterey in the quaint seaside town of Pacific Grove, was the first oceanic research laboratory on the West Coast and only the second in the country (the Marine Biological Laboratory in Woods Hole, Massachusetts, was established four years earlier).

6.   R. L. Switzer, E. R. Stadtman, and T. C. Stadtman, "H. A. Barker: November 29, 1907–December 24, 2000," in *Biographical Memoirs* (Washington, DC: National Academies Press, 2004).

7.   A. J. Kluyver and H. J. L. Donker, "Die Einheit in der Biochemie," *Chemie der Zelle und Gewebe* 13 (1926): 134–190.

8.   Four decades later, in proposing the universality of the genetic code, Jacques Monod, one of the recipients of the 1965 Nobel Prize in Physiology or Medicine, would borrow the same sentiment: "Tout ce qui est vrai pour le Colibacille est vrai pour l'éléphant" (All that is true for the *Escherichia coli* bacteria is true for the elephant). H. G. Friedmann, "From *Butyribacterium* to *E. coli*: An Essay on Unity," *Biochemistry Perspectives in Biology and Medicine* 47 (2004): 47–66.

9.   Barker did not have to travel far from the lab to discover new bacteria to explore. The city of Delft is named for the canal, or delft (from the Dutch phrase "to dig"), on which it was sited. All the way back to the late seventeenth century, the city's waterways were a rich source of microorganisms for study. In 1677, a local resident, Antonie Philips van Leeuwenhoek (later anointed "the Father of Microbiology"), began using microscopes to study bacteria found in the rich sediment of Delft's canals, thereby establishing the existence of single-celled organisms, which he characterized as "animalcules." The Delft School of Microbiology continued that tradition, isolating, cataloging, and studying many other bacteria derived from the canals.

10. H. A. Barker and S. M. Taha, "*Clostridium kluyverii*, an Organism Concerned in the Formation of Caproic Acid from Ethyl Alcohol," *Journal of Bacteriology* 43 (1942): 347–363.

11. Switzer et al., "H. A. Barker."

12. E. R. Stadtman, "How I Became a Biochemist," *International Union of Biochemistry and Molecular Biology—Life* 54 (2002): 39–40.

13. Stadtman, An Oral History Conducted on February 13, 2001, by Buhm Soon Park. It is hard to imagine a compelling military need for naturally colored dried apricots, but that was the project assigned to Stadtman. Troops fighting in the jungles of the South Pacific needed lightweight, compact food rations, and dried or dehydrated foods were essential. Dried apricots were included in these jungle meals (or "J-Rations"), but after two or three weeks in the heat the apricots would turn an unappealing brown. Stadtman was assigned the task of trying to prevent the fruit from darkening—an exercise that may not have won the war but did result in Stadtman's first laboratory experience.

14. E. R. Stadtman, H. A. Barker, V. A. Haas, and E. M. Mrak, "The Influence of Temperature on the Deterioration of Dried Apricots," *Industrial and Engineering Chemistry* 38 (1946): 541–543.

15. E. R. Stadtman, H. A. Barker, E. M. Mrak, and G. Mackinney, "Studies on the Storage of Dried Fruit: Experimental Methods and the Influences of Moisture and Sulfur Dioxide on the Rate of Deterioration of Dried Apricots," *Industrial and Engineering Chemistry* 38 (1946): 99–104.

16. E. R. Stadtman, H. A. Barker, V. A. Haas, E. M. Mrak, and G. Mackinney, "Studies on the Storage of Dried Fruit: Gas Exchange During Storage of Dried Apricots and the Influence of Oxygen on the Rate of Deterioration," *Industrial and Engineering Chemistry* 38 (1946): 324–329.

17. V. A. Haas, E. R. Stadtman, F. H. Stadtman, and G. Mackinney, "Deterioration of Dried Fruits. I. The Effects of Sugars and Furfurals," *Journal of the American Chemical Society* 70 (1948): 3576–3579.

18. A. Goldstein, "A Duo's Great Chemistry," *Washington Post*, January 26, 2004.

19. N. L. Söhngen, *Het ontstaan en verdwijnen van waterstof en methaan onder den invloed van het organische leven* (Delft: Technische Hoogeschool, 1906).

20. T. C. Stadtman and H. A. Barker, "Studies on the Methane Fermentation. X. A New Formate-Decomposing Bacterium, *Methanococcus Vannielii*," *Journal of Bacteriology* 62 (1952): 269–280.

21. T. C. Stadtman and L. S. McClung [1951], "*Clostridium Sticklandii* Nov. Spec," *Journal of Bacteriology* 73, no. 2: 218–219 (1957).

22. Barker and Taha, "*Clostridium kluyverii*."

23. Barker's collaborator from the radiation facility was a physical chemist named Dr. Martin Kamen. In February 1940, Kamen and his colleague Sam Ruben demonstrated that a long-lived radioactive isotope of carbon, known as carbon-14 and occurring once in a trillion carbon atoms in nature, could be made to order in the laboratory. This feat was accomplished by smashing the nuclei of a heavy isotope of hydrogen into the ordinary carbon of graphite, producing overweight carbon atoms that could be traced easily. Because carbon is the essential ingredient of organic compounds, the ability to trace

a stable radioactive isotope of carbon opened new doors of opportunity for biochemists. For the first time, researchers had the ability to study the pathways by which organic compounds are constructed and deconstructed within living organisms.

24. H. A. Barker, M. D. Kamen, and B. T. Bornstein, "The Synthesis of Butyric and Caproic Acids from Ethanol and Acetic Acid by *Clostridium kluyveri*," *Proceedings of the National Academy of Sciences* 31 (1945): 373–381.

25. E. R. Stadtman, T. C. Stadtman, and H. A. Barker, "Tracer Experiments on the Mechanisms of Synthesis of Valeric and Caproic Acids by *Clostridium kluyveri*," *Journal of Biological Chemistry* 178 (1949): 677–682.

26. Stadtman, "How I Became a Biochemist."

27. E. R. Stadtman and H. A. Barker, "Fatty Acid Synthesis by Enzyme Preparations of *Clostridium kluyveri*. I. Preparation of Cell-Free Extracts That Catalyze the Conversion of Ethanol and Acetate to Butyrate and Caproate," *Journal of Biological Chemistry* 180 (1949): 1085–1093.

28. F. Lipmann, "Generation and Utilization of Phosphate High Energy Bonds," *Advances in Enzymology and Related Areas of Molecular Biology* 1 (1941): 99–162.

29. F. Lipmann, N. O. Kaplan, L. Novelli, C. Tuttle, and B. M. Guirard, "Coenzyme for Acetylation: A Pantothenic Acid Derivative," *Journal of Biological Chemistry* 167 (1947): 869–870.

30. Typically, coenzymes are derived from vitamins or other nutrients. CoA is a small molecule that has three subcomponents: vitamin B_5; a high-energy generator; and a sulfur-containing hitch that is used to attach two-carbon building blocks onto other molecules. The "A" in CoA stands for "activation of acetate," referring to the two-carbon building blocks that it either adds or removes from the compound on which it is operating. The chemical "hitch" for the two-carbon acetyl group is relatively unstable, meaning that the attached two-carbon fragments can be transferred on and off with great ease. CoA plays a key role in multiple metabolic pathways, including the breakdown of sugars, proteins, and lipids, as well as the construction of fatty acids.

Lipmann's work on CoA was of great interest to Stadtman. During his doctoral studies with Barker, they observed that extracts of a Delft mud bacterium contained an enzyme involved in the transfer of two-carbon building blocks for fatty acids. E. R. Stadtman and H. A. Barker, "Fatty Acid Synthesis by Enzyme Preparations of *Clostridium kluyveri*. VI. Reactions of Acylphosphates," *Journal of Biological Chemistry* 184 (1950): 769–793. It occurred to them that CoA, with its helper role in two-carbon transfer reactions, might be a partner to their enzyme. This was a bit of a leap of faith, as Barker and Stadtman had been studying bacterial enzymes and Lipmann was working with animal material. Their hunch proved to be correct, however: Coenzyme A was indeed a facilitator of their enzyme. Equally important, when they mixed the bacterial enzyme with Lipmann's pigeon liver tissue extract, the metabolic machinery worked to perfection. E. R. Stadtman, G. D. Novelli, and F. Lipmann, "Coenzyme A Function in and Acetyl Transfer by the Phosphotransacetylase System," *Journal of Biological Chemistry* 191 (1951): 365–376.

In other words, these particular biochemical processes were identical in a mud-dwelling, oxygen-hating, single-cell organism and a high-flying, navigationally gifted, intelligent vertebrate. A quarter-century after Albert Kluyver first proposed the principle of "Unity in Biochemistry," his scientific progeny performed an elegant validation, in part deploying a bacterium named after the Dutch master himself. Although this was certainly not the first (nor the last) interspecies demonstration of a common metabolic pathway, surely the old professor whose career was interrupted by the Nazi occupation of the Netherlands felt personally connected to this discovery. This same sense of belonging to an intergenerational family is how Fritz Lipmann ran his laboratory.

31.   Goldstein, "A Duo's Great Chemistry."
32.   A. N. Schechter, "Christian B. Anfinsen, 1916–1995," in *Biographical Memoirs* (Washington, DC: National Academy of Sciences, 2015).
33.   In the defense of the Philippines in 1942, for example, it is estimated that a third of American and Filipino military personnel suffered from malaria. Worse, the supply of the one known antimalarial drug, quinine, had been disrupted by the Japanese. In what became the medical counterpart to the Manhattan Project, around 14,000 compounds were tested for antimalarial effect, resulting in the approval of quinacrine in 1943 and chloroquine a few years later. L. B. Slater, *War and Disease: Biomedical Research on Malaria in the Twentieth Century* (New Brunswick, NJ: Rutgers University Press, 2009).
34.   M. A. Shampo and R. A. Kyle, "Hugo Theorell—Nobel Prize for Study of Enzymes," *Mayo Clinic Proceedings* 73 (1998): 147. Theorell returned to Stockholm as director of the Biochemical Department of the Medical Nobel Institute, where one particular focus was the process by which the liver breaks down alcoholic compounds. This work would lead to his selection as the 1955 recipient of the Nobel Prize in Physiology and Medicine.
35.   T. C. Stadtman, "A Gold Mine of Fascinating Enzymes: Those Remarkable Strictly Anaerobic Bacteria, *Methanococcus vannielli* and *Clostridium sticklandii*," *Journal of Biological Chemistry* 277 (2002): 49091–49100.
36.   B. S. Park, "The Development of the Intramural Research Program at the National Institutes of Health after World War II," *Perspectives in Biology and Medicine* 46 (2003): 383–402.
37.   Park, "Development of the Intramural Research Program."
38.   E. R. Stadtman, An Oral History Conducted on February 6, 2001, by Buhm

Soon Park [interview no. 2] (Bethesda, MD: National Institutes of Health, 2001).

39. J. Axelrod, interview by Bernhard Witkop, November 25, 2003, National Institutes of Health, Bethesda, MD.

40. Most important to the collaborative culture at NIH in its formative years were the personalities of the scientists who worked there. Kornberg is an excellent example: with several of his colleagues, he established a daily luncheon seminar on enzyme research. The colleagues met every day, including holidays, to discuss work in the burgeoning field of enzymology, including research done at NIH's labs and elsewhere. C. W. Tabor and H. Tabor, "It All Started on a Streetcar in Boston," *Annual Reviews in Biochemistry* 68 (1999): 1–32.

41. R. McManus, "Era of Distinction Ends for Building 3," *NIH Record* (Bethesda, MD: National Institutes of Health, May 1, 2001).

42. T. C. Stadtman, "On the Metabolism of an Amino Acid Fermenting *Clostridium*," *Journal of Bacteriology* 67 (1954): 314–320.

43. T. C. Stadtman, P. Elliott, and L. Tiemann, "Studies on the Enzymic Reduction of Amino Acids. III. Phosphate Esterification Coupled with Glycine Reduction," *Journal of Biological Chemistry* 231 (1958): 961–973.

44. D. C. Turner and T. C. Stadtman, "Purification of Protein Components of Clostridial Glycine Reductase System and Characterization of Protein A as a Selenoprotein," *Archives of Biochemistry and Biophysics* 154 (1973): 366–381.

45. J. E. Cone, M. del Rio, J. N. Davis, and T. C. Stadtman, "Chemical Characterization of the Selenoprotein Component of Clostridial Glycine Reductase: Identification of Selenocysteine as the Organo-Selenium Moiety," *Proceedings of the National Academy of Sciences* 73 (1976): 2659–2663.

46. R. H. McCoy, C. E. Meyer, and W. C. Rose, "Feeding Experiments with Mixtures of Highly Purified Amino Acids. VIII. Isolation and Identification of a New Essential Amino Acid," *Journal of Biological Chemistry* 112 (1935): 283–302.

47. E. R. Stadtman, "The Net Enzymatic Synthesis of Acetyl Coenzyme A," *Journal of Biological Chemistry* 196 (1952): 535–546.

48. U. S. Neill, "A Conversation with Roy Vagelos," *Journal of Clinical Investigation* 124 (2014): 2291–2292.

49. "P. Roy Vagelos, M.D.: 1991 Maxwell Finland Award" (Bethesda, MD: National Foundation for Infectious Diseases, 1991) [no author].

50. A. Marks, "A Conversation with P. Roy Vagelos," *Annual Reviews Conversations* (Palo Alto, CA: Annual Reviews, 2011). See also P. R. Vagelos and L. Galambos, *Medicine, Science, and Merck* (Cambridge, UK: Cambridge University Press, 2004), 42.

51. P. R. Vagelos, "Personal Notes," *Archives of Biochemistry and Biophysics* 397 (2002): 449.

52. Vagelos, "Personal Notes."
53. E. R. Stadtman, G. N. Cohen, G. Le Bras, and H. de Robichon-Szulmajster, "Feedback Inhibition and Repression of Aspartokinase Activity in *Escherichia coli* and *Saccharomyces cerevisiae*," *Journal of Biological Chemistry* 286 (1961): 2033–2038.
54. E. R. Stadtman, An Oral History Conducted on January 23, 2001, by Buhm Soon Park [interview no. 1] (Bethesda, MD: National Institutes of Health, 2001).
55. C. A. Woolfolk and E. R. Stadtman, "Cumulative Feedback Inhibition in the Multiple End Product Regulation of Glutamine Synthetase Activity in *Escherichia coli*," *Biochemical and Biophysical Research Communications* 17 (1964): 313–319.
56. H. S. Kingdon, "Earl R. Stadtman, Ph.D.: Citizen of the World," *Archives of Biochemistry and Biophysics* 397 (2002): 452.
57. Kingdon, "Earl R. Stadtman," 452.
58. Kingdon, "Earl R. Stadtman," 452.
59. D. Atkinson, "Personal Notes," *Archives of Biochemistry and Biophysics* 397 (2002): 453.
60. R. McManus, "Nobelist Prusiner Draws Homecoming Crowd," *NIH Record* 50, no. 22 (November 3, 1998) (Bethesda, MD: National Institutes of Health).
61. I. H. Pastan, "Personal Notes," *Archives of Biochemistry and Biophysics* 397 (2002): 450.
62. Pastan, "Personal Notes," 450.
63. McManus, "Nobelist Prusiner Draws Homecoming Crowd."

CHAPTER 9: IN EARL'S COURT

1. M. S. Brown, personal communication, May 6, 2017.
2. L. Laster and R. Laster, interview by Joan Ash, March 5, 1999, Oregon Health and Science University, Portland.
3. Laster and Laster, interview by Joan Ash, March 5, 1999.
4. M. S. Brown, interview by Raymond S. Greenberg, July 27, 2017, University of Texas Southwestern Medical Center, Dallas.
5. Brown, interview by the author, July 27, 2017.
6. J. D. Gardner, M. S. Brown, and L. Laster, "The Columnar Epithelial Cell of the Small Intestine: Digestion and Transport. First of Three Parts," *New England Journal of Medicine* 283 (1970): 1196–1202; J. D. Gardner, M. S. Brown, and L. Laster, "The Columnar Epithelial Cell of the Small Intestine. Digestion and Transport. Second of Three Parts," *New England Journal of Medicine* 283 (1970): 1264–1271; and J. D. Gardner, M. S. Brown, and L. Laster, "The Columnar Epithelial Cell of the Small

Intestine. Third of Three Parts," *New England Journal of Medicine* 283 (1970): 1317–1324.

7. National Commission for the Protection of Human Subjects of Biomedical and Behavioral Research, *National Commission for the Protection of Human Subjects of Biomedical and Behavioral Research: The Belmont Report* (Washington, DC: Government Printing Office, 1978).

8. Brown, interview by the author, July 27, 2017.

9. H. Alter, quoted in National Institutes of Health, *Clinical Center 50th Anniversary Celebration: Celebrating 50 Years of Clinical Research* (Bethesda, MD: National Institutes of Health, July 9, 2003).

10. Brown, interview by the author, July 27, 2017.

11. Brown, interview by the author, July 27, 2017.

12. Brown, interview by the author, July 27, 2017.

13. With the patient sedated, the physician inserts a thin, lighted, flexible tube, called an endoscope, that has a camera and a tissue-sampling device built into it. The physician can easily feed the endoscope from the mouth, through the esophagus and the stomach, and into the small intestines to snag a small piece of tissue.

14. In those days, the patient would swallow a large oval stainless-steel capsule connected to a plastic tube. The physician would position the patient to allow the capsule to pass into the desired location while monitoring its progress with X-ray images. When the capsule was in the correct position, suction was applied through the tube into a small opening in the capsule, pulling the intestinal wall against the capsule. Then, by pressing a trigger, the physician would activate a spring-loaded knife in the capsule that would slice off a small piece of tissue.

15. Brown, interview by the author, July 27, 2017.

16. Brown, interview by the author, July 27, 2017.

17. Brown, interview by the author, July 27, 2017.

18. Brown, interview by the author, July 27, 2017.

19. Laster and Laster, interview by Joan Ash, March 5, 1999.

20. Laster and Laster, interview by Joan Ash, March 5, 1999.

21. Z. Wang, *In Sputnik's Shadow: The President's Science Advisory Committee and Cold War America* (New Brunswick, NJ: Rutgers University Press, 2009), 295–296.

22. R. D. Lyons, "Science Adviser to Nixon Leaving for Industry Job," *New York Times*, January 3, 1973.

23. Brown, interview by the author, July 27, 2017.

24. E. H. Fischer and E. G. Krebs, "Conversion of Phosphorylase B to Phosphorylase A in Muscle Extracts," *Journal of Biological Chemistry* 216 (1955): 121–132.

25. P. Cohen, "The Origins of Protein Phosphorylation," *Nature Cell Biology* 4 (2002): E127–130.

26.   Brown, interview by the author, July 27, 2017.

27.   B. M. Shapiro, H. S. Kingdon, and E. R. Stadtman, "Regulation of Gluta-mine Synthestase, VII. Adenylyl Glutamine Synthetase: A New Form of the Enzyme with Altered Regulatory and Kinetic Properties," *Proceedings of the National Academy of Sciences* 58 (1967): 642–649.

28.   M. L. Yarbrough, Y. Li, L. N. Kinch, N. V. Grishin, H. L. Ball, and K. Orth, "AMPylation of Rho GTPases by Vibrio VopS Disrupts Effector Binding and Downstream Signaling," *Science* 323 (2009): 269–272.

29.   Brown, interview by the author, July 27, 2017.

30.   Brown, interview by the author, July 27, 2017.

31.   Brown, interview by the author, July 27, 2017.

32.   Brown, interview by the author, July 27, 2017.

33.   U. S. Neill and H. A. Rockman, "A Conversation with Robert Lefkowitz, Joseph Goldstein, and Michael Brown," *Journal of Clinical Investigation* 122 (2012): 1586–1587.

34.   Brown, interview by the author, July 27, 2017.

35.   Brown, interview by the author, July 27, 2017.

36.   Brown, interview by the author, July 27, 2017.

37.   Brown, interview by the author, July 27, 2017.

38.   M. S. Brown, A. Segal, and E. R. Stadtman, "Modulation of Glutamine Synthetase: Adenylylation and Deadenylylation is Mediated by Metabol-ic Transformation of P11-Regulatory Protein," *Proceedings of the National Academy of Sciences* 68 (1971): 2949–2953; E. R. Stadtman, A. Ginsburg, W. B. Anderson, A. Segal, M. S. Brown, and J. R. Ciardi, "Regulation of Glutamine Metabolism in *E. coli* by Enzyme Catalyzed Adenylylation and Deadenylylation of Glutamine Synthetase," *Acta Cientfica Venezolana* 22 (1971): R-2–8; and A. Segal, M. B. Brown, and E. R. Stadtman, "Metabolic Regulation of the State of the Adenylylation of Glutamine Synthetase," *Archives of Biochemistry and Biophysics* 161 (1974): 319–327.

CHAPTER 10: HARMONY IN HORMONES

1.   E. H. Starling, "The Chemical Correlation of the Functions of the Body," *Lancet* 166 (1905): 339–341.

2.   P. Valent, B. Groner, and U. Schumacher et al., "Paul Ehrlich (1854–1915) and His Contributions to the Foundation and Birth of Translational Medicine," *Journal of Innate Immunity* 8 (2016): 111–120.

3.   Ehrlich's theory included the notion that the receptors and the bacteria or toxins to which they link fit together like a lock and key. Ehrlich's use of the lock-and-key metaphor was borrowed from its application a few years earlier by the Nobel laureate Emil Fischer in describing the action of en-zymes. According to Fischer's construct, an enzyme must have a specific

three-dimensional configuration that matches up with the site where it exerts its action. F. Bosch and L. Rosich, "The Contributions of Paul Ehrlich to Pharmacology: A Tribute on the Occasion of the Centenary of His Nobel Prize," *Pharmacology* 82 (2008): 171–179.

4. W. M. Fletcher, "John Newport Langley: In Memorium," *Journal of Physiology* 18 (1926): 4–15.

5. J. N. Langley, "On the Physiology of the Salivary Secretion. Part II. On the Mutual Antagonism of Atropin and Pilocarpin, Having Especial Reference to Their Relations in the Sub-Maxillary Gland of the Cat," *Journal of Physiology* 1 (1878): 339–369.

6. J. N. Langley, "On the Reaction of Cells and of Nerve-Endings to Certain Poisons, Chiefly as Regards the Reaction of Striated Muscle to Nicotine and to Curari," *Journal of Physiology* 33 (1905): 374–413.

7. At best they were an odd couple. The German Ehrlich was a moody, competitive, hard-driving, and hard-drinking chain-smoker of strong black cigars. The Englishman Langley was reserved and athletic.

8. H. H. Dale, "Modes of Drug Action: General Introductory Address," *Transactions of the Faraday Society* 39 (1943): 319–322.

9. R. Ahlquist, "Adrenergic Receptors: A Personal and Practical View," *Perspectives in Biology and Medicine* 17 (1973): 119–122.

10. J. Black, "Learning by Doing" (Interview), *Molecular Interventions* 4 (2004): 139–142.

11. J. Roth, "An Oral History Conducted on June 4, 2011, by Michael Chappelle," *The Endocrine Society* (Chevy Chase, MD: The Clark Sawin Library, 2011).

12. I. Pastan, interview by Jason Gart, September 24, 2008, interview no. 1, Oral History Project, NCI Laboratory of Molecular Biology, National Cancer Institute, Bethesda, MD.

13. I. Pastan, "Certain Functions of Isolated Thyroid Cells," *Endocrinology* 68 (1961): 924–931.

14. I. Pastan and J. B. Field, "*In Vitro* Stimulation of Glucose Oxidation in Thyroid by Serotonin," *Endocrinology* 70 (1962): 656–659.

15. Pastan, interview, NCI Oral History Project.

16. I. Turgenev, *Fathers and Sons: A Novel* (New York: Leypoldt and Holt, 1867).

17. J. P. Fitzpatrick, ed., *The Writings of George Washington from the Original Sources, 1745–1799*, 37 vols. (Washington, DC: US Government Printing Office, 1940), vol. 33: 175–176.

18. E. R. Stadtman, T. R. Stadtman, I. Pastan, and L. D. Smith, "*Clostridium barkeri* sp. n," *Journal of Bacteriology* 110 (1972): 758–760.

19. Roth, "An Oral History."

20. Robert Barnes was a wealthy banker in St. Louis. Among his many wise decisions, he loaned money to Adolphus Busch to start a brewery; he

died without heirs in 1892 and left a bequest to build a "modern general hospital for sick and injured persons, without distinction of creed." Barnes Hospital opened in 1914 as the principal teaching hospital of Washington University.

21. Roth, "An Oral History."

22. J. E. Rall, *Solomon A. Berson: 1918–1972. A Biographical Memoir* (Washington, DC: National Academy of Sciences, 1990), 54–70.

23. A. Friedman, "Remembrance: The Berson and Yalow Saga," *Journal of Clinical Endocrinology and Metabolism* 87 (2002): 1925–1928.

24. I. A. Mirsky, "The Etiology of Diabetes in Man," *Recent Progress in Hormone Research* 7 (1952): 437–467.

25. S. A. Berson, R. S. Yalow, A. Bauman, M. A. Rothschild, and K. Newerly, "Insulin-I[131] Metabolism in Human Subjects: Demonstration of Insulin Binding Globulin in the Circulation of Insulin Treated Subjects," *Journal of Clinical Investigation* 35 (1956): 170–190.

26. Clinging tight to this dogma, at two separate scientific journals, outside reviewers of the Berson and Yalow paper recommended its rejection.

27. C. R. Kahn and J. Roth, "Berson, Yalow, and the JCI: The Agony and the Ecstasy," *Journal of Clinical Investigation* 114 (2004): 1051–1054.

28. R. S. Yalow and S. A. Berson, "Immunoassay of Endogenous Plasma Insulin in Man," *Journal of Clinical Investigation* 39 (1960): 157–175.

29. Examples of the range of uses of this technology today include monitoring levels of drugs (legal and illegal), detecting infectious agents such as viruses, and screening for early markers of cancer.

30. She was honored with two other corecipients, Roger Guilleman and Andrew Schally, who studied the release of hormones from the brain.

31. R. S. Yalow, "Radioimmunoassay: A Probe for Fine Structure of Biologic Systems," Nobel Lecture, Stockholm, Sweden, December 8, 1977.

32. Roth, "An Oral History."

33. S. M. Glick, "An Oral History Conducted on April 2, 2000, by Adolph Friedman, M.D.," *The Endocrine Society* (Chevy Chase, MD: The Clark Sawin library, 2009).

34. Roth, "An Oral History."

35. Glick, "An Oral History."

36. Glick, "An Oral History."

37. Glick, "An Oral History."

38. Roth, "An Oral History."

39. Roth, "An Oral History."

40. S. M. Glick, J. Roth, R. S. Yalow, and S. A. Berson, "Immunoassay of Human Growth Hormone in Plasma," *Nature* 199 (1963): 784–787; J. Roth, S. M. Glick, R. S. Yalow, and S. A. Berson, "Hypoglycemia: A Potent Stimulus to Secretion of Growth Hormone," *Science* 140 (1963): 987–988; J. Roth, S. M.

Glick, R. S. Yalow, and S. A. Berson, "Secretion of Human Growth Hormone: Physiologic and Experimental Modification," *Metabolism* 12 (1963): 577–579; and J. Roth, S. M. Glick, R. S. Yalow, and S. A. Berson, "The Influence of Blood Glucose on the Plasma Concentration of Growth Hormone," *Diabetes* 13 (1964): 355–361.

41. Glick, "An Oral History."
42. Roth, "An Oral History."
43. Roth, "An Oral History."
44. Roth, "An Oral History."
45. I. Pastan, J. Roth, and V. Macchia, "Binding of Hormone to Tissue: The First Step in Polypeptide Hormone Action," *Proceedings of the National Academy of Sciences* 56 (1966): 1802–1809.

CHAPTER 11: PRIEST AND PROPHET

1. J. Roth, telephone interviews by Raymond S. Greenberg, May 30 and June 3, 2017.
2. Roth, telephone interviews by the author, May 30 and June 3, 2017.
3. Roth, telephone interviews by the author, May 30 and June 3, 2017.
4. R. J. Lefkowitz, interview by Raymond S. Greenberg, August 16, 2017, Duke University Medical Center, Durham, NC.
5. Lefkowitz, interview by the author, August 16, 2017.
6. Roth, telephone interviews by the author, May 30 and June 3, 2017.
7. Roth, telephone interviews by the author, May 30 and June 3, 2017.
8. Roth, telephone interviews by the author, May 30 and June 3, 2017.
9. The name "pituitary gland" was coined by the sixteenth-century Flemish anatomist Andreas Vesalius, often considered the originator of modern anatomy because of his extensive, carefully described dissections of human cadavers. Vesalius referred to the pituitary in Latin as *glans in quam pituita destillat*, which sounds much more elegant than its English translation: "gland in which slime drips." Given the gland's location, Vesalius assumed that the tiny structure must be the source of the watery mucus lining the adjacent nasal passages. Even after it was shown later that the pituitary had absolutely nothing to do with nasal secretions, the slimy name stuck. For those who prefer a more flattering name, the gland has an alias—"hypophysis," which derives from the Greek *hupophusis*, meaning "attachment underneath."
10. Originally isolated by the biochemist Edward Kendall at the Mayo Clinic and labeled by him as "Compound F."
11. R. S. Yalow, S. M. Glick, J. Roth, S. Roth, and S. A. Berson, "Radioimmunoassay of Human Plasma ACTH," *Journal of Clinical Endocrinology and Metabolism* 24 (1964): 1219–1225.

12. S. A. Berson and R. S. Yalow, "Radioimmunoassay of ACTH in Plasma," *Journal of Clinical Investigation* 47 (1968): 2725–2751.

13. O. D. Taunton, J. Roth, and I. Pastan, "Studies of the Adrenocorticotropic Hormone-Activated Adenyl Cyclase of a Functional Adrenal Tumor," *Journal of Biological Chemistry* 244 (1969): 247–253.

14. Taunton et al., "Studies of the Adrenocorticotropic."

15. Roth, telephone interviews by the author, May 30 and June 3, 2017.

16. J. Roth, "An Oral History Conducted on June 4, 2011, by Michael Chappelle," *The Endocrine Society* (Chevy Chase, MD: The Clark Sawin Library, 2011).

17. Lefkowitz, interview by the author, August 16, 2017.

18. Roth, telephone interviews by the author, May 30 and June 3, 2017.

19. R. J. Lefkowitz, "Nobel Prize in Chemistry," interviewed for the Academy of Achievement, September 13, 2014, San Francisco, achievement.org/achiever/robert-lefkowitz-m-d/#interview.

20. R. J. Lefkowitz, interview by Duke University President Richard Brodhead for *Duke Forward*, February 3, 2015, Duke University, Durham, NC.

21. Lefkowitz, interview by the author, August 16, 2017.

22. R. J. Snyderman, "Introduction of Robert J. Lefkowitz," *Journal of Clinical Investigation* 121 (2011): 4192–4200.

23. "The Chemistry of Discovery," *Duke Magazine* (November 5, 2012) [no author].

24. R. J. Lefkowitz, "The Reluctant Scientist" (Keynote Address), North Carolina School for Science and Mathematics, Durham, NC, March 15, 2013.

25. Lefkowitz, "The Reluctant Scientist."

26. Lefkowitz, interview by the author, August 16, 2017.

27. Lefkowitz, interview by the author, August 16, 2017.

28. Lefkowitz, interview by the author, August 16, 2017.

29. R. J. Lefkowitz, "The Art of Mentoring," interview by Sim B. Sitkin, February 22, 2015, Levin Jewish Community Center, Durham, NC.

30. Lefkowitz, "The Art of Mentoring."

31. I. Pastan, interview by Jason Gart, September 24, 2008, interview no. 1, Oral History Project, NCI Laboratory of Molecular Biology, National Cancer Institute, Bethesda, MD.

32. Pastan, interview, NCI Oral History Project.

33. I. Pastan, telephone interview by Raymond S. Greenberg, May 30, 2017.

34. Roth, "An Oral History."

35. J. Chamberlain, "'Priests and Prophets': Diabetes Branch Alumni Toast Mentors," *NIH Record* 57, no. 4 (February 15, 2005): 579.

36. Roth, telephone interviews by the author, May 30 and June 3, 2017.

37. Lefkowitz, interview by the author, August 16, 2017.

38. Lefkowitz, interview by the author, August 16, 2017.

39. J. Chamberlain, "'Priests and Prophets.'"

40. Lefkowitz, interview by the author, August 16, 2017.

41. Lefkowitz, interview by the author, August 16, 2017.

42. R. J. Lefkowitz, J. Roth, W. Pricer, and I. Pastan, "ACTH Receptors in the Adrenal: Specific Binding of ACTH-125I and Its Relation to Adenylate Cyclase," *Proceedings of the National Academy of Sciences* 65 (1970): 745–752.

43. R. J. Lefkowitz, J. Roth, and I. Pastan, "Effects of Calcium on ACTH Stimulation of the Adrenal: Separation of Hormone Binding from Adenyl Cyclase Activation," *Nature* 228 (1970): 864–866; also R. J. Lefkowitz, J. Roth, and I. Pastan, "Radioreceptor Assay of Adrenocorticotropic Hormone: New Approach to Assay of Polypeptide Hormones in Plasma," *Science* 170 (1970): 633–635.

44. Roth, "An Oral History."

45. Lefkowitz, interview by the author, August 16, 2017.

46. Lefkowitz, interview by the author, August 16, 2017.

47. R. J. Lefkowitz and B. K. Kobilka, interview by Adam Smith, December 6, 2012, Stockholm, for NobelPrize.org and Nobel Media AB, nobelprize.org/prizes/chemistry/2012/lefkowitz/interview; and nobelprize.org/prizes/chemistry/2012/kobilka/interview.

48. Lefkowitz, interview by Duke University President Richard Broadhead, February 3, 2015.

49. Lefkowitz, interview by the author, August 16, 2017.

50. Lefkowitz, interview by the author, August 16, 2017.

51. Lefkowitz, interview by the author, August 16, 2017.

52. Lefkowitz, interview by the author, August 16, 2017.

53. Lefkowitz, interview by the author, August 16, 2017.

54. Lefkowitz, interview by the author, August 16, 2017.

55. Roth, "An Oral History."

56. Roth, "An Oral History."

CHAPTER 12: OVERCOMING REPRESSION

1. With interests in the social side of medicine, Perlman pursued clinical training at Bellevue—an inner-city hospital that served an underprivileged population. A subsequent planned posting in Ghana to conduct public health research was canceled when a civil war broke out there. In this somewhat circuitous fashion and almost by default, Perlman ended up as a trainee at NIH.

2. A physical chemist in the Clinical Endocrinology Branch at the National Institute of Arthritis and Metabolic Diseases, Edelhoch's particular interest was how two thyroid hormones—one with three iodine atoms, the other

with four—are formed. Edelhoch launched these investigations upon arriving at NIH in the late 1950s and continued this line of research until his death in 1986. In all, he produced more than forty papers on this topic and coauthored the sixteenth and seventeenth publications in that forty-paper series on thyroid hormone. In all, Perlman and Edelhoch wrote a half-dozen papers together, all of which focused on protein structure and function.

3. R. L. Perlman, interview by Jason Gart, November 7, 2008, Oral History Project, NCI Laboratory of Molecular Biology, National Cancer Institute, Bethesda, MD.

4. Perlman, interview, NCI Oral History Project.

5. R. S. Makman and E. W. Sutherland, "Adenosine 3',5'-Phosphate in *Escherichia coli,*" *Journal of Biological Chemistry* 240 (1965): 1309–1314.

6. I. Pastan, telephone interview by Raymond S. Greenberg, May 30, 2017.

7. Pastan, telephone interview by the author, May 30, 2017.

8. Pastan, telephone interview by the author, May 30, 2017.

9. F. Jacob, D. Perrin, C. Sanchez, and J. Monod, "Operon: A Group of Genes with the Expression Coordinated by an Operator," *Comptes Rendus Hebdomadaires des Séances de L'Académie des Sciences* 250 (1960): 1727–1729.

10. A. B. Pardee, F. Jacob, and J. Monod, "The Genetic Control and Cytoplasmic Expression of Inducibility in the Synthesis of β-galactosidase in *E. coli,*" *Journal of Molecular Biology* 1 (1959): 165–178.

11. F. Jacob and J. Monod, "Genetic Regulatory Mechanisms in the Synthesis of Proteins," *Journal of Molecular Biology* 3 (1961): 318–356.

12. W. Gilbert and B. Müller-Hill, "Isolation of the Lac Repressor," *Proceedings of the National Academy of Sciences* 56 (1966): 1891–1898.

13. Pastan, telephone interview by the author, May 30, 2017.

14. Pastan, telephone interview by the author, May 30, 2017.

15. Perlman, interview, NCI Oral History Project.

16. Humans use a different enzyme, lactase, to break down lactose into its digestible component parts. The condition of lactose intolerance, characterized by indigestion following consumption of dairy products, can result when the lactase enzyme is deficient. When added to dairy products, beta-galactosidase can break down lactose, thereby diminishing digestive problems for people with lactose intolerance.

17. Perlman, interview, NCI Oral History Project.

18. Perlman, interview, NCI Oral History Project.

19. Perlman, interview, NCI Oral History Project.

20. Perlman, interview, NCI Oral History Project.

21. R. L. Perlman and I. Pastan, "Regulation of β-galactosidase Synthesis in *Escherichia coli* by Cyclic Adenosine 3',5'-Monophosphate," *Journal of Biological Chemistry* 243 (1968): 5420–5427; also I. Pastan and R. L. Perlman, "The Role of the Lac Promoter Locus in the Regulation of β-galactosidase

Synthesis by Cyclic 3',5'-Monophosphate," *Proceedings of the National Academy of Sciences* 61 (1968): 1336–1342.

22. Pastan, telephone interview by the author, May 30, 2017.

23. Pastan, telephone interview by the author, May 30, 2017.

24. H. Varmus, *The Art and Politics of Science* (New York: W. W. Norton & Company, 2009).

25. Varmus, *Art and Politics of Science.*

26. Varmus, *Art and Politics of Science.*

27. Pastan, telephone interview by the author, May 30, 2017.

28. Varmus, *Art and Politics of Science.*

29. A. Jha, "In Conversation with Harold Varmus," *Mosaic: The Science of Life* (London: Wellcome Trust, July 22, 2014).

30. H. R. Bourne, *Paths to Innovation: Discovering Recombinant DNA, Oncogenes, and Prions, in One Medical School, over One Decade* (San Francisco: University of California Medical Humanities Consortium, 2011).

31. Bourne, *Paths to Innovation.*

32. Pastan, telephone interview by the author, May 30, 2017.

33. Varmus, *Art and Politics of Science.*

34. H. Varmus, R. L. Perlman, and I. Pastan, "Regulation of Lac Messenger Ribonucleic Acid Synthesis by Cyclic Adenosine 3',5'-Monophophate and Glucose," *Journal of Biological Chemistry* 245 (1970): 2259–2267.

35. M. Emmer, B. deCrombrugghe, I. Pastan, and R. Perlman, "Cyclic AMP Receptor Protein of *E. coli*: Its Role in the Synthesis of Inducible Enzymes," *Proceedings of the National Academy of Sciences* 66 (1970): 480–487.

36. H. E. Varmus, R. L. Perlman, and I. Pastan, "Regulation of Lac Transcription in *Escherichia coli* by Cyclic Adenosine 3',5'-Monophosphate," *Journal of Biological Chemistry* 245 (1970): 6366–6372.

37. S. Adhya and S. Garges, "How Cyclic AMP and Its Receptor Protein Act in *Escherichia coli*," *Cell* 29 (1982): 287–289.

38. Perlman, interview, NCI Oral History Project.

39. Pastan, telephone interview by the author, May 30, 2017. Pastan found that the offer on the West Coast opened doors of opportunity much closer to home: "I played tennis every Wednesday with a guy named Mort Lipsett, who was an endocrinologist working in the [National] Cancer Institute. I said to Mort one day: 'I can't see you next week. I'm going to look at a job at Stanford.' . . . So, I went to Stanford and I looked at this job—Stanford is beautiful . . . and it was a great job." I. Pastan, interview by Jason Gart, September 24, 2008, interview no. 1, Oral History Project, NCI Laboratory of Molecular Biology, National Cancer Institute, Bethesda, MD.

40. Pastan, interview, NCI Oral History Project. Upon making the transition, Pastan was interested in bringing his collaborator, Perlman, along for the ride. However, Perlman decided that he "would prefer to stay as an

independent investigator [in the National Institute of Arthritis and Metabolic Diseases].... So, I stayed when Ira moved ... I did not see any reason to move if we could continue to work together if we wanted to, even if we were in different Institutes. So that's what we did."

41. Pastan, interview, NCI Oral History Project.

42. Pastan, interview, NCI Oral History Project. See also Perlman, interview, NCI Oral History Project.

43. Although Perlman chose not to move with Pastan to the tenth floor of the Clinical Center, and they continued to work together, it was not long before Perlman began to see greener grass elsewhere. Having spent five productive years at NIH, he was ready for a change, which came the following year when he accepted a faculty position in the Department of Physiology at Harvard.

44. Jha, "In Conversation with Harold Varmus."

45. Jha, "In Conversation with Harold Varmus."

46. Jha, "In Conversation with Harold Varmus."

47. H. Varmus, "How Tumor Virology Evolved into Cancer Biology and Transformed Oncology," *Annual Reviews in Cancer Biology* 1 (2017): 1–18.

48. Bourne, *Paths to Innovation.*

CHAPTER 13: THE TEXAS TWO-STEP

1. A. G. Motulsky (as told to M. C. King), "The Great Adventure of an American Human Geneticist," *Annual Reviews of Genomics and Human Genetics* 17 (2016): 1–15.

2. Motulsky (as told to M. C. King), "The Great Adventure," 1–15.

3. C. Müller, "Angina Pectoris in Hereditary Xanthomatosis," *Archives of Internal Medicine* 64 (1939): 675–700.

4. A. K. Khachadurian, "The Inheritance of Essential Familial Hypercholesterolemia," *American Journal of Medicine* 37 (1964): 402–407.

5. M. F. Boudet, "Nouvelle Recherches Sur La Composition du Serum du Sang Humain," *Annales de Chimie et de Physique* 52 (1833): 337–348.

6. A. Windaus, "Uber der Gehalt Normaler und Atheromatoser Aorten an cholesterol und Cholesterinester," *Zeitschrift für Physiologishe Chemie* 67 (1910): 174.

7. N. Anitschkow and S. Chalatow, "Ueber Experimentelle Cholesterinsteatose und ihre Bedeutung für die Entstehung Einiger Pathologischer Prozesse," *Allgemeine Pathologie und Pathologische Anatomie* 24 (1913): 1–9.

8. J. W. Gofman, L. Rubin, J. P. McGinley, and H. B. Jones, "Hyperlipoproteinemia," *American Journal of Medicine* 17 (1954): 514–520.

9. Gofman et al., "Hyperlipoproteinemia."

10. J. L. Goldstein, W. R. Hazzard, H. G. Schrott, E. L. Bierman, and A. G. Motulsky, "Hyperlipidemia in Coronary Heart Disease. I. Lipid Levels in

500 Survivors of Myocardial Infarction," *Journal of Clinical Investigation* 52 (1973): 1533–1543.

11. J. L. Goldstein, H. G. Schrott, W. R. Hazzard, E. L. Bierman, and A. G. Motulsky, "Hyperlipidemia in Coronary Heart Disease. II. Genetic Analysis of Lipid Levels in 176 Families and Delineation of a New Inherited Disorder, Combined Hyperlipidemia," *Journal of Clinical Investigation* 52 (1973): 1544–1568.

12. J. L. Goldstein, interview by Raymond S. Greenberg, June 5, 2017, University of Texas Southwestern Medical Center, Dallas.

13. D. Linder and S. M. Gartler, "Glucose-6-Phosphate Dehydrogenase Mosaicism: Utilization as a Cell Marker in the Study of Leiomyomas," *Science* 150 (1965): 67–69.

14. S. M. Gartler, "Apparent HeLa Cell Contamination of Human Heteroploid Cell Lines," *Nature* 217 (1968): 750–751.

15. G. P. Jarvik, "2016 Victor A. McKusick Leadership Award Introduction: Stanley Gartler," *American Journal of Human Genetics* 100 (2017): 401–402.

16. Goldstein, interview by the author, June 5, 2017.

17. M. S. Brown, interview by Raymond S. Greenberg, July 27, 2017, University of Texas Southwestern Medical Center, Dallas.

18. Brown, interview by the author, July 27, 2017.

19. One was John Dietschy, who, like Brown, trained as a gastroenterologist. Dietschy came to Dallas in 1963 for a two-year fellowship with Marvin Siperstein. A physician with a PhD in physiology, Siperstein was a leader in the field of cholesterol research. He was known for his work on HMG-CoA reductase, demonstrating how its activity rose or fell in relation to the body's need for cholesterol. M. D. Siperstein and V. M. Fugan, "Feedback Control of Mevalonate Synthesis by Dietary Cholesterol," *Journal of Biological Chemistry* 241 (1966): 602–609. By the time Brown arrived, Siperstein's former trainee, Dietschy, had become a professor, having made important contributions to understanding how cholesterol is absorbed in the diet and manufactured by the liver, as well as the balancing act that goes on between the two sources.

20. M. S. Brown, S. E. Dana, J. M. Dietschy, and M. D. Siperstein, "3-Hydroxy-3-Methylglutaryl Coenzyme A Reductase: Solubilization and Purification of a Cold-Sensitive Microsomal Enzyme," *Journal of Biological Chemistry* 248 (1973): 4731–4738.

21. Brown, interview by the author, July 27, 2017.

22. R. Williams, Joseph Goldstein, and Michael Brown, "Demoting Egos, Promoting Success," *Circulation Research* 106 (2010): 1006–1010.

23. Williams, Goldstein, and Brown, "Demoting Egos, Promoting Success."

24. J. L. Goldstein and M. S. Brown, interview by Adam Smith, December 10, 2012, Stockholm, for NobelPrize.org and Nobel Media AB, nobelprize.org/prizes/medicine/1985/goldstein/interview.

25. Brown, interview by the author, July 27, 2017.
26. Brown, interview by the author, July 27, 2017.
27. Southwestern Research Foundation, *Cholesterol Metabolism: The Work of Drs. Brown and Goldstein* (Dallas: Southwestern Research Foundation, May 4, 2012).
28. Brown, interview by the author, July 27, 2017.
29. J. L. Goldstein and M. S. Brown, "The LDL Receptor," *Arteriosclerosis, Thrombosis, and Vascular Biology* 29 (2009): 431–438.
30. Brown, interview by the author, July 27, 2017.
31. Brown, interview by the author, July 27, 2017.
32. Brown, interview by the author, July 27, 2017.
33. T. E. Starzl, C. W. Putnam, H. P. Chase, and K. A. Porter, "Portacaval Shunt in Hyperlipoproteinaemia," *Lancet* 2 (1973): 940–944.
34. T. E. Starzl, C. W. Putnam, and L. J. Koep, "Portacaval Shunt and Hyperlipidemia," *Archives of Surgery* 113 (1978): 71–74.
35. T. E. Starzl, H. P. Chase, and E. H. Ahrens et al., "Portacaval Shunt in Patients with Familial Hypercholesterolemia," *Annals of Surgery* 198 (1983): 273–283.
36. Southwestern Research Foundation, *Cholesterol Metabolism.*
37. Southwestern Research Foundation, *Cholesterol Metabolism.*
38. Southwestern Research Foundation, *Cholesterol Metabolism.*
39. Brown, interview by the author, July 27, 2017.
40. J. Davignon and M. Roy, "Familial Hypercholesterolemia in French-Canadians: Taking Advantage of the Presence of a 'Founder Effect,'" *American Journal of Cardiology* 72 (1993): 6D–10D.
41. Goldstein, interview by the author, June 5, 2017.
42. Brown, interview by the author, July 27, 2017.
43. J. L. Goldstein and M. S. Brown, "Familial Hypercholesterolemia: Identification of a Defect in the Regulation of 3-Hydroxy-3-Methylglutaryl Coenzyme A Reductase Activity Associated with Overproduction of Cholesterol," *Proceedings of the National Academy of Sciences* 70 (1973): 2804–2808.
44. Goldstein and Brown, "Familial Hypercholesterolemia."
45. Southwestern Research Foundation, *Cholesterol Metabolism.*
46. Southwestern Research Foundation, *Cholesterol Metabolism.*
47. Williams, Goldstein, and Brown, "Demoting Egos, Promoting Success."
48. M. S. Brown, S. E. Dana, and J. L. Goldstein, "Regulation of 3-Hydroxy-3-Methylglutaryl Coenzyme A Reductase Activity in Cultured Human Fibroblasts: Comparison of Cells from a Normal Subject and from a Patient with Homozygous Familial Hypercholesterolemia," *Journal of Biological Chemistry* 249 (1974): 789–796.
49. M. S. Brown and J. L. Goldstein, "Familial Hypercholesterolemia: Defective Binding of Lipoproteins to Cultured Fibroblasts Associated with Impaired Regulation of 3-Hydroxy-3-Methylglutaryl Coenzyme A

Reductase Activity," *Proceedings of the National Academy of Sciences* 71 (1974): 788–792.

50. J. L. Goldstein and M. S. Brown, "Binding and Degradation of Low Density Lipoproteins by Cultured Human Fibroblasts," *Journal of Biological Chemistry* 249 (1974): 5153–5162.

51. N. Kresge, R. D. Simoni, and R. L. Hill, "30 Years of Cholesterol Metabolism: The Work of Michael Brown and Joseph Goldstein," *Journal of Biological Chemistry* 281 (2006): e25–e28.

52. Southwestern Research Foundation, *Cholesterol Metabolism*.

53. Williams, Goldstein, and Brown, "Demoting Egos, Promoting Success."

54. Southwestern Research Foundation, *Cholesterol Metabolism*.

55. Goldstein and Brown, interview by Adam Smith, December 10, 2012.

56. Southwestern Research Foundation, *Cholesterol Metabolism*.

57. Williams, Goldstein, and Brown, "Demoting Egos, Promoting Success."

58. Williams, Goldstein, and Brown, "Demoting Egos, Promoting Success."

59. J. L. Goldstein, S. K. Basu, G. Y. Brunschede, and M. S. Brown, "Release of Low Density Lipoprotein from its Cell Surface Receptor by Sulfated Glycosaminoglycans," *Cell* 7 (1976): 85–95.

60. M. S. Brown, S. E. Dana, and J. L. Goldstein, "Receptor-dependent Hydrolysis of Cholesteryl Esters Contained in Plasma Low Density Lipoprotein," *Proceedings of the National Academy of Sciences* 72 (1975): 2925–2929.

61. R. G. W. Anderson, M. S. Brown, and J. L. Goldstein, "Role of the Coated Endocytic Vesicle in the Uptake of Receptor-Bound Low Density Lipoprotein in Human Fibroblasts," *Cell* 10 (1977): 351–364.

62. W. J. Schneider, U. Beisiegel, J. L. Goldstein, and M. S. Brown, "Purification of the Low Density Lipoprotein Receptor, an Acidic Glycoprotein of 164,000 Molecular Weight," *Journal of Biological Chemistry* 257 (1982): 2664–2673.

63. T. Yamamoto, C. G. Davis, M. S. Brown, W. J. Schneider, M. L. Casey, J. L. Goldstein, and D. W. Russell, "The Human LDL Receptor: A Cysteine-Rich Protein with Multiple Alu Sequences in Its mRNA," *Cell* 39 (1984): 27–38.

64. T. C. Südhof, J. L. Goldstein, M. S. Brown, and D. W. Russell, "The LDL Receptor Gene: A Mosaic of Exons Shared with Different Proteins," *Science* 228 (1985): 815–822.

65. M. S. Brown and J. L. Goldstein, "A Receptor-Mediated Pathway for Cholesterol Homeostasis," *Science* 232 (1986): 34–47.

66. S. Leigh, curator, "LDLR (Low Density Lipoprotein Receptor): Unique Variants in Gene LDLR" (Leiden, Netherlands: Leiden Open Variation Database, Leiden University Medical Center, databases.lovd.nl/shared/variants/LDLR/unique).

67. M. S. Brown, J. R. Faust, and J. L. Goldstein et al., "Induction of 3-Hydroxy-3-Methylglutaryl Coenzyme A Reductase Activity in Human

Fibroblasts Incubated in Compactin (M. L.-236B), a Competitive Inhibitor of the Reductase," *Journal of Biological Chemistry* 253 (1978): 1121–1128.

68. P. T. Kovanen, D. W. Bilheimer, and J. L. Goldstein et al., "Regulatory Role for Hepatic Low Density Lipoprotein Receptors In Vivo in the Dog," *Proceedings of the National Academy of Sciences* 78 (1981): 1194–1198.

69. R. J. Havel, D. B. Hunninghake, and D. R. Illingworth et al., "Lovastatin (Mevinolin) in the Treatment of Heterozygous Familial Hypercholesterolemia: A Multicenter Study," *Annals of Internal Medicine* 107 (1987): 609–615.

70. Lovastatin Study Group II, "Therapeutic Response to Lovastatin (Mevinolin) in Nonfamilial Hypercholesterolemia: A Multicenter Study," *Journal of the American Medical Association* 256 (1986): 2829–2834.

71. Southwestern Research Foundation, *Cholesterol Metabolism.*

72. Southwestern Research Foundation, *Cholesterol Metabolism.*

73. J. G. Hanna, "A Nobel Prize: Dr. Joseph Goldstein, '63, Honored for Medical Research," *Alumni Magazine of Washington and Lee* 60 (1985): 2–7.

74. Southwestern Research Foundation, *Cholesterol Metabolism.*

CHAPTER 14: ADRENALINE RUSH

1. R. J. Lefkowitz, "A Tale of Two Callings," *Journal of Clinical Investigation* 121 (2011): 4201–4203.

2. R. P. Ahlquist, "Adrenergic Receptors: A Personal and Practical View," *Perspectives in Biology and Medicine* 17 (1973): 199–122.

3. Lefkowitz, "A Tale of Two Callings."

4. "The Chemistry of Discovery," *Duke Magazine* (November–December 2012) [no author].

5. "The Chemistry of Discovery" [no author].

6. D. Kroll, "Duke's Bob Lefkowitz Wins the Nobel Prize: At Last, a Nice Guy Finishes First," *Indy Week*, January 9, 2013.

7. R. J. Lefkowitz, "A Serendipitous Scientist," *Annual Reviews of Pharmacology and Toxicology* 58 (2018): 17–32.

8. Kroll, "Duke's Bob Lefkowitz Wins the Nobel Prize."

9. Kroll, "Duke's Bob Lefkowitz Wins the Nobel Prize."

10. Kroll, "Duke's Bob Lefkowitz Wins the Nobel Prize."

11. R. J. Lefkowitz, "A Serendipitous Scientist."

12. M. G. Caron and R. J. Lefkowitz, "Solubilization and Characterization of the Beta-Adrenergic Receptor Binding Sites in Frog Erythrocytes," *Journal of Biological Chemistry* 251 (1976): 2374–2384.

13. J. L. Benovic, R. G. L. Schorr, and M. G. Caron et al., "The Mammalian Beta2-Adrenergic Receptor: Purification and Characterization," *Biochemistry* 23 (1984): 4510–4518.

14. J. W. Regan, H. Nakata, and R. M. DeMarinis et al., "Purification and Characterization of the Human Platelet Alpha 2-Adrenergic Receptor," *Journal of Biological Chemistry* 261 (1986): 3894–3900.

15. J. W. Lomasney, M. F. Leeb-Lundberg, and S. Cotecchia et al., "Mammalian Alpha 1—Adrenergic Receptor: Purification and Characterization of the Native Receptor Ligand Binding Unit," *Journal of Biological Chemistry* 261 (1986): 7710–7716.

16. R. A. Cerione, B. Strulovici, and J. L. Benovic et al., "Reconstitution of beta-Adrenergic Receptors in Lipid Vesicles: Affinity Chromatography-Purified Receptors Confer Catecholamine Responsiveness on a Heterologous Adenylate Cyclase System," *Proceedings of the National Academy of Sciences* 80 (1983): 4899–4903.

17. R. J. Lefkowitz, "Inspiring the Next Generation of Physician-Scientists," *Journal of Clinical Investigation* 125 (2015): 2905–2907.

18. R. A. Dixon, B. K. Kobilka, and D. J. Strader et al., "Cloning of the Gene and cDNA for Mammalian Beta-Adrenergic Receptor and Homology with Rhodopsin," *Nature* 321 (1986): 75–79.

19. R. J. Lefkowitz, interview by Duke University President Richard Brodhead, November 2, 2012, Duke University, Durham, NC.

20. M. Rodbell, L. Birnbaumer, and S. L. Pohl et al., "The Glucagon-Sensitive Adenyl Cyclase System in Plasma Membranes of Rat Liver. V. An Obligatory Role of Guanyl Nucleotides in Glucagon Action," *Journal of Biological Chemistry* 246 (1971): 1877–1882.

21. C. Londos, Y. Salomon, and M. C. Lin et al., "5'-Guanylylimidodiphosphate: A Potent Activator of Adenyl Cyclase Systems in Eukaryotic Cells," *Proceedings of the National Academy of Sciences* 71 (1974): 3087–3090.

22. E. M. Ross and A. G. Gilman, "Resolution of Some Components of Adenylate Cyclase Necessary for Catalytic Activity," *Journal of Biological Chemistry* 252 (1977): 6966–6969.

23. B. K. K. Fung, J. B. Hurley, and L. Stryer, "Flow of Information in the Light-Triggered Cyclic Nucleotide Cascade of Vision," *Proceedings of the National Academy of Sciences* 78 (1981): 152–156.

24. D. R. Manning and A. G. Gilman, "The Regulatory Components of Adenylate Cyclase and Transducin: A Family of Structurally Homologous Guanine Nucleotide-Binding Proteins," *Journal of Biological Chemistry* 258 (1983): 7059–7063.

25. Dixon et al., "Cloning of the Gene and cDNA."

26. T. Frielle, S. Collins, and K. W. Daniel et al., "Cloning of the cDNA for the Human Beta 1-Adrenergic Receptor," *Proceedings of the National Academy of Sciences* 84 (1987): 7920–7924.

27. B. K. Kobilka, H. Matsui, and T. S. Kobilka et al., "Cloning, Sequencing, and Expression of the Gene Coding for the Human Platelet Alpha 2-Adrenergic Receptor," *Science* 238 (1987): 650–656.

28. S. Cotecchia, D. A. Schwinn, and R. R. Randall et al., "Molecular Cloning and Expression of the cDNA for the Hamster Alpha 1-Adrenergic Receptor," *Proceedings of the National Academy of Sciences* 85 (1988): 7159–7163.

29. Other orphan receptors are less fortunate—the largest set of which pertain to odor perception, accounting for nearly half of all G protein–coupled receptors, most of which do not have an identified messenger. Among sensory receptors, greater success in assigning functions has been achieved with those associated with taste. R. J. Lefkowitz, "Seven Transmembrane Receptors—A Brief Personal Perspective," *Biochimica et Biophysica Acta* 1768 (2007): 748–755.

30. R. J. Lefkowitz, "A Brief History of G-Protein Coupled Receptors (Nobel Lecture)," *Angewandte Chemie International Edition* 52 (2013): 6367–6378.

31. J. M. Stadel, P. Nambi, and T. N. Lavin et al., "Catecholamine-Induced Desensitization of Turkey Erythrocyte Adenylate Cyclase," *Journal of Biological Chemistry* 257 (1982): 9242–9245.

32. J. L. Benovic, P. H. Strasser, and M. G. Caron et al., "Beta-Adrenergic Receptor Kinase: Identification of a Novel Protein Kinase That Phosphorylates the Agonist-Occupied Form of the Receptor," *Proceedings of the National Academy of Sciences* 83 (1986): 2797–2801.

33. W. Lorenz, K. Inglese, and J. J. Palczewski et al., "The Receptor Kinase Family: Primary Structure of Rhodopsin Kinase Reveals Similarities to the Beta-Adrenergic Receptor Kinase," *Proceedings of the National Academy of Sciences* 88 (1991): 8715–8719.

34. M. J. Lohse, J. L. Benovic, and J. Codina et al., "Beta-arrestin: A Protein That Regulates Beta-Adrenergic Receptor Function," *Science* 248 (1990): 1547–1550.

35. Kroll, "Duke's Bob Lefkowitz Wins the Nobel Prize."

36. Kroll, "Duke's Bob Lefkowitz Wins the Nobel Prize."

37. A. Pang, "This Is New York: Robert Lefkowitz on Winning a Nobel Prize," *The Epoch Times*, October 9, 2013.

38. J. Shamp, "Nobel Calling? Lefkowitz Finally Gets It," North Carolina Biotechnology Center. Story reprinted from *Durham Herald-Sun*, October 19, 2003.

39. "An Interview with Robert J. Lefkowitz," *Trends in Pharmaceutical Sciences* 33 (2012): 51–52 [no author].

40. R. Williams, "Robert Lefkowitz: Godfather of the G Protein–Coupled Receptors," *Circulation Research* 106 (2010): 812–814.

41. Lefkowitz, "Inspiring the Next Generation."

42. Lefkowitz, "Inspiring the Next Generation."

43. Lefkowitz, "Inspiring the Next Generation."

44. Lefkowitz, "Inspiring the Next Generation."

45. Williams, "Robert Lefkowitz: Godfather."

46. E. C. Head, "An Interview with Bob Lefkowitz, Five Years after His Nobel," *Duke Today*, November 9, 2017.

CHAPTER 15: INFECTIOUS ENTHUSIASM

1. H. M. Temin, "The Effects of Actinomycin D on Growth of Rous Sarcoma Virus in vitro," *Virology* 20 (1963): 577–582.
2. S. Mukherjee, *The Emperor of All Maladies: A Biography of Cancer* (New York: Scribner, 2010), 352–354.
3. H. M. Temin and S. Mizutani, "Viral RNA-dependent DNA Polymerase: RNA-dependent DNA Polymerase in Virions of Rous Sarcoma Virus," *Nature* 226 (1970): 1211–1213; also D. Baltimore, "Viral RNA-dependent DNA Polymerase: RNA-dependent DNA Polymerase in Virions of RNA Tumor Viruses," *Nature* 226 (1970): 1209–1211.
4. H. R. Bourne, *Paths to Innovation: Discovering Recombinant DNA, Oncogenes, and Prions, in One Medical School, Over a Decade* (San Francisco: University of California Medical Humanities Consortium, 2011).
5. G. S. Martin, "Rous Sarcoma Virus: A Function Required for the Maintenance of the Transformed State," *Nature* 227 (1970): 1021–1023.
6. H. Varmus, *The Art and Politics of Science* (New York: W. W. Norton & Company, 2009).
7. J. M. Bishop, *How to Win the Nobel Prize: An Unexpected Life in Science* (Cambridge, MA: Harvard University Press, 2003).
8. Bishop, *How to Win the Nobel Prize.*
9. He was told many years later that his letter had been posted in the dean's office, where it served as light entertainment for a staff who mostly dealt with applicants swooning to be admitted to Harvard.
10. Bishop, *How to Win the Nobel Prize.*
11. The first step toward addressing that was taken after his second year. Bishop took a leave of absence to work in the Pathology Department of Massachusetts General Hospital.
12. Pfefferkorn was known to generations of students, first at Harvard and then at Dartmouth, and introduced Bishop to what would become his lifelong pursuit: the study of viruses.
13. Bishop, *How to Win the Nobel Prize.*
14. Bourne, *Paths to Innovation.* Unfortunately, few things in life are more inflexible than medical school curricula. Much to his credit as a negotiator, however, Bishop was able to strike an unprecedented compromise: if he would complete the required two-month clerkship in internal medicine, he would be excused from the other courses in order to pursue his research. Bishop was sufficiently impressive on the internal medicine rotation at MGH that he was accepted into the highly competitive internship and residency there.
15. Bishop, *How to Win the Nobel Prize.*

16. The two scientists also shared a passion for music and developed a personal chemistry that bridged the fourteen-year gap in their ages and experience. Bishop described their typical interaction: "Leon sat at his desk, he read, and he would discuss my day with me. I was semi-independent because I was doing stuff he had never done. Leon was definitely an alter ego, a sage advisor and a pretty good critic." Bishop, *How to Win the Nobel Prize*. The research that Bishop undertook was to investigate the replication of poliovirus.

17. Bishop, *How to Win the Nobel Prize*.

18. M. Drake and R. Schindler, "Interview with Nobel Laureates Harold Varmus, M.D., and J. Michael Bishop, M.D.," *Bulletin—Alumni Faculty Association, School of Medicine, University of California, San Francisco* (Spring 1990): 6–9. With Levintow's advocacy, Bishop received institutional support when he needed bridge funding for trainees. He remembered the feeling of security that this benevolence engendered: "I had people who clearly thought I belonged here and wanted to keep me here and that's all that mattered." Bourne, *Paths to Innovation*.

19. Drake and Schindler, "Interview with Nobel Laureates Harold Varmus, M.D., and J. Michael Bishop, M.D."

20. P. Rous, "A Transmissible Avian Neoplasm (Sarcoma of the Common Fowl)," *Journal of Experimental Medicine* 12 (1910): 696–705.

21. Rous, "A Transmissible Avian Neoplasm."

22. P. Rous, "A Sarcoma of the Fowl Transmissible by an Agent Separable from the Tumor Cells," *Journal of Experimental Medicine* 13 (1911): 397–411.

23. The outbreak of World War I redirected Rous's attention to work on blood transfusions. Rous later returned to the study of cancer causation, demonstrating that benign, virally mediated warts of rabbits could be induced to become malignant.

24. P. Rous, "The Challenge to Man of the Neoplastic Cell," Nobel Lecture, December 13, 1966, in *Nobel Lectures, Physiology or Medicine, 1963–1970* (Singapore: World Scientific Publishing Company, 1999), 220–231.

25. H. Varmus, "How Tumor Virology Evolved into Cancer Biology and Transformed Oncology," *Annual Reviews of Cancer Biology* 1 (2017): 1–18.

26. P. H. Duesberg and P. K. Vogt, "Differences Between the Ribonucleic Acids of Transforming and Nontransforming Avian Tumor Viruses," *Proceedings of the National Academy of Sciences* 67 (1970): 1673–1680.

27. D. Stehelin, R. V. Guntaka, H. E. Varmus, and J. M. Bishop, "Purification of DNA Complementary to Nucleotide Sequences Required for Neoplastic Transformation of Fibroblasts by Avian Sarcoma Virus," *Journal of Molecular Biology* 101 (1976): 349–365.

28. Bourne, *Paths to Innovation*.

29. Bishop, *How to Win the Nobel Prize*.

30. D. Stehelin, H. E. Varmus, J. M. Bishop, and P. K. Vogt, "DNA Related to the Transforming Gene(s) of Rous Sarcoma Virus Is Present in Normal Avian DNA," *Nature* 260 (1976): 170–173.

31. Bourne, *Paths to Innovation.*

32. D. H. Spector, H. E. Varmus, and J. M. Bishop, "Nucleotide Sequences Related to the Transforming Gene of Avian Sarcoma Virus are Present in the DNA of Uninfected Vertebrates," *Proceedings of the National Academy of Sciences* 75 (1978): 4102–4106.

33. J. M. Bishop, interview by Peter Sylwan, May 11, 2004, Stockholm, for Nobel Media AB, nobelprize.org/prizes/medicine/1989/bishop/interview.

34. Bishop, *How to Win the Nobel Prize.*

35. J. S. Brugge and R. L. Erikson, "Identification of a Transformation-Specific Antigen Induced by an Avian Sarcoma Virus," *Nature* 269 (1977): 346–348.

36. M. S. Collett and R. L. Erikson, "Protein Kinase Activity Associated with the Avian Sarcoma Virus src Gene Product," *Proceedings of the National Academy of Sciences* 75 (1978): 2021–2024.

37. A. D. Levinson, H. Opperman, L. Levintow, H. E. Varmus, and J. M. Bishop, "Evidence That the Transforming Gene of Avian Sarcoma Virus Encodes a Protein Kinase Associated with a Phosphoprotein," *Cell* 15 (1978): 561–572.

38. D. Sheiness, L. Fanshier, and J. M. Bishop, "Identification of Nucleotide Sequences Which May Encode the Oncogenic Capacity of Avian Retrovirus M. C.29," *Journal of Virology* 28 (1978): 600–610.

39. D. Sheiness and J. M. Bishop, "DNA and RNA from Uninfected Vertebrate Cells Contain Nucleotide Sequences Related to the Putative Transforming Gene of Avian Myelocytomatosis Virus," *Journal of Virology* 31 (1979): 514–521.

40. Varmus, "How Tumor Virology Evolved."

41. Drake and Schindler, "Interview with Nobel Laureates Harold Varmus, M.D., and J. Michael Bishop, M.D."

42. Varmus, *Art and Politics of Science.*

43. Bishop, *How to Win the Nobel Prize.*

44. Varmus, *Art and Politics of Science.*

45. Bourne, *Paths to Innovation.*

46. Varmus, *Art and Politics of Science.*

47. Bourne, *Paths to Innovation.*

48. Bourne, *Paths to Innovation.*

49. Varmus, *Art and Politics of Science.*

50. Varmus, *Art and Politics of Science.*

EPILOGUE

1. M. Perutz, "The Medical Research Council Laboratory of Molecular Biology," July 1, 1997, nobelprize.org.

2. S. Connor, "Inside the Nobel Prize Factory," *The Independent*, October 12, 2002.

3. Perutz, "The Medical Research Council Laboratory."

4. V. Raper, "A Nobel Prize-Winning Culture," *Science* 333 (July 8, 2011): 131, sciencemag.org.

5. Connor, "Inside the Nobel Prize Factory."

6. W. Bynum, "What Makes a Great Lab?" *Nature* 490 (2012): 31–32.

7. J. B. Wyngaarden, "The Clinical Investigator as an Endangered Species," *New England Journal of Medicine* 301 (1979): 1254–1259.

8. J. L. Goldstein, "On the Origin and Prevention of PAIDS (Paralyzed Academic Investigator's Disease Syndrome)," *Journal of Clinical Investigation* 78 (1986): 848–854.

9. J. L. Goldstein and M. S. Brown, "The Clinical Investigator: Bewitched, Bothered, and Bewildered—But Still Beloved," *Journal of Clinical Investigation* 99 (1997): 2803–2812.

10. H. H. Garrison and A. M. Deschamps, "Physician Scientists: Assessing the Workforce," *Federation of American Societies of Experimental Biology* (December 11, 2013).

11. R. E. McKinney, "The Daunting Career of the Physician-Investigator," *Academic Medicine* 92 (2017): 1368–1370.

12. D. Pratt, "What Makes a Nobel Laureate?" *Los Angeles Times*, October 9, 2013.

13. R. J. Lefkowitz, "A Serendipitous Scientist," *Annual Reviews of Pharmacology and Toxicology* 58 (2018): 17–32.

14. M. S. Brown, "How to Win a Nobel Prize—Nine Simple Steps," *TEDx*, November 7, 2014, Dallas.

15. J. L. Goldstein and M. S. Brown, "What Should You Look for in a Mentor?" *Nobel Inspiration Initiative* (Cambridge, UK, October 2014).

16. J. L. Goldstein and M. S. Brown, "What Did Your Early Mentors Teach You?" *Nobel Inspiration Initiative* (Cambridge, UK, October 2014).

17. R. J. Lefkowitz, interview by Raymond S. Greenberg, August 16, 2017, Duke University Medical Center, Durham, NC.

18. J. Roth, telephone interview by Raymond S. Greenberg, May 30, 2017.

19. H. Varmus, interview by Raymond S. Greenberg, October 4, 2017, Weill Cornell Medical College, New York, NY.

20. T. Veblen, "The Intellectual Preeminence of Jews in Modern Europe," *Political Science Quarterly* 29 (1919): 33–43.

21. G. Cochran, J. Hardy, and H. Harpending, "Natural History of Ashkenazi Intelligence," *Journal of Biosocial Science* 38 (2006): 659–693.

22. Lefkowitz, interview by the author, August 16, 2017.

23. R. B. Ferguson, "How Jews Became Smart: Anti-'Natural History of Ashkenazi Intelligence,'" Department of Sociology and Anthropology, Rutgers University, Newark, NJ, 1–48.

24. Lefkowitz, interview by the author, August 16, 2017.

25. N. J. Efron, *Judaism and Science: A Historical Introduction* (Westport, CT: Greenwood Press, 2007).

26. M. S. Brown, interview by Raymond S. Greenberg, July 27, 2017, University of Texas Southwestern Medical Center, Dallas.

27. P. Burstein, "Jewish Educational and Economic Success in the United States: A Search for Explanations," *Sociological Perspectives* 50 (2007): 209–228.

28. Roth, telephone interview by the author, May 30, 2017.

29. Roth, telephone interview by the author, May 30, 2017.

30. C. V. Harding, M. H. Akaba, and O. S. Anderson, "History and Outcomes of 50 Years of Physician-Scientist Training in Medical Scientist Training Programs," *Academic Medicine* 92 (2017): 1390–1398.

BIBLIOGRAPHY

INTERVIEWS
PERSONAL INTERVIEWS BY THE AUTHOR

Boat, T. F. Telephone interview by Raymond S. Greenberg, June 27, 2017.

Buja, L. M. Telephone interview by Raymond S. Greenberg, June 7, 2017.

Brown, M. S. Interview by Raymond S. Greenberg, July 27, 2017. University of Texas Southwestern Medical Center, Dallas.

Caskey, C. T. Telephone interview by Raymond S. Greenberg, June 2, 2017.

DeLong, M. R. Telephone interview by Raymond S. Greenberg, July 19, 2017.

Goldstein, J. L. Interview by Raymond S. Greenberg, June 5, 2017. University of Texas Southwestern Medical Center, Dallas.

Lefkowitz, R. J. Interview by Raymond S. Greenberg, August 16, 2017. Duke University Medical Center, Durham, NC.

———. Telephone interview by Raymond S. Greenberg, October 9, 2017.

Lovejoy, W. Telephone interview by Raymond S. Greenberg, October 20, 2017.

Pastan, I. Telephone interview by Raymond S. Greenberg, May 30, 2017.

Roth, J. Telephone interviews by Raymond S. Greenberg, May 30 and June 3, 2017.

Schechter, A. Interview by Raymond S. Greenberg, May 3, 2017. National Institutes of Health, Bethesda, MD.

Varmus, H. Interview by Raymond S. Greenberg, October 4, 2017. Weill Cornell Medical Center, New York, NY.

THIRD-PARTY INTERVIEWS AND ORAL HISTORIES

Axelrod, J. Interview by Bernhard Witkop, November 25, 2003. National Institutes of Health, Bethesda, MD.

Caskey, C. T. Interview by Ruth Roy Harris, 1995. National Institutes of Health, Bethesda, MD.

Fauci, A. S. Interview by Victoria A. Harden, March 7, 1989. Office of History, National Institutes of Health, Bethesda, MD.

Fauci, A. S. Interview by Melissa K. Klein, July 16, 1998. Office of History, National Institutes of Health, Bethesda, MD.

Fredrickson, D. S. Interview by Melissa K. Klein, July 8, 1998. Office of History, National Institutes of Health, Bethesda, MD.

Gallo, R. Interview by Sandeep Khot, August 7, 2001. National Institutes of Health, Bethesda, MD.

Kimball, H. R. Interview by Melissa K. Klein, July 16, 1997. Office of History, National Institutes of Health, Bethesda, MD.

Kimball, H. R. Telephone interview by Melissa K. Klein, July 16, 1997. Philadelphia.

Laster, L., and R. Laster. Interview by Joan Ash, March 5, 1999. Oregon Health and Science University, Portland.

Lefkowitz, R. J. "The Art of Mentoring." Interview by Sim B. Sitkin, February 22, 2015. Levin Jewish Community Center, Durham, NC.

Lefkowitz, R. J. Interview by Duke University President Richard Brodhead, November 2, 2012. Duke University, Durham, NC.

Lefkowitz, R. J. Interview by Duke University President Richard Brodhead for *Duke Forward*, February 3, 2015. Duke University, Durham, NC.

Metzger, H. Interview by Sandeep Khot, July 30, 2001. National Institutes of Health, Bethesda, MD.

Metzger, H. Interview by Melissa K. Klein, June 10, 1998. Office of History, National Institutes of Health, Bethesda, MD.

Nirenberg, M. Interviews by Ruth Roy Harris between September 20, 1995, and January 24, 1996. National Institutes of Health, Bethesda, MD [2008] ("Harris Interviews").

Pastan, I. Interview by Jason Gart, September 24, 2008. Interview no. 1, Oral History Project, NCI Laboratory of Molecular Biology, National Cancer Institute, Bethesda, MD.

Perlman, R. L. Interview by Jason Gart, November 7, 2008. Oral History Project, NCI Laboratory of Molecular Biology, National Cancer Institute, Bethesda, MD.

Rosen, S. Interview by Melissa K. Klein, July 23, 1997. National Institutes of Health, Bethesda, MD.

Schechter, A. Interview by Sandeep Khot, July 23, 2001. National Institutes of Health, Bethesda, MD.

Scolnick, E. Interview by Gretchen A. Case, June 24, 1998. Oral History Project, NCI Laboratory of Molecular Biology, Merck Laboratories, West Point, PA, and Bethesda, MD.

Stadtman, E. R. An Oral History Conducted on January 23, 2001, by Buhm Soon Park [interview no. 1]. National Institutes of Health, Bethesda, MD, 2001.

Stadtman, E. R. An Oral History Conducted on February 6, 2001, by Buhm Soon Park [interview no. 2]. National Institutes of Health, Bethesda, MD, 2001.

Stadtman, E. R. An Oral History Conducted on February 13, 2001, by Buhm Soon Park [interview no. 3]. National Institutes of Health, Bethesda, MD, 2001.

OTHER PUBLISHED INTERVIEWS

Bishop, J. M. Interview by Peter Sylwan, May 11, 2004. Stockholm, for Nobel-Prize.org and Nobel Media AB. nobelprize.org/prizes/medicine/1989/bishop/interview.

Black, J. "Learning by Doing." Interview. *Molecular Interventions* 4 (2004): 139–142.

[Varmus, H., and M. Bishop.] Drake, M., and R. Schindler. "Interview with Nobel Laureates Harold Varmus, M.D., and J. Michael Bishop, M.D." *Bulletin— Alumni Faculty Association, School of Medicine, University of California, San Francisco* (Spring 1990): 6–9.

Glick, S. M. "An Oral History Conducted on April 2, 2000, by Adolph Friedman, M.D." *The Endocrine Society*. Chevy Chase, MD: The Clark Sawin library, 2009.

Goldstein, J. "Retiring Editor Interviews Bernard Baruch." *The Boll Weevil* (Kingstree High School, Kingstree, SC) 271 (February 28, 1958): 1.

Goldstein, J. L., and M. S. Brown. Interview by Adam Smith, December 10, 2012. Stockholm, for NobelPrize.org and Nobel Media AB. nobelprize.org/prizes/medicine/1985/goldstein/interview.

Jha, A. "In Conversation with Harold Varmus." *Mosaic: The Science of Life*. London: Wellcome Trust, July 22, 2014.

[Leder, P.] Mukhopadhyay, R. "A 'Mad Race to the Finish': A Conversation with Philip Leder on the Genetic Code Experiment That He Began 50 Years Ago." *American Society for Biochemistry and Molecular Biology Today* (February 2012).

Lefkowitz, R. J. "Nobel Prize in Chemistry." Interviewed for the Academy of Achievement, September 13, 2014, San Francisco. achievement.org/achiever/robert-lefkowitz-m-d/#interview.

[Lefkowitz, R. J.] Head, E. C. "An Interview with Bob Lefkowitz, Five Years after His Nobel." *Duke Today,* November 9, 2017.

[Lefkowitz, R. J.] "An Interview with Robert J. Lefkowitz." *Trends in Pharmaceutical Sciences* 33 (2012): 51–52 [no author].

[Lefkowitz, R., J. Goldstein, and M. Brown.] Neill, U. S., and H. A. Rockman. "A Conversation with Robert Lefkowitz, Joseph Goldstein, and Michael Brown." *Journal of Clinical Investigation* 122 (2012): 1586–1587.

Lefkowitz, R. J., and B. K. Kobilka. Interview by Adam Smith, December 6, 2012. Stockholm, for NobelPrize.org and Nobel Media AB. nobelprize.org/prizes/chemistry/2012/lefkowitz/interview; and nobelprize.org/prizes/chemistry/2012/kobilka/interview.

Nirenberg, M. *A Conversation with Dr. Marshall Nirenberg, Summer 2009.* Bethesda, MD: Office of the Director, National Institutes of Health, 2009.

Roth, J. "An Oral History Conducted on June 4, 2011, by Michael Chappelle." *The Endocrine Society.* Chevy Chase, MD: The Clark Sawin Library, 2011.

Scolnick, E. Interview by Franklin H. Portugal, December 11, 2012. Quoted in Portugal, *The Least Likely Man: Marshall Nirenberg and the Discovery of the Genetic Code.* Cambridge, MA: MIT Press, 2015.

[Vagelos, R.] Marks, A. "A Conversation with P. Roy Vagelos." *Annual Reviews Conversations.* Palo Alto, CA: Annual Reviews, 2011.

[Vagelos, R.] Neill, U. S. "A Conversation with Roy Vagelos." *Journal of Clinical Investigation* 124 (2014): 2291–2292.

GOVERNMENT PUBLICATIONS AND DOCUMENTS

Berger, C., ed., and J. S. Ballard et al. *The United States Air Force in Southeast Asia, 1961–1973: An Illustrated Account* (Washington, DC: Office of Air Force History, 1977.

Cowdrey, A. E. *The Medic's War: United States Army in the Korean War.* Washington, DC: United States Army Center of Military History, 1987.

Fitzpatrick, J. P., ed. *The Writings of George Washington from the Original Sources, 1745–1799.* 37 vols. Washington, DC: US Government Printing Office, 1940, vol. 33: 175–176.

Holmes, J. G., H. W. Marean, N. P. Neill, A. S. Root, A. T. Sweet, and W. E. McLendon. *Soil Survey of the San Bernardino Valley, California.* Washington, DC: US Department of Agriculture, Government Printing Office, 1905.

Kennedy, J. F. "Remarks at a Dinner Honoring Nobel Prize Winners of the Western Hemisphere." April 29, 1962. In *American Presidency Project,* ed. G. Peters and J. T. Woolley. Santa Barbara: University of California, Santa Barbara, n.d.

Klein, M. K. *The Legacy of the "Yellow Berets": The Vietnam War, the Doctor Draft, and the NIH Associate Training Program* (Manuscript). Bethesda, MD: NIH History Office, National Institutes of Health, 1998, 1–33.

McNees, P. *A Brief History of the Clinical Center: Selections from Building Ten at Fifty.* Bethesda, MD: National Institutes of Health, 2003.

National Commission for the Protection of Human Subjects of Biomedical and Behavioral Research. *National Commission for the Protection of Human Subjects of Biomedical and Behavioral Research: The Belmont Report.* Washington, DC: Government Printing Office, 1978.

National Institutes of Health. *Clinical Center 50th Anniversary Celebration: Celebrating 50 Years of Clinical Research.* Bethesda, MD: National Institutes of Health, July 9, 2003.

———. *NIH Factbook: Guide to National Institutes of Health Programs and Activities*, 1st ed. Chicago: Marquis Academic Media, 1976.

———, Clinical and Professional Education Branch. *Appointment of Associateships for 1967 at the National Institutes of Health* (Public Health Reports) 80 (1965): 370–371.

———, Office of Research Information. "News from NIH: New Class of 101 New Physicians Join NIH Research Training Programs." Bethesda, MD: National Institutes of Health, July 1963.

Public Papers of the Presidents of the United States: Lyndon B. Johnson, 1965. Washington, DC: Government Printing Office, 1965, Book 2.

Public Papers of the Presidents of the United States: Lyndon B. Johnson, 1967. Washington, DC: Government Printing Office, 1968, Book 2, 1018.

Public Papers of the Presidents of the United States: Lyndon B. Johnson, 1968–69. Washington, DC: Government Printing Office, 1970, Book 1.

Thomason, P. *Historic Resources of Kingstree: Partial Inventory: Historic and Architectural Properties.* Washington, DC: National Register of Historic Places Inventory—Nomination Form, US Department of the Interior, January 1, 1981.

United States Congress. Tonkin Gulf Resolution, Publ. Law No. 88-408, 78 Stat. 384, 88th Cong. (August 7, 1964). General Records of the United States Government, Record Group II, National Archives.

———. Public Laws Enacted during the Second Session of the Eighty-First Congress of the United States, 1950, Chapter 939, 826–828. loc.gov/law/help/statutes-at-large/81st-congress.php.

United States House of Representatives. *Concurrent Resolution 175: Code of Ethics for Government Service*, 72 Stat. B12. Washington, DC: United States Congress, July 11, 1958.

US Department of Commerce, Bureau of the Census. *Consumer Income: Income in 1968 of Families and Persons in the United States* (December 23, 1969): Series P-60, No. 66, Table 6, 21.

———. *Population Characteristics: Educational Attainment in the United States: March 1968—Detailed Tables.* Washington, DC: US Department of Commerce, Bureau of the Census, April 28, 1969. Series P-20, No. 182, Table 1.

———. *Statistical Abstract of the United States: 1977,* 98th ed. Washington, DC: US Department of Commerce, Bureau of the Census, 1977.

———. *Vietnam Conflict—U.S. Military Forces in Vietnam and Casualties Incurred: 1961 to 1972.* Table 590. In *Statistical Abstract of the United States, 1977.* Washington, DC: US Department of Commerce, Bureau of the Census, 1980.

US Department of Defense, Defense Manpower Data Center, Office of the Secretary of Defense. *Vietnam Conflict Extract Data File.* Washington, DC: National Archives and Record Administration, April 2008.

———, Office of the Assistant Secretary of Defense (Health and Medical). *Information Bulletin: Armed Forces Reserve Medical Officer Commissioning and Residency Consideration Program.* Washington, DC: US Government Printing Office, 1959, 1–10.

———, Office of the Historian. *Department of Defense: Foreign Relations of the United States, 1964–1968.* Vol. 27, Mainland Southeast Asia, no. 53.

US Department of Health, Education, and Welfare, National Center for Health Statistics. *Vital Statistics of the United States, 1967,* vol. II—Mortality, Part A. Washington, DC: US Department of Health, Education, and Welfare, 1969, Table 1-25, 1-100-1.

———, Office of Information, National Institutes of Health. *The National Institutes of Health Almanac.* Washington, DC: US Department of Health, Education, and Welfare, 1970.

US Department of Labor, Bureau of Labor Statistics. *Employment and Earnings and Monthly Reports of the Labor Force* 15 (July 1968). Table A-12, 28.

Villard, E. *The 1968 Tet Offensive Battles of Quang Tri City and Hue.* Fort McNair, Washington, DC: US Army Center of Military History, 2008.

ARTICLES & ESSAYS

"213th Commencement Week Events Get Underway This Week." *Ring-tum Phi: Washington and Lee Semi-Weekly Newspaper* 57 (June 6, 1962): 1. hdl.handle. net/11021/29107.

Adhya, S., and S. Garges. "How Cyclic AMP and Its Receptor Protein Act in *Escherichia coli*." *Cell* 29 (1982): 287–289.

Adler, R. "Screen: 'Green Berets' as Viewed by John Wayne: War Movie Arrives at the Warner Theater." *New York Times,* June 20, 1968.

Agre, P. C. "Fifty Years Ago: Linus Pauling and the Belated Nobel Peace Prize." *Science and Diplomacy* 2, no. 4 (December 2013). sciencediplomacy.org/ letter-field/2013/fifty-years-ago-linus-pauling-and-belated-nobel-peace-prize.

Ahlquist, R. P. "Adrenergic Receptors: A Personal and Practical View." *Perspectives in Biology and Medicine* 17 (1973): 199–122.

Anderson, R. G. W., M. S. Brown, and J. L. Goldstein. "Role of the Coated Endocytic Vesicle in the Uptake of Receptor-Bound Low Density Lipoprotein in Human Fibroblasts." *Cell* 10 (1977): 351–364.

Angell, R. "Comment." *The New Yorker* (June 15, 1968).

Anitschkow, N., and S. Chalatow. "Ueber Experimentelle Cholesterinsteatose und ihre Bedeutung für die Entstehung Einiger Pathologischer Prozesse." *Allgemeine Pathologie und Pathologische Anatomie* 24 (1913): 1–9.

"April 5, 1968: Chicago Explodes One Day after the Death of Martin Luther King Jr." *Chicago Tribune* (updated August 16, 2018), graphics.chicagotribune.com/riots-chicago-1968-mlk/index.html.

Atkinson, D. "Personal Notes." *Archives of Biochemistry and Biophysics* 397 (2002): 453.

Babior, B. M. Quoted in B. S. Park, "The Development of the Intramural Research Program at the National Institutes of Health after World War II." *Perspectives in Biology and Medicine* 46 (2003): 383–402.

Balsam, L. B., and A. DeAnda. "Historical Perspectives of the American Association for Thoracic Surgery: Frank B. Berry (1892–1976)." *Journal of Thoracic and Cardiovascular Surgery* 142 (2011): 253–256.

Baltimore, D. "Viral RNA-dependent DNA Polymerase: RNA-dependent DNA Polymerase in Virions of RNA Tumor Viruses." *Nature* 226 (1970): 1209–1211.

Barker, H. A., M. D. Kamen, and B. T. Bornstein. "The Synthesis of Butyric and Caproic Acids from Ethanol and Acetic Acid by *Clostridium kluyveri*." *Proceedings of the National Academy of Sciences* 31 (1945): 373–381.

Barker, H. A., and S. M. Taha. "*Clostridium kluyverii*, an Organism Concerned in the Formation of Caproic Acid from Ethyl Alcohol." *Journal of Bacteriology* 43 (1942): 347–363.

Bartter, F. C., P. Pronove, J. R. Gill, and R. G. MacCardle. "Hyperplasia of the Juxtaglomerular Complex with Hyperaldosteronism and Hypokalemic Alkalosis. A New Syndrome." *American Journal of Medicine* 33 (1962): 811–828.

Benovic, J. L., R. G. L. Schorr, and M. G. Caron et al. "The Mammalian Beta 2-Adrenergic Receptor: Purification and Characterization." *Biochemistry* 23 (1984): 4510–4518.

Benovic, J. L., P. H. Strasser, and M. G. Caron et al. "Beta-Adrenergic Receptor Kinase: Identification of a Novel Protein Kinase That Phosphorylates the Agonist-Occupied Form of the Receptor." *Proceedings of the National Academy of Sciences* 83 (1986): 2797–2801.

Berry, F. B. "How the Berry Plan Got Started." *Medical Times* 98 (1970): 104–106.

———. "The Story of 'The Berry Plan.'" *Bulletin New York Academy of Medicine* 52 (1976): 278–282.

Berson, S. A., and R. S. Yalow. "Radioimmunoassay of ACTH in Plasma." *Journal of Clinical Investigation* 47 (1968): 2725–2751.

Berson, S. A., R. S. Yalow, A. Bauman, M. A. Rothschild, and K. Newerly. "Insulin-I¹³¹ Metabolism in Human Subjects: Demonstration of Insulin Binding Globulin in the Circulation of Insulin Treated Subjects." *Journal of Clinical Investigation* 35 (1956): 170–190.

Bosch, F., and L. Rosich. "The Contributions of Paul Ehrlich to Pharmacology: A Tribute on the Occasion of the Centenary of His Nobel Prize." *Pharmacology* 82 (2008): 171–179.

Boudet, M. F. "Nouvelle Recherches Sur La Composition du Serum du Sang Humain." *Annales de Chimie et de Physique* 52 (1833): 337–348.

Bowman, R. L. Quoted in B. S. Park, "The Development of the Intramural Research Program at the National Institutes of Health after World War II." *Perspectives in Biology and Medicine* 46 (2003): 383–402, at 392.

Brenner, S., F. Jacob, and M. Meselson. "An Unstable Intermediate Carrying Information from Genes to Ribosomes for Protein Synthesis." *Nature* 190 (1961): 576–580.

Brown, M. S. "How to Win a Nobel Prize—Nine Simple Steps." *TEDx*. November 7, 2014, Dallas.

Brown, M. S., S. E. Dana, J. M. Dietschy, and M. D. Siperstein. "3-Hydroxy-3-Methylglutaryl Coenzyme A Reductase: Solubilization and Purification of a Cold-Sensitive Microsomal Enzyme." *Journal of Biological Chemistry* 248 (1973): 4731–4738.

Brown, M. S., S. E. Dana, and J. L. Goldstein. "Receptor-dependent Hydrolysis of Cholesteryl Esters Contained in Plasma Low Density Lipoprotein." *Proceedings of the National Academy of Sciences* 72 (1975): 2925–2929.

———. "Regulation of 3-Hydroxy-3-Methylglutaryl Coenzyme A Reductase Activity in Cultured Human Fibroblasts: Comparison of Cells from a Normal Subject and from a Patient with Homozygous Familial Hypercholesterolemia." *Journal of Biological Chemistry* 249 (1974): 789–796.

Brown, M. S., J. R. Faust, and J. L. Goldstein et al. "Induction of 3-Hydroxy-3-Methylglutaryl Coenzyme A Reductase Activity in Human Fibroblasts Incubated in Compactin (M. L.-236B), a Competitive Inhibitor of the Reductase." *Journal of Biological Chemistry* 253 (1978): 1121–1128.

Brown, M. S., and J. L. Goldstein. "A Receptor-Mediated Pathway for Cholesterol Homeostasis." *Science* 232 (1986): 34–47.

———. "Familial Hypercholesterolemia: Defective Binding of Lipoproteins to Cultured Fibroblasts Associated with Impaired Regulation of 3-Hydroxy-3-Methylglutaryl Coenzyme A Reductase Activity." *Proceedings of the National Academy of Sciences* 71 (1974): 788–792.

Brown, M. S., A. Segal, and E. R. Stadtman. "Modulation of Glutamine Synthetase: Adenylylation and Deadenylylation is Mediated by Metabolic Transformation of Pii-Regulatory Protein." *Proceedings of the National Academy of Sciences* 68 (1971): 2949–2953.

Brugge, J. S., and R. L. Erikson. "Identification of a Transformation-Specific Antigen Induced by an Avian Sarcoma Virus." *Nature* 269 (1977): 346–348.

Burstein, P. "Jewish Educational and Economic Success in the United States: A Search for Explanations." *Sociological Perspectives* 50 (2007): 209–228.

Bynum, W. "What Makes a Great Lab?" *Nature* 490 (2012): 31–32.

Capecchi, M. R. "Polypeptide Chain Termination *In Vitro*: Isolation of a Release Factor." *Proceedings of the National Academy of Sciences* 58 (1967): 1144–1151.

Caron, M. G., and R. J. Lefkowitz. "Solubilization and Characterization of the Beta-Adrenergic Receptor Binding Sites in Frog Erythrocytes." *Journal of Biological Chemistry* 251 (1976): 2374–2384.

Caspersson, T., and J. Schultz. "Pentose Nucleotides in the Cytoplasm of Growing Tissues." *Nature* 143 (1939): 602–603.

Cerione, R. A., B. Strulovici, and J. L. Benovic et al. "Reconstitution of beta-Adrenergic Receptors in Lipid Vesicles: Affinity Chromatography-Purified Receptors Confer Catecholamine Responsiveness on a Heterologous Adenylate Cyclase System." *Proceedings of the National Academy of Sciences* 80 (1983): 4899–4903.

Chamberlain, J. "'Priests and Prophets': Diabetes Branch Alumni Toast Mentors." *NIH Record* 57, no. 4 (February 15, 2005): 579.

Charlton, B. G. "Scientometric Identification of Elite 'Revolutionary Science' Research Institutions by Analysis of Trends of Nobel Prizes, 1947–2006." *Medical Hypotheses* 68 (2007): 931–934.

"The Chemistry of Discovery." *Duke Magazine* (November 5, 2012) [no author].

Cochran, G., J. Hardy, and H. Harpending. "Natural History of Ashkenazi Intelligence." *Journal of Biosocial Science* 38 (2006): 659–693.

Cohen, P. "The Origins of Protein Phosphorylation." *Nature Cell Biology* 4 (2002): E127–130.

Collett, M. S., and R. L. Erikson. "Protein Kinase Activity Associated with the Avian Sarcoma Virus src Gene Product." *Proceedings of the National Academy of Sciences* 75 (1978): 2021–2024.

Cone, J. E., M. del Rio, J. N. Davis, and T. C. Stadtman. "Chemical Characterization of the Selenoprotein Component of Clostridial Glycine Reductase: Identification of Selenocysteine as the Organo-Selenium Moiety." *Proceedings of the National Academy of Sciences* 73 (1976): 2659–2663.

Connor, S. "Inside the Nobel Prize Factory." *The Independent*, October 12, 2002.

Cooper, R. A. "Medical Schools and Their Applicants." *Health Affairs* 22 (2003): 71–84.

Cotecchia, S., D. A. Schwinn, and R. R. Randall et al. "Molecular Cloning and Expression of the cDNA for the Hamster Alpha 1-Adrenergic Receptor." *Proceedings of the National Academy of Sciences* 85 (1988): 7159–7163.

Crick, F. H. C. "Cracking the Genetic Code." In Frontiers of Knowledge Series, no. 256. British Broadcasting Corporation, January 22, 1962.

Culliton, B. J. "NIH Policymaker: A Fundamentalist Takes the Number Two Spot at NIH." *Science News* 95 (1969): 263–264.

Dale, H. H. "Modes of Drug Action: General Introductory Address." *Transactions of the Faraday Society* 39 (1943): 319–322.

Dans, P. E. "David Seegal: Ic Ne Wat and Other Maxims of a Master Teacher." *Pharos* (Autumn 2014): 5–8.

Davignon, J., and M. Roy. "Familial Hypercholesterolemia in French-Canadians: Taking Advantage of the Presence of a 'Founder Effect.'" *American Journal of Cardiology* 72 (1993): 6D–10D.

Dixon, R. A., B. K. Kobilka, and D. J. Strader et al. "Cloning of the Gene and cDNA for Mammalian Beta-Adrenergic Receptor and Homology with Rhodopsin." *Nature* 321 (1986): 75–79.

"Dr. David Seegal of Columbia Dies." *New York Times*, July 27, 1972 [no author].

Duesberg, P. H., and P. K. Vogt. "Differences Between the Ribonucleic Acids of Transforming and Nontransforming Avian Tumor Viruses." *Proceedings of the National Academy of Sciences* 67 (1970): 1673–1680.

"Editorial Opinion: Bill Clinton's Vietnam Test." *New York Times*, February 14, 1992.

Emmer, M., B. deCrombrugghe, I. Pastan, and R. Perlman. "Cyclic AMP Receptor Protein of *E. coli*: Its Role in the Synthesis of Inducible Enzymes." *Proceedings of the National Academy of Sciences* 66 (1970): 480–487.

Evans, R., and R. Novak. "Inside Report: Medicare Crisis." *Herald Tribune*, March 3, 1966.

Ferguson, R. B. "How Jews Became Smart: Anti-'Natural History of Ashkenazi Intelligence.'" Department of Sociology and Anthropology, Rutgers University, Newark, NJ, 1–48.

"Fifty-one Groups of Apartment Buildings Will House 12,000 Families." *New York Times*, May 5, 1939, 47.

Fischer, E. H., and E. G. Krebs. "Conversion of Phosphorylase B to Phosphorylase A in Muscle Extracts." *Journal of Biological Chemistry* 216 (1955): 121–132.

Fletcher, W. M. "John Newport Langley: In Memorium." *Journal of Physiology* 18 (1926): 4–15.

Florida, R. "The Role of the University: Leveraging Talent, Not Technology." *Issues in Science and Technology* 15 (1999): 67–73.

Fredrickson, D. S., P. H. Altrocchi, L. V. Avioli, D. S. Goodman, and H. C. Goodman. "Tangier Disease." *Annals of Internal Medicine* 55 (1961): 1016–1031.

Friedman, A. "Remembrance: The Berson and Yalow Saga." *Journal of Clinical Endocrinology and Metabolism* 87 (2002): 1925–1928.

Friedmann, H. G. "From *Butyribacterium* to *E. coli*: An Essay on Unity." *Biochemistry Perspectives in Biology and Medicine* 47 (2004): 47–66.

Frielle, T., S. Collins, and K. W. Daniel et al. "Cloning of the cDNA for the Human Beta 1-Adrenergic Receptor." *Proceedings of the National Academy of Sciences* 84 (1987): 7920–7924.

Fung, B. K. K., and J. B. Hurley, and L. Stryer. "Flow of Information in the Light-Triggered Cyclic Nucleotide Cascade of Vision." *Proceedings of the National Academy of Sciences* 78 (1981): 152–156.

Gardner, J. D., M. S. Brown, and L. Laster. "The Columnar Epithelial Cell of the Small Intestine: Digestion and Transport. First of Three Parts." *New England Journal of Medicine* 283 (1970): 1196–1202.

———. "The Columnar Epithelial Cell of the Small Intestine. Digestion and Transport. Second of Three Parts." *New England Journal of Medicine* 283 (1970): 1264–1271.

———. "The Columnar Epithelial Cell of the Small Intestine. Third of Three Parts." *New England Journal of Medicine* 283 (1970): 1317–1324.

Garnett, C. "NIH-NIMH Vietnam Moratorium Committee Reunites for Posterity." *NIH Record* 58, no. 2 (January 27, 2006), 586.

Garrison, H. H., and A. M. Deschamps. "NIH Research Funding and Early Career Physician Scientists: Continuing Challenges in the 21st Century." *FASEB Journal* 28 (2014): 1049–1058.

———. "Physician Scientists: Assessing the Workforce." *Federation of American Societies of Experimental Biology* (December 11, 2013).

Gartler, S. M. "Apparent HeLa Cell Contamination of Human Heteroploid Cell Lines." *Nature* 217 (1968): 750–751.

Gilbert, W., and B. Müller-Hill. "Isolation of the Lac Repressor." *Proceedings of the National Academy of Sciences* 56 (1966): 1891–1898.

Ginsberg, D. "Chamber Music Series' 40 Years of Concerts Ends on a Wistful Note." *Washington Post*, April 5, 2008.

Glick, S. M., J. Roth, R. S. Yalow, and S. A. Berson. "Immunoassay of Human Growth Hormone in Plasma." *Nature* 199 (1963): 784–787.

Goethals, T. R. "Americans First." *New England Journal of Medicine* 243 (1950): 896–897.

Gofman, J. W., L. Rubin, J. P. McGinley, and H. B. Jones. "Hyperlipoproteinemia." *American Journal of Medicine* 17 (1954): 514–520.

"Goldstein Wins Phi Beta Kappa Soph Award." *Ring-tum Phi: Washington and Lee Semi-Weekly Newspaper* 603 (March 11, 1960), 1.

Goldstein, A. "A Duo's Great Chemistry." *Washington Post*, January 26, 2004.

Goldstein, J. L. "On the Origin and Prevention of PAIDS (Paralyzed Academic Investigator's Disease Syndrome)." *Journal of Clinical Investigation* 78 (1986): 848–854.

———. Presentation at "A Tribute to Dr. Marshall Nirenberg." October 2, 2010. National Institutes of Health, Bethesda, MD.

Goldstein, J. L., S. K. Basu, G. Y. Brunschede, and M. S. Brown. "Release of Low Density Lipoprotein from its Cell Surface Receptor by Sulfated Glycosaminoglycans." *Cell* 7 (1976): 85–95.

Goldstein, J. L., A. L. Beaudet, and C. T. Caskey. "Peptide Chain Termination with Mammalian Release Factor." *Proceedings of the National Academy of Sciences* 67 (1970): 99–106.

Goldstein, J. L., and M. S. Brown. "A Century of Cholesterol and Coronaries: From Plaques to Genes and Statins." *Cell* 161 (2015): 161–172.

———. "Binding and Degradation of Low Density Lipoproteins by Cultured Human Fibroblasts." *Journal of Biological Chemistry* 249 (1974): 5153–5162.

———. "The Clinical Investigator: Bewitched, Bothered, and Bewildered—But Still Beloved." *Journal of Clinical Investigation* 99 (1997): 2803–2812.

———. "Familial Hypercholesterolemia: Identification of a Defect in the Regulation of 3-Hydroxy-3-Methylglutaryl Coenzyme A Reductase Activity Associated with Overproduction of Cholesterol." *Proceedings of the National Academy of Sciences* 70 (1973): 2804–2808.

———. "A Golden Era of Nobel Laureates." *Science* 338 (2012): 1033–1034.

———. "The LDL Receptor." *Arteriosclerosis, Thrombosis, and Vascular Biology* 29 (2009): 431–438.

———. "What Did Your Early Mentors Teach You?" *Nobel Inspiration Initiative.* Cambridge, UK, October 2014.

———. "What Should You Look for in a Mentor?" *Nobel Inspiration Initiative.* Cambridge, UK, October 2014.

Goldstein, J. L., and C. T. Caskey. "Peptide Chain Termination: Effect of Protein S on Ribosomal Binding of Release Factors." *Proceedings of the National Academy of Sciences* 67 (1970): 537–543.

Goldstein, J. L., W. R. Hazzard, H. G. Schrott, E. L. Bierman, and A. G. Motulsky. "Hyperlipidemia in Coronary Heart Disease. I. Lipid Levels in 500 Survivors of Myocardial Infarction." *Journal of Clinical Investigation* 52 (1973): 1533–1543.

Goldstein, J. L., G. Milman, E. Scolnick, and T. Caskey. "Peptide Chain Termination. VI. Purification and Site of Action of S." *Proceedings of the National Academy of Sciences* 65 (1970): 430–437.

Goldstein, J. L., H. G. Schrott, W. R. Hazzard, E. L. Bierman, and A. G. Motulsky. "Hyperlipidemia in Coronary Heart Disease. II. Genetic Analysis of Lipid Levels in 176 Families and Delineation of a New Inherited Disorder, Combined Hyperlipidemia." *Journal of Clinical Investigation* 52 (1973): 1544–1568.

Haas, V. A., E. R. Stadtman, F. H. Stadtman, and G. Mackinney. "Deterioration of Dried Fruits. I. The Effects of Sugars and Furfurals." *Journal of the American Chemical Society* 70 (1948): 3576–3579.

Hallin, D. C. *The "Uncensored War": The Media and Vietnam.* New York: Oxford University Press, 1986.

Halperin, E. C. "The Jewish Problem in U.S. Medical Education." *Journal of the History of Medicine and Allied Sciences* 56 (2001): 140–167.

Hanna, J. G. "A Nobel Prize: Dr. Joseph Goldstein, '63, Honored for Medical Research." *Alumni Magazine of Washington and Lee* 60 (1985): 2–7.

Harding, C. V., M. H. Akaba, and O. S. Anderson. "History and Outcomes of 50 Years of Physician-Scientist Training in Medical Scientist Training Programs." *Academic Medicine* 92 (2017): 1390–1398.

Havel, R. J., D. B. Hunninghake, and D. R. Illingworth et al. "Lovastatin (Mevinolin) in the Treatment of Heterozygous Familial Hypercholesterolemia: A Multicenter Study." *Annals of Internal Medicine* 107 (1987): 609–615.

Hewlett, H. W. "Amherst's New Curriculum in its First Year." *Journal of Higher Education* 19 (1948): 365.

Hostetler, Z. Quoted in C. Garnett, "NIH-NIMH Vietnam Moratorium Committee Reunites for Posterity." *NIH Record* 58, no. 2 (January 27, 2006), 588.

Interlandi, J. "Fighting the Cancer War." *Columbia College Today* (May/June 2007).

Jacob, F., and J. Monod. "Genetic Regulatory Mechanisms in the Synthesis of Proteins." *Journal of Molecular Biology* 3 (1961): 318–356.

Jacob, F., D. Perrin, C. Sanchez, and J. Monod. "Operon: A Group of Genes with the Expression Coordinated by an Operator." *Comptes Rendus Hebdomadaires des Séances de L'Académie des Sciences* 250 (1960): 1727–1729.

Jarvik, G. P. "2016 Victor A. McKusick Leadership Award Introduction: Stanley Gartler." *American Journal of Human Genetics* 100 (2017): 401–402.

Johnson, D. "Yale's Limit on Jewish Enrollment Lasted Until Early 1960's, Book Says." *New York Times*, March 4, 1986.

Jones, B. F. "Age and Great Invention." *Review of Economics and Statistics* 92 (2010): 1–14.

Jones, O. W., and M. W. Nirenberg. "Qualitative Survey of RNA Codewords." *Proceedings of the National Academy of Sciences* 48 (1962): 2115–2123.

Kahn, C. R., and J. Roth. "Berson, Yalow, and the JCI: The Agony and the Ecstasy." *Journal of Clinical Investigation* 114 (2004): 1051–1054.

Karp, D. "Valencia Oranges, under Siege in California, Fight to Survive." *Los Angeles Times*, July 5, 2013.

Keefe, F. Quoted in K. Honey, "True Dedication to Clinical Research: The Clinical Center of the National Institutes of Health Receives the 2011 Mary Woodard Lasker Award for Public Service." *Journal of Clinical Investigation* 121 (2011): 3778–3781.

Kennedy, T. J. "James A. Shannon and the Beginnings of the Laboratory of Kidney and Electrolyte Metabolism of the National Institutes of Health." *Kidney International* 55 (1999): 326–333.

Kevles, D. "Big Science and Big Politics in the United States: Reflections on the Death of the SCC and the Life of the Human Genome Project." *Historical Studies in the Physical and Biological Sciences* 27 (1997): 269–297.

Khachadurian, A. K. "The Inheritance of Essential Familial Hypercholesterolemia." *American Journal of Medicine* 37 (1964): 402–407.

Khot, S., B. S. Park, and W. T. Longstreth. "The Vietnam War and Medical Research: Untold Legacy of the U.S. Doctor Draft and the NIH 'Yellow Berets.'" *Academic Medicine* 86 (2011): supplemental digital content, download.lww. com/.../ACADMED_86_4_2011_01_21_KHOT_202393_SDC1.pdf.

Kingdon, H. S. "Earl R. Stadtman, Ph.D.: Citizen of the World." *Archives of Biochemistry and Biophysics* 397 (2002): 452.

Kluyver, A. J., and H. J. L. Donker. "Die Einheit in der Biochemie." *Chemie der Zelle und Gewebe* 13 (1926): 134–190.

Kobilka, B. K., and H. Matsui, and T. S. Kobilka et al. "Cloning, Sequencing, and Expression of the Gene Coding for the Human Platelet Alpha 2-Adrenergic Receptor." *Science* 238 (1987): 650–656.

Korn, E. D. "Retrospective: Earl R. Stadtman (1919–2008)." *American Society of Biochemistry and Molecular Biology Today* (2008): 11–13.

Kovanen, P. T., D. W. Bilheimer, and J. L. Goldstein et al. "Regulatory Role for Hepatic Low Density Lipoprotein Receptors In Vivo in the Dog." *Proceedings of the National Academy of Sciences* 78 (1981): 1194–1198.

Kresge, N., R. D. Simoni, and R. L. Hill. "30 Years of Cholesterol Metabolism: The Work of Michael Brown and Joseph Goldstein." *Journal of Biological Chemistry* 281 (2006): e25–e28.

Kroll, D. "Duke's Bob Lefkowitz Wins the Nobel Prize: At Last, a Nice Guy Finishes First." *Indy Week*, January 9, 2013.

Langley, J. N. "On the Physiology of the Salivary Secretion. Part II. On the Mutual Antagonism of Atropin and Pilocarpin, Having Especial Reference to Their Relations in the Sub-Maxillary Gland of the Cat." *Journal of Physiology* 1 (1878): 339–369.

———. "On the Reaction of Cells and of Nerve-Endings to Certain Poisons, Chiefly as Regards the Reaction of Striated Muscle to Nicotine and to Curari." *Journal of Physiology* 33 (1905): 374–413.

Lardner G., and L. Romano. "At Height of Vietnam, Bush Picks Guard." *Washington Post*, July 28, 1999.

Lee, C. "The History of Citrus in California." *California Country* (March/April 2010).

Lefkowitz, R. J. "A Brief History of G-Protein Coupled Receptors (Nobel Lecture)." *Angewandte Chemie International Edition* 52 (2013): 6367–6378.

———. "Inspiring the Next Generation of Physician-Scientists." *Journal of Clinical Investigation* 125 (2015): 2905–2907.

———. "The Reluctant Scientist." Keynote Address. North Carolina School for Science and Mathematics, Durham, NC, March 15, 2013.

———. "A Serendipitous Scientist." *Annual Reviews of Pharmacology and Toxicology* 58 (2018): 17–32.

———. "Seven Transmembrane Receptors—A Brief Personal Perspective." *Biochimica et Biophysica Acta* 1768 (2007): 748–755.

———. "A Tale of Two Callings." *Journal of Clinical Investigation* 121 (2011): 4201–4203.

Lefkowitz, R. J., J. Roth, and I. Pastan. "Effects of Calcium on ACTH Stimulation of the Adrenal: Separation of Hormone Binding from Adenyl Cyclase Activation." *Nature* 228 (1970): 864–866.

———. "Radioreceptor Assay of Adrenocorticotropic Hormone: New Approach to Assay of Polypeptide Hormones in Plasma." *Science* 170 (1970): 633–635.

Lefkowitz, R. J., J. Roth, W. Pricer, and I. Pastan. "ACTH Receptors in the Adrenal: Specific Binding of ACTH-125I and Its Relation to Adenylate Cyclase." *Proceedings of the National Academy of Sciences* 65 (1970): 745–752.

Leigh, S., curator. "LDLR (Low Density Lipoprotein Receptor): Unique Variants in Gene LDLR." Leiden, Netherlands: Leiden Open Variation Database, Leiden University Medical Center, databases.lovd.nl/shared/variants/LDLR/unique.

Lengyel, P. "Memories of a Senior Scientist: On Passing the Fiftieth Anniversary of the Beginning of Deciphering the Genetic Code." *Annual Review of Microbiology* 66 (2012): 27–38.

Lengyel, P., J. F. Speyer, and S. Ochoa. "Synthetic Polynucleotides and the Amino Acid Code." *Proceedings of the National Academy of Sciences* 47 (1961): 1936–1942.

Levinson, A. D., H. Opperman, L. Levintow, H. E. Varmus, and J. M. Bishop. "Evidence That the Transforming Gene of Avian Sarcoma Virus Encodes a Protein Kinase Associated with a Phosphoprotein." *Cell* 15 (1978): 561–572.

Linder, D., and S. M. Gartler. "Glucose-6-Phosphate Dehydrogenase Mosaicism: Utilization as a Cell Marker in the Study of Leiomyomas." *Science* 150 (1965): 67–69.

Lipmann, F. "Generation and Utilization of Phosphate High Energy Bond." *Advances in Enzymology and Related Areas of Molecular Biology* 1 (1941): 99–162.

Lipmann, F., N. O. Kaplan, L. Novelli, C. Tuttle, and B. M. Guirard. "Coenzyme for Acetylation: A Pantothenic Acid Derivative." *Journal of Biological Chemistry* 167 (1947): 869–870.

Lohrmann, R., D. Stöll, H. Hayatsu, E. Ohtsuka, H. G. Khorana. "Studies of Polynucleotides: LI. Synthesis of the 64 Possible Ribotrinucleotides Derived from the Four Major Ribomononucleotides." *Journal of the American Chemical Society* 88 (1966): 819–829.

Lohse, M. J., J. L. Benovic, and J. Codina et al. "Beta-arrestin: A Protein That Regulates Beta-Adrenergic Receptor Function." *Science* 248 (1990): 1547–1550.

Lomasney, J. W., M. F. Leeb-Lundberg, and S. Cotecchia et al. "Mammalian Alpha1—Adrenergic Receptor: Purification and Characterization of the Native Receptor Ligand Binding Unit." *Journal of Biological Chemistry* 261 (1986): 7710–7716.

Londos, C., Y. Salomon, and M. C. Lin et al. "5′-Guanylylimidodiphosphate: A Potent Activator of Adenyl Cyclase Systems in Eukaryotic Cells." *Proceedings of the National Academy of Sciences* 71 (1974): 3087–3090.

Lorenz, W., K. Inglese, and J. J. Palczewski et al. "The Receptor Kinase Family: Primary Structure of Rhodopsin Kinase Reveals Similarities to the Beta-Adrenergic Receptor Kinase." *Proceedings of the National Academy of Sciences* 88 (1991): 8715–8719.

Lovastatin Study Group II. "Therapeutic Response to Lovastatin (Mevinolin) in Nonfamilial Hypercholesterolemia: A Multicenter Study." *Journal of the American Medical Association* 256 (1986): 2829–2834.

Lyons, R. D. "Science Adviser to Nixon Leaving for Industry Job." *New York Times*, January 3, 1973.

MacPherson, M. "Dan Quayle and the Vietnam Question." *Washington Post*, August 19, 1988.

Makman, R. S., and E. W. Sutherland. "Adenosine 3′,5′-Phosphate in *Escherichia coli.*" *Journal of Biological Chemistry* 240 (1965): 1309–1314.

Manning, D. R., and A. G. Gilman. "The Regulatory Components of Adenylate Cyclase and Transducin: A Family of Structurally Homologous Guanine Nucleotide-Binding Proteins." *Journal of Biological Chemistry* 258 (1983): 7059–7063.

Marshall, E. "N.I.A.I.D's Anthony Fauci." *Science* 292 (2001): 1990.

Martin, G. S. "Rous Sarcoma Virus: A Function Required for the Maintenance of the Transformed State." *Nature* 227 (1970): 1021–1023.

Martin, R. G. "A Revisionist View of the Breaking of the Genetic Code." In DeWitt Stetten Jr., ed., *NIH: An Account of Research in Its Laboratories and Clinics.* Orlando, FL: Academic Press, 1984.

Matthaei J. H., and M. W. Nirenberg. "Characteristics and Stabilization of DNAse Sensitive Protein Synthesis in *E. coli* Extracts." *Proceedings of the National Academy of Sciences* 47 (1961): 1580–1588.

———. "The Dependence of Cell-Free Protein Synthesis in *E. coli* upon RNA Prepared from Ribosomes." *Biochemical and Biophysical Research Communications* 4 (1961): 404–408.

Matthews, K. R. W., et al. "The Aging of Biomedical Research in the United States." *PloS one* 6 (2011): e29738.

McCoy, R. H., C. E. Meyer, and W. C. Rose. "Feeding Experiments with Mixtures of Highly Purified Amino Acids. VIII. Isolation and Identification of a New Essential Amino Acid." *Journal of Biological Chemistry* 112 (1935): 283–302.

McKinney, R. E. "The Daunting Career of the Physician-Investigator." *Academic Medicine* 92 (2017): 1368–1370.

McManus, R. "Era of Distinction Ends for Building 3." *NIH Record*. Bethesda, MD: National Institutes of Health, May 1, 2001.

———. "FAES Marks 50th Year at NIH." *NIH Record* 61 (August 7, 2009).

———. "Nobelist Prusiner Draws Homecoming Crowd." *NIH Record* 50, no. 22 (November 3, 1998). Bethesda, MD: National Institutes of Health.

McNees, P. "An Abnormal Reunion." *The Scientist* (March 1, 2008).

"Medicare Is Launched into Shambles." *Life* (September 3, 1965): 52B-58 [no author].

Milman, G., J. Goldstein, E. Scolnick, and T. Caskey. "Peptide Chain Termination. III. Stimulation of *In Vitro* Termination." *Proceedings of the National Academy of Sciences* 63 (1969): 183–190.

Mirsky, I. A. "The Etiology of Diabetes in Man." *Recent Progress in Hormone Research* 7 (1952): 437–467.

Moffatt, C. "Deciphering the Genetic Code: A 50 Year Anniversary." *Circulating Now*. Bethesda, MD: National Library of Medicine, January 21, 2015.

"Monitoring Media Attitudes." Roper Center, Cornell University, *Public Perspective Online* 1, no. 5 (July/August 1990): 95–101.

Mooney, M. J. "The Father of Dallas Medicine." *D Magazine* (October 2013).

Motulsky A. G. (as told to M. C. King). "The Great Adventure of an American Human Geneticist." *Annual Reviews of Genomics and Human Genetics* 17 (2016): 1–15.

Müller, C. "Angina Pectoris in Hereditary Xanthomatosis." *Archives of Internal Medicine* 64 (1939): 675–700.

"The NIH Looks for Research Associates." *Medical World News*, February 22, 1974.

Nirenberg, M. "Historical Review: Deciphering the Genetic Code—A Personal Account." *Trends in Biochemical Sciences* 29 (2004): 46–54.

Nirenberg, M., T. Caskey, R. Marshall, R. Brimacombe, D. Kellogg, B. Doctor, D. Hatfield, J. Levin, F. Rottman, S. Pestka, M. Wilcox, and F. Anderson. "The RNA Code and Protein Synthesis." *Cold Spring Harbor Symposium on Quantitative Biology* 31 (1966): 11–24.

Nirenberg, M. W., O. W. Jones, P. Leder, B. F. C. Clark, W. S. Sly, and S. Pestka. "On the Coding of Genetic Information." *Cold Spring Harbor Symposium on Quantitative Biology* 28 (1963): 549–557.

Nirenberg, M. W., and P. Leder. "RNA Codewords and Protein Synthesis. I. The Effect of Trinucleotides Upon the Binding of sRNA to Ribosomes." *Science* 145 (1964): 1399–1407.

Nirenberg, M. W., and J. H. Matthaei. "The Dependence of Cell-Free Protein Synthesis in *E. coli* upon Naturally Occurring or Synthetic Polyribonucleotides." *Proceedings of the National Academy of Sciences* 47 (1961): 1588–1602.

Nishimura, S., D. S. Jones, E. Ohtsuka, H. Hayatsu, T. M. Jacob, and H. G. Khorana. "Studies of Polynucleotides: XLVII. The *In Vitro* Synthesis of Homopeptides as Directed by a Ribopolynucleotide Containing a Repeating Trinucleotide Sequence. New Codon Sequences for Lysine, Glutamic Acid and Arginine." *Journal of Molecular Biology* 13 (1965): 283–301.

"Obituaries: Barry Sadler, 49, Balladeer, Dies." *New York Times*, November 6, 1989.

Oransky, I. "Giulio Cantoni." *The Lancet* 366 (2005): 888.

"P. Roy Vagelos, M.D.: 1991 Maxwell Finland Award." Bethesda, MD: National Foundation for Infectious Diseases, 1991 [no author].

Pang, A. "This Is New York: Robert Lefkowitz on Winning a Nobel Prize." *The Epoch Times*, October 9, 2013.

Pardee, A. B., F. Jacob, and J. Monod. "The Genetic Control and Cytoplasmic Expression of Inducibility in the Synthesis of β-galactosidase in *E. coli.*" *Journal of Molecular Biology* 1 (1959): 165–178.

Park, B. S. "The Development of the Intramural Research Program at the National Institutes of Health after World War II." *Perspectives in Biology and Medicine* 46 (2003): 383–402.

Pastan, I. H. "Certain Functions of Isolated Thyroid Cells." *Endocrinology* 68 (1961): 924–931.

———. "Personal Notes." *Archives of Biochemistry and Biophysics* 397 (2002): 450.

Pastan, I., and J. B. Field. "*In Vitro* Stimulation of Glucose Oxidation in Thyroid by Serotonin." *Endocrinology* 70 (1962): 656–659.

Pastan, I., and R. L. Perlman. "The Role of the Lac Promoter Locus in the Regulation of β-galactosidase Synthesis by Cyclic 3′,5′-Monophosphate." *Proceedings of the National Academy of Sciences* 61 (1968): 1336–1342.

Pastan, I., J. Roth, and V. Macchia. "Binding of Hormone to Tissue: The First Step in Polypeptide Hormone Action." *Proceedings of the National Academy of Sciences* 56 (1966): 1802–1809.

Patterson, P. "The Truth about Tonkin." *Naval History Magazine* 22, no. 1 (February 2008): 22.

Perlman, R. L., and I. Pastan. "Regulation of β-galactosidase Synthesis in *Escherichia coli* by Cyclic Adenosine 3′,5′-Monophosphate." *Journal of Biological Chemistry* 243 (1968): 5420–5427.

Perutz, M. "The Medical Research Council Laboratory of Molecular Biology." July 1, 1997. nobelprize.org.

"Phi Eta Sigma Honor Group Adds Sophomore, 9 Freshmen." *Ring-tum Phi: Washington and Lee Semi-Weekly Newspaper* 592 (February 20, 1959), 1.

Poen, M. M. "National Health Insurance." In R. S. Kirkendall, ed., *The Harry S. Truman Encyclopedia*. Boston: G. K. Hall & Co., 1989.

Pratt, D. "What Makes a Nobel Laureate?" *Los Angeles Times*, October 9, 2013.

Ransdell, J. E. "The National Institute of Health." *Radiology* 18 (1932): 942–947.

Raper, V. "A Nobel Prize-Winning Culture." *Science* 333 (July 8, 2011): 131. sciencemag.org.

Regan, J. W., H. Nakata, and R. M. DeMarinis et al. "Purification and Characterization of the Human Platelet Alpha 2-Adrenergic Receptor." *Journal of Biological Chemistry* 261 (1986): 3894–3900.

Reiff, J. L., D. Keating, and J. R. Grossman. "West Madison Street, 1968." In *Encyclopedia of Chicago*. Chicago: Chicago Historical Society, 2004.

Reiss, D. Quoted in C. Garnett, "NIH-NIMH Vietnam Moratorium Committee Reunites for Posterity." *NIH Record* 58, no. 2 (January 27, 2006): 587.

"Revolutionary Center for Medical Research Dedicated." *New York Times,* July 3, 1953.

Rich, A., and J. D. Watson. "Some Relations Between DNA and RNA." *Proceedings of the National Academy of Sciences* 40 (1954): 759–764.

Rodbell, M., L. Birnbaumer, and S. L. Pohl et al. "The Glucagon-Sensitive Adenyl Cyclase System in Plasma Membranes of Rat Liver. V. An Obligatory Role of Guanyl Nucleotides in Glucagon Action." *Journal of Biological Chemistry* 246 (1971): 1877–1882.

Roosevelt, F. D. "Dedication of the National Institute of Health." October 31, 1940. Cited in M. Lyons, *70 Acres of Science: The National Institute of Health Moves to Bethesda.* Bethesda, MD: DeWitt Stetten, Jr., Museum of Medical Research, National Institutes of Health, 2006.

Ross, E. M., and A. G. Gilman. "Resolution of Some Components of Adenylate Cyclase Necessary for Catalytic Activity." *Journal of Biological Chemistry* 252 (1977): 6966–6969.

Roth, J., S. M. Glick, R. S. Yalow, and S. A. Berson. "Hypoglycemia: A Potent Stimulus to Secretion of Growth Hormone." *Science* 140 (1963): 987–988.

———. "The Influence of Blood Glucose on the Plasma Concentration of Growth Hormone." *Diabetes* 13 (1964): 355–361.

———. "Secretion of Human Growth Hormone: Physiologic and Experimental Modification." *Metabolism* 12 (1963): 577–579.

Rous, P. "A Sarcoma of the Fowl Transmissible by an Agent Separable from the Tumor Cells." *Journal of Experimental Medicine* 13 (1911): 397–411.

———. "A Transmissible Avian Neoplasm (Sarcoma of the Common Fowl)." *Journal of Experimental Medicine* 12 (1910): 696–705.

Sadler, B., and R. Moore. "Ballad of the Green Berets." New York: RCA Victor, Catalogue No. 47-8739, 1966.

Saxon, W. "Gaylord Harnwell, Physicist and President of Penn, Dies." *New York Times,* April 19, 1982.

Schechter, A. N. "Christian B. Anfinsen, 1916–1995." In *Biographical Memoirs.* Washington, DC: National Academy of Sciences, 2015.

Schenker, S. "In Memorium: Burton Combes, M.D." *Hepatology* 59 (2014): 1655–1656.

Schneider, W. J., U. Beisiegel, J. L. Goldstein, and M. S. Brown. "Purification of the Low Density Lipoprotein Receptor, an Acidic Glycoprotein of 164,000 Molecular Weight." *Journal of Biological Chemistry* 257 (1982): 2664–2673.

Scipioni, J. "Meet the Most Powerful Doctor in America." Fox Business, June 10, 2015. foxbusiness.com/features/2015/06/11/meet-most-powerful-man-in-us-medicine.html.

Scolnick, E. "Marshall Nirenberg, 1927–2010." *Cell* 140 (2010): 450–451.

Scolnick, E., R. Tompkins, T. Caskey, and M. Nirenberg. "Release Factors Differing in Specificity for Terminator Codons." *Proceedings of the National Academy of Sciences* 61 (1968): 768–774.

Segal, A., and M. B. Brown, and E. R. Stadtman. "Metabolic Regulation of the State of the Adenylylation of Glutamine Synthetase." *Archives of Biochemistry and Biophysics* 161 (1974): 319–327.

Seger, B. (under the attribution D. Dodger). "Ballad of the Yellow Beret." Performed by the Beach Bums. Produced and arranged by Doug Brown and the Omens. Detroit: Are You Kidding Me Records, 1966.

Shamp, J. "Nobel Calling? Lefkowitz Finally Gets It." North Carolina Biotechnology Center. Story reprinted from *Durham Herald-Sun*, October 19, 2003.

Shampo, M. A., and R. A. Kyle. "Hugo Theorell—Nobel Prize for Study of Enzymes." *Mayo Clinic Proceedings* 73 (1998): 147.

Shapiro, B. M., and H. S. Kingdon, and E. R. Stadtman. "Regulation of Glutamine Synthestase, VII. Adenylyl Glutamine Synthetase: A New Form of the Enzyme with Altered Regulatory and Kinetic Properties." *Proceedings of the National Academy of Sciences* 58 (1967): 642–649.

Sheiness, D., and J. M. Bishop. "DNA and RNA from Uninfected Vertebrate Cells Contain Nucleotide Sequences Related to the Putative Transforming Gene of Avian Myelocytomatosis Virus." *Journal of Virology* 31 (1979): 514–521.

Sheiness, D., L. Fanshier, and J. M. Bishop. "Identification of Nucleotide Sequences Which May Encode the Oncogenic Capacity of Avian Retrovirus M. C.29." *Journal of Virology* 28 (1978): 600–610.

Siperstein, M. D., and V. M. Fugan. "Feedback Control of Mevalonate Synthesis by Dietary Cholesterol." *Journal of Biological Chemistry* 241 (1966): 602–609.

"Sixteen Tapped for Phi Beta Kappa." *Ring-tum Phi: Washington and Lee Semi-Weekly Newspaper* 614 (February 28, 1961), 1.

Snyderman, R. J. "Introduction of Robert J. Lefkowitz." *Journal of Clinical Investigation* 121 (2011): 4192–4200.

Sokoloff, L. "The Rise and Decline of the Jewish Quota in Medical School Admissions." *Bulletin of the New York Academy of Medicine* 68 (1992): 497–518.

Spector, D. H., H. E. Varmus, and J. M. Bishop. "Nucleotide Sequences Related to the Transforming Gene of Avian Sarcoma Virus are Present in the DNA of Uninfected Vertebrates." *Proceedings of the National Academy of Sciences* 75 (1978): 4102–4106.

Spock, B. Quoted in "A Wrap-Up on the Washington, DC Moratorium." Recorded in Washington, DC, broadcast on WBAI, and distributed by Pacifica Radio Archives (October 15, 1969). North Hollywood, CA: Pacifica Radio Archives, Number: BB3743., 1969, 7–12.

Stadel, J. M., P. Nambi, and T. N. Lavin et al. "Catecholamine-Induced Desensitization of Turkey Erythrocyte Adenylate Cyclase." *Journal of Biological Chemistry* 257 (1982): 9242–9245.

Stadtman, E. R. "How I Became a Biochemist." *International Union of Biochemistry and Molecular Biology—Life* 54 (2002): 39–40.

———. "The Net Enzymatic Synthesis of Acetyl Coenzyme A." *Journal of Biological Chemistry* 196 (1952): 535–546.

Stadtman, E. R., and H. A. Barker. "Fatty Acid Synthesis by Enzyme Preparations of *Clostridium kluyveri*. VI. Reactions of Acylphosphates." *Journal of Biological Chemistry* 184 (1950): 769–793.

———. "Fatty Acid Synthesis by Enzyme Preparations of *Clostridium kluyveri*. I. Preparation of Cell-Free Extracts That Catalyze the Conversion of Ethanol and Acetate to Butyrate and Caproate." *Journal of Biological Chemistry* 180 (1949): 1085–1093.

Stadtman, E. R., H. A. Barker, V. A. Haas, and E. M. Mrak. "The Influence of Temperature on the Deterioration of Dried Apricots." *Industrial and Engineering Chemistry* 38 (1946): 541–543.

Stadtman, E. R., H. A. Barker, V. A. Haas, E. M. Mrak, and G. Mackinney. "Studies on the Storage of Dried Fruit: Gas Exchange During Storage of Dried Apricots and the Influence of Oxygen on the Rate of Deterioration." *Industrial and Engineering Chemistry* 38 (1946): 324–329.

Stadtman, E. R., H. A. Barker, E. M. Mrak, and G. Mackinney. "Studies on the Storage of Dried Fruit: Experimental Methods and the Influences of Moisture and Sulfur Dioxide on the Rate of Deterioration of Dried Apricots." *Industrial and Engineering Chemistry* 38 (1946): 99–104.

Stadtman, E. R., G. N. Cohen, G. Le Bras, and H. de Robichon-Szulmajster. "Feedback Inhibition and Repression of Aspartokinase Activity in *Escherichia coli* and *Saccharomyces cerevisiae*." *Journal of Biological Chemistry* 286 (1961): 2033–2038.

Stadtman, E. R., A. Ginsburg, W. B. Anderson, A. Segal, M. S. Brown, and J. R. Ciardi. "Regulation of Glutamine Metabolism in *E. coli* by Enzyme Catalyzed Adenylylation and Deadenylylation of Glutamine Synthetase." *Acta Cientfica Venezolana* 22 (1971): R-2–8.

Stadtman, E. R., G. D. Novelli, and F. Lipmann. "Coenzyme A Function in and Acetyl Transfer by the Phosphotransacetylase System." *Journal of Biological Chemistry* 191 (1951): 365–376.

Stadtman, E. R., T. C. Stadtman, and H. A. Barker. "Tracer Experiments on the Mechanisms of Synthesis of Valeric and Caproic Acids by *Clostridium kluyveri*." *Journal of Biological Chemistry* 178 (1949): 677–682.

Stadtman, E. R., T. R. Stadtman, I. Pastan, and L. D. Smith. "*Clostridium barkeri* sp. n." *Journal of Bacteriology* 110 (1972): 758–760.

Stadtman, T. C. "A Gold Mine of Fascinating Enzymes: Those Remarkable Strictly Anaerobic Bacteria, *Methanococcus vannielli* and *Clostridium sticklandii*." *Journal of Biological Chemistry* 277 (2002): 49091–49100.

———. "On the Metabolism of an Amino Acid Fermenting *Clostridium*." *Journal of Bacteriology* 67 (1954): 314–320.

Stadtman, T. C., and H. A. Barker. "Studies on the Methane Fermentation. X. A New Formate-Decomposing Bacterium, *Methanococcus Vannielii.*" *Journal of Bacteriology* 62: 269–280.

Stadtman, T. C., P. Elliott, and L. Tiemann. "Studies on the Enzymic Reduction of Amino Acids. III. Phosphate Esterification Coupled with Glycine Reduction." *Journal of Biological Chemistry* 231 (1958): 961–973.

Stadtman, T. C., and L. S. McClung [1951]. "*Clostridium Sticklandii* Nov. Spec." *Journal of Bacteriology* 73, no. 2 (1957): 218–219.

Starling, E. H. "The Chemical Correlation of the Functions of the Body." *Lancet* 166 (1905): 339–341.

Starzl, T. E., H. P. Chase, and E. H. Ahrens et al. "Portacaval Shunt in Patients with Familial Hypercholesterolemia." *Annals of Surgery* 198 (1983): 273–283.

Starzl, T. E., C. W. Putnam, H. P. Chase, and K. A. Porter. "Portacaval Shunt in Hyperlipoproteinaemia." *Lancet* 2 (1973): 940–944.

Starzl, T. E., C. W. Putnam, and L. J. Koep. "Portacaval Shunt and Hyperlipidemia." *Archives of Surgery* 113 (1978): 71–74.

Stehelin, D., R. V. Guntaka, H. E. Varmus, and J. M. Bishop. "Purification of DNA Complementary to Nucleotide Sequences Required for Neoplastic Transformation of Fibroblasts by Avian Sarcoma Virus." *Journal of Molecular Biology* 101 (1976): 349–365.

Stehelin, D., H. E. Varmus, J. M. Bishop, and P. K. Vogt. "DNA Related to the Transforming Gene(s) of Rous Sarcoma Virus Is Present in Normal Avian DNA." *Nature* 260 (1976): 170–173.

"Students Selected for 1961 Who's Who." *Ring-tum Phi: Washington and Lee Semi-weekly Newspaper* 12 (October 31, 1961). hdl.handle.net/11021/29056.

Südhof, T. C., J. L. Goldstein, M. S. Brown, and D. W. Russell. "The LDL Receptor Gene: A Mosaic of Exons Shared with Different Proteins." *Science* 228 (1985): 815–822.

Switzer, R. L., E. R. Stadtman, and T. C. Stadtman. "H. A. Barker: November 29, 1907–December 24, 2000." In *Biographical Memoirs.* Washington, DC: National Academies Press, 2004.

Tabor, C. W., and H. Tabor. "It All Started on a Streetcar in Boston." *Annual Reviews in Biochemistry* 68 (1999): 1–32.

Taunton, O. D., J. Roth, and I. Pastan. "Studies of the Adrenocorticotropic Hormone-Activated Adenyl Cyclase of a Functional Adrenal Tumor." *Journal of Biological Chemistry* 244 (1969): 247–253.

Temin, H. M. "The Effects of Actinomycin D on Growth of Rous Sarcoma Virus in vitro." *Virology* 20 (1963): 577–582.

Temin, H. M., and S. Mizutani. "Viral RNA-dependent DNA Polymerase: RNA-dependent DNA Polymerase in Virions of Rous Sarcoma Virus." *Nature* 226 (1970): 1211–1213.

Truman, H. Quoted in J. I. Gallin, "The NIH Clinical Center and the Future of Clinical Research." *Nature Medicine* 17 (2011): 1221–1223.

Tscheschlok, E. "Long Time Coming: Miami's Liberty City Riot of 1968." *Florida Historical Quarterly* 74 (1996): 440–460.

Turner, D. C., and T. C. Stadtman. "Purification of Protein Components of Clostridial Glycine Reductase System and Characterization of Protein A as a Selenoprotein." *Archives of Biochemistry and Biophysics* 154 (1973): 366–381.

Vagelos, P. R. "Personal Notes." *Archives of Biochemistry and Biophysics* 397 (2002): 449.

Valent, P., B. Groner, and U. Schumacher et al. "Paul Ehrlich (1854–1915) and His Contributions to the Foundation and Birth of Translational Medicine." *Journal of Innate Immunity* 8 (2016): 111–120.

Varmus, H. "How Tumor Virology Evolved into Cancer Biology and Transformed Oncology." *Annual Reviews in Cancer Biology* 1 (2017): 1–18.

Varmus, H. E., R. L. Perlman, and I. Pastan. "Regulation of Lac Messenger Ribonucleic Acid Synthesis by Cyclic Adenosine 3′,5′-Monophosphate and Glucose." *Journal of Biological Chemistry* 245 (1970): 2259–2267.

———. "Regulation of Lac Transcription in *Escherichia coli* by Cyclic Adenosine 3′,5′-Monophosphate." *Journal of Biological Chemistry* 245 (1970): 6366–6372.

Veblen, T. "The Intellectual Preeminence of Jews in Modern Europe." *Political Science Quarterly* 29 (1919): 33–43.

"W&L Grad Wins Nobel." *Ring-tum Phi: Washington and Lee University* 855 (October 17, 1985), 1, 4.

Watson, J. D., and F. H. C. Crick. "Genetical Implications of the Structure of Deoxyribonucleic Acid." *Nature* 171 (1953): 964–967.

———. "Molecular Structure of Nucleic Acids." *Nature* 171 (1953): 737–738.

Williams, R. "Robert Lefkowitz: Godfather of the G Protein–Coupled Receptors." *Circulation Research* 106 (2010): 812–814.

Williams, R. "Joseph Goldstein, and Michael Brown. Demoting Egos, Promoting Success." *Circulation Research* 106 (2010): 1006–1010.

Windaus, A. "Uber der Gehalt Normaler und Atheromatoser Aorten an cholesterol und Cholesterinester." *Zeitschrift für Physiologishe Chemie* 67 (1910): 174.

Woolfolk, C. A., and E. R. Stadtman. "Cumulative Feedback Inhibition in the Multiple End Product Regulation of Glutamine Synthetase Activity in *Escherichia coli*." *Biochemical and Biophysical Research Communications* 17 (1964): 313–319.

Wyngaarden, J. B. "The Clinical Investigator as an Endangered Species." *New England Journal of Medicine* 301 (1979): 1254–1259.

Yalow, R. S. "Radioimmunoassay: A Probe for Fine Structure of Biologic Systems." Nobel Lecture, Stockholm, Sweden, December 8, 1977.

Yalow, R. S., and S. A. Berson. "Immunoassay of Endogenous Plasma Insulin in Man." *Journal of Clinical Investigation* 39 (1960): 157–175.

Yalow, R. S., S. M. Glick, J. Roth, S. Roth, and S. A. Berson. "Radioimmunoassay of Human Plasma ACTH." *Journal of Clinical Endocrinology and Metabolism* 24 (1964): 1219–1225.

Yamamoto, T., C. G. Davis, M. S. Brown, W. J. Schneider, M. L. Casey, J. L. Goldstein, and D. W. Russell. "The Human LDL Receptor: A Cysteine-Rich Protein
with Multiple Alu Sequences in Its mRNA." *Cell* 39 (1984): 27–38.

Yarbrough, M. L., Y. Li, L. N. Kinch, N. V. Grishin, H. L. Ball, and K. Orth.
"AMPylation of Rho GTPases by Vibrio VopS Disrupts Effector Binding and
Downstream Signaling." *Science* 323 (2009): 269–272.

Young, J. Q., S. R. Ranji, R. M. Wachter, C. M. Lee, B. Niehaus, and A. D. Auerback. "'July Effect': Impact of the Academic Year-End Changeover on Patient Outcomes: A Systematic Review." *Annals of Internal Medicine* 155 (2011):
309–115.

BOOKS AND DISSERTATIONS

Anderson, D. L. *The Columbia Guide to the Vietnam War.* New York: Columbia
University Press, 2002.

Association of American Medical Colleges. *2016 AAMC Data Book.* Washington,
DC: AAMC, 2016, 41, Table B-12: "U.S. Medical School Women Enrollment
and Graduates."

Bishop, J. M. *How to Win the Nobel Prize: An Unexpected Life in Science.* Cambridge, MA: Harvard University Press, 2003.

Blight, J. G., and J. M. Lang. *The Fog of War: Lessons from the Life of Robert S.
McNamara.* Lanham, MD: Rowman & Littlefield, 2005.

Boddie, W. W. *History of Williamsburg.* Columbia, SC: The State Company, 1923.

Bonior, D. E., S. M. Champlain, and T. S. Kolly. *The Vietnam Veteran: A History
of Neglect.* New York: Praeger Publishers, 1984.

Bonner, T. N. *Becoming a Physician in Britain, France, Germany, and the United
States, 1750–1945.* Baltimore: Johns Hopkins University Press, 1995.

Boomhower, R. E. *Robert F. Kennedy and the 1968 Indiana Primary.* Bloomington:
Indiana University Press, 2008.

Bourne, H. R. *Paths to Innovation: Discovering Recombinant DNA, Oncogenes,
and Prions, in One Medical School, over One Decade.* San Francisco: University
of California Medical Humanities Consortium, 2011.

Brown, M. S. *Origins of a 40-Year Partnership.* Cambridge, UK: University of
Cambridge, Nobel Prize Inspiration Initiative, Nobel Media AB, 2014. nobel-
prizeii.org/videos/michael-brown-cambridge-lecture.

Brown, S. *Faces of Power: Constancy and Change in the United States Foreign Policy
from Truman to Obama.* New York: Columbia University Press, 2015.

Buhite, R. D. *Call to Arms: Presidential Speeches, Messages, and Declarations of
War.* Wilmington, DE: Scholarly Resources, 2003.

Carson, C., and K. Shepard. *A Call to Conscience: The Landmark Speeches of Martin Luther King, Jr.* New York: Warner Books, 2001.

Crick, F. *What Mad Pursuit: A Personal View of Scientific Discovery.* New York:
Basic Books, 1988.

Csicsek, A. "Spiro Agnew and the Burning of Baltimore." In J. I. Elfenbein, T. L. Hallowak, and E. M. Nix, eds. *Baltimore '68: Riots and Rebirth of an American City*. Philadelphia: Temple University Press, 2011.

Dallek, R. *Flawed Giant: Lyndon Johnson and His Times*. New York: Oxford University Press, 1998.

De Kruif, P. *Microbe Hunters*. San Diego: Harcourt, 1996.

Dennis, E. E., and W. L. Rivers. *The New Journalism in America*. New Brunswick, NJ: Transaction Publishers, 2011.

Drew, D. M. *Rolling Thunder 1965: Anatomy of a Failure*. Maxwell AFB: Air University Press, 1986.

Edgerton, G. R. *The Columbia History of American Television*. New York: Columbia University Press, 2002.

Editors of Boston Publishing Company. *The American Experience in Vietnam: Reflections on an Era*. Minneapolis: Zenith Press, 2014.

Efron, N. J. *Judaism and Science: A Historical Introduction*. Westport, CT: Greenwood Press, 2007.

Eldridge, L. A. *Chronicles of a Two Front War: Civil Rights and Vietnam in the African American Press*. Columbia: University of Missouri Press, 2011.

Finger, M. *31 Hours, 28 Minutes*. Memphis: The City Magazine, April 1, 2008.

Fleming, A. *Martin Luther King, Jr.: A Dream of Hope*. New York: Sterling, 2008.

Flexner, A. *Medical Education in the United States and Canada: A Report to the Carnegie Foundation for the Advancement of Teaching*. Bulletin No. 4. New York: The Carnegie Foundation for the Advancement of Teaching, 1910, 326.

Fry, M. *Landmark Experiments in Molecular Biology*. London: Academic Press, 2016.

Gallup News Service. *Americans Look Back at Vietnam War*. Princeton, NJ: Gallup, November 17, 2000.

Garrison, H. H., B. Drehman, and E. Neu. *NIH Research Funding Trends: FY 1995–2013*. Bethesda, MD: Office of Public Affairs, Federation of American Societies of Experimental Biology, 2013.

Gilbert, B. *Ten Blocks from the White House*. New York: Praeger, 1969.

Grant, J. *Bernard M. Baruch: The Adventures of a Wall Street Legend*. New York: John Wiley and Sons, 1997.

Graves, M. P., and D. Fillingim. *More Than Precious Memories: The Rhetoric of Southern Gospel Music*. Macon, GA: Mercer University Press, 2004.

Grossman, M. *World Military Leaders: A Biographical Dictionary*. New York: Facts on File, 2007.

Harmon, M. D. *Found, Featured, Then Forgotten: U.S. Network TV News and the Vietnam Veterans Against the War*. Knoxville: University of Tennessee Libraries, 2011.

Harris, N. L., and R. C. Scully. "The Clinicopathological Conferences (CPCs)." In D. N. Louis and R. H. Young, eds., *Keen Minds to Explore the Dark Continents of Disease.* Boston: Department of Pathology, Massachusetts General Hospital, 2011.

Honey, M. K. *Going Down Jericho Road: The Memphis Strike, Martin Luther King's Last Campaign.* New York: W. W. Norton, 2007.

Isaacson, W. *Profiles in Leadership: Historians on the Elusive Quality of Greatness.* New York: W. W. Norton & Company, 2010.

Johnson, D. D. P., and D. Tierney. *Failing to Win: Perceptions of Victory and Defeat in International Politics.* Cambridge, MA: Harvard University Press, 2006.

Kastor, J. A. *The National Institutes of Health, 1991–2008.* New York: Oxford University Press, 2010.

Kennedy, T. J. *James Augustine Shannon, 1904–1994: A Biographical Memoir.* Washington, DC: National Academies Press, 1998.

Key, L. E. *Who Wrote the Book of Life? A History of the Genetic Code.* Stanford: Stanford University Press, 2000.

Kornberg, A. *For the Love of Enzymes: The Odyssey of a Biochemist.* Cambridge, MA: Harvard University Press, 1989, 310–313.

Kusch, F. *Battleground Chicago: The Police and the 1968 Democratic National Convention.* Westport, CT: Praeger, 2004.

Lefkowitz, Robert J. In *The Nobel Prizes, 2012.* Sagamore Beach, MA: Science History Publications/USA, 2013.

Lorell, M., and C. Kelley. *Casualties, Public Opinion, and Presidential Policy During the Vietnam War.* Santa Monica, CA: Rand Corporation, 1985.

Miller, A. *On the Shooting of Robert Kennedy.* New York: The New York Times, June 8, 1968.

Mukherjee, S. *The Emperor of All Maladies: A Biography of Cancer.* New York: Scribner, 2010.

Mullan, F. *Plagues and Politics: The Story of the United States Public Health Service.* New York: Basic Books, 1989.

Nixon, Richard. "Address Accepting the Presidential Nomination of the Republican National Convention in Miami Beach, Florida" (August 8, 1968). In G. Peters and J. T. Woolley, comps., *The American Presidency Project* (Santa Barbara: University of California, Santa Barbara). presidency.ucsb.edu.

Old York Road Historical Society. *Cheltenham Township.* Charleston, SC: Arcadia Publishing, 2001.

Perlmutter, D. D. *Photojournalism and Foreign Policy: Icons of Outrage in International Crises.* Westport, CT: Praeger, 1998.

Portugal, F. H. *The Least Likely Man: Marshall Nirenberg and the Discovery of the Genetic Code.* Cambridge, MA: MIT Press, 2015.

Rall, J. E. *Solomon A. Berson: 1918–1972. A Biographical Memoir.* Washington, DC: National Academy of Sciences, 1990.

Rosenberg, C. E. *No Other Gods: On Science and American Social Thought.* Baltimore: Johns Hopkins University Press, 1997.

Rous, P. "The Challenge to Man of the Neoplastic Cell." Nobel Lecture, December 13, 1966. *Nobel Lectures, Physiology or Medicine, 1963–1970.* Singapore: World Scientific Publishing Company, 1999.

Safer, M. *Flashbacks: On Returning to Vietnam.* New York: Random House, 1990.

Saldin, R. P. *War, the American State, and Politics since 1898.* New York: Cambridge University Press, 2011.

Schmitz, D. F. *The Tet Offensive: Politics, War, and Public Opinion.* Lanham, MD: Rowman & Littlefield, 2005.

Schrödinger, E. *What Is Life?* Cambridge: Cambridge University Press, 1944.

Scott, D. *Remembering Cheltenham Township.* Charleston, SC: The History Press, 2009.

Shea, D. M., and M. B. Harward. *Presidential Campaigns: Documents Decoded.* Santa Barbara, CA: ABC-CLIO, 2013.

Skipper, J. C. *The 1964 Republican Convention: Barry Goldwater and the Beginning of the Conservative Movement.* Jefferson, NC: McFarland & Company, 2016.

Slater, L. B. *War and Disease: Biomedical Research on Malaria in the Twentieth Century.* New Brunswick, NJ: Rutgers University Press, 2009.

Smyth, D. J. *Freedom of the Press and National Security in Four Wars: World War I, World War II, the Vietnam War, and the War on Terrorism.* Master's thesis in public policy. College Park: University of Maryland, 2007.

Söhngen, N. L. *Het ontstaan en verdwijnen van waterstof en methaan onder den invloed van het organische leven.* Delft: Technische Hoogeschool, 1906.

Southwestern Research Foundation. *Cholesterol Metabolism: The Work of Drs. Brown and Goldstein.* Dallas: Southwestern Research Foundation, May 4, 2012.

Stetten, J. D., ed. *NIH: An Account of Research in Its Laboratories and Clinics.* Orlando, FL: Academic Press, 1984.

Tuchman, B. W. *The March of Folly.* New York: Knopf, 1984.

Turgenev, I. *Fathers and Sons: A Novel.* New York: Leypoldt and Holt, 1867.

Vagelos, P. R., and L. Galambos. *Medicine, Science, and Merck.* Cambridge, UK: Cambridge University Press, 2004.

Varmus, H. *The Art and Politics of Science.* New York: W. W. Norton & Company, 2009.

Wang, Z. *In Sputnik's Shadow: The President's Science Advisory Committee and Cold War America.* New Brunswick, NJ: Rutgers University Press, 2009.

Ward, P. S. *Simon Baruch: Rebel in the Ranks of Medicine, 1840–1921.* Tuscaloosa: University of Alabama Press, 1994.

Watson, J. D. *The Double Helix: A Personal Account of the Discovery of the Structure of DNA.* New York: Atheneum, 1968.

Watson, J. D., A. Berry, and K. Davies. *DNA: The Story of the Genetic Revolution.* New York: Alfred A. Knopf, 2017.

Westmoreland, W. C. *A Soldier Reports.* New York: Doubleday, 1976.

Willibanks, J. H., ed. *The Vietnam War: The Essential Reference Guide*. Santa Barbara, CA: ABC-CLIO, 2013.

Woods, R. B. *Prisoners of Hope: Lyndon B. Johnson, the Great Society, and the Limits of Liberalism*. Philadelphia: Basic Books, 2016.

Zuckerman, H. *Scientific Elite: Nobel Laureates in the United States*. New York: The Free Press, 1977.

INDEX